SKEPTICISM AND FREEDOM

A VOLUME IN THE SERIES

STUDIES IN LAW AND ECONOMICS
Edited by William M. Landes and
J. Mark Ramseyer

ALSO IN THIS SERIES

Pervasive Prejudice? Unconventional Evidence of Race and Gender Discrimination, by Ian Ayres

Politics and Property Rights: The Closing of the Open Range in the Postbellum South, by Shawn Everett Kantor

Are Predatory Commitments Credible? Who Should the Courts Believe? by John R. Lott Jr.

More Guns, Less Crime: Understanding Crime and Gun Control Laws, Second Edition, by John R. Lott Jr.

Japanese Law: An Economic Approach, by J. Mark Ramseyer and Minoru Nakazato

Measuring Judicial Independence: The Political Economy of Judging in Japan, by J. Mark Ramseyer and Eric B. Rasmusen

When Rules Change: An Economic and Political Analysis of Transition Relief and Retroactivity, by Daniel Shaviro

Smoke-Filled Rooms: A Postmortem on the Tobacco Deal, by W. Kip Viscusi

Richard A. Epstein

SKEPTICISM AND
Freedom

A

MODERN CASE

FOR

CLASSICAL

LIBERALISM

The University of Chicago Press

Chicago and London

RICHARD A. EPSTEIN is the James Parker Hall Distinguished
Service Professor of Law at the University of Chicago and the
Peter and Kirsten Senior Fellow at the Hoover Institution. He is
the author of many books, among which are *Simple Rules for a
Complex World*, *Principles for a Free Society: Reconciling
Individual Liberty and the Common Good*, and *Takings: Private
Property and the Power of Eminent Domain*.

The University of Chicago Press, Chicago 60637
The University of Chicago Press, Ltd., London
© 2003 by Richard A. Epstein
All rights reserved. Published 2003
Printed in the United States of America

12 11 10 09 08 07 06 05 04   2 3 4 5

ISBN: 0-226-21300-5 (cloth)

Library of Congress Cataloging-in-Publication Data

Epstein, Richard A.
    Skepticism and freedom : a modern case for classical
liberalism / Richard A. Epstein.
        p.   cm. — (Studies in law and economics)
    Includes bibliographical references and index.
    ISBN: 0-226-21304-8 (cloth : alk. paper)
        1. Liberty.   2. Skepticism.   3. Law—Philosophy.   I. Title.
II. Series.

    K487.L5 E67   2003
    340'.1—dc21

                                    2002152211

⊗The paper used in this publication meets the minimum
requirements of the American National Standard for Information
Sciences—Permanence of Paper for Printed Library Materials,
ANSI Z39.48–1992.

CONTENTS

▉ ACKNOWLEDGMENTS

THIS BOOK HAS HAD A LONG PERIOD OF GESTATION. It contains ideas that have evolved slowly in my mind over the past twenty-five years. My intellectual odyssey has been from a staunch libertarian who distrusted consequentialist explanations to a classical liberal who embraces these explanations. The transformation of self almost always takes place in gradual stages and it is quite impossible to pin down the one single moment that marks either its inception or its completion. I only wish it were possible to thank by name the many people who over the years have aided my intellectual journey, first as a student at Oxford and Yale, where I did my legal studies, then as a member of the faculty at the University of Southern California, and for the last thirty years at the University of Chicago Law School. I shall mention here only Robert Nozick, whose own work in *Anarchy, State, and Utopia* made me realize the close connections between political theory and legal thought.

It is also proper to acknowledge those who have helped me in working through this particular project. I am grateful for having had the opportunity to present portions of this book at workshops at the University of Chicago, in the Law School, the Economics Department, the MacLean Center for Clinical Medical Ethics, and the Cultural Policy Center. I have spoken on various problems that this book examines in lectures and workshops at other universities and think tanks—among them the American Enterprise Institute, the Cato Institute, the Federalist Society, the Hoover Institution, the Institute for Humane Studies, the Manhattan Institute, Queen's University in Ontario, the Social Philosophy and Policy Center in Ohio, St. Gallen University, Stanford University—and in lectures presented in New Zealand on tours organized by Roger Kerr of the New Zealand Business Round Table in 1990, 1995, and 1999. I have also benefited from David Friedman's and Mark Ramseyer's detailed comments on the entire manuscript and from valuable comments on various portions of the book from Philip Hamburger, Peter Huang, Charles Larmore, Bentley McCloud, Andrei Shleifer, Cass Sunstein, Adrian Vermeule, and David Weisbach, as well as countless others over the years. I owe a debt of gratitude to my research assistants at the University of Chicago

Law School—Jamil Jaffer, Jonathan Mitchell, and Jenny Silverman. I have profited from the able library assistance of Margaret Duczynski. For secretarial help, I thank my long-time secretary Katheryn Kepchar. I am also appreciative of the help I have received on this project from Lynn Chu and Glen Hartley, my literary representatives. I also thank Geoffrey Huck, my first editor at the University of Chicago, and John Tryneski who worked with me thereafter.

Most of all I thank my wife, Eileen, and my children, Melissa, Benjamin, and Elliot, who have put up with the distracted musings of husband and father in developing a set of arguments of which they do not entirely approve.

Why Classical Liberalism?

The Positive Case for a Negative Book

THIS VOLUME IS MY THIRD, and perhaps last, in a series of books written about the intersection of law and political theory. The first two were *Simple Rules for a Complex World* (1995), and *Principles for a Free Society: Reconciling Individual Liberty with the Common Good* (1998). In both those works, my purpose was to defend a version of what has been variously described as libertarian theory, laissez-faire economics, or classical liberalism. I included the words "classical liberalism" in the title of this book in order to emphasize that I do not think that "free markets," let alone "capitalism," supply the answer to all the questions of social organization—a connotation that is sometimes attached to the terms "laissez-faire" and "libertarianism" by their most ardent defenders.[1] I also have consciously inserted the word "modern" in the title to indicate that methodological approaches that I use to defend this outcome are of recent origin. I use the word "classical" to indicate that I use modern techniques to reaffirm traditional rules and outlooks, which were often—and still are—defended on very different grounds.

To many the views adopted here will be regarded as extreme, but I write without apology because I do not think that this charge should be accepted. My version of classical liberalism sees a large place for the operation of voluntary markets under legal protection. Yet at the same time, it is clear that markets do not operate in a void, but, as Hernando de Soto, among others, so forcefully reminds us, also depend on a social infrastructure that often only the state can create. The market depends even—make that *especially*—on such mundane but critical acts as the creation of a consistent and accurate record of land titles and a published set of addresses to facilitate quintessential private acts, such as the purchase or mortgage of real property.[2] Markets depend on governments; governments of course depend on markets. The key question is not to exclude one or the other from the mix, but to assign to each its proper role.

Classical liberal theories, by whatever name, seek to maintain that proper balance. Evaluated for their similarities and not their differences, classical liberalism, libertarianism, or laissez-faire lay out a small set of powerful principles to guide ordinary social interaction. The relevant rules respect the autonomy of the individual. They account for the emergence of a strong system of private property by allowing land and movables to be reduced to private ownership by occupation, and animals by a rule of capture. They provide voluntary exchange as the one means for people to sell their labor or possessions to others who might value it more highly. Finally, to ensure the supremacy of the voluntary transfer of ownership of labor and property, the legal rules contain a strong prohibition against the use of force or fraud as means for altering the balance of entitlements and obligations in interpersonal relations.

The simplicity and generality of these rules should not conceal the complexity of the relationships that their consistent application facilitates. The autonomy rule provides a near-costless way to assign the labor of each person to the one who values it most—himself. The first possession rule represents an inexpensive way to remove things from the state of nature to private ownership, without extended political deliberations. These rights can then be brought together in endless combinations through voluntary exchanges that embody win-win transactions, which have the further virtue of setting the stage for subsequent voluntary arrangements that produce similar improvements. At the same time, the prohibitions against force and fraud prevent win-lose situations, where regrettably the losses routinely exceed, even dwarf, the gains. For most individuals, conformity with these principles in their daily lives goes largely unnoticed, which is why the natural lawyers often regarded their work as descriptive and not normative—a close observation and documentation of the standard rules that in an unreflective fashion organized social exchange and cooperation. But, noticed or not, these principles organize the routine transactions on which human prosperity and, indeed, bodily integrity depend.

It would be nice to say that these four rules are the end of the story. And for some ardent libertarians of a natural law bent, perhaps they are. But any examination of real-world institutions and practices makes it painfully clear that embracing these four rules leaves two intellectual tasks largely ignored. The first is to articulate a principled justification for these rules. The second is to identify a place for justified legal coercion. It is useful to say a few words about each at the outset.

Natural Justice and Consequentialist Thought

It is possible to insist that "natural" rules of conduct rest on immutable principles of justice or self-evident truths. It is, in the deontological tradition, "just wrong" to break promises, take property, or harm other people. But those dogmatic explanations, even when offered by lawyers as influential as William Blackstone or philosophers as great as Immanuel Kant, fall on barren ground today. Blackstone could write, without embarrassment: "When he [God] created man, and endued him with freewill to conduct himself in all parts of life, he laid down certain immutable laws of human nature, whereby that freewill is in some degree regulated and restrained, and gave him also the faculty of reason to discover the purport of those laws."[3] That protestation of faith will not cut it today. There is simply too much dispute over the proper foundations of a just legal order for claims of natural justice or natural law to carry the day by fiat.

One aim of my earlier writings has been to explain how a coherent consequentialist theory avoids the *ipse dixit* of traditional theories. The trick here is to avoid the pitfalls of crude utilitarian thought, which posits some indefinable entity that is separate and apart from the desires and aspirations of the individuals that compose it. Yet at the same time it becomes important to offer strong functional justifications for these traditional legal rules, and to oppose many common forms of regulation that sought, for example, to reject or cripple the principle of freedom of contract. The natural law theorists did us the great service of isolating the core *presumptions* of a working legal system, without indicating why they continue to hold sway and when or how they could be rebutted. It is only when these presumptions are treated as a first step in an exercise of successive approximations to some desirable social objective that their full place can be understood. The sensible form of consequentialism recognizes that the deontological imperatives form the first step in that journey, but do not complete the task. The prohibition against the use of force must make room for a privilege of self-defense. The obligation to honor promises must excuse people from having to perform in full when the other party is in breach. A comprehensive theory of liberty must work out these limitations in order to be true to its own premises.

Modern welfarist theories often posit some abstract goal of utility or wealth maximization in a wide range of institutional settings without the foggiest notion of how to achieve them. Thus in their recent study *Fairness versus Welfare*,[4] Louis Kaplow and Steven Shavell offer a comprehensive description of what counts as individual well-being in their effort to explain why matters of fairness should always be regarded as subordinate to claims of utility. The root of their claim is one that I have also defended in the works mentioned above: it is not possible to articulate any acceptable principle of social justice or fairness that explains why it is that in a two-person society if A and B both prefer alternative 1 to alternative 2, they should be required in the name of justice or fairness to accept alternative 2 over alternative 1. Any effort to force them into paths that they do not like will only result in a state of affairs that leaves both worse off than they would otherwise be. The principle generalizes to any number of individuals, no matter how complicated its application might become.

At one level, the strength of this welfarist insight explains why no system of deontological reasoning can survive this one consequentialist challenge. The claim seems clearly right insofar as it establishes a criterion by which to evaluate various social rules and practices. Why would anyone oppose making someone better off if it did not make anyone else worse off? But in order to make this claim convincing, what is needed is more than an abstract justification for how this system would work in practice, for ordinary individuals are deeply suspicious of large overarching claims that cut against the ordinary habits of mind and moral intuitions of their daily life. People have used terms like "justice" and "fairness" all their lives, and they are not about to rip them out of their vocabulary because learned lawyers and economists have concluded that they are either otiose on the one hand, or subsumed in more sophisticated accounts of welfare on the other.

In order to ease the gap between ordinary discourse and sophisticated thought, therefore, what is needed is a strong translation mechanism that links ordinary sensibilities to a more systematic theory. Typically none is supplied. Indeed much of the history of legal thought is defined by the inability to breach this gap. The tale really begins as early as Roman law. Gaius, like Justinian after him, begins his discussion of law by noting that each nation is governed by both "its own peculiar law and . . . the common law of mankind."[5] The former, described by him as the *ius civile*, includes special procedures and forms, for example, the formalities for a contract or conveyance, such as oaths or recordation, that can and do vary from nation to nation. But at the same time, Gaius is equally insistent in noting an opposition between the *ius civile* and the *ius naturale:* "while the law that natural reason establishes among all mankind is followed by all peoples alike, and is called the *ius gentium* (law of nations, or law of all people), as being the law observed by all mankind."[6] In effect Gaius points to some elusive notion of "natural reason" that is yoked with the idea that these laws are the ones that are in common use in all civilizations. This invites the obvious response that slavery was (in the ancient law) both common on the one hand and in opposition to natural reason on the other. Justinian acknowledges the conflict by observing:

"Slavery . . . is an institution of the law of all peoples; it makes a man the property of another, contrary to the law of nature."[7] The necessary correspondence between common practice and natural reason is shattered in a single sentence.

What is needed in their stead is a way to coordinate these twin impulses of natural reason and common practice. Slavery to one side, the use of common practice often *does* point the way to what a sensible system of abstract norms would require. Justinian seeks to fill the gap by noting, however briefly, that "nature" instills a respect for these laws in all creatures, not only man, and then observes, "From it [the law of nature] comes intercourse between male and female, which we call marriage; also the bearing and bringing up of children." He thus makes an early, if feeble, effort to link the emergence of social laws to biological imperatives, a task that, when explored in connection with modern sociobiology, yields substantial dividends. After all, the basic institutions of property, contract, and tort that Gaius does describe have managed to survive more or less intact down to the present time because they have worked well to organize the daily affairs of most individuals most of the time. Slavery represents an odious practice that the ins impose on the outs, but most customs that relate to contract and tort both bind and benefit members of the in group in roughly equal proportions. At this point the survival of these laws, norms, and practices are grist for the intellectual mill that no serious consequentialist should ignore. Often it is better to presume the soundness of instincts that survive, even if one does not quite understand why they flourish. Learning does not take place only from the top down. It also takes place from the bottom up, so that in the end the best results are likely to be achieved by having top-down theory and bottom-up experience meet somewhere in the middle. Hopefully, as the knowledge base grows the two will converge, or so I shall argue here.

The Legitimate Uses of Coercion

The second difficulty with the four core legal rules of ordinary life is that, even after these emendations are made, they offer an incomplete account of the necessary features of any sustainable political order. No matter how one combines notions of autonomy, property, contract, and tort, they *cannot* independently provide for the social infrastructure and public goods that secure the very rights they are meant to recognize and protect. It is easy to imagine that individuals could form voluntary protective associations, and that these could interact with one another in ways that produce some stable threat positions, one against another. That mechanism surely works to some degree in international situations, where in the simplest models territorial boundaries may prove stable when each nation has enough force to block attacks by the other but insufficient force to mount such attacks by themselves, except if they are intent upon a Pyhrric victory. But it is almost inconceivable in practice that informal alliances of individuals who mingle with each other on a daily basis would be sufficient to police everything from petty street crime to strong-arm warlords, especially if tensions are exacerbated by serious racial or religious differences. The void at the center would lead to one gang's proving itself stronger than the others, taking control over the social landscape, and decreeing itself into a state. In this somber sense, some form of government is always with us. The key is to make sure that we choose it, so that it is not imposed by conquest. A complete legal system, therefore, must go outside the narrow parameters of private property and voluntary exchange in order to sustain its own operation as a sociological fact.

Critics of all forms of laissez-faire repeatedly urge this position by noting that markets require government backup for their operation. The social critic on the Left takes as his motivation the desire to demonstrate how it is impossible to find any way to erect a coherent theory of limited government that stops short of the modern social welfare state. That same observation also has been made with a different intention by thoughtful defenders of limited government and classical liberalism. The conscious shift from "contract" to "social contract" in the theory of political organization could be (mis)read as a desperate effort to rely on fictional consent across the generations even when the bare rudiments of offer and acceptance are wholly absent. As such, it could not explain how millions of people, both alive and unborn, could have reached and sustained such an agreement. But there is a better way to think about the issue. The "social contract" language is better understood as having the opposite meaning, namely, as a signal that ordinary voluntary contracts among citizens cannot provide the social and legal infrastructure that allows for the state protection of autonomy and property or the enforcement of voluntary contracts. The transactional barriers to unanimous, voluntary agreements are too great to be overcome so long as a tiny fraction of self-interested individuals are prepared to hold out against some cooperative solution—as, lamentably, they always are. The force of the word "social" in the phrase "social contract" signals the use of state *coercion* with the intention to produce a set of outcomes that meets the test of ordinary contracts—the win-win arrangements for all individuals who are part of the social system.

In this view, one main task of political and legal theory is to explain the public use of coercion—coercion is *justified* on the ground that it allows all individuals to achieve a higher state of well-being than they could do by their own efforts, either as individuals or as portions of small voluntary groups that are formed under rules that meet the test for creating ordinary contracts. A fuller theory of political obligation requires that individual consent for political obligation yield to a principle that justifies the state's use of force so long as it both supplies compensation to the individual against whom coercion is used and offers them a fair division of the social surplus that is created by public action. Elsewhere I have argued that these principles are more or less embedded in our constitutional order by a consistent interpretation of the Takings Clause: "Nor shall private property be taken for public use, without just compensation."[8] These principles can explain why a system of proportionate taxation allows the state to obtain whatever resources it needs (in peace or in war) to discharge its central mission, without altering the balance of advantage among individuals in whose service it works. It also explains why the state, through regulation and taxation, should normally acquire property through the payment of just compensation, not by confiscation. And it explains why the state need supply no compensation at all when it invokes state force to prevent various forms of aggression (such as the creation of pollution) by one or more citizens against another.

The missing, or at least suppressed, element of many classical libertarian theories is that they do not offer a comprehensive explanation of the role of *forced exchanges* in structuring a political system. The principle of autonomy never permits a draft in times of war.[9] The principle of first possession does not respond to the exhaustion of the common pool. The principle of freedom of contract cannot distinguish between an ordinary sale and a cartel arrangement. A categorical prohibition against taking does not recognize any privilege to take property of others in time of necessity. The stripped-down libertarian theories, with their extreme voluntaristic orientation, precludes the use of taxation, condemnation, and the state provision of infrastructure. These practices were part and parcel of government action long before the rise of the modern welfare state. Figuring out why these institutions are needed and how they should be designed and funded requires a major correction to the starker versions of libertarian theory, which is what the classical liberal approach seeks to supply.

Yet by the same token, the effort to respond to these difficulties does not require us to abandon the vision of limited government and fall into the deadly embrace of the welfare state. Even after all these adaptations are made, government would occupy a far smaller place than it holds under contemporary political theory and constitutional law. The dominant modern sentiment, held on both the Left and the Right, is that finely spun political theories are just the thing that legislatures should consider in deciding what laws to pass, but that notions of liberty and property are also subordinate to the political institutions of the state. To reach this result, they place an enormous stress on the importance of deliberative democracy, but often give no clue as to the proper subjects of deliberation, nor the arguments that should carry the day in these deliberations.

No one can argue in response that deliberation is irrelevant to the success of social institutions. Private associations, regardless of their purpose, build deliberative structures into the ground floor. Directors and trustees are encouraged to speak. The communication is of value not only to those who speak but also to those who listen, which is why the right to speak is not auctioned off to the highest bidder. But the secret of private deliberation is that it is focused on those issues that are common to the enterprise, and not to the private affairs of the individual members of the corporation or private organization. By analogy, deliberation in the political context is directed to the wrong target when it decides the wages that firms can pay workers or the prices at which firms should buy and sell goods. In contrast, public deliberation is needed to decide the size of a national budget or whether to form alliances with foreign nations, or to declare war against them. No general discussion of political theory can state how these political decisions should be decided in the abstract; nor do rules on deliberation guarantee that any nation has in place the leaders who are able to meet the challenges that lie before them. What that theory *can* do is to indicate which decisions fall outside political deliberation, to be decided by individual citizens on their own behalf, and which decisions only the government can undertake, such as securing the rights of citizens, either to a set of initial liberties or to compensation for their deprivation. The real question here is the distribution of decisions between private and public bodies. One task of this book is to place limits on the scope of public deliberation by showing that a theory of limited government can be defended against any and all its critics.

Taking on All Comers

To achieve that end, I first summarize the positive case for the positions that I have adopted. Accordingly, chapter 1 defends the proposition that all important legal propositions rest not on deductive necessities, but on powerful empirical regularities of human conduct, which explains why the same basic set of principles have received such widespread attention from so many different writers and in so many different social settings. In one sense, this is an effort to make good Justinian's cryptic suggestion of how biological demands shape legal institutions. In another sense, it suggests that the key object of comparative law is to show how the similarities across legal systems dominate the differences. From this account emerges, I believe, an understanding of the relationship between skepticism and freedom—the topic to which this book is devoted. I argue for a form of skepticism that rightly shuns a priori argument on the one hand but refuses to fall prey to the delusive trap that no moral judgment about the shape of political institutions is better than any other. In order to achieve this end, it is not sufficient to argue abstractly in defense of a rational legal order. Instead, it is necessary to build on that wise skepticism that exhibits two virtues. First, it refuses to claim that any person knows the intensity and preferences of other individuals. Second, it uses social awareness of that systematic ignorance to shape a set of legal rules that maximizes the overall sphere on human choice. We may not know the shape of individual preferences, but we can grasp the great Humean insight about how the nature of ordinary individuals—limited self-interest in a world of scarcity—shapes the central questions of political organization. [10]

Chapter 2 sets out that affirmative case by articulating the rules needed to develop a system of liberty and its relationship to the legal and political infrastructure of a political order. It rests on a form of naïve assumptions, which, while not universal truths, do wear well with time. The first of these concerns human preferences and behavior, and assumes that these preferences by and large are well ordered, even if they cannot be fully communicated to or measured by other individuals. From these building blocks it organizes the domains of individual choice with those for collectively supplied social institutions on which they depend. I defend a position that I have taken before that seeks to merge the strong protection of individual liberties with the state provision of key public goods, including the infrastructure needed to make this system work.

From this point forward, my intention is to beat back the manifold arguments from different quarters that have been advanced to show either the incoherence or downright confusion of the classical liberal order that I have sought to defend. For these purposes, these attacks come in three different types: moral, conceptual, and psychological. Each type in its own ways seeks to show that one pillar of the classical liberal synthesis has to fall. Moral theories become arbitrary. Conceptual distinctions become arid, pointless, or confused. Behavioral profiles of individual psychology undermine the orderliness, stability, and rationality of human preference on which individual choice turns. Chapters 3–10 address these claims in turn.

Chapter 3 begins the inquiry by confronting the claim of skepticism directly, and argues that our inability to gauge the preferences of others counts as one of the strongest reasons to respect their liberty of choice with respect to their own lives. It also attacks those more aggressive forms of skepticism, closely associated with Oliver Wendell Holmes and, more recently, Richard Posner, that purport to establish on pragmatic grounds that moral relativism becomes the order of the day because of the deep-seated inability to prove even the most rudimentary social and moral truths.

Chapter 4 then develops in a systematic way the method of presumptions making it possible, by successive approximations, to show the close connection between the generalized propositions of ordinary life and the more precise requirements of a consequentialist theory. In so doing, it becomes critical to begin with the easy cases of ordinary life and only then address the more difficult cases of "necessity," dealing with such matters as abortion and rescue, which receive so much attention in the legal and philosophical literature.

Next, chapter 5 addresses the conceptual and terminological objections raised against classical liberal theory. At its root this approach depends on the ability to articulate general commands. It is not possible to form systems of constitutional governance if freedom and coercion can be yoked together as though they shared a single meaning. Yet it is just this approach that conceptual critics of classical liberalism such as Robert Lee Hale and Gerald Cohen seek to achieve. But a more patient analysis helps explain why it is coherent to speak of voluntary choices in competitive markets, and recognizes the need for distinct legal responses to the power that a monopolist can enjoy over those with whom he deals.

Chapter 6 then offers a bridge between the previous conceptual discussion and the behavioral issues that follow. The key behavioral element of the classical liberal system depends on the ability of individuals to organize their preferences over time. Indeed, without this ability it is doubtful that any organism could be able to stay the course that allows it to raise its own offspring to their maturity. Yet one common attack on the classical liberal order, mounted by Jon Elster and Amartya Sen, is that individual preferences are so inconsistent or malleable, or both, that they do not serve as a sensible basis for crafting legal rules or social institutions. Chapter 7 then extends that inquiry by studying the extent to which Prisoner's Dilemma games frustrate the emergence of a classical liberal order. The short answer to the descriptive claims is that they seem to be largely wrong. But even if they have a grain of truth, these difficulties in the formation and expression of preferences in no event justify the grant of extensive powers to state officials, whose own internal preference structures cannot be considered beyond reproach.

Chapters 8 and 9 turn to the newer developments of behavioral economics, which purport to establish the empirical foundations for the claims about the instability of preferences and the inability of people to adopt rational means to achieve their own ends. Chapter 9 turns specifically to an examination of problems of cognitive bias, especially as they relate to issues of decisionmaking under uncertainty in financial and nonfinancial markets. In so doing, these critiques are meant to undermine the neoclassical economic assumption that, in a world of scarce resources, most individuals act in roughly rational fashion to protect themselves and their loved ones. Accordingly many modern writers argue that individual preferences do not have the stability or internal rationality that classical liberalism presupposes, or that individuals suffer from systematic behavioral quirks and anomalies that make it foolhardy to assume that strong property rights and freedom of contract will yield optimal social results.

In both cases, the opposition is overdrawn. The first line of defense of classical theories is that it is dangerous to attach too much weight to the anomalies of human behavior founded on experimental research with naïve subjects. Real-world markets are not simulations, and they create institutional mechanisms that shape expectations and correct the mistakes so frequent to experimental subjects. While these biases may come into play in a few extreme cases, they are not widespread enough to warrant any revision in the basic rules. The second line of defense argues that, to the extent that these behavioral anomalies and cognitive biases do exist, they strengthen the case for the classical legal order. Simple rules are more immune to these errors, and thus should be one major objective of public order. Similarly, the decentralized decisionmaking associated with private ordering creates a form of redundancy, which works to the relative advantage of those individuals, groups, and firms that are most resistant to these irrational tendencies. No system of legal rules and private precaution can eliminate all biases in human behavior. But the classical liberal order does better than its rivals.

In dealing with these moral, conceptual, and psychological critiques, I seek to examine and criticize in detail the strongest statements of the position I disagree with. My hope is to learn from them in ways that allow us to preserve their insights while avoiding their mistakes. The task, if successfully completed, should work as a defense of classical liberalism by showing that it can meet the skeptical objections that are lodged against it from all corners of the intellectual landscape. Thus this book's title, *Skepticism and Freedom,* expresses its aim of showing the proper relationship between freedom and skepticism. Once that relationship is understood, then the purpose of the subtitle becomes clearer. This book offers a modern defense of classical liberalism, one which gains in strength in light of the many obstacles that by persistent effort it is able to overcome.

I Two Forms of Skepticism

Law and Everything

THE STUDY OF LAW IN THE UNITED STATES can no longer be regarded as an autonomous discipline, if it ever was. To its credit, law is now a net importer of scholarship done in a wide range of contiguous disciplines: anthropology, biology (both evolutionary and social), economics, feminism, government, history, literary theory, philosophy, psychology, and sociology. This massive importation from other disciplines offers a sharp, systematic contrast to the incremental process of hunch and analogy characteristic of the common law method. The story of the common law runs as follows. Cases, not principles, are said to be the dominant focus. Generalizations were viewed warily lest any court go beyond the secure factual base for its decision. Only when a consensus accrued over time could some overarching precedent gain a measure of permanence. Each branch of law was treated as though it rested on its own separate bottom. Intuitions abounded; results were often justified by earnest appeals to fairness and justice, only to be easily parried. The skepticism toward systematic theory made it quite possible for judges and scholars to take first one approach to labor law, and a second to product liability. Different legal subjects were carefully distributed into self-contained legal boxes, devoid of any overriding theoretical structure linking one substantive area of law to another.

Given this ad hoc approach to legal issues, intelligent legal reform turned on incremental improvement of existing bodies of law, based on the difficulties in application that emerged through practice and experience. The diligent law professor sought to iron out the inconsistencies that crept into the decisional law, or to suggest some modest statutory reform of a problem that proved especially thorny in practice. The development of the Uniform Commercial Code from the extensive case law of sales, secured transactions, and negotiable instruments offers one successful illustration from the 1950s and 1960s. But any search for comprehensive first principles was, if thought of at all, dismissed as an idle pastime, the indulgence of airy philosophers, but not worthy of professional lawyers.

Yet appearances can easily deceive. However limited the pretensions of the common law lawyers, the results of their halting method were uniformly far more impressive than my description of this ad hoc process suggests. Sometimes intuitions are good; sometimes judges extend sound principles by careful analogies; sometimes the parts cohere in spite of the particularistic aims of the judges. Although it is premature to celebrate the virtues of "one case at a time,"[1] an incremental approach to case law issues allows for a conversation over the centuries to which many contribute but in which no one voice dominates. It is easy to find unresolved disputes on hard questions of little practical consequence: issues that really matter do get decided one way or another, and are not just allowed to linger. It is also foolish to overlook broad areas of defensible consensus on matters of great practical importance.

The common law presents a deceptive subject matter. Its sprawling case-by-case development suggests that the subject is one in which the dominant virtue is judgment—that is, the capacity to intuit which cases fall on which side of some imaginary line. The haphazard organization of the materials looks to be the antithesis of any systematic theory. Again, however, appearances on this matter are deceiving. No one can pretend that thousands of individual decisions can be reconciled into a unified whole. Nor can one insist that the judicial articulation of reasons for decisions will always prove persuasive after searching examination. But, that said, I am convinced that behind the endless array of discrete cases lies a series of coherent principles whose value in application survives the multiple false turns of judicial reasoning. Properly pruned and refined, these principles allow us to establish a complete and well-defined set of relationships between private individuals that meet simultaneously the practical concerns of ordinary individuals, the moral concerns of philosophers, and the efficiency concerns of economists. Properly extended, this body of law allows one to tackle the still more difficult question of the proper relationship between the individual and the state. Put most simply, the material of the common law forms a vast depository of the raw data (which no moral philosopher could hope to duplicate by unaided reflection) needed to fashion a sound set of legal rules for our political and social institutions. And when that task is done, the final product stands in stark contrast to the general statist outlook that until recently had come to dominate both twentieth-century political thought and, more important, twentieth-century political behavior. With the start of a new millennium, it is more imperative to set out the basic outlines of the system. In doing so, I hope to transcend the judicial origins of the basic system, and to demonstrate that the principles articulated here are defensible against the multitude of hard challenges raised about this view of the relationship between the individual and the state.

In dealing with this issue, the claim is meant to cover more than the laws and institutions of the United States. Over the past years, I have spoken on these topics in places as diverse as Belgium, Brazil, the Czech Republic, Germany, Great Britain, Israel, New Zealand, South Africa, and Switzerland. I have talked and argued with lawyers, economists, and political scientists from around the globe. The legal systems and cultural traditions that I have encountered differ very much from ours and from one another in their historical backgrounds and their legal terminology. Their legal codes necessarily contain variations on matters of statutory form and implementation. For example, all these nations may have systems for licensing drivers, but the requirements may well vary from nation to nation. Yet I have never once found that geographical separation, cultural differences, historical accident, or variation in administrative schemes has impeded dialogue across these borders.

More concretely, my intellectual outlook has more in common with a small government libertarian in some remote corner of the world than it does with my liberal Hyde Park neighbors, near the University of Chicago, who remain devotees of the modern welfare state. I suspect that the same statement can be made by traditional social democrats or modern feminists, looking at local and worldwide discourse from their own perspective. Powerful ideas, like new fashions, move quickly across geographical and cultural boundaries, for good or for ill. Different settings simply bring forth new circumstances that illustrate a theory and test its limitations. Cultural and political differences do not create impassable barriers to discourse, but offer opportunities to test general principles in new settings. People often disagree, but their serious disagreements turn on substance, not on terminological oddities. I may well be wrong in what I believe. But I am definite in my opinions and, if wrong, have no desire to be wrong in a small way. I should be disappointed if the principles I defend are simply regarded as inappropriate for Bombay, Moscow, or New York because of some local nuance of which I am unaware. Better to be flat wrong across the board so that everyone can learn from my mistakes.

Deductive Truths about Human Nature?

These opening assertions necessarily commit me to a form of legal universalism, which stands in apparent contrast to the cautiously skeptical approach of the common lawyer. From whence can that position arise?

And how may it be defended? Many thinkers, typically in the natural law tradition, who preach the gospel of universalism do so from the vantage point of *deductive* truth. It is easy to say (as I emphatically do not) that all just legal rules are necessarily immutable across time and space; that they are known through the application of pure reason or intuitive apprehension, or by some combination of these two unruly bedfellows. Sometimes these rules are said to be "immanent" in social relations—a learned word that conceals far more than it reveals. Empirical evidence counts for little in assessing the soundness of these rules whose normative punch is said to make resistance futile. It is this form of moral inevitability that Kant seems to have in mind when he writes: "Empirical principles are wholly unsuited to serve as the foundation for moral laws. For the universality with which such laws ought to hold for all rational beings, without exception (the unconditional practical necessity imposed by moral laws upon such beings) is lost if the basis of these laws is taken from the particular constitution of human nature or from the accidental circumstances in which such nature is placed."[2]

This form of natural law thought has often been associated with conservative strands of thought, although there is no necessary reason for treating that level of conviction as the handmaiden of the *status quo ante:* a radical could argue that major social changes are required because existing societies have adopted legal rules that violate natural law principles (as indeed they often do). To the extent that I have flirted with the natural law tradition, it has been not exclusively as a defender of some established legal practice, but often as a critic of the status quo, now in the form of the welfare state. But even when natural law is given a reformist or radical slant, it has been consistently vulnerable to attack by lawyers and social critics whose sociological and historical orientation quickly draws them to the differences in time, space, and culture. Legal rules are not proved like mathematical theorems; nor are they found like elements in the periodic table. These laws are, we are constantly reminded, contingent rules that evolve with time in accordance with the tastes and the needs of society. The most famous war cry on behalf of this realist tradition is Holmes's, who said (but did not practice) that "[t]he life of the law has not been logic: it has been experience."[3] In more modern lingo, these rules are regarded as social constructions made by its members from within a society, rather than commands imposed on society from without, be it by nature or by God. The effort to find common elements within a legal system, let alone across legal systems, is often derided as hopeless nonsense or facile generalization. Instead, scholars in countless specialties can take a certain perverse delight in showing how particular outcomes stymie and frustrate the general theories which natural lawyers strived to achieve but could never reach. Far from dealing with the power of logic and the fear of self-contradiction, we are dealing with a pliable set of social materials that generates an incredible diversity of legal rules across time and locations.

The challenge facing the conservative intellectual is to reestablish the soundness of his position without falling into the deductive traps that sap credibility from the natural law tradition. I think that it is possible to do this by beating the sociological approach at its own game. It is evident that the natural law approach is exposed to two kinds of objections, one logical and the other sociological. The former point is that the natural law theorist cannot show any linkage between what is natural and what is good. The second is that the natural law theory cannot explain the oasis of universality, given the wide variety of practices found in societies that have functioned successfully over time. Nor can it take into account the corrosive effects that the irreducible uncertainty in human and natural events has on the operation of any system that claims to talk in the language of deductive truth.

Human Desire and Human Good

The initial step in this inquiry is to establish some relationships between natural or human events and some normative test of the good. Within the naturalist tradition, one quest has always been to find ways to link some abstract conception of the good to the desires or wants of discrete individuals. The most common form of the proposition, articulated in definitional form, is that "A desires X" is treated as an equivalent to "X is good," or "X is desirable."[4] A moment's reflection shows that this simple effort to reduce the normative to the natural fails. There are obvious differences in meaning between the two expressions, as the former appears to refer to the condition of the thing itself and the latter to one person's view of it. Practically, a giant roadblock is the common case where A desires X and B desires not-X, so that X becomes both good and bad in itself. Likewise, there is no contradiction in saying that something that someone desires is undesirable. It becomes important, in a sense, to relearn the lesson taught by David Hume—that major legal truths are not deductions from empirical facts or natural laws—for the passage of more than 250 years has not allowed us to derive logically propositions that contain "ought" from those which contain only "is."[5]

This logical objection, however, hardly shows that there is no lower-level connection between individual desire and a responsible conception of the good. Thus, it would be odd to assert that X is good because A *dislikes* it, or bad because A *likes* it, or oddly that X is good because no one likes it. The obvious response is that the mere fact that A likes X counts as a *reason* why X should be regarded as a good, even if that reason is not conclusive in and of itself. Simply put, we can establish *ceteris paribus* that the desire of A for X is presumptive evidence of the goodness of X. We might have to work a bit to deal with how these desires are formed—a topic taken up in detail in chapter 5—but most of the objections to this simple proposition are better understood as weakening the inference, not undermining it altogether. In addition (in a theme that dominates this book), it is strictly necessary to show how this approach can take into account the desires of *all* individuals to avoid the problem of differing sentiments.

Some cases seem easy. If A likes X, and everyone else is indifferent as to whether X is or is not the case, then the inference that X is good appears to hold. And if all persons should prefer X to not-X, then the case for X's being good is stronger still. The hard cases, therefore, all involve situations in which there is a difference of opinion about the merits of X, and here the philosophical literature never did span the gap between the individual and social judgments of desire. But within the economic tradition, that extension has been made. Often X is not the outcome of a particular instance, but rather the articulation of some general rules of conduct. The rules then become desirable to the extent that all people prefer X to not-X, which is another way of stating the usual condition of Pareto superiority: somebody is better off and no one is worse off. And by a like measure, we have a trickier job in reaching this conclusion by saying that the winners like X enough such that they could compensate those who prefer not-X and still come out ahead. In effect, these subjective evaluations of various states of affairs, when coupled with compensation (real or hypothetical), offer a sensible way to link natural states of affairs with some ethical judgment as to their overall desirability. The definitional ploy to link desire and desirability may fail, but the presumptive link between them can be established. The core of good sense of the naturalist position remains on the choice of criterion: to link up questions of good and bad with some natural state of the world.

Necessary and Contingent Truths

The second step in defending a revised natural law position lies in exposing the ambiguity in the word "contingent" as a way to describe the social truths or social constructions of a given time and place. Here the critical ambiguity comes from the failure to distinguish between the logical and empirical use of the term. I would freely concede that all social truths about legal rights and duties are "contingent" in the logical sense that they are not derived from some inevitable principles, the truth of which can be denied only on pain of self-contradiction. Political and moral theory, however, need *not* be "contingent" in the empirical sense, which stresses their irregularity and unpredictability, or even the unexpected twists of circumstance and history.

Once we no longer treat political and legal theory as a matter of pure logic, or even, one might add, as being governed by the universal laws of physics, the challenge is to identify those empirical regularities across time, space, and culture to which any viable legal system will have to respond. That task is far harder indeed if the question is to explain the fall of the Roman Empire, the rise of Christianity, or the failure of democracy in China. Those events were so sweeping in nature that it becomes well-nigh impossible to identify some set of repetitive pattern of events into which these transformational historical moments fall. Without that backdrop it becomes far harder to isolate some common element that demonstrates the regularities in human behavior that shaped these events. But, in dealing with the more prosaic acts of buying and selling, marrying and divorcing, educating and working, the huge size of the sample makes it possible to find the elements of order hidden in the swirl of human events. Finding these regularities is not simply a matter of consulting some legal text, or even some grand economic theory. Indeed, the first part of the task is simply the collection and organization of information, which is how the natural lawyers began. In their effort to define, for example, the contract of sale, or to specify the duties of both buyer and seller, they did not begin with deductive abstractions. Rather, they observed how these transactions took place successfully on a daily basis, and then sought to recount and classify what they observed, much as the early biologists did when they organized members of the plant and animal kingdom into different groups and species. Their guiding principle was that things ought to be as they commonly are, so that customary practices and natural law went, from the earliest time, hand in hand.

Nor does this procedure run smack into the Humean gap by insisting on the functional connection between "is" and "ought," for, again, no one is (or should be) claiming any *necessary* connection between the two. Rather, the appeal rests on a test of durability: those principles and practices that endure generally do so because they serve well the communities of which they are a part. The claim is that any system that broadly flunks either or both the tests of social welfare—customary practice or cost-benefit analysis—is not likely to stand the test of time. The connection between the two lies in the way in which customs, at least within close-knit communities, gravitate to the solution that a sound cost-benefit analysis would dictate. The presumption, therefore, is that what ordinarily is the case ought to be the case, so that the natural ways of doing business become the desirable ways of doing it. Or as the ancient lawyers used to say in defining water rights: water ought to flow where it flows.

The reliance on classification and the implicit normative value of standard practices offers an additional reason why the term "natural," in its less mysterious sense of regular or commonplace, exerted such a strong hold over legal theory in its formative period. This older method may require a certain degree of imagination, but it has the great virtue of using the knowledge acquired in ordinary life as the source of legal definitions and legal rules, a process that I defend in chapter 5, which is devoted to moral incrementalism. Any more ambitious effort to understand and deal with legal matters requires a mastery of what these earlier scholars learned and accomplished, just as the wonders of modern biomedical technology still require a working knowledge of gross anatomy that has been accumulating at least from the time of Galen.

Yet it is quite clear that an understanding of legal rules does not end with classification and observation. When these are understood, there is an inescapable tendency to aim at articulating the fundamental principles around which the particulars are organized. Natural law thinkers, both in law and philosophy, thought that their method was equal to this task, for the term "natural," as in natural reason, is often used to justify certain practices like self-defense, or to condemn others as unnatural acts.

To take but one example, Aristotle resorted to this practice on numerous occasions.[6] But his intuitions were all too often far off the mark. Thus he decreed that the increase in wealth through household management is "natural," but that which is obtained through the retail trade is "justly censured; for it is unnatural, and a mode by which men gain from each other." Here Aristotle adopts what might be called a "principle of mutual exploitation," which does the Marxist one better by opening the way to attack transactions from which *both* sides benefit. By his lights usury is of course the worst sin of all, because money is meant to facilitate exchange, such that it is unnatural for it to be lent, it appears, at any interest at all. The howlers in this set of propositions are a source of stunned embarrassment. Retailing should be praised to the extent that it allows for gains from trade, which relieve the pressure on the household to make shoes from leather and clothes from textiles. Forward transactions in money (for example, business lines of credit and home mortgages) are the staple of an exchange economy. Let the term "natural" be pressed into causes so ignorant, and it is no wonder that the term falls into disgrace.

Philosophical fashions have, however, a way of working themselves pure within the law. The rhetorical flourishes remain, but the need to decide cases within the framework of an established set of social practices prevents the well-socialized lawyer from engaging in Aristotelian fits of fantasy. From Roman times to the present, knotty legal points have often been evaded by an appeal to natural law, natural reason, and natural right. Justinian grandly wrote that "[t]he law of nature is that which she has taught all animals; a law that is not peculiar to the human race, but shared by all living creatures, whether denizens of the air, the dry land, or the sea."[7] This general proposition operates at all the critical junctures within a legal system. It is natural obligation that requires parents to raise and protect their children. The acquisition of property by capture is described as the natural mode of acquisition.[8] The same logic covers self-defense: "So if I kill your slave who is lying in wait to rob me, I shall be safe: for natural reason allows a person to defend himself against danger."[9]

Nothing here has the same loopy feel as Aristotle's denunciation of usury and the retail trade. But that said, the methodology of natural law nevertheless starts to look shaky. Invocation of the "natural" looks more like a placeholder for an explanation, and less like an explanation in and of itself. And any forthcoming explanation introduces clear consequentialist overtones.[10] Parents (in large part because of their genetic connection) have the strongest interest in the welfare of their children and are best positioned to offer them optimal protection. Acquisition of property by possession gives things an easily identifiable owner, who can then preserve or consume, develop or sell the thing in question. The use of force in self-defense both deters aggression and forces the assailant, not his victim, to bear the costs of harm. To be sure, the these twin explanations show a certain level of tension: in the case of self-defense, for example, the emphasis could either be on the overall social reduction in violence or, more specifically, a correction of the imbalance between the parties that was worked by the assailant's wrongful act. But the difference in emphasis does not lead to any obvious contradiction in outcome, for each explanation gains in strength when it is reinforced by the other.

At this point the central challenge is to come up with a simple and coherent set of principles that explain both the common and diverse elements across legal systems. Here I think it best to begin with those elements that are common, and then move to those that account for the evident diversity across cultures and over time.

Twin Impulses to Universalism: Scarcity and Self-Interest

In our constant fascination with the regulatory or cost-benefit state, it is easy to forget that these issues of basic social order occupied a much larger place in earlier legal and philosophical systems than they do to-day.[11] The use and limits of self-defense, for example, occupied a central place in early deliberations, and it should be regarded as a useful window on some larger enterprise, by seeking to identify those contingent facts on which the main outlines of any sound legal order must rest. So the effort to find the key to human institutions required a different approach, one which relies less on deductive economic theory and more on the contingent regularities of human nature. H. L. A. Hart is very much in this tradition when he writes: "It is merely a contingent fact that human beings need food, clothes, and shelter; that these do not exist at hand in limitless abundance; but are scarce, have to be grown or won from nature, or have to be constructed by human toil."[12]

In this connection, the key external feature to which any sound legal and social system must respond is the condition of *scarcity,* which ensures that human wants always exceed the means to satisfy them. That scarcity in turn has a powerful influence on the kinds of living entities that will survive and prosper. In a word, it is those individuals who develop a keen sense of self-interest that survive.

The pursuit of individual self-interest—I will address the key qualification in a moment—presupposes that individuals have objects of their own that they wish to achieve, based on who they are and what they need. Any theory of natural law must therefore ask what things individuals value and how much they value them. On both frontiers we must confront the inexorable tug of subjective and objective valuation. In one sense, both individually and collectively, we are confident that we can make some objective valuations of what is good and bad. Those things that supply the resources allowing us to survive and flourish count as goods. Those things that frustrate our life plans count as bads.

Ordinary language captures this common impulse quite nicely when it speaks of "goods," not as some philosophical abstraction, but as a synonym for "merchandise," as in "dry goods" whose sale is covered, naturally, by the Sale of Goods Act. There is in general very little difference in sentiment across individuals as to what items count as goods and what count as bads (household "junk" is a nice borderline case, some of which is thrown out while some is kept as memorabilia). Stated otherwise, our common biological origins help shape the patterns of socialization whereby most people most of the time tend to value the same things, either positively or negatively. Food counts as a good; poison counts as a bad, at least if we have to consume it ourselves. The line between goods and bads, such as waste materials, is fairly strong. The market for emissions controls is strong. The market for pollutants is nonexistent.

With that said, there is a second sense in which valuation is subjective. Individuals all have different circumstances and endowments. Nothing says that all individuals value all goods, or dislike all bads, in the same way or with the same intensity. In this regard, value turns out to be subjective. Left to their own devices, different individuals will take a given sum of cash and spend it on different goods on a trip to the supermarket. The positive prices for the goods in question can be maintained even if most people value the goods at less than their cost, so long as those who value them at above cost can be found in sufficient numbers.

The question then becomes how these goods can be matched with their proper owners, and for that task nothing compares with the marketplace, which allows individuals to sort themselves by their purchasing decisions. The same can be said about other key life choices, from marriage to business, as well. It does not take an exact knowledge of the preferences and tastes of any person to understand that his choices will not be distributed evenly across any population. Yet our knowledge of the variance in the population is enough to caution us about collective solutions for the allocation of goods and services, or for the central dictation of social relations. When common law judges say that the value of goods and services received in exchange is for the parties to evaluate, they do not commit themselves to the proposition that valuation is so arbitrary that it lacks any internal coherence. They rest on the proposition that individuals should be given their head in organizing their own lives because they are likely to have better knowledge—which need not be perfect knowledge—of what their own self-interest requires than any one who might choose to act on their behalf.

The exact meaning of self-interest is worth a brief discussion. In its crudest form, the term could be construed atomistically to mean that persons will satisfy whatever appetites they have in the short run, wholly without regard to the welfare of other persons. Self-interest, taken in this uncritical sense, is hardly enlightened, but rather constitutes a polite way of describing persons as being merely selfish. A moment's reflection should indicate that this account does not even appear to apply to most animals (which care for their young), and in any event does not capture anything like the full richness of human experience. Evolution, which has taken place over countless generations, can hardly stop dead in its tracks in a single generation. Individuals are not born full grown into this world, but are raised as part of families and larger communities in which (as every coach knows—"There is no 'I' in 'Team'") human interaction and cooperation count every bit as much as the competition and rivalry that are wrongly said to constitute the full range of self-interested behavior. The parent who is indifferent to the fate of his or her helpless children may well take actions that prevent them from reaching maturity and thus continuing the cycle of life. Children who do not learn how to share trust within the family can rarely function well outside of it. Parents have to take into account the welfare of their children, and for parents to do that they have to take into account the welfare of each other.[13] Throughout it all, they must be able to interact with extended family and larger groups in ways that allow them to obtain sufficient caloric intake to discharge the ordinary functions of life, and to resolve their differences in ways that do not fatally compromise their bodily integrity and their ability to carry out purposive activity.

Self-interest, then, is *inclusive* of those with whom one has a genetic bond; it certainly includes the capacity to feel love to another individual so as to facilitate raising family; it presupposes an ability to engage in some cooperative behavior with strangers; and it covers the ability to avoid force inflicted by others every bit as much, if not more, than the use of force against others. The exact ways in which these cooperative and familial tasks are discharged may differ in detail from place to place and culture to culture; and they surely depend in large measure on the means of production and exchange available at any stage in human development. But, with all that said, the elemental imperatives place powerful constraints on what individuals are allowed to do to, for, and with each other. It is quite inconceivable (in the practical, not the logical sense) to envision a society in which parents are routinely allowed to abandon their young; in which the use of force within the community prompts no social disapproval; in which promises are as easily broken as kept; or in which all individuals are encouraged to freeload off the efforts of others.

Indeed, experimental and psychological research on the issue of group interests indicates the power of self-interest. Mancur Olson's classical exposition of the theory of group behavior asserts that self-interested individuals will not necessarily advance the interest of the group they are a part of. Unless coerced, or tempted with some private benefit, they have a tendency to free ride with respect to goods that they prefer to acquire. When that tendency is universalized, goods and services that everyone wants become just those goods that no one will voluntarily and unilateral supply. "Indeed, unless the number of individuals in a group is quite small, or unless there is coercion or some other special device to act in their common interest, *rational, self-interested individuals will not act to achieve their common or group interests.*"[14] That theory has, as Olson well understood, clear application to group activity at the political level, for it suggests the unhappy conclusion that rational, self-interested individuals would never cooperate with each other in order to achieve a collective end, of which peace and good order is the most obvious. As he observes, notwithstanding the appeals to patriotism and national ideology, as strengthened by the bonds of common culture, "no state in modern history has been able to support itself through voluntary dues or contributions."[15] The simple logic is that each individual can receive the public benefits (which are by definition nonexclusive) whether or not he contributes labor or resources to support them. But every person is in exactly the same position, so that all persons refuse to cooperate so that nothing gets produced even though these same players would by their own lights have been better off if all of them had contributed to the preservation of public goods from which each would benefit.

Thus if each of one hundred people could contribute goods and services worth fifty dollars that produce one hundred dollars, shared equally, then if everyone participated, the total cost of five thousand dollars would yield ten thousand dollars in benefits. However, since each person can feast on the contribution of others even if he makes none himself, the prediction is that all will hold back unless a powerful state force coerces them to act in their collective benefit. But that model presupposes that the consequences of holding out leave one no worse off than he was before. Yet in nature the failure to cooperate can often lead to death, so that any individuals who learn to cooperate with each other have a better chance of survival than the pure egotists who brave it alone. Cooperation among kin offers obvious genetic advantages. And since evolution is, by definition, a most imperfect instrument, the usual principles of natural selection should lead to some, probably normal, distribution of tastes on the willingness to cooperate, in which cooperators will on average be more likely to survive than noncooperators. The net result is that there is no reason to accept the radical Hobbesian account of individual selfishness, or its corollary that a state of nature is productive of an anarchy that can be curbed only with a unitary state governed by an absolute sovereign. Quite to the contrary, one of the great dangers of the centralization of power is that it tends to sap informal methods of social control of their strength. Individuals exhibit higher levels of cooperation in unregulated environments when their prior breaches of legal rules are *not* subject to legal sanctions.[16] Evidently, faced with success or failure on their own, they develop cooperative strategies.

But it hardly follows that every person must follow these informal rules all the time for any society to survive. Hence some individuals will always seek to disobey the rules, or, even better for them, to carve out exceptions and privileges to general rules of unquestioned validity. Some individuals might wish to abandon their young, or at least impose the cost of raising their own children on others; some individuals seek to use force to their own ends while holding all others to the general prohibition. Some individuals seek to evade their own promises, while holding others to theirs; some individuals seek a privileged status that allows them to live off the resources owned and gathered by others. For every good rule, there are impulses for a few principled exceptions and a thousand unprincipled ones.

It is from insights as simple as these that the practical case for the ordinary and general rules of individual liberty, private property, and contractual obligations is born. The process here was not deductive, but followed, ironically perhaps, an evolutionary path that once again hearkens back to the implicit logic of the common law. The basic distribution of rights and duties were, like speech and grammar, learned and obeyed before anyone could formalize their content.[17] As Hayek stressed so often and so well, they did not arise from some central plan created from on-high.[18] "[R]ecent developments in evolutionary theory and supporting empirical research provide strong support for the assumption that modern humans have inherited a propensity to learn social norms, similar to our inherited propensity to learn grammatical rules."[19] In their original form these norms evolved by a process of trial and error, such that those primitive groups unable to control excessive egoism within their ranks did not survive in competition with those who could present a more unified front to the rest of the world.

Those instincts should survive, at least in attenuated form, as extended familial groups become larger political institutions. But the instincts become much more jumbled, for the old loyalties remain even as new ones are added. Today we have, or should have, a greater awareness of the social and economic reasons that lie behind the legal rules. Our cautious evolutionary sense should warn us against lurching from one extreme to another. Just as we need to have private institutions, so we must be sure that we understand the role and scope for public institutions. The enduring need to maintain cooperative behavior places limits on the extent to which the important legal rights speak only of separation and exclusion. If homes are private, streets and rivers are likely to be held in common. If the use of force is to be prohibited, the maintenance of order by force and the collection of tax revenues to fund these public endeavors is strictly required. The constraints may appear to be slight, but they bind with a great deal of power.

The Sources of Variation

This discussion thus far still leaves open the question of how one can account for the extensive *variation* in observed legal rules and practices in a world that respects, albeit for consequentialist or utilitarian reasons, these natural law rules. At this point, the best way to get a handle on this situation is to stress the limited objective of the original natural law theorists, which was to explain the basic set of relationships that defined rights and wrongs between people. The system thus did well in delineating these rights, but at a philosophical level it had little if anything to say about the choice and articulation of remedies once a violation to those rights had been threatened or realized. It is with respect to the choice of remedies that we can locate much of the variation in the structure of legal rules across cultures and over time.[20]

Any responsible effort to deal with this ever-recurrent remedial issue requires an appreciation of the ubiquity of midlevel *trade-offs* and the serious questions of institutional design they create. A simple sale may go astray. What remedy should be afforded the innocent party? Even if valuation is subjective, some collective measurement has to be made about damages. In the first instance, this practice might be left to the parties. But in some cases they will be silent and some legal intervention will have to sort out the mess. An unflagging allegiance to subjective value opens the way for the aggrieved party to inflate his losses without fear of contradiction. So virtually every legal system places some form of "objective" constraint on valuation in order to control that abuse. We are forced to abandon the ideal measure of damages as unworkable and substitute some serviceable proxy in its place.

This one example represents only the tip of the iceberg. The problem of remedies mushrooms at every area of the law. The question is whether we should give a remedy before the wrong has been committed or only after it has been done. If it is before, should it be publicly administered or privately administered? If it is afterward, should it be an award in damages or the restoration of some thing in kind? Does one prefer an administrative remedy by the state, or a class action brought by members of a class? Does one require the use of some standard form, for example, a contract in writing, so as to ease the burden of enforcement after the fact, or does one shun these formalities in order to allow the joint realization of any expression of the intentions of the parties?

The range of responses to these questions is broad, to say the least, and often the relative merits of these alternative systems are hard to rank. How many ordinary people have any strong sense of how to deal with the questions of anticipatory breach, restitution, reliance, or expectation damages, specific performance, and injunctive relief that form so much of the law of contracts? To someone in the nonimperialist side of the law and economics tradition (that is, someone who thinks that law and economics is only one powerful tool among many), this simple demonstration of remedial uncertainty shows the implicit trade-offs in everything the law touches. The so-called debate between rules and standards picks up one corner of this challenge when it asks, in the most general form, whether we have a hard-edged rule ("only people over eighteen may enter into contracts") or a looser standard ("only people of full competence may enter into contracts"). In practice, even this stark opposition understates the complexity of the matter, for a sound institution frequently adopts a *mixed* solution, which contains, for example, a minimum age requirement for entering into (some) contracts, and then recognizes additional incapacities for persons with special disabilities, for example, insanity or retardation at any age. The question is how to minimize the sum of error and administrative costs, relative to an object—the enforcement of contracts, the protection of property—that is itself uncontroversial under the general natural law principles.

At this point, it is easy to see why different legal systems take different approaches on the full range of remedial institutions. The level of formality required for marriages or real estate contracts or legal settlements may well vary. Sometimes we ask for a writing, other times for notaries, and still other times for witnesses, but always with the object of improving the security of transactions at reasonable costs. In principle, no one should be daunted by the need to face these objects, so long as the ends are proper and the trade-offs to reach them are transparent. But in some intellectual circles, the messiness of the remedial enterprise is said to infect the operation of the entire system. For example, one major thrust of the now dormant Critical Legal Studies movement has been to expose the soft underbelly of the classical legal system (precisely because it rests on these natural law principles of individual choice, private property, and freedom of contract) by showing that it is unable to deal with these questions effectively.

That critique would be quite welcome if it proceeded in good incremental fashion to show why one system of recordation was superior to another. But here the choice of rhetoric raises the stakes. No longer do we deal with inescapable trade-offs in the operation of any complex legal system. Rather, we face *contradictions* in the internal constitution of the legal system as a whole. The choice of language is not inadvertent. Trade-offs are frequent and can be managed for better or worse. Contradictions are fatal in life as in logic. For example, in his careful explication of Duncan Kennedy's work,[21] Mark Kelman stressed "the contradiction between a commitment to mechanically applicable rules as the appropriate form of resolving disputes (thought to be associated in complex ways with the political tradition of self-reliance and individuals) and a commitment to situation-sensitive, ad hoc standards (thought to correspond to sharing and altruism)."[22]

This talk of "contradictions" in Critical Legal Studies forms an odd couple with the "necessity" arguments in favor of natural law. Just as the natural lawyers overclaimed for their position by appealing to deductive logic, so it is that the Critical Legal Scholars exaggerated their claim by elevating every important remedial and institutional trade-off into a contradiction worthy of Karl Marx's critique of capitalism generally. Necessity, impossibility and contradiction are logical constructs, none of which does well in handling the messy materials of the law. Armchair empiricism is, at times, the best tool we have to resolve these matters. These trade-offs in institutional design are not unique to a system of private law. They are endemic in every piece of legislation of the modern state, regardless of its substantive regulation. Similar trade-offs can be found in setting up every state-run cartel, in enforcing every minimum wage law, in subsidizing every agricultural crop, and in determining eligibility and payment in every public welfare program. The sensible questions to ask about these schemes touch both the selection of their ends and the choice of means. If the basic natural law position is wrong on ends, why bother to debate the questions of institutional and remedial design? There is a reason why the Critical Legal Studies program became moribund. Once it launched its initial salvo, it disabled itself from saying anything constructive about the actual choices that required resolution. Like the strong natural rights theory, its demise was guaranteed because its critique was too powerful for its own good.

The dangers of this categorical approach become most vivid in thinking about the choice of remedies in those cases in which it is uncertain whether violations of the law have been committed. In these cases, we have resolved the fundamental question of entitlement by deciding, uncontroversially, that fraud is bad. The remedial question is how to stop it. The first principle is to avoid some unworkable extremes—ban all contracts for the sale of goods in order to avoid fraud in one case in a million. The harder choices flirt with mandatory disclosures, minimum terms, cooling-off periods, and the like. Here, moreover, it is possible to adopt different strategies.[23] The legislature could invest heavily in detailed rules to achieve its ends, in order to reduce the costs of compliance by individuals who gain greater knowledge of what the rule requires. To ensure automobile safety, the front bumper of any car must be able to resist a force of X; no wheelchair ramp can have a slope of more than Y degrees. The alternative strategy is to articulate general standards: build a car that is reasonably safe; make reasonable accommodations for the disabled so long as these do not impose undue costs. Our dilemma is that general standards are cheaper to articulate, but are by the same token more difficult to interpret and apply. Any range of intermediate specificity can be easily imagined, where one goal is to minimize the sum of the costs needed first for their promulgation and then for their interpretation. This problem can be further complicated because the legislature need not articulate the standards itself, but could delegate that responsibility to some administrative body.

The pros and cons of these arrangements are always difficult to sort out. Viewed solely as a matter of information costs, it is never quite clear who is in the best position to reduce these communication costs, the speaker or the audience. Wisdom is another issue. A badly calibrated rule may raise compliance costs excessively, while a broad standard could easily invite an abuse of discretion by those in charge of its implementation. The durability of the rule is yet another concern. Specific rules may well need constant revision as technology changes, while general standards have greater durability, even if their application requires constant reinterpretation. There is no cheap or easy solution to any of these so-called contradictions.

It is not my purpose to untangle this ball of yarn here, but rather to suggest that the daunting nature of that task counsels in favor of a sharp contraction of the areas in which government intervention is justified in the first place. But it is critical to stress that, to the extent that diversity arises out of response to these institutional and remedial issues, we have a powerful explanation of how a small set of core normative principles can mushroom into a rich array of legal practices and institutions. Happily enough, since it is easy to replace the word "contradiction" with "trade-off," even readers who have no truck with the grandiose political claims of the Critical Legal Studies movement have much to learn from their more sober examination of the soft spots in traditional legal regimes.[24]

An additional word of caution should be added about this second prong of the Kennedy-Kelman thesis. There is, quite simply, no necessary linkage between the rules/standards debate and the egoism/altruism debate. Rather, in this context the fatal temptation is to assume any one-to-one correspondence between the choice of remedy and the attitudes of the party who urges it. The point, easily generalized, is conveniently made in connection with long-term commercial contracts, whose performance is impeded by some unwelcome or unforeseen event.[25] From the *ex ante* perspective, the parties may well choose a rule that calls on them to share the risk in the event of an adverse event, or that may place all (or most) of the loss on one party. In principle, the parties have all the right incentives to place the risk of future loss in ways that maximize the joint value of the contract to them. If, therefore, they choose to place all the loss on one party (so as, for example to minimize the risk of certain occurrences), then the uncooperative party is the one that seeks to divide a loss that the contract allocates to him exclusively. Similarly, in a contract that calls for a proportionate division of the losses between the parties, then that outcome does not demonstrate altruism, but only the interplay of market forces. The choice of remedial rules—be it rules or standards, apportionment or not—gives *no* insight into whether a society has strong individualistic or communitarian routes. That question can only be answered by looking elsewhere, by seeing the level of voluntary and state transfers, to persons in need. On this dimension at least, the choice of remedy reveals very little about the ultimate constitution of society. For that we have to turn to the basic determinants of human behavior on which natural law theories implicitly rely.

2 The System of Liberty

Laissez-Faire, Cautiously Defined

THE PURPOSE OF THE FIRST CHAPTER was to offer, within a consequentialist framework, a skeptical defense of a general system of liberty built on the natural law tradition. Those words will ring hollow unless some content is given to the rules that deserve such universal observance. In dealing with these matters, my overall position is to endorse a sensible version of laissez-faire—as its proponents, and not its critics, would define it. For these purposes, Jacob Viner proposed a good working definition some years ago when he used the term "to mean what the pioneer systematic exponents of it, the Physiocrats and Adam Smith, argued for, namely, the limitation of governmental activity to the enforcement of peace and of 'justice' in the restricted sense of 'commutative justice,' to defense against foreign enemies, and to public works regarded as essential and as impossible or highly improbable of establishment by private enterprise, or, for special reasons, unsuitable to be left to private operation."[1] A similar account of the classical liberal position is offered by Charles Murray, who recognizes the need for government to supply, with tax revenues, key public goods and infrastructure.[2] Both these accounts are far more sophisticated than Grant Gilmore's oft-quoted bon mot: "I suppose that laissez-faire economic theory comes down to something like this: If we all do exactly as we please, no doubt everything will work out for the best."[3]

Even if we put Gilmore's piquant account to one side, the issue is one of real consequence, because many purported refutations of laissez-faire and libertarian thought are premised on the view that laissez-faire falls once it is shown that government action is necessary to preserve the liberties it prizes. One recent example of this tradition is offered by Stephen Holmes and Cass Sunstein in—the title tells all—*The Cost of Rights: Why Liberty Depends on Taxes.*[4] Their work starts out with the observation that any and all claims of rights, regardless of their content, will necessarily require the use of public institutions and public officials to enforce. That argument could be contested by those, like David Friedman, who point to Homeric Greece and early Icelandic history to show that some human societies have created stable institutions without the intervention of the nation-state.[5] But the real lesson to learn from these limited examples is, in my view, precisely the opposite. The utter lack of modern examples of this nongovernmental extreme shows that as territories become larger, and populations more diverse, some level of centralized power is needed to ensure political stability. In modern times, it is wishful thinking to assume that some kind of libertarian order is viable in which minimal state involvement becomes no involvement at all.

That said, it hardly follows that the dependence of liberty on taxation justifies any scheme of taxation that the mind of man can propose, for it is equally true that some systems of taxation are so excessive and confiscatory as to pose major threats to the system of liberty they are supposed to undergird. The first pressing question asks, What counts as an optimal system of taxation? This inquiry is not answered sufficiently by a showing that this level of taxation is greater than zero. Just as taxes can be too low, they can be too high or too skewed. Chief Justice Marshall did not speak idly when he intoned: "The power to tax involves the power to destroy."[6] Yet Holmes and Sunstein offer no judgment on the multitude of tax policy questions: Should the tax base be on consumption or income? Should taxes be flat or progressive? How should capital gains be taxed? Nor do they give any account of which functions of government they regard as appropriate and which ones they do not. Certainly it is a misconception of laissez-faire to assume that because it thinks that recordation of preexisting property interests necessarily promotes the security of possession, it also welcomes all forms of government regulation that "protect" private property, such as the provision of below-market insurance against natural catastrophes brought on by hurricanes or earthquakes.

A similar set of confusions from a similar launch point is found in Liam Murphy and Thomas Nagel's *The Myth of Ownership*,[7] a recent defense of the social welfare state and the extensive system of taxation that it presupposes. Here our authors are not content to make functional arguments against the classical liberal position. They desire to achieve a clean conceptual kill by showing that it is "deeply incoherent." "There is no market without government and no government without taxes; and what type of market there is depends on laws and policy decisions that government must make."[8] To which it could be added that the type of government depends equally on the type of private institutions that are allowed to develop. In this regard, moreover, their critique depends not only on the insistence of an implicit baseline of state ownership. It also depends on the question of what modifications from that baseline they are prepared to accept as part of their theory. Thus a government without a market economy will produce very little, and therefore will have nothing to tax at all. It could then grant individuals weak and partial property rights in order to secure the revenues that it needs to fulfill its own functions. But once the government is supposed to design optimal social institutions, then it can no longer act in a fashion that seeks to maximize solely the revenues that fall into state coffers. It must do so in a way that maximizes the social welfare of all citizens that live within its borders (and perhaps beyond), which it can only do by placing limits on its own powers to confiscate, tax, and regulate. If the goal is some optimal system of social welfare, it is easy to see how this all-powerful state will come to cede most of its powers to the extent that it thinks that private institutions can outperform public ones over a large sphere of behavior. In a sense, therefore, the question of finding the optimal mix of public and private resources should not in principle depend on which baseline we choose. So long as corrections and emendations are made, we should end up at the same point in the middle no matter which extreme we start from.[9] In practice, however, each transition is fraught with difficulty, such that the key question is which corner we start from. If, as I believe, the optimal mix of private and state behavior has large components of the former and limited ones of the latter, then we should start with the naïve assumption of no government in the state of nature, and not with the authoritarian assumption that some nameless, all powerful state is needed to make markets run.

An analysis of laissez-faire, then, requires a far more precise definition, and far more work. As a first stab, crudely speaking, laissez-faire stands for the proposition that the government should keep its "hands off" the economy. But that inexact formulation lacks the precision of Viner's account, and should not be taken as rejecting all government regulation—legislative, administrative, or judicial—of economic affairs. Rather, the well-articulated system of laissez-faire recognizes the need for national defense. It has also accepted, more cautiously, the state financing and operation of infrastructure, such as sewers and highways, although it acknowledges with regard to both that it can be financed by a set of user fees instead of general taxes, and that large portions of their operations can be contracted out to private parties. The system also recognizes in principle a place for the antitrust law to prevent monopolies when competitive markets work, or even—although the execution is difficult—to regulate natural monopolies, when competitive markets are not feasible.[10] The system of property under laissez-faire depends heavily on a system of mandatory recordation that protects the security of transactions in real estate and personal property; it includes a system of bankruptcy that allows for the orderly liquidation and reorganization of bankrupt individuals and firms; it accepts a rule of limited liability that encourages investment in the corporate form; it requires the rigorous legal protection of property from trespasses and nuisance, including pollution. Laissez-faire also recognizes the mandatory formalities for contracting, such as writing requirements; and, of course, it depends heavily on judicial enforcement of a contract when one (or both) sides to it are in breach.

That list of state functions is by no means trivial. But it is also not exhaustive. Equally important are the possible ends for state power that are excluded from the list. Most centrally, the parties, not the state, should determine terms and conditions of ordinary contracts, with respect to goods and services. It is for that reason that the theory of laissez-faire rejects the effort of governments to set maximum hours or minimum wages; to impose antidiscrimination laws on private competitive industries; to ban yellow dog contracts, whereby employees accept as a condition of employment the obligation not to belong to a union; and to establish price controls for agricultural commodities, gasoline, or apartment rents. These are all grounded in skepticism about government power: the parties know better than anyone else what is in their own interest, so that any public dictation of contractual terms is a limitation of the freedom of both parties to the transaction which necessarily harms their economic welfare.

Articulating that bare-bones vision of laissez-faire, however, neither explains the account of human nature on which it rests nor delineates the legal rules that make it all possible. I set out what I regard as the template for both those tasks in my 1995 book *Simple Rules for a Complex World*. Here the initial question can be formulated as follows: Given the general knowledge that we have of human psychology, human behavior, and the external world, what tasks must any stable legal system discharge? By putting the question this way, it should be clear that we are not engaged in some sterile deductive activity. Rather, we are supplying a functional foundation to rights that have over time been widely respected and enforced in successful societies.

The Building Blocks of Private Law

Autonomy

The first component of a system of liberty is easy to state. Any adequate theory of rights has to establish some assignment of right between persons and objects, so it is known who has control over whom and what.

The first part of that inquiry asks how it is that individuals come to have rights over themselves. To be sure, there has not been a universal empirical answer to this question, for history has been filled with societies that have prospered on the backs of their slaves. But does the infinite variety of sociological norms justify the relativist argument that slavery was just to the slaves in the societies that practiced it? Or was it a rule that was tolerated because of the perceived self-interest from the practice? The Romans had an extensive system of slaves. But they were under no illusion as to its supposed justice under a system of natural law. Justinian, in his *Institutes,* states the central proposition loud and clear: "[B]y the law of nature all men from the beginning were born free."[11]

The alternative position to slavery is one that accords each individual some measure of autonomy, by which I mean self-rule, in order to beat back so odious a legal system. From this it is but a short step to the familiar Lockean position that all persons are born free, equal, and independent in the state of nature.[12] By this it is not meant that there are no families or associations, or that individuals have their characters forged from birth without human guidance or social intervention. Rather, the claim is more modest: that outside the family individuals should interact as legal equals with one another. Dominance and authority of one stranger over another is not an acceptable option. After all, what form would this asymmetrical allocation of power take? Who would dominate whom, to what extent, and how long? The one condition of legal equality stands in stark opposition to an infinite variety of positions of inequality. Historically many of these inequalities emerged from conquest, which treated slavery as an act of mercy for those otherwise condemned to death. But that argument just pushes back the inquiry one level: Why was it that the victors (who were often aggressors) had the right to conquer in the first place? Apologetics aside, no one has ever made the case for the dominance that slave institutions presuppose.

The acceptance of equality, of course, does not quite carry the day without some conception of the ways in which equality expresses itself. It is here that the emphasis on freedom, or "natural liberty" as it has been called, becomes critical. We could have a system of equality in which all persons are free to kill one another at will and subject them to slavery. Or we could have a system of equality that requires each person to respect the autonomy of the other. At this point some informal but powerful utilitarian judgments back up the presumption in favor of natural liberty. One reason is that the autonomy principle is capable of being universalized. No matter how many individuals there are, no matter when and where they are born, each can be accommodated into a system of natural liberty without having constantly to rejigger the rules of the game, or to communicate to members of the community the content of their new obligations. The simple clear message works well to a large and diverse audience.[13] Forbearance against the use of force as a general obligation works as well in a society of a million as it does in one of a thousand.

But why do we want that prohibition? To appreciate its staying power, just ask one simple question over and over again. Assume that there is some deviation from the principle of equality that gives one person an advantage over another, as with slavery. To use John Rawls's famous phrase, place yourself behind a "veil of ignorance," and then deliberate as to the proper set of social choices.[14] If you did not know whether you would be the winner or loser under this scheme, but had equal chances of being either, would you choose slavery in preference to a system that secured the equality of rights associated with the Lockean formation? There is no airtight answer to that question. But it is instructive that very few free individuals have ever chosen to sell themselves into slavery even when there was no prohibition against their so doing. The gains to the winners do not exceed or justify the losses imposed on the losers.

Speaking more generally, a world in which we tolerate ad hoc advantages in entitlements is one in which legal rights will remain essentially contested. A world that fixes those entitlements equally across individuals allows for a long-term solution to emerge, under a norm of equality of rights. One can easily think of small variations in how autonomy is expressed that will move across cultures. But it is very difficult to think of cultural variations that will justify widespread deviations from the autonomy principle. If it is A who faces the risk of a dangerous surgery to relieve a threatening medical condition, it would be odd indeed for any legal system to say that the decision whether A should proceed should be left to some randomly chosen B, instead of to A or (when competence is an issue) the members of A's immediate family. The result is rejected as absurd not because it is logically contradictory, but because it is socially counterproductive.

This mistake of the natural lawyers was a logical one. It was to assume that a proposition that was practically unworkable or self-destructive was equivalent to one that was internally self-contradictory. The mistake is easy to make. Even today we often use the words "reason" and "rational" to describe the connections between logical propositions. Simultaneously, we use the words "unreasonable" and "irrational" to describe most undesirable social affairs, doubtless because of the inveterate tendency to transmute socially necessary truths into logically necessary ones. But just because the natural lawyers were guilty of overpromotion did not mean that classification and observation led to the wrong conclusions. To revert to our previous example, A will surely not benefit from medical treatment when his right to receive or refuse that treatment is assigned to a randomly chosen B; and B will surely not benefit if rights to his medical treatment are lodged either in A or in some randomly chosen C, and so on down the line. Assigning the rights over any particular person to that person is a dominant solution for the patients of Galen as it is for the enrollees in a modern health plan.

Property

The principle of autonomy does not operate in a void, for individuals all need space and nourishment to survive and reproduce. A system of liberty may well give each person rights over his or her own person, but it does not in and of itself do much to assign ownership rights over things in the external world. To make that assignment, it has often been suggested that we should collectively seek some form of unanimous consent to make those decisions affecting ownership rights. The argument is that no one can protest an allocation to which he has agreed. True enough perhaps, but a moment's reflection will indicate that this agreement will never be consummated, for each individual, acting out of self-interest, will always claim a little more for himself than he is willing to cede for to others. If under a condition of scarcity wants exceed needs, then we can be confident that any simple system of self-revealed preferences will be satisfied only if a society can conjure up more land, more food and water than it is capable of finding or producing. Yet by the time any such grand agreement is reached, we should all be dead.

The well-nigh universal response to this problem in primitive societies is to allow individuals to acquire unowned land by occupation and unowned animals by capture. This simple device will invite certain inequality of outcomes, as some individuals may have advantages born of luck of speed, strength, or position. And in some cases it might result in the premature occupation of land before it is needed for productive use. There are surely costs to this general rule, as there are to any other. But lest we be consumed by these disadvantages, on this, as in so many other matters, we must heed David Hume's injunction: "Justice, in her decisions, never regards the fitness or unfitness of objects to particular persons, but conducts herself by more extensive views."[15] To dwell on the unsatisfactory state of outcomes in particular cases, to lament the triumph of this miser over that generous man, is to overlook the general benefits that follow from these broad-gauged allocation decisions. All things now have a determinate owner who can make decisions about consumption, use, or disposition in a self-interested matter. The question of equity in the original division of useful things turns out to be far less important in practice than the creation of a clear and powerful set of ownership rights over things that will permit intelligent decision over their development, use, sale, and consumption. So while virtually all legal systems fret about following these rules of occupation and capture for land, movables, and animals, they also have found it very hard to deviate from them—except when rules of conquest have given the new sovereign the whip hand, to the exclusion of ordinary citizens.

For all our doubts, it is useful to reflect on the appeal of the first possession to mediate disputes between different ethnic groups. Whether one speaks of the various Indian tribes in the United States or Canada, the Maori in New Zealand, or the aborigines of Australia, the question of who owns the land often starts with the question of who occupied it first. No one can say that first possession is the only thing that matters, for history is rarely kind enough to preserve the orderly transmission of property over time. Treaties are made, misunderstood, violated, rejected, and disregarded—and it is never quite sure by whom.[16] Voluntary exchange is often displaced by theft, and evidence of both is lost in the mists of time. But before we dismiss too quickly the power of the proposition that prior in time is higher in right, we should reflect on what alternative regime will be implemented once the classical legal rule is pronounced irrelevant. Do we want last in time to be highest in right? Or a rule that gives the property to the deserving party, determined by a set of rules that no one could quite articulate or defend? Do we want to allocate rights by lottery to avoid all thorny factual questions? But if we do so, do we displace all people in current occupation of land, even if they have expended time, money, and labor to improve their property? It is hard to beat something with nothing, and here, as in other social issues, the question is never whether a proposed legal solution is perfect. It is only whether it is at least as good, all things considered, as some rival, and imperfect, social alternative.

In making these statements about land and chattels, it is important not to claim too much. One fair criticism of John Locke is that he envisioned a world in which it was undesirable for anything to be held permanently in the commons. The object of a set of legal rules was to secure private ownership of natural resources in the quickest way possible. But a moment's reflection reveals that every legal system has preserved elements of common property, most notably in the air and in the water, and often in the seashore, which operates as a buffer between the private spaces on one side, and the public spaces on the other.[17] Indeed, we quickly discover in the evolution of English common law—and, I dare say, in Maori tribal law—that private and communal property institutions are adopted cheerfully and simultaneously within a single society.

There are good economic reasons why this division is observed. To see why, just ask whether it would be a matter of simple fortuity if the arrangements were reversed, so that large bodies of flowing water could be routinely privatized by individuals who built dams across rivers, while land had to perpetually remain held in common no matter how intensive the investments necessary to make it suitable for cultivation or for the construction of factories and homes. Do we really think that the level of social satisfaction would increase if, with the advancement of agriculture, no one could be secure enough in the possession of land to be confident that crops he planted today he could harvest tomorrow? The original justification of property was often couched in the agricultural metaphor that proclaimed only those who sowed may reap, and for good reason. Only if the gain is internalized will self-interested individuals make the investment to improve the soil so as to eke out a living from it. The long time horizons obviated potentially devastating temporal externalities.

But with water, total privatization results in the destruction of flowing rivers, of navigation, recreation, fishing, and aesthetics. To be sure, one could conceive of a way in which one person could first privatize a river and then sell it back to the public at large, but the high transaction costs preclude such a maneuver. Far better, therefore, to start with what is secured as common property, first by custom and then by the state, to preserve the natural advantages of public access to flowing water, than it is to privatize it all. Thereafter individual rights of appropriation of limited quantities can be made secure by custom or positive enactment, until some regime of mixed public and private uses inches its way to a system with high levels of social stability.

To make the point more generally, the choice between private and common property is a choice between two sets of benefits and two sets of costs, both of which exist in different amounts in different resource settings. One of these costs is the pain of excluding nonowners and the other is the difficulty of coordination between co-owners. With land, exclusion comes at a far lower price because of the sharp boundaries and the easy ability to develop or sell land once it is owned separately. With water, coordination among separate autonomous owners presents the far greater difficulty, so that common solutions are almost universally required. With the groundwater the solution is often in doubt and usually depends on the intensity of the use: where it is light a rule of capture tends to dominate because of its low administrative costs.[18] But when use becomes heavier, so that the interactive effects loom larger, a rule that respects "correlative rights" is generally invoked to limit the levels of removal in settings where the transaction costs among an indeterminate set of neighbors is likely to be high. As one might imagine, the transition between legal regimes is often likely to be messy and uncertain. But lest one be blinded by the details in the individual case, the implicit logic is to minimize the sum of the two costs. To be sure, these allocations are not constant over time, either with land or water. Before agriculture, there was little investment that one could make in land, so why not have individuals in a hunter-gatherer society move about at will? But with reaping and sowing came the privatization of land and the rules that limit the rights to remove water, be it for consumption or irrigation. Just that pattern of development emerges in response to technical innovation, be it in the English common law or the customary law of indigenous people in Hawaii[19] or Japan.[20] Private investment will only take place on private property.

Contract

Thus far I have articulated relatively simple rules to establish the ownership of labor and property. But once assigned, these initial rights, when privately held, are normally capable of transfer, usually by contract, although also by gift or bequest. Moral and legal philosophers often take the position that promises are binding of their own inherent force. That mysterious conclusion contains a large element of truth, but its underlying moral intuition needs some functional grounding. All to often, the promises made or received in the classical legal texts have no apparent direction or focus. A promise to touch the surface of the moon may well be of more philosophical interest, because of its obvious impossibility,[21] than one to sell a bushel of wheat, which has the academic misfortune to make perfectly good commercial sense. But to grasp the moral force of promising, as everywhere in law, we should avoid the temptation to skip over the routine and dwell on exotic undertakings. The important element is to recognize that self-interest and scarcity shape the promises that are exchanged. You promise to do or deliver that which costs you less than what you receive in exchange by way of cash, services, or property. I do the same.

The key issue is why go through this exercise at all. And here it is the subjective account of value that explains the transaction. Each side attaches its own unique value to the objects that are exchanged, surrendering that which they value less in exchange for that which they value more. In most cases, there is no reason to attempt to reproduce the calculations that each side made. Rather, it is best to rely on the cautious skepticism that recognizes first our collective knowledge of general rules of human behavior (which alone makes law possible), and second our collective ignorance of individual valuations (which makes voluntary exchange the preferred method of transferring resources).

This point need not be demonstrated afresh in each individual transaction to which it applies. Promises are presumptively enforced because, on average, they generate gains to both parties to the arrangement. The gains to both parties then set up opportunities for further transactions with additional gains, so that one sound principle is capable of millions of distinct and successive applications. The cycle of exchange stops only with consumption or use, and both of these are determined by the current owner, not by the state.

Anyone who doubts the importance of gains from trade should then ask what our reaction to promises would be if we thought, as Marxist theories of exploitation suggest,[22] that on average they impoverished *both* sides to the transaction. We should ban them, of course. Most people would have the same reaction to mutual promises between strangers, excluding gifts, that helped one side only to hurt the other. This class of win-lose transactions would be scarcely distinguishable in outcome from theft, whereby one party profits only at the expense of the other. There is no guarantee, indeed little likelihood, that if put to the test the thief would (even if fully solvent) be ready and willing to buy the thing at a price set by the owner. Indeed just this one-sided result is obtained when one party receives the performance from the other without making good on its return promise.

The situation only gets worse if the original promise was made when there was no intention to keep it, for now subsequent nonperformance is compounded by initial deceit. The Kantian point is that "a man who intends to make a false promise will immediately see that he intends to make use of another man merely as a means to an end which the latter does not hold."[23] Even when couched in Kantian language, the point is the soul of common sense. The false promise is just a subtle form of theft: a transaction from which one side necessarily gains and the other loses. Treating a person as "an end in himself" is just another way of saying that each person should benefit from any transaction to which he is a part, or that in any social calculation the utility of each person should count along with that of anyone else. Notwithstanding Kant's dogged nonconsequentialism, his basic position offers a defense of win-win transactions, which are stable, and a rejection of win-lose transactions, which are not.

From this comes the third major feature of a legal system: a strong presumption in favor of the enforcement of private agreements. This maximizes the gains from the redeployment of labor and property, once their ownership has been secured under our first two rules of autonomy and property. The basic principle here is capable of easy extension to complex transactions. A contract need not take the form of a simple exchange of goods or services for cash between two parties. It could easily involve multiple parties; and it could easily involve the pooling of economic resources into a common venture, such as a partnership, from which each contributor receives some portion of the shared gain. These arrangements are hardly risk free, but contracts are not made by parties oblivious to the peril that some parties will necessarily take out less than they put in, or even less than other partners receive for taking the same risk. To counter that ever-present risk of implicit wealth transfer out of pooling arrangements, partnership agreements frequently adopt two kinds of prophylactic rules. First, they may specify nondiscriminatory rules for the distribution of capital and profits to minimize this risk of the diversion of their wealth—a private form of confiscation. It is hard for A and B to extract ill-concealed gains from a partnership if they have to pay equal amounts to their partner, C. But this rule is not ideal in all circumstances. It works reasonably well in the context of limited partners whose passive position in the business makes it possible to treat them in a lockstep position. But the rule is only a presumption. In many arrangements partners strike specific deals that call for consciously asymmetrical roles and returns. A nondiscrimination rule may not be needed when the partners know each other's worth and can monitor their respective contributions. And it does not in and of itself determine who gets to direct the business. Second, at the very least, the nondiscrimination rules must be married to a system of voting control that allows some group to set the business course that binds all. By joining these two sets of rules together (and throwing in some supermajority voting protection for major transactions),[24] collective business agreements seek to preserve the prospects of *ex ante* gain that draw people into these arrangements in the first place.

The needed variations can easily become more complex. Let insiders take the corporation private, and outside shareholders must be paid the "fair value" for their shares. If they are paid less, then some portion of their returns will be siphoned off by the insider group. Here is not the place to discuss the full range of evasive stratagems, and the provisions used to counter them.[25] The parties themselves, and not any outside commentator or observer, determine the range and variety of these voluntary arrangements. The process has no externally mandated ending point. The assets acquired in one transaction may be resold or recombined and then exchanged in yet another. The role of the state is to reduce the cost of transacting, which in turn allows ordinary parties to maximize their gains from trade.

The full richness of these consensual arrangements is easy to overlook by stressing those exotic cases where events turn sour and end up in litigation. Occasionally, these cases represent novel circumstances and unexpected events. Most often they represent refusals to perform where the law is clear. Sometimes litigation raises difficult disputes over questions of fact. But looking at disputed cases to understand mainstream institutions is like gazing down the wrong end of the barrel of a gun. In understanding how contracts work, whether between two parties or two hundred, we have to keep our eyes on the dominant pattern. Most contracts run the course from birth to death, from formation to discharge, without serious complication or legal intervention. Often times, they are modified without fanfare during their life. Most disputes that arise in negotiation address known issues whose pros and cons have been thoroughly ventilated by the parties. It may not be possible to draft the perfect contingent-state contract that covers each and every possibility that arises. But good lawyers can get close. It is possible to draft standard contracts that cover the routine questions of when and where delivery should be made; what form of payment is required and when; what quality of goods is expected; and what remedies are available in the event of breach. Additional legal rules mark the time when negotiations end and contractual agreement begins (a writing requirement), or guard against fraud, duress, and undue influence (provide a weaker party with independent advice).

These "conventional" arrangements will vary from across time and place, as a reflection of technology and custom. In some cases a writing might be required; in others a handshake might suffice. A close study of the forms chosen would, I think, reveal that the patterns of business are far from random. Real estate transactions are infrequent; they usually proceed slowly because they create or transfer permanent interests of great value. It is no surprise that they require a high degree of formality; hence they are in writing, and usually witnessed and recorded. Yet even that conclusion is not universal. Sometimes sales (or leases) involve a transfer of only partial interests, where the seller (or lessor) wishes to constrain the ability of the buyer (or lessee) to resell (or sublease) the property. Keeping the deeds from the buyer (so that he cannot resell the property) offers one way to prevent unwanted transactions that could compromise the value of the retained interest.

The velocity of transfers shifts with fungible goods, which have no unique physical or spatial properties, and to which their owners attach no subjective value. Trades on the stock exchange are done quickly and by word of mouth. It is no surprise that these disputes are frequently settled on the day by arbitration, given the frequency of transactions. But having different trading conventions for different settings only improves the odds of reaching the right result. It does not create perfect protection against failure. The set of cases that makes it into court even under the best of legal rules is usually the worst, or most atypical, cases from the original group. It is dangerous to draw any negative inference about the power of contractual mechanisms or the commercial behavior of market participants solely by looking at contracting failures that end in litigation. That group constitutes a biased and unrepresentative sample. What matters most is the integrity of the routine sales or loan transaction. Conventions may come and conventions may go. Yet throughout it all, the full and prompt enforcement of most contractual arrangements should be regarded as one of the highest priorities of any system of public policy.

The celebration of voluntary contracts should not be understood as adopting a universal hands-off policy. Contracts by ordinary persons to kill innocent people are not, and should not be, enforced by any legal system. The great use of ordinary contracts is that they increase the resources available to achieve legitimate ends. Given that simple consequence, most successful contracts have *positive* externalities, for by expanding wealth and satisfaction they increase the opportunities to other individuals. Yet here again the law works by successive approximations, not by necessary truths. Let the end of any transaction be illegitimate, then the law has to set its face against the contractual devices that increase their possibility of success. Now partnership becomes a conspiracy to kill or combination in restraint of trade; cooperation becomes aiding and abetting. To be sure, a subset of contracts that harm third persons might be rehabilitated in turn: posses hunt down escaped convicts; certain kinds of horizontal arrangements are necessary for clearinghouse operations. But in each case the question one has to ask is whether the systemwide external losses (that is, from bank to bank) on net (for these effects may be both negative and positive) outweigh the gains from trade to the parties. Most ordinary contracts of sale, hire, lease, or partnership do not begin to rub up against this constraint. The competitive harm that they cause is of the same kind and quality their disappointed competitors would cause them if they had available better products or lower prices. We ban either all these routine transactions or none: that choice seems clear if one looks at how alternative regimes of free trade and no trade play out over time, for the one set of institutional arrangements produces the very wealth that the second stifles. Some consequentialist judgments are easy to make.

Tort

Contracts to kill or maim third persons open an instructive window on the law of tort, isolating the greatest peril to the social arrangements that combine rules of autonomy, property, and contract into a single whole. The overwhelming majority of people willing to play by these rules should not have their own voluntary arrangements subverted by the few people who do not understand the rules or who refuse to abide by them. In the midst of modern tumult over professional, product, occupier's, and employer's liability, it should never be forgotten that the first office of the law of tort is to prevent aggression and deception against strangers, even by one person acting alone. No society can afford to allow a tiny fraction of its population to compel the rest of the population to live in fear, so these twin prohibitions against force and fraud become the bedrock principle on which all legal systems rest, and the obvious source of the priority of what Isaiah Berlin (not quite accurately) called "negative liberty."[26]

The greatest danger lies in the deliberate use of force, which allows someone to pick his targets in ways that inflict maximum harm on others at minimum cost to himself. The strongest justification for the use of state power is to prevent the unilateral and forcible circumvention of the basic protections offered to autonomy, property, and contract. A general prohibition against deliberate harms supplies an uncontroversial start, but in and of itself cannot produce the social optimum because it does not target harms to strangers caused by carelessness or simple accident. It is to those conceptually tricky cases that much of modern tort law is devoted, with its immense vacillation between the rule of negligence and that of strict liability. I have long favored the strict liability rule, which allows all individuals to recover presumptively for any infliction of harm caused by force, leaving it to each person to decide what level of precautions to adopt to avoid those negative external effects. But others have insisted that the standard is inapplicable because it holds people liable to others when they have taken the same level of care appropriate for the protection of their own person and property. Those refinements are unimportant in the grand scheme of things, even if they loom large in the fraction of cases that wend their way through the courts to appellate review, and it is best to defer the choice between negligence and strict liability until later.[27] The central point here is the solid foundation of the libertarian quartet: the rules of autonomy, property, exchange, and protection do not capture all that is needed in a legal system. But they form the first approximation of the set of rules that any liberal society must adopt in order to prosper.

Private Monopoly

The most uncompromising libertarian position reflects the view that the role of the state begins and ends with the faithful enforcement of the basic rules on autonomy, property, exchange, and protection.[28] The history of the common law, however, also reveals a continuous concern with the role of monopolies, especially monopolies and franchises created by the state and protected by law against new entry by rivals. Theoretically, one great appeal of any system of freedom of contract depends on the ability of private individuals and firms to choose from a large number of potential trading partners before entering into voluntary exchanges. Although the dangers of economic monopoly are small relative to those arising from the unconstrained use of force, the fundamentals of contract are altered for the worse when one party—or worse, both—faces no competition from any source. Charles Murray, a strong libertarian, takes up this theme by sensing that "a natural monopoly can engage in something close to coercion."[29] Clearly force and fraud are not involved, so that the resemblance stems from the way in which monopoly power, whenever it arises, can undermine some consequentialist conception of social welfare.

These problems are, moreover, ubiquitous. That monopoly position could arise in ordinary cases of necessity, as when one person during a storm must take refuge at the dock of another to save his ship.[30] It can arise, as Murray notes, in the context of natural monopoly with public utilities where a single supplier who bears the front-end cost becomes the cheapest supplier of some standard commodity or good, such as electricity and power. Even though contracts entered into with these parties will secure mutual gain, the overall social situation, in principle, could be improved *if* (and it is a big if) the terms of contracts were restricted by law so as to reduce the dangers of monopoly profit, without forcing the dominant supplier to sell goods and services at below their initial cost.[31] The great challenge is to develop a set of rules that manages to weave its way between these two dangers—*firm* exploitation of customers on the one hand, and *state* confiscation of firm property on the other.[32]

The common law has always been sensitive to these twin concerns. From the earliest times, royal grants, licenses, and franchises carried with them correlative duties to supply goods and services to all comers, without discrimination, at a reasonable price. Situational monopolies created by good fortune were subject to the same general rule. This obligation to serve all comers primarily achieves economic ends. But it has a critical political function as well, by helping to ensure that well-placed political operatives do not favor their friends with sweetheart deals while burdening their adversaries with petty regulations, or, in extreme cases, depriving their enemies of the common necessities of life. In this context, some explicit protection against discrimination between customers is commonly invoked to backstop the initial obligation of universal service at a reasonable price. What good does it do to require that someone be served if the terms offered are so onerous as to invite instant rejection? Note that as an economic matter this norm is *not* needed in competitive markets, where the credible threat of switching to another supplier prevents a seller from singling out any person or group for invidious or discriminatory treatment. The desires of one side constrain the excesses of the other, and drive prices down and wages up to their competitive levels so that, without state interference, all parties pay the same prices and receive the same wages, subject to the usual quality adjustments.

The regulation of legal monopolies is never an easy task. The commonly used antidiscrimination norm must be carefully interpreted so that it does not itself become an instrument of abuse. Most emphatically, that norm does not mean that a seller is obliged to provide all customers with the same service at the same price. Quite the opposite, its conscientious application requires that the prices charged to different customers be adjusted to reflect differences in the cost of providing their respective services. The basic theory thus draws a sharp distinction between those forms of price discrimination designed to extract monopoly profits from buyers, and those cost-justified forms of price discrimination designed to prevent the emergence of undesirable cross-subsidies between different classes of consumers.

Monopoly power in private businesses, however, is not fully countered by the norm against discrimination. The monopolist who charges a single price to identical customers still has it within its power to cause major resource misallocations by setting prices to all consumers in excess of the marginal costs of production. The duty that the prices be reasonable—

that is, sufficient to cover costs with an allowance for standard economic profit—is the best approximate response to counter the risk of supra-competitive prices charged by the natural monopolist. Implementing that ideal, however, was fraught with difficulties in the regulation of railroads (and the interconnection between railroad lines) a century ago, and it raises similar vexatious issues today with the integration of independent and competing carriers into a single coherent telecommunications net-work, both national and worldwide.[33] Forging the connections that al-low all parties to work within a single network requires regulators to set the correct prices for these forced interconnections. Set them too high, and the newcomers are warded off while the incumbent firm continues to reap monopoly profits. Set them too low, and the newcomer can pilfer the network elements of the incumbent without making any social investment of his own.

The history of regulated industries shows that the delicate mission of walking between extremes has been discharged, at best, with mixed suc-cess. Nothing frustrates the task of setting rates more than expanding the traditional obligation of universal service to embrace an extensive program of income redistribution among users, which works at cross-purposes to the control of monopoly behavior.[34] Thus telecommunica-tions regulators have routinely required commercial users to subsidize service to residential users, and, at enormous cost, urban users to subsi-dize rural users. The demand for universal medical care (where private monopoly power is usually weak) has also become an insistent plea for massive redistribution to some groups of consumers (often the older and wealthy) at the expense of others (often younger and with more limited incomes).

No one can claim that this cautious approach to monopoly power is perfectly self-enforcing. In application it can and has gone astray. But the technical mistakes in rate regulation pale into insignificance in compari-son with one dominant strategy of the modern administrative state: first, subject competitive markets to state regulation that makes them operate under monopoly conditions; next, try to figure out what duties should be imposed on the relevant actors to make them behave as though they lacked the bargaining advantage that the state had just conferred upon them. Just this incoherent pattern emerges in labor markets under the current American system of mandatory collective bargaining that allows the majority of workers in a bargaining unit to select a union bargaining agent, which is then under an obligation to bargain with the employer in good faith. In principle, it is as hard to be against good faith as it is to be for bad faith. But in these complex negotiations good faith does not require simple honesty, but seeks to counteract the inveterate tendency to set one's prices to extract monopoly profits from the other side.

This method to control temptation comes in a distant second to ordinary market transactions. It replaces a steady stream of small market adjustments with stilted negotiations frequently marked by excessive posturing, rigidity, and protectionism. Often the bitter pace of negotiations does not reach public attention because the breakdown does not result in strike. But the dangers of holdouts are always there, and often small differences are sufficient to produce deadlocks. In the transportation industry, pilot strikes at a single carrier can bring the entire transportation network to its knees.[35] Even though the common impression is that both sides will learn to "split the difference," that undramatic outcome does not always come about, and even when it does, it does not carry with it the same implications as two friends splitting the cost of a tank of gas: the pilots still end up with a hefty premiums over the competitive wage level.

Similar outcomes are observed in education. One recent study noted that the differences between the final offer positions of teacher unions and school districts were on the order of 1 percent per annum.[36] That is sufficient to create the holdout and produce supercompetitive wages when the two sides do settle. More dramatically, in 1999 the National Basketball Association and its players union bargained to impasse even though they left about $2 billion dollars (plus lost revenues from player endorsements and sales of licensed club products) on the table over differences that could not have exceeded 5 percent per annum. It may well be that in league situations the problem of monopoly power is inescapable since each of the competitive teams must cooperate with its rivals. But no justification of that sort is ever available in the ordinary labor markets in which collective bargaining had its original roots.

State Monopoly and Just Compensation

The functions of the state, then, are properly limited to the control of force and fraud on the one hand, and to the regulation and constraint of monopoly behavior on the other. The irony of this system is that the creation of the state poses risks of the very evil that it is supposed to negate. One need only think of those not-uncommon government regimes in the twentieth century alone that committed mass slaughter of individuals grouped together by race, creed, or national origin. The use of unbridled force by government is still the greatest peril to any sound system of governance. Yet even when those massive failures are effectively checked, as they largely are in today's modern democracies, the dangers of state monopoly, factionalism, and favoritism are too large to be ignored. Governments are not only good at protecting the goods and services produced by ordinary individuals. Often they are adept—too adept—at shifting opportunities, advantages, and property from one group to another, especially by allowing political majorities to control the destinies of the minorities that live under their rule. What else can be said of rent control, price supports, and most (but not all) zoning regulations?

None of these abuses should be welcomed as a matter of first principle. The task is to develop a set of institutions that compel the state to respect the limitations on its use of force that are consistent with its role as a protector, not destroyer, of individual rights. That problem will be addressed only when we persuade ourselves that state power is a necessary evil rather than an unqualified blessing. That outlook, in turn, will come only when we recognize that the dark side of human nature does not disappear just because fallible human beings have assumed the trappings of public office. What are needed are clear rules that define the ends to which public force may be directed.

That task lies at the heart of any robust social contract theory. To be sure, the phrase "social contract" conjures up images of hypothetical and obscure political arrangements, with a hint of Rousseau's "general will" thrown in for good measure. But its commonsense core helps generate the more specialized norms that govern well-structured societies. The trick is to be literal in attaching sufficient weight to both terms in the expression. The term "contract" hearkens back to voluntary arrangements that yield on formation an expected gain for all their participants. Translated to the political sphere, the objective of government is to make all individuals better off in society under its protection than they would be otherwise. The phrase "better than" connotes an implicit comparison to some alternative state of affairs. Selecting that baseline is done through the normative theory that depends on the fundamental principles of autonomy, property, exchange, and protection derived from the basic theory of private rights set out above.

It is commonplace among liberal and progressive theorists to claim that the social contract behind laissez-faire economics fills an impoverished moral niche by stressing how each new right necessarily generates an equal and opposite correlative duty. Garry Wills, for example, condemns the Lockean conception of the state for insisting that under it "we are faced with a zero-sum game. Any power given to the government is necessarily subtracted from the liberty of the governed."[37] Later on, Wills returns to this zero-sum theme by claiming that "John Locke's social contract . . . teaches that government is founded on a necessary *loss* of freedom, not on the *enhancement* of liberty."[38] The clear implication of his message is that defenders of laissez-faire necessarily condemn government to idleness, even as they shrink from the implication that it should be abolished.

Unfortunately, Wills misunderstands what zero-sum games are about. Every shift of rights between individuals, or from individuals to government, necessarily conserves the sum of legal rights. Two individuals cannot possess the same rights over the same thing at the same time. Likewise, in politics, every accretion of government power necessarily shrinks rights left to individuals. Conceded. But to understand the social situation, we have to apply the zero-sum concept not to *rights,* but to *utilities.* A transfer or reassignment of rights rarely, if ever, operates as a zero-sum game in the domain of utility. It is for just that reason that people enter into voluntary exchanges: even though their rights as against the rest of the world are neither increased or decreased, their joint utilities improve because of the exchange. To the Lockean social contract theorist (among whom I happily include myself), the ideal is to support only those forced transfers of legal rights that create positive-sum games in, of course, the domain of utility, while spurning proposed transfers that create negative or zero-sum results.

Unfortunately, Wills's criticism of the Lockean position captures only a partial truth about zero-sum games. Under the Lockean view, the "government," as such, has no rights. Rather the individuals who possess sovereign power act as agents for those individuals who are benefited by their particular actions. It bears repetition that, just as every transaction between a shareholder and a corporation can in reality be disaggregated into transactions among shareholders,[39] every interaction between the state and individuals can likewise be reduced into transactions among individuals. Given the strict correlative relationship between rights and duties, every shift of rights between individuals, or from individuals to government, necessarily conserves the *sum* of legal rights even as it changes their location. Likewise, in politics, every advance of state power necessarily shrinks rights retained by individuals in their individual capacity. That point is one that we should insist on, not timidly concede, for without it there is no reason to worry about the configuration of legal rights and responsibilities in the first place.

Because Wills cannot clearly articulate the Lockean vision, he is unable to isolate the cases where his vision of the New Deal, social welfare state parts company with its Lockean precursor. His prime example to show that government is "a necessary good" lies in its building and management of public highways. The state can define rules of the road, require drivers to wear seatbelts and helmets, license drivers, charge tolls, and the like. No Lockean disputes categorically this general branch of public power, but a Lockean would limit the ability of government to allow some people to drive without licenses or without paying tolls. Yet Wills never articulates a set of political or constitutional constraints that he would place on state-run highways, or for that matter, on the state regulation of public utilities, even though these areas have been the subject of enormous debate and litigation.

Criticisms such as Wills's should not, however, be allowed to cloud the central point that no libertarian theory of individual rights is capable of practical implementation on its own terms. Stated otherwise, we cannot credibly conceive of a set of voluntary transactions from a set of widely dispersed individual and property rights that results in the creation of a sovereign power. No voluntary agreements will ever bind the millions of people alive today who must contract not only among themselves, but also with future, unborn generations. The term "social" in the phrase "social contract" therefore is meant to sanction coercive arrangements fashioned by the state so long as they achieve the same distribution of ends—that is, mutual advantage—as the voluntary agreements on which they are modeled.

In order to achieve that goal, strong restrictions must be placed on the illicit use of government force while, at the same time, permitting the use of state force to constrain private acts of violence. The entire organization of local police forces and self-help regimes is designed to achieve that objective, without falling prey to the risks of favoritism and prejudice that may be otherwise injected into matters of public administration. It is therefore necessary to devise rules and customs that prevent the full force of the state from being directed to single individuals or isolated groups. The objective contains a powerful message for our age of identity politics. If a chasm separates different social and economic groups, if immigration, internal migration, and intermarriage continue to stir the melting pot now more than in previous days, then the manifest implication is to gravitate toward a *smaller* government than might have been optimal in earlier days when national populations were both smaller and more homogeneous. As individual and group preferences start to diverge, it becomes ever harder for state coercive behavior to replicate the win-win outcomes generated by the simple voluntary exchange. The kinds of education that one group wants are anathema to another, as the struggles over teaching both evolution and creationism in public schools so clearly indicate. The set of activities that satisfy the win-win constraint is more likely to be found only when the state confines itself to a minimal role that is consistent with the basic subjective preferences of all its members. Looking for the common elements across diverse peoples drives us back, inexorably, to the classical government roles: the preservation of order against foes, domestic and foreign, and the provision of familiar public goods, such as highways. Separate individuals who routinely use their own property for their own diverse ends can all be accommodated on the same highway grid. When the state supplies only these basics, then each individual or private group can treat those public services as an input for ends that it alone shares, without having to surrender its distinctive goals and objectives. It is for good reasons that individual ratepayers don't become partners with a public utility. Power and light can be used to advance faith by one group and preach heresy by another, without the two coming into necessary conflict.

The same need to counter factions helps explain the case for using a flat tax as a general tool for public finance. The intellectual origins of the flat tax come from the benefit theory of taxation, which asks that all individuals be taxed in relationship to the benefits that they receive from government action. As is typical on this matter, writers in the classical liberal tradition all start out by looking for the appropriate private analogy to taxation, and find it in the ordinary partnership. Thus Adam Smith, in *The Wealth of Nations,* writes: "The subjects of every state ought to contribute towards the support of the government, as nearly as possible, in proportion to their respective abilities; that is, in proportion to the revenue which they respectively enjoy under the protection of the state."[40] Nor is he alone. Aristotle, in speaking of distributive justice generally, notes: "The just, then, is a species of the proportionate.[41] That broad conception is thereafter linked to taxation by John Locke: " 'Tis true Governments cannot be supported without great Charge, and 'tis fit every one who enjoys his share of the Protection, should pay out of his Estate his proportion for the maintenance of it."[42] Similarly, Hayek notes: "[A] person who commands more of the resources of society will also gain proportionately more from what the government has contributed," and thus should be taxed proportionately.[43] And I have taken the same position myself.[44] No one in the libertarian tradition has ever been under any allusion that the protection of legal rights comes free.

Yet why the support? Here the uniform impulse of all these thinkers is to strive for that tax structure that, on average, will yield the highest net gain over the costs of their imposition. The flat tax is easier to administer than its rivals because it avoids the complexities of income splitting and joint returns that arise under any system of progressive taxation. Its application to a broad base tends to reduce the distortion between various forms of private activities. To the extent, moreover, that each individual so taxed receives government benefits equal to or greater than his own contribution, this system should not diminish the economic incentives for production. The use of the flat tax, moreover, is tied to the traditional function of states, the provision of nonexcludable public goods. Once appropriate government functions are limited, then the flat rate structure dulls the constant jockeying for position that comes from trying to impose first regressive and then progressive taxation, where in each case the raison d'être is to make some anonymous or targeted persons within society pay the lion's share of the cost while the winning faction snaps up the lion's share of the benefit. Nor does the flat tax commit any nation to resources that are insufficient to meet its collective challenges. The flat tax does not impose any absolute dollar or percentage limitation on the amount of social resources that are subject to government direction. That course of action would, of course, be foolish in the extreme because the appropriate mix of state and private expenditures is heavily dependent on the external state of the world. Government expenditures rightly rose during World War II, just as they may have to rise again in order to combat the terrorist menace of Bin Laden and Al Qaeda.

This concern with confiscation does not apply only to taxation. It also explains why we normally require the state to pay whenever it takes land or other property for public use. These political risks arise not only when the government occupies land once privately owned, but also when for the direct benefit of others it restricts the use of land that remains in private possession. On any sensible rule, the restrictions that should call forth the obligation to compensate are only those that go above and beyond the ordinary obligations that neighbors have to each other under the law of nuisance:[45] after all, the state can perform a useful service when it prevents harm from happening to a broad group of individuals, none of whom has enough at stake to sue to prevent harm before its inception. The state uses its coercive power to coordinate the response of individual victims who are too spread out to organize their litigation efforts against the wrongdoer. This statement of the principle also contains its own limits. We should look with profound suspicion on efforts to compel some persons to leave their lands idle or underdeveloped so that their neighbors can continue to enjoy uninterrupted views. These lopsided zoning rules are exactly the kind of restrictions that, if implemented at all, should be done only if compensation is paid to the burdened landowner. With land, as with speech, the imposition of selective restrictions on isolated groups of individuals is the hallmark of the dark side of democratic politics, as we all too often discover. The previous discussion indicated how private monopolies have to be limited in the scope of their power, while guaranteed a competitive rate of return. The state monopoly should be subject to the same limitation: it may take or regulate for public advantage when it is prepared to pay its way. Otherwise it should stay its hand.

This unified treatment of regulation and confiscation marks the critical transition from private to public law. Yet, it would be a great mistake to assume that, in shuttling between private and public law questions, we should radically alter our mode of analysis. In particular, our entry into the dizzying world of public policy does not give us a free hand in adopting rules that deviate from the traditional common law treatment of landlords and tenants, or ordinary boundary disputes between neighbors. To the contrary, our thinking about small problems is capable of generalization by careful increments in dealing with public law issues. To the extent that we reject this linkage, we effectively set up two sets of books, whereby private law disputes are resolved by one set of principles and the analogous public law disputes by another. That duality in turn creates two inconsistent centers of power, and creates wasteful controversy to choose the arena in which any particular dispute will be played out. Sooner or later disputes in one area will spill over to the other, and the resulting clash will leave us with jarring inconsistencies at the margins that even ingenious lawyers and clever economists will not be able to avoid or resolve.

This cautionary note does not rob the public/private distinction of all its salience. Presumptively, public and private powers are subject to different regimes. Generally speaking, most private individual agents act on their own account, without possessing monopoly power. The only time they stand accountable to other individuals for their own business decisions is when they assume, by agreement, fiduciary obligations toward others. In that universe they can act as they please so long as they obey the familiar constraints, and respect the liberty and property of others. The entire framework of voluntary transactions is placed in jeopardy when notions of nondiscrimination and fairness are allowed to override freely entered private arrangements. But paradoxically, public officials must be subjected to those limitations precisely because their decisions bind ordinary individuals, who have done no wrong, without their individual consent. Public officials are always fiduciaries who should be held accountable for their actions to all their citizens.

Once we are alert to the dangers of public law, it should be possible—not easy, but possible—to fashion a state that is strong enough to provide for social order and constrained enough not to become a threat to the social order that it supports. But it takes constant attention to basic theory to reach that end. From what has just been said, it would be a mistake to assume that those who are in favor of limited government are necessarily in favor of weak government. Nothing could be further from the truth. The task here is to find ways to target government energies on clearly demonstrable tasks where public resources can do the most good. When that mission is well defined, several things happen at once. First, state enforcement enjoys the highest level of legitimacy, because it is directed against activities that everyone opposes in principle, no matter how much they may privately deviate from that principle in practice. For that reason it is better to make murder a crime than to prohibit the sale of handguns, for the former concentrates on aggression as such, while the latter may be more likely to remove weapons from those who resist aggression than from those who commit it.[46] Second, the dangers of excessive taxation and regulation are effectively negated, because the state does not move into contentious areas (such as wage and price regulation) where public opinion and economic effects are likely to divide along various political and social axes. Political power is a scarce resource that must be husbanded for the few ends that it can serve best, for otherwise the level of care and attention that hard matters receive is diluted by the ever-expanding role of government authority.

Redistribution

The burden of this last section is to restrict the scope of government intervention to deal, albeit imperfectly, with the two pervasive problems of any liberal order: aggression and coordination in the creation of public goods from which all benefit. The next question is whether the state has a third function, the redistribution of wealth in accordance with some principle of social need. The simplest and most persuasive argument for redistribution rests on the diminishing marginal utility of wealth. That principle seems evident enough in the decisionmaking behavior of ordinary individuals seeking to juggle their time and resources over multiple activities. At some point in time the next unit of leisure becomes more important than the next unit of wealth, and vice versa.

Yet at the same time the question is often more complicated than this simple account allows.[47] It is one thing to note that at some point diminishing marginal utility of wealth sets in for all persons. But the earlier discussion on the pervasive nature of individual variations means that for some people the point of diminishing returns comes later than it does for others. One distinct possibility, therefore, is that those individuals who labor mightily to accumulate wealth are, *ceteris paribus,* just those for whom additional increments of wealth hold their highest marginal utility. It is therefore not possible to assume across the board that the next unit of wealth is always worth less to the person who already has accumulated a greater store of wealth. Some differences in wealth are better accounted for by looking at the differential demand for income and not solely to differences in productive capabilities, as the traditional account provides.

Yet this argument as well is subject to its own limitations, for surely in many, if not most cases, it would be a sensible guess to assume that lower stores of wealth correlated positively with the higher value of an additional unit of wealth. That result would, moreover, gain strength when the disparities in wealth were pronounced, and even more so when hunger and starvation were in the offing. If people entertained deep philosophical objections to *inter*personal comparisons of utility, then it would be doubtful whether *any* transfer designed to ease disparities of wealth between A and B, either voluntary or coerced, improved the overall social situation. Yet the widespread practice of charitable transfers would be baffling if ordinary people acted on the assumption that these interpersonal comparisons were unintelligible. Few people contest the traditional view that some transfers of wealth from the relatively well-to-do are appropriate to counteract the dangers of extreme want.

Commonsense thought on the question suggests, therefore, that the same logic could apply to transfers of wealth between individuals: a dollar in the hands of a poor person yields a greater increment in utility than a dollar in the hands of a rich person. In principle, therefore, one can increase the overall level of utility, even at the cost of reducing overall wealth, by introducing a set of forced exchanges between individuals.

The question remains whether this ideal can be realized in practice. The first point is a methodological caveat. As a matter of general political theory, the question of redistribution should always be taken up *last.* Before embarking on a set of win-lose transactions, it is imperative to see that we have exhausted all the win-win transactions that are possible. That requires the control of force and fraud, the creation of sensible infrastructure, the removal of barriers of entry to competition, and the control over various forms of natural monopoly. Making those changes should exert a profound upward influence on the overall levels of wealth. That shift will surely increase the absolute lot of those at the bottom of the ladder, even if it may, under some circumstances, increase the disparity of wealth from top to bottom. If the criterion for redistribution of wealth were the elimination of wealth disparities, then it would not matter whether A were at $1,000 and B at $10,000, or A at $100,000 and B at $1,000,000. But instincts on redistribution are clearly divided on this point, with some, probably most, individuals worrying more about redistribution to avoid extreme poverty than about relative wealth regardless of absolute levels. In the aggregate, the doubts over redistribution will increase with any increase in overall wealth levels. The initial strategy must therefore be to reduce the scope of the problem by improving overall patterns of social output.

The next issue is whether redistribution should proceed by coercive or only voluntary means. Voluntary redistribution poses no theoretical problem, for charitable gifts are every bit as legitimate as gifts within families or between friends. This approach cautions strongly, however, against state systems for mandatory redistribution of wealth in society, which is now the target of an ever-greater portion of state power. Indeed, sometimes political power is defined as taking property from A and giving it to B. In going against that grain, I still subscribe to the classical position that obligations of beneficence are real, indeed imperative, but are best supported by voluntary social norms and practices.[48] Often these activities are extensive, and it is a mistake to assume that laissez-faire stifles the expression of individual compassion. Laissez-faire is *not* a form of social Darwinism; it does *not* prohibit voluntary assistance to those in need on the ground that it weakens human fiber in the long run. No one should deny that charitable activity carries this risk, but at most it counsels caution on potential donors,[49] not a total ban. Charitable activity was commonplace for robber barons. No government founded the University of Chicago; John D. Rockefeller did. Similar stories can be told of Barnard, Vassar, Stanford, and Johns Hopkins. The Mellon Foundation, the Carnegie Foundation, the Ford Foundation, the Sloan Foundation, the Hewlett Foundation, the Gates Foundation—the list can go on—were all named after their charitable founders.

Modern political institutions have dulled many of those charitable impulses. When the state takes responsibility for the care of the needy, it crowds out private benevolence with public coercion. Its decision could easily spawn a more selfish society by negating direct personal appeals that simply state: "Joe, the people there are hungry. If you don't help them nobody else will." The welfare state makes those impulses seem almost naïve and, by degrees, turns potential donors into potential recipients. From behind that proverbial veil of ignorance it is easy to claim that we would all opt for minimum support as a right, even when it is not possible to state just how generous that right should be. But I have my doubts about the systematic consequences of the broad articulation of welfare rights and think that we would do better with the nineteenth-century model than we do today, once we solve the other problems of political life. Nothing in laissez-faire economics places people under a legal obligation to be selfish or greedy. The system simply recognizes that giving each person the right to make choices about the use of his or her talents and resources is a strong spur to their efficient allocation. Even if five individuals are thoroughly selfish and greedy, ninety-five others are not. We are better off relying on their individual initiative rather than attempting to rope in the recalcitrant 5 percent through coercive redistributive mechanisms that operate as a huge drain on general welfare.

The actual pattern of charitable giving should not, however, be easily displaced by simple slogans that point to the imperfections that arise in a world devoid of state redistribution. Thus Anatole France said famously that the law, in all its majesty, allows rich and poor to sleep on park benches. The rhetoric has undeniable power until it is asked who, if anyone, should be allowed to sleep in public parks. Everyone? No one? Only poor people? Some people, for particular purposes, such as political protests from parades to sleep-ins?[50] And the issue gets no easier when the question is whether cities are able to prevent the homeless from sleeping on park benches, given the serious security and health problems that can follow as other law-abiding citizens abandon their public spaces. France's aphorism provides no answer to these questions; nor does it offer a clue to designing social programs to keep everyone from having, or wanting, to sleep on park benches. Surely it is not wise to introduce class legislation that gives formal sleeping rights to the rich that are denied to the poor, or vice versa. Nor should clearing the park benches commit the government to funding major programs of poverty relief—programs with flaws all their own. Homeless shelters can easily become places of violence; and their very availability may induce families to cast out wayward members, knowing that the state will take care of them. As with every program, there is reason to beware of the pitfalls as well as the obvious advantages. A far more constructive approach is to look for ways to neutralize the impact of zoning laws, building codes, and rent control systems, all of which drive up the price and constrict the supply of housing. Removing barriers to entry increases rather than constricts the size of the pie, and thus is not subject to the ever treacherous trade-offs between aggregate social wealth and its preferred distribution.

No short summary will, I fear, dissuade people from their theoretical endorsement of welfare rights backed by the power of the state. My sense is that they will remain unbowed, even if they acknowledge that higher levels of welfare support will increase the number of people who will come to depend on them. But it may be possible to point to one or two reasons to blunt the enthusiasm for these rights. The first is that the exercise is often counterproductive. It is a melancholy truth that in practice redistribution often works in favor of those who have political power and not those who have genuine need. The only moral case for redistribution is to overcome differences of wealth in the service of those with real human needs. Once redistribution becomes a legitimate function of government, it is likely to be unleashed in ways that flatly contradict this purpose. One tragic illustration is how long-standing constitutional limitations on the power of the state to regulate prices and wages was swept aside in *Nebbia v. New York*,[51] which upheld mandatory minimum prices for milk and other dairy products during the Depression, to the great detriment of the urban poor. Some workers have insufficient skills to join a union, but it is easy to block their advancement with minimum wage laws, zoning laws, and safety laws that operate as *de facto* barriers to entry. Before committing yourself to the magic of redistribution, ask in which direction it will operate. There is many a slip between cup and lip.

Today's vast reservoirs of political discretion often operate for the benefit of the rich and famous, who receive their preferences in the name of the poor and needy. Many farm subsidy programs use beaten-down individual farmers as icons to conceal the far larger transfers made to corporate operations. Similarly, age discrimination laws protect the position of high-paid older workers (often white males) who are allowed to disclaim bargains calling for their retirement while keeping the pensions and benefits set up for just that eventuality. Medicare provides care at bargain rates for the same class of preferred recipients who also claim much of the payout under Medicaid for their nursing home allowances. Never forget that the big dollars in redistribution follow political influence, not social compassion. What are hard to find are decisive counterexamples that result in net benefits to the poor.

The second drawback to coerced redistribution is that it always requires the sacrifice of productive labor. No one should argue skeptically that the need for the marginal dollar is as great for the billionaire as it is for the person on the edge of poverty. Private charity is a coherent and durable institution only because people widely reject that skeptical view of the relative need for additional amounts of wealth. But coerced redistribution does not rely on compassion and the sense of identification between giver and receiver. Because of the institutional distances between the parties, it often provokes self-interested individuals to manipulate an anonymous system for their own advantage. In open and subtle ways, state coercion reduces the incentives to produce for rich and poor alike. It shrinks the size of the pie by redirecting individual and group efforts to obtain or resist transfers of wealth. Production benefits all; redistribution by coercive means benefits some at the expense of others. Yet once in place it is difficult to dislodge, for it is difficult to critique a system in the political realm when the concealed mechanisms of regulation make it so difficult to calculate both costs and benefits.

With all this said, redistribution should not be condemned as a simple form of theft given the level of social deliberation and ratification that accompanies it. But political deliberation hardly insulates these programs from a critique of their corrosive effects on human behavior. The more assistance that is offered, the greater the numbers of people who will flock to it. The number of people who claim disabilities in the United States today has more than doubled since 1990 because of the gains disability status now confers under the law.[52] It is simply a mistake to assume that the high-minded motives that accompany the introduction of a new program will determine how people respond to it in practice. A huge number of small, but selfish, decisions can easily overcome the loftiest of collective ambitions.

Nor is there any reason to think that these programs work once we look beyond their short-term intended effects. One useful approach is the "trend line" test of Charles Murray.[53] Just look at the percentage of individuals below the poverty level relative to the number of dollars spent on welfare program, and see if the increase in expenditures results in an amelioration of the basic condition. Any reader interested in the American scene can find a useful collection of data in Michael Tanner's *The End of Welfare,* published in 1996 by the Cato Institute.[54] Perhaps the most dramatic of these figures are those that correlate the levels of expenditure on welfare with the percentage of individuals living below the poverty line (see figure 1). The curves move in opposite directions. From about 1949 through about 1969, the actual expenditures on welfare remained low, both in aggregate and individual terms. During that period the level

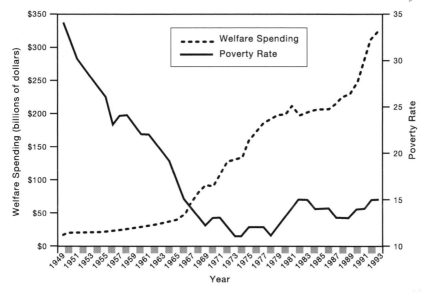

Figure 1 Welfare spending versus poverty

Source: Adapted from Michael Tanner, *The End of Welfare: Fighting Poverty in the Civil Society,* fig. 3.1, p. 70 (1996). Data from Bureau of the Census, Current Population Surveys, Series P60, various numbers; and Robert Rector and William Lauber, *America's Failed $5.4 Trillion War on Poverty,* table 1, pp. 92–93 (1995).

of individuals living below the poverty line fell from close to 35 percent in 1949 to about 12 percent in 1969. But starting in 1965, with Lyndon Johnson's Great Society programs, the levels of welfare expenditure, both in the aggregate and per capita, started to rise, to around 15 percent. Yet throughout the 1970s the poverty levels did not decline any further, and as the increases in welfare expenditures continued to mount sharply in the 1980, the percentage of individuals living below the poverty line rose slightly. These consequences were hardly intended, but they offer some approximate measure of the long-term incentives of welfare programs. The strongest objection to welfare is the humdrum practical point that these programs, when administered by government, are not likely to work, especially in the long run.

Many will regard these practical objections as overdrawn, or even as cloaks for selfish behavior by wealthy individuals desperate to keep what they have. To these doubters, my appeal takes a somewhat more restrained form. You cannot redistribute what you do not produce. Therefore you should try to make the entire process as transparent as possible so that the objects of benevolence and the costs of benevolence are clearly revealed. In addition, it becomes imperative to preserve basic institutions of liberty, property, exchange, and protection to secure the wealth base that makes sensible redistribution—that is to say, redistribution based on need and not on age, race, or political influence—work. Covert tools are bad tools, as the great American legal philosopher and contracts scholar Karl Llewellyn said long ago. And so it is with the politics of redistribution. Many of the subsidies buried in labor and pricing policies could not survive political outrage if made explicit.

In sum, no political philosophy or legal theory is worth defending unless it can be defended in a wide range of social contexts. Those who are skeptical therefore about the power of the theories advanced here are encouraged to read on to see whether they work better than their alternatives. I am confident that they do and that the strong presumption in favor of government regulation and intervention should be reversed in favor of the earlier tradition that used government intervention to control force, fraud, and monopoly, and then called it a day.

3 Moral Relativism

Defending the Edifice?

ONCE THE FUNDAMENTAL FRAMEWORK OF classical liberalism has been established, it remains to determine whether it can meet the various attacks lodged against it. The classical defenders of the traditional order stress the importance of durability and continuity within the law and lament the puffed-up ignorance of reformers who meddle with law's richly textured rules and practices. The chief modern proponent of this view was Friedrich von Hayek, who, in his later work—*The Constitution of Liberty*,[1] *Law, Legislation and Liberty*,[2] *The Fatal Conceit*[3]—developed a near mystical appreciation for the spontaneous evolution of legal (by which he largely meant the common law, or at least judge-made) rules that could never be outperformed by the arbitrary commands of the modern administrative state. The guiding principle of social organization, according to Hayek, is "the impossibility for anyone of knowing all the particular facts on which the overall order of the activities in a Great Society is based."[4]

Given this assumption about the diffusion of knowledge in society, Hayek's ultimate defense of markets does not rest on the Pollyannish view that perfect competition leads necessarily to the best outcome in the best of all possible worlds. Rather, it rests on the incremental ability of each individual to capitalize on his or her own partial knowledge through a system of voluntary exchange. A seller may know why it is that he values the money he receives more than the goods he sells. The buyer may know why he values the goods he receives more than the money he pays for them. Abstractly, neither side need have the barest inkling of the motivations and private purposes of the other side for an anonymous exchange to work.[5] But of course it is hard to sell to customers while ignorant of their needs, so the exchange of goods and services can be speeded up, when necessary, by the techniques of modern marketing that allow firms to identify their customer base, tailor their products to customer needs, and make frequent small adjustments in response to the feedback they receive. Astute merchants can thus make enduring local improvements, even though they operate without knowledge of the overall determinants of economic growth. Recognizing how this tacit coordination tends to stabilize markets, political actors, at the very least, should be aware of the risk that any government intervention or legal reform will lead us further away from the hard-fought equilibrium achieved by the voluntary transactions protected by the common law.

Hayek's unflagging devotion to open markets prevents his fascination with ignorance from turning him into a moral relativist. He is confident of the sources of collective wisdom and private knowledge, and thus uses a temporal skepticism to direct decisions to those places where the knowledge base is strongest. Often, however, skepticism about the limits on human knowledge takes more mischievous forms, which attack in one way or another the capacity to develop a rational legal order. There are, I think, three major intellectual trends that tend to undercut the viability of economic markets and the social and political institutions on which they depend. The first of these dangers is *moral relativism,* which disputes the capacity to make any kind of objective moral judgments about the relative soundness of alternative legal rules, not only in close cases, but in any case where someone refuses to acquiesce in the claims of his rivals. The second is *linguistic and terminological,* and insists that the only possible building blocks of legal theory—language—are so indeterminate that no one can delineate propositions with sufficient clarity to allow one to state coherently the principles strong enough to give guidance on how to constrain the relentless expansion of government power. The third impediment is, broadly speaking, *psychological and behavioral,* which seeks to undermine the behavioral assumptions, chiefly those of human rationality, on which the soundness of the traditional legal order depends.

Each line of attack represents a grave and misguided effort to undermine both the rule of law and the principle of individual liberty with which it is usually linked. What all of these practices share is the desire to give the comeuppance to the commonsense ways in which ordinary people both behave and talk about their behavior. Arguments against common sense are staples of philosophical discourse: just think of the number of sophisticated philosophical arguments that have been raised to disprove the existence of the external world. But in the end we are all naïve realists, for it is only on that view that we can make intelligible progress in any area from physics to human emotions. In both ethics and in metaphysics, common sense reluctantly leads to the right result, not because it solves every difficult problem the first time through, but because it supplies the needed vocabulary and the shared social expectations that allow us first to understand the easy cases, and then use that hard-fought knowledge to make progress on the difficult ones. Too often intellectual obscurantism masks itself as intellectual sophistication. In truth, a measured skepticism yields a better understanding of the legal system than Hayek's view, stressed in his later writings, that human knowledge of complex systems was so limited that no theoretical framework could articulate or defend sound principles of government that departed from the gradual evolution of custom. Let us take these points up in order.

Holmes: *Abrams* and *Lochner*

The common attitude of moral relativism is not to embrace positions that are repugnant to the world at large, but to claim that there are no authoritative moral grounds on which to attack these positions. Within the legal system, our most famous legal skeptic is Oliver Wendell Holmes, whose transformative experience as a young soldier during the Civil War formed, or perhaps scarred, him for the next seventy years of his long professional life. As a sitting judge and a technical lawyer, there was little, apart from the elegant aphorism, to distinguish Holmes from his less brilliant peers. For Holmes it was a mistake to assume that law operated as a "brooding omnipresence"[6] detached from its enforcement by public officials in any particular jurisdiction. From here it is easy to take the next step, which Holmes, as one of the forebears of legal realism, was prepared to take: to mount an attack on natural law by a pervasive skepticism about our individual or collective ability to generate any legal principles that merit adoption as a universal standard.[7] Having seen men in battle charge heedlessly to their death for causes they so little understood, Holmes despaired that anyone could articulate a coherent set of moral beliefs that could work as necessary truths to guide and constrain human conduct. For him, human behavior consisted of a long list of "can't helps," that is, those beliefs that he, or any person, cannot help but act on even if it is not possible to give some precise account of the reasons for so acting. Any allusion to "absolute truth" fell on deaf ears.[8] Any effort at grand synthesis was sure to run aground on some hidden shoal; so better not to try.

The key question for our purposes is how Holmes's philosophical speculation translates itself into common law and, more important, constitutional adjudication. At its most pervasive level, unbounded moral skepticism corrodes the possibilities of principled decisionmaking. Yet it is easy to overlook that the exact form of skepticism matters. One form of skepticism takes a leaf from Hayek and prizes the system of voluntary exchange because it harnesses the partial knowledge of trading partners for desirable social ends. The second leads, in constitutional terms, to the pathless fields of judicial deference to legislative action. So long as the judge has no clear conception of right and wrong, then any broad philosophical generalization is too empty to supply precise guidance for hard cases. If so, then by all means let the legislature, with its democratic imprimatur, call the shots.

Holmes, as he was wont, embraced both forms of skepticism simultaneously and was thus pulled in both directions. We see his intelligent skepticism best at work in *Abrams v. United States*.[9] Holmes invoked the First Amendment guarantee—"Congress shall make no law abridging the freedom of speech"—to dissent from the conviction of socialists and anarchists for subverting the war effort against Germany by circulating anonymous leaflets attacking an American expedition to Russia as a covert attempt to undermine Lenin's new communist revolution. It is easy today to think that Holmes was on the side of the angels, but matters were quite different in the immediate post–World War I period. Fierce anti-German passions provoked, for example, John Wigmore into writing a vehement denunciation of Holmes for his willingness to exonerate these hapless Russian anarchists, knowing how close the German July 1918 offensive came to breaking the resistance of the United States, Great Britain, and France on the western front.[10] None of this fazed Holmes, who wrote: "But when men have realized that time has upset many fighting faiths, they may come to believe even more than they believe the very foundations of their own conduct that the ultimate good desired is better reached by free trade in ideas—that the best test of truth is the power of the thought to get itself accepted in the competition of the market. . . . That at any rate is the theory of our Constitution. It is an experiment, as all life is an experiment."[11]

Everything is right in this short, moving passage. His initial reference to "fighting faiths" is an implicit attack on the kind of dogmatic fundamentalism that sparks individuals to use force against anyone who opposes their own views. Holmes recognizes that people who believe deeply about anything are all too often prone to the error of thinking that they must eradicate those who think differently from themselves. In his next breath he hopes that rational reflection ("they may come to believe") will lead them to develop the necessary separation between their own bedrock beliefs and embrace a neutral principle—the free trade in ideas—as the *test* of truth.[12] The word "test" concedes that error may come from following this principle, but simultaneously, and rightly, presupposes that under conditions of uncertainty we should embrace that strategy that in the long run is likely to lead to the best outcome. That there are no certainties in the world, we can freely concede, but we must also insist that there are better and worse outcomes. As stated, it looks as though Holmes thinks that freedom of speech prevents the government from imposing any limitations on the use of words. But the legs are cut out from under that incautious proposition by Holmes's curt remark in the earlier case of *Schenck v. United States:* "The most stringent protection of free speech would not protect a man in falsely shouting fire in a theatre and causing a panic."[13]

So the question then is where to draw the line between the forms of speech that can be regulated and those that cannot. Holmes ultimately held that it was best to err on the side of liberty: "[W]e should be eternally vigilant against attempts to check the expression of opinions that we loathe and believe to be fraught with death, unless they so imminently threaten immediate interference with the lawful and pressing purposes of the law that an immediate check is required to save the country."[14] Holmes need have only tied the ribbon to the package, by pointing out the many steps that must intervene between the circulation of an idle leaflet and a physical attack on government activities or personnel. The substantive evil to be prevented is not some criticism of government conduct, but tangible interference with war efforts, as by blocking government officials in doing their work or offering direct inducements for them to breach their contractual and public duties,[15] and it is notable that the fact in *Abrams* itself contains no hint that any of the defendants' activities had any impact whatsoever on the overall conduct of the war effort.

So construed, Holmes's skepticism about right and wrong does not degenerate into a constitutional regime where anything goes. Nor does it fail to generate a legal principle capable of general application. Quite the opposite; with time his dissent came to organize and control this branch of the law.[16] In good Hayekian sense, our collective ignorance of the pros and cons in particular disputes provides the reason for allowing everyone to have his say before collective decisions are made. Freedom of speech thus serves as a counterweight to government monopoly, a problem that exists not only in the United States but wherever sovereign authority is exerted, which is to say everywhere.

Yet much of Holmes's perceived greatness inheres in his enigmatic status. Unfortunately, on matters of economic regulation his skepticism turned sour and led to his acquiescence in the unwarranted expansion of government power. The pivotal case, which captures the mood, is *Lochner v. New York,*[17] in which a divided Supreme Court struck down a New York criminal statute that provided that no employee shall "work in a biscuit, bread or cake bakery or confectionary establishment more than

sixty hours in any one week, or more than ten hours in any one day."
Speaking for the court, Justice Peckham held that the statute limited the
contractual freedom of employer and employee alike; as such it was "a labor law, pure and simple" that could not be justified as a means to protect
public health. The logic in *Lochner* recognized a strong prima facie case
for striking down the statute, based on liberty of contract, which in turn
was subject to a narrow class of justifications not met in the case. The
baker could decide for himself whether to accept or reject the contract
offer. The state had no warrant to intervene on his behalf.

Holmes would have none of this:

> The liberty of the citizen to do as he likes so long as he does not interfere
> with the liberty of others to do the same, which has been a shibboleth for
> some well-known writers, is interfered with by school laws, by the Post
> Office, by every state or municipal institution which takes his money for
> purposes thought desirable, whether he likes it or not. The 14th Amend-
> ment does not enact Mr. Herbert Spencer's Social Statics. . . . [A] Constitu-
> tion is not intended to embody a particular economic theory, whether of
> paternalism and the organic relation of the citizen to the State or of laissez-
> faire. It is made for people of fundamentally differing views.[18]

The upshot was

> I think that the word "liberty," in the 14th Amendment, is perverted when
> it is held to prevent the natural outcome of dominant opinion, unless it can
> be said that a rational and fair man necessarily would admit that the stat-
> ute proposed would infringe fundamental principles as they have been un-
> derstood by the traditions of our people and our law.[19]

These oft-quoted passages exhibit a very different form of skepticism
from that found in *Abrams*. We do not see Holmes make the argument
that in a system of voluntary exchange each person gives up something in
order to receive something that he values more.[20] But his insistence that
the ordinary meaning of liberty (which surely covers more than freedom
from imprisonment) is "perverted" when extended to cover freedom of
contract (which should be understood as a subset of the freedom of action
that liberty normally protects) shows the nastier side of Holmes: his powerful use of language to force everything to yield to "dominant opinion"
unless the case becomes so clear to admit of no exception. With this attitude, it is not surprising that he misses the strongest argument for limited
skepticism: from our perch outside the transaction, we (the people) are
not privy to the opportunities and costs of the transacting parties, and

are thus ill equipped to override their judgment on matters that fall closer to their well-being than to our own. Holmes thus gets the presumption backward. He allows state intervention unless there is a strong reason to think otherwise. The proper approach is that, mindful of our collective infirmities, we should stay our hand and let the parties take their course unless we can advance some strong justification for interfering. In this context, the case name—*Lochner v. New York*—virtually cries out for nonintervention. We must be especially suspicious of criminal penalties imposed on an employer whose workers do not protest, for these penalties could easily operate solely for the benefit of the firm's competitors whose cost of compliance with the statute was lower. Reformist zeal is often a thin cover for partisan legislation.

Nor need we leave the point to abstract speculation. Some evidence is on the face of the statute itself: only certain classes of bakers are covered, even though there is no evidence that the perils they face are greater than those bakers who are excluded from the act. A public-spirited view of contract regulation should cover all types of bakers if it covers any. The selective element here, however, has a more ominous explanation in light of interest group pressures. The broader statute could attract opposition from both firms and laborers whose production could have been compromised by the statute. But the differential pressure of the maximum hour limitation imposed few restraints on larger manufacturers who used two shifts of workers, one to prepare bread in the evening and a second to package it after baking in the morning. Lochner's bakers worked a single shift by sleeping on the job, which they could no longer do. And the telltale sign of the differential effect: the other provisions of the statute that regulated the sleeping conditions of workers while on the job![21]

The demonstration of the particular political forces at work is not, however, necessary to support a general principle that requires the state to respect the liberty of each person to dispose of his own labor or capital as he sees fit, unless he interferes with the like liberty of other individuals. The earlier case law, which Peckham himself had endorsed, had extended this principle to allow the state to limit contracts in restraint of trade, such as price-fixing between competitors.[22] Ironically, that position does not limit state power to the strict libertarian prohibitions on force and fraud. Quite the opposite, it presupposes that the state can choke off the ability of competitors to deal with each other, which the strong libertarian theory allows private parties to do. That emendation of the basic theory can, moreover, be defended only on the grounds that the systematic social losses from monopoly are great enough to entitle the state to determine the shape of the market. This approach rests freedom of contract on the same limited skepticism used to defend freedom of speech, for it relies on general regularities in human conduct to shape the scope of the legislative power. In answering this position, it does Holmes no good to say that *a* constitution does not rest on any particular theory: *our* Constitution does, and it is most emphatically a theory of limited government and vested individual rights. So long as laissez-faire is understood to allow government action for the provision of infrastructure and public goods,[23] then our Constitution does embrace, if not in so many words, the principle of laissez-faire over the broad range of social activities.

Holmes's well-chosen epithet "shibboleth" does nothing to undermine these basic principles; nor do any of his counterexamples touch the case before him. It is quite possible to defend laws that require the education of children while attacking limitations on the ability of adults to contract on their own behalf: a discussion of vouchers shows how it might be done. The Constitution may authorize the federal operation of the Post Office, but it hardly requires it to run at a deficit, to offer cross-subsidies between different classes of service, or to insulate the postal monopoly from the competition of Federal Express and United Parcel Service. State taxation of one class of individuals for the exclusive benefit of another may not be an interference of contract but should nonetheless be condemned on the kindred principle that condemns any law "that takes property from A and gives it to B."[24]

At this point, we can identify the perils associated with the interference in private contract—two winners are made into two losers. So why then does Holmes, in contrast with his *Abrams* dissent, cut the state so much slack so that its interference with private contracts is tolerated unless a "rational" man would "necessarily" condemn its action? Of course, individuals have sharp divisions of opinion over the desirability of state regulation of private contracts, just as they have sharp divisions over regulations needed to nip subversive speech in the bud. But the same position is true with respect to subversive speech at the end of World War I; yet that division of sentiment did not prevent Holmes from casting a heavy burden on the state in *Abrams* (when the dangers of intervening too late could be the overthrow of political institutions). Why not impose a similar burden in this case?

One obvious response is that freedom of speech is necessary for the preservation of political democracy while the institution of private property is not. But the defense of private property has its political as well as its economic dimension. Start with the extreme. Let the state own all the land, such that ordinary people are dependent on it for the houses in which they live and the jobs in which they work. What possible reason is there to hope that individuals with that level of dependency would be able to muster either the resources or the courage to criticize government activity? Right now we know that firms in regulated industries are reluctant to speak out lest they invite the burden of legislation on them. More generally, it is hard enough to curb government retaliation against its critics when state power is limited. It would become nearly impossible if all private property were swallowed up into public hands so that newspapers and broadcast stations were everywhere under state ownership and control. In good times, with good leaders, free institutions might flourish for at least a while. But come bad times, and the cumulative weight of government power will overwhelm everyone subject to it. The independence that strong property rights afford has a political dimension that makes it dangerous to compartmentalize government action into discrete political and economic spheres.

Notwithstanding its good sense, the outcome of *Lochner* is frequently condemned, if not reviled, both in Holmes's time and at our own.[25] That case, which to some defines no less than an era, was the prime target of the Progressive movement before its fall in the aftermath of the 1937 judicial revolution. But on the merits, Holmes's brand of misguided constitutional skepticism does not come within a country mile of undermining Peckham's methodical attack on the industry-specific maximum hours legislation. The only way to make out Holmes's case is through some showing that the state intervention would improve the efficiency of the contracting process, as by eliminating serious sources of worker misinformation. But the disputed term on hours was a matter evident to both parties, and the present set of regulations has led to the comedy of interest group politics and enforcement errors under the Occupational Safety and Health Act.[26] And so it is that the wrong form of skepticism leads to judicial deference.

Posner: Pragmatism, (Social) Darwinism, and Nazism

The question of moral skepticism is not confined to the constitutional setting. While cases like *Lochner* and *Abrams* have generated much philosophical and constitutional passion, they have occurred within a tradition that responds to arguments on both sides of the intellectual and social divide. In a sense, therefore, neither case raises in starkest form the question of moral relativism, because those cases are more about how moral theories are incorporated into law than they are about whether there are any moral theories at all. On this first question, one possible view of the matter is that the existence of law is one thing and its merit or demerit is another. The position thus presupposes the logical separation of law and morals, even though it expects that most of the time legal rules will be influenced by moral concerns. The case that tests this ostensible separation most profoundly arises in connection with Nazi rule, where the settled legal view was that the secret commands of the führer were considered to have the force of law even though they countermanded the requirements of a published statute.[27] In order to fight that result, Lon Fuller argued that all laws, to count as law, had to meet minimum procedural requisites, such as publication and the right to be heard. Stated more generally, do we accord the status of law to any command of the sovereign (which Hitler was, owing to his effective control over German territory and more), or is there some indisputable moral minimum that must be met before any such command of the statute can be raised to the level of law? The famous Hart-Fuller debate of the 1950s grappled inconclusively with that question.[28] The debate is in part definitional (and in part an effort to hold Nazis in the dock at Nuremberg). My own view is that Hart has the better of their debate on legal positivism insofar as he insists that we should all be the wiser if we recognize that the existence of law is one thing, and its demerit is quite another.

The dispute of moral relativism, however, is agnostic about the resolution of this debate, whether it deals with the Nazis or anything else. In order to defeat moral relativism, it is only necessary to show that Nazi law, even if law, can be condemned on independent moral grounds. Most ordinary folk do not hesitate to think that condemnation is possible. Indeed, part of the outburst against Friedrich Hayek is attributable to his defense of decentralized power in *The Road to Serfdom,* which begins with the (overstated) fear that concentrated state power under democratic socialism will lead inexorably to the horrors of Nazism.[29] The historical record now seems clear that a system that has strong elements of private property can resist tyranny, even if it allows extensive regulation in other areas, which our system does.

Holmes's skepticism, however, can be taken that extra mile to ask whether there is any moral theory from which law can be separated in the first place. Here the argument is that it is not possible to develop any set of moral principles that allow us to mount some generalized attack on law, in particular the Nazi version of law, as immoral in the first place. Holmes himself did not push hard on the particulars of this program, but the campaign has as its most articulate spokesman Judge Richard A. Posner, for whom Holmes has near-deified status. Posner has defended in a "pragmatic voice" what amounts to, if not fully acknowledged as, a form of moral relativism. He mocks—the choice of word is deliberate—

those who purport to find moral universals sufficient to guide human conduct or to persuade dissenters of the wrongness of their actions.[30] The disjunctions in this exposition are evident. At one level, Posner, as a skilled academic, is capable of articulating a nuanced, if indeterminate, account of pragmatism. Thus he describes it variously as an attitude or an approach that seeks to avoid the false illusion that there is, in Ronald Dworkin's language, "one right answer" to any legal question.[31] With maddening elegance, Posner states that "the brand of pragmatism that I like emphasizes the scientific virtues (open-minded, no-nonsense inquiry), elevates the process of inquiry to the results of inquiry, prefers ferment to stasis, dislikes distinctions that make no practical difference—in other words, dislikes 'metaphysics,'—is doubtful of finding 'objective truth' in any area of inquiry, is uninterested in creating an adequate philosophical foundation for its thought and action, likes experimentation, likes to kick sacred cows, and within the bounds of prudence, prefers shaping the future to maintaining continuity with the past."[32]

At one level it is hard to disagree with this to-and-fro account of the preferred methodology; it has a flexibility sufficient to accommodate any but the most nondogmatic approach. In the same vein, there is little to disagree with Posner's statement that he adopts "skepticism" in its lay, rather than in its philosophical, sense, that is, as an attitude toward the world rather than a philosophical denial of knowledge of the external world.[33]

Yet the reasons for uneasiness are evident: Just what is the cash value of a position that is open to everything and commits to nothing, and takes pride in its elusive quality, and refuses to offer any systematic defense of any set of institutional arrangements? In essence, the approach offers skilled oral advocates the possibility of taking any side of any legal dispute and coming out the better for it. Needless to say, armed with this approach, Posner no longer takes the sunny view of the efficiency of the common law that characterized his earlier writings.[34] But he also takes after the mission, which he rightly associates with my own work, of seeking to use or understand the basic or "natural" impulses of human behavior as a guide to what counts as right or wrong in human affairs.[35]

Unfortunately, too much gets lost in the translation. Thus an affinity for natural law gets transformed into the deadly embrace of social Darwinism, and crude utilitarianism—the greatest good for the greatest number—now allows for just about any sacrifice of individual rights for the benefit of the whole, with collectivist overtones that libertarians, like myself, hold in deep suspicion.[36] As a rhetorical matter, this is surely just the right tactic: it is a modern-day version of Holmes's effort to trash the majority decision in *Lochner* by linking it with the social Darwinist movement. Taken historically, the equation of any version of natural law with Darwinism seems false. At least two close examinations of the jurisprudence of the "old Court"—that infamous body of men who comprised the Supreme Court between the end of the Civil War and the constitutional transformation of 1937—shows that there was less jurisprudential novelty in the period than meets the eye. James W. Ely has shown quite conclusively that social Darwinism had little role to play in the jurisprudence of the old Court.[37] He has also shown, at least to my satisfaction, that the principles of "substantive due process" were not an oxymoronic perversion of the original constitutional language of the Due Process Clauses of the Fifth and Fourteenth Amendments, but represent a continuous view of interpretation that dates back to the Magna Carta, or at least to the substantive interpretations that it had received long before founding period.[38]

Likewise, Howard Gillman reached the same conclusion, noting that the efforts of the old Court (including the decision in *Lochner*) to define the appropriate uses and limitations of the police power never so much as flirted with any conception, Darwinist or otherwise, of radical individualism.[39] The quest there was to draw the line between those limitations on property and contract that were needed to protect the safety, health, morals, and, under some formulations, "general welfare" of the public at large. Figuring out which statutes met this test and which did not was not done in the modern language of law and economics, but it seemed quite clear that the judges understood the risks of the major sources of market failure: monopoly, externalities, and misinformation. The key villain of the piece was often "labor law"—those statutes that protected certain individuals from competition by rival firms or that sought to give legal protection to labor monopolies, as an impermissible form of "class legislation."[40] Holmes stood utterly alone in *Lochner* for good reason: he was the only one of the justices on either side of the case who refused to conduct any in-depth discussion of the police power issue.

Posner's unhappy conflation of natural law with Darwinist theories also fails as a conceptual matter. A belief in natural law does not champion nature red in tooth and claw, or even the survival of the fittest; treating charity as an imperfect obligation of benevolence is a powerful feature of natural law that has no place in a Darwinist conception. Rather, it only asks what the traditional inquiries into the police power sought to explicate: that legal rules be organized in ways that bring out the best and suppress the worst in human behavior, given what we know about human psychology and behavior—which is not altogether pretty. No sensible version of utilitarianism lets utility monsters gobble up their fellow men. If anything, they treat each person as though he "counts for one and only one."[41] Indeed, it is just the concern with the boundaries between persons that leads me to believe that the better form of consequentialism places the autonomy assumption front and center (on the grounds that it looks to be strongly Pareto superior to the state of nature, and its attendant difficulties),[42] and then asks that any deviation from that rule be one that improve the lot of all individuals subject to the regulation. In the alternative, there are occasions when it is so difficult to implement that position that we gravitate toward the weaker Kaldor-Hicks test, under which as a practical matter we accept some relatively small compromise of individual entitlements in order to achieve major advantages for the public at large. Yet even here the winners, in principle, should be able to pay the losers and still remain better off. The ability to find some substantial social surplus becomes the substitute for just compensation.

We can go further: if this principle is consistently applied to a substantial number of legislative initiatives, then the Kaldor-Hicks formula starts to blend into the Paretian formula, for it becomes ever less likely that the same individuals will be systematically short-changed by a series of unrelated statutes, all of which have substantial net benefits. Let there be a society in which there are ten statutes each of which benefits the winners by $10,000 per head and costs the losers only $100. In each case, 90 percent of the people come out winners, and only 10 percent losers. If the statutes were randomly chosen, the individual who was on the winning side only once would still end up $9,100 ahead ($10,000 − 9 × $100). The odds that he would lose the $1,000 depend on his being on the short side in each case. But the chance of losing ten times in succession is only 1 in 10^{10}, a number that is small enough to ignore. Let the basic payoffs be as advertised, and it is easy to see how some individuals could get a disproportionate share of the surplus. But it is hard to see how many individuals are likely to come out net losers.

Working through the implications of this mixed position is not easy. It requires us to recognize that specific rules, such as the autonomy principle, do excellent work over broad portions of the legal terrain, but may well fail under extreme circumstances, where they should be suitably circumscribed. The ordinary approach to these matters is one of sensible incrementalism. One consistent set of implications from this position is that it leads, as Posner acknowledges, to the conclusion that "a variety of

widely accepted norms, including the keeping of certain promises, the ab-
horrence of the unjustified killing of human beings, and perhaps even the
sanctity of property rights, promote the adaptation of the human species
to its environment. But so does genocide." [43]

Zowie! The passage just quoted begins with too much equivocation.
Why only the keeping of "certain" promises, what counts as an "unjustified killing," does the protection of property rights require their "sanctity?" But all these small points can be resolved using the usual tools of
common law interpretation. When is there an intention to create legal
relations? Are certain promises against public policy? Is provocation a
justification for killing? Does the sanctity of property prohibit all takings
of private property? The shock value of the last sentence is a rhetorical
device that Posner borrows from Holmes. But it badly misfires: it shows
that the man who prides himself on his steely ability to cut through legal
malarkey lacks the most elementary sense of proportion, or, dare one say
it, judgment, not to say any appreciation of the tragedies of human suffering. Despite his protestations to the contrary, his form of pragmatism
morphs into a cruel form of moral skepticism. The very possibility that
this position could be squared with a utilitarian account would, if correct, be a devastating indictment of that venerable system. But of course,
he cannot cite any utilitarian who would embrace that position, so how
does he come by it? Not by starting with the view that treats all persons
as though they count for one and only one. Those who are hunted and
exterminated are left with nothing at all. No utilitarian could live with a
result that shrinks massively the number of human beings to gratify the
desires of a select few. If it is hard to get a utilitarian justification for
garden-variety murder, it is no easier to find one for mass murder. The
same results are, if anything, clearer under any criterion that explicitly
requires us to generate real or hypothetical gains to all participants, as
the Pareto and Kaldor-Hicks standards do. Whatever one's doubts about
the scope of enforceable promises, the segue from limited government to
genocide takes a determined form of moral blindness open only to the
totally inept or the devilishly brilliant.

Posner, of course, does not evaluate this statement against these cri-
teria but reverts to his crude form of social Darwinism by noting that
"the race that exterminates other races spreads its members' genes. If the
Nazis' geopolitical ambitions had been fulfilled, Hitler would have been
entitled to kudos from those who believe that Darwinism is a source of
moral norms." [44] His thoughtless transition from the natural law tradition
to his caricature of the Darwinist position comes at a very high price.

Is there any way to dislodge this kind of fatal conceit? For Posner, the standard is: unless you can force me to confess error, I can wreck your conventional wisdom by taking the stance of the sole moral holdout, and thus deny your position universal acceptance. The quoted passage above is not some misguided exaggeration. Defiantly, he repeats his taunts on another occasion by insisting that no person steeped in the values of Western democracy could persuade a determined Nazi to abandon his own deeply held convictions. The bluntness of his language has to be quoted to be appreciated:

> It was right to try the Nazi leaders rather than to shoot them out of hand in a paroxysm of disgust. But it was *politically* right. It created a trustworthy public record of what the Nazis had done. And it exhibited "rule of law" virtues to the German people that made it less likely that Germany would again embrace totalitarianism. But it was not right because a trial could produce proof that the Nazis *really* were immoralists; they were, but according to our lights, not theirs. [45]

The passage starts out all right because what the Nazis did was disgusting, and it was politically right to punish them in order to preserve the rule of law, although one could argue whether Nuremberg offered the right forum. [46] But from those conventional moral beginnings the relativism of the last sentence hardly follows: Why retreat now to the difference between their lights and ours? For Posner, the logic of this position is in the supposed difference between moral relativism and moral skepticism. The former allows for the development of "local"—that is, culture-specific—tests of truth and falsity that could be applied to moral propositions, including those governing the proper use of state power. Hence the moral relativist is also a moral skeptic. But the downside of moral relativism is that, like moral skepticism, it rejects the proposition that these truths can be made universal. The most resourceful moral thinker in one culture cannot persuade an oafish holdout in a second culture to abandon his boorish position. It is this distinction that prevents us from attacking on moral grounds the Nazis or indeed any other alien practice that disgusts our own sensibility.

This question of cross-cultural moral discourse is, of course, not confined to the Nazis. Posner offers the example of suttee—the immolation of a widow on her husband's bier, which may or may not be voluntary—as yet another kind of practice that we find repellent and might, as Westerners, ban, as much for our aesthetic comfort as anything else. [47] But here the most obvious question is the counterfactual one, whether that practice could survive in a political system in which women were accorded equal political rights with men. Stated otherwise, could the practice have survived if it were debated in an open forum, even if the only participants were the Hindus who engaged in it? To an outsider this practice looks less like a moral choice of those who suffer and more like the powerful imposing their own destructive preferences on the weak. (It is hard to divine which way it cuts that "suttee" in Sanskrit literally means "true woman" or "good woman.") If it did, then we would face the question that classical liberal theory has always divided: Do we accept the appropriate nature of suicide, given that the choice once made cannot be undone?[48] We need not plumb the depths of that debate here to recognize that this odd example would serve as a testament to cultural relativism if we had seen it spread in the same fashion as universal civil capacity and universal suffrage. But otherwise, we should treat it as nothing more than a crabbed exception that proves the value of the general principles of autonomy around which every social system is concluded. To the extent that moral skepticism erodes that principle, it corrodes the only rules ever found to give individuals a decent chance to live in peace and harmony with each other. That is a terrible price to pay to embrace a moral relativism, which in the end always decays into an indefensible moral skepticism.

The same point can be made in reply to the issue of the Nazis. Once again, it seems quite clear that the principles announced did not take place under conditions of full and free debate of the ideas in question. The systematic suppression of all opposition by ruthless tactics precluded that condition. So it is hard to see how "they" reached any position on the question when most of "them" were silenced. More generally, the purported distinction between moral skepticism and moral relativism collapses under its own weight once we deconstruct the elusive "we" in Posner's phrase "our lights" in order to ask how one person persuades another person in the *same* locality or social community of the soundness of some given moral point of view. One possibility is that all of us share the same common moral framework, in which case the argument is both easy and uninteresting: logical deduction and empirical verification of facts is all that is required. The second possibility is that these individuals share no moral premise, at which point the task of suasion would be hopeless even among ourselves, no matter how local our culture. But of course it is not. The test of whether a moral theory is good or bad does not depend on the willingness of the most resistant and perverse person to accept its logical force. When faced with disputes of this sort, the sensible counterstrategy is to adopt the stance of some impartial observer who is tied to neither party to help adjudicate the claims between them.[49] Or it is to appeal to one of those universals that seem bland until they are put to the test: "Thou shall not kill," for starters.

Either way, however, Posner's entire argument presupposes some inexplicable unity within any given culture whose boundaries are left curiously undefined in either space or time. His "we" includes radical feminists, religious fundamentalists, and everyone in between. If members of this community can engage in moral discourse with right and wrong answers, then why does moral discourse stop at some national boundary line? What barriers, for example, prevent us from asking the same questions of the Nazis that could have been asked by contemporary members of the German resistance who were not won over by Hitler's propaganda machine?[50] Why was the American of 1940 unable to pose to the Nazi of 1940 the identical question as his German interrogator could have posed at that time, or indeed, in 1946? The boundaries of space and time simply do not block the free movement of public moral discourse across communities. To deny the possibility of argument across cultures is to deny them within cultures, or indeed between individual persons, each of whom could stoutly defend any moral proposition to the bitter end. There is, quite simply, no way to preserve moral relativism from the ravages of moral skepticism. If individuals in different cultures are helpless to resolve differences in the face of disagreement, then individuals within the same culture are equally helpless to persuade as well. Likewise, if people can communicate within cultures, then they can communicate between cultures.

But does that communication take place? In one sense, anyone who listens to the ravings of Hitler or Goebbels would have to say that they had lost their moral compass. But listen a bit closer. They never attacked any of those bland universals on which Western civilization rests. They could never have carried the German population with them if they preferred cowardice to bravery, deceit to honor, aggression to self-defense, filth to cleanliness, or selfishness to sacrifice. The simple truth is the Germans, Nazi or not, had to maintain a viable social order within their own preferred group, and the fundamental glue of any social group is what Posner disparages when he writes that "[t]he only nonlocal facts are the useless rudimentary principles of social cooperation"[51] contained in such "uninteresting" universals as murder is wrong and that promises should be kept. Substitute "fundamental" for "useless rudimentary" and the error in his position becomes apparent. In his book, he softens the point a little when he writes:

There are a handful of rudimentary principles of social cooperation—
such as don't lie *all* the time, or break promises without *any* reason or kill
your relatives or neighbors indiscriminately—that may be common to all
human societies, and if one wants to call these rudimentary principles the
universal moral law, that is fine with me. But they are too abstract to be
criterial.[52]

Yet either way, his basic point is false because it misses the generative
power of these basic norms. The principles of cooperation are the basis
not only for social order but also for legal contract, which comprehends
not only spot transactions of exchange but also the long-term relational
interests common to such institutions as marriage and partnership. For
its part, the tautological principle that murder—or theft, or rape, or robbery, or other forms of aggression—is wrong is what stands between us
and the horrors that the Nazis inflicted on both their own people and
the rest of the world.[53] There are dangers of being too cute: the point
is not that the Nazis killed "indiscriminately"; quite the opposite, they
picked their targets with grim precision. Side by side with our history of
mass slaughters, it is impossible to find any variation in the private law
of murder from the Code of Hammurabi to the German Civil Code that
offered up a colorable reason to excuse or justify these killings.

We all know the stuff of which the Model Penal Code, and every
known legal system, is made. Its offenses are murder, theft, and rape.
It may take a bit of time to explicate fine points of mental states, or
to distinguish between murder and manslaughter; and we can have extensive debates over the limits of insanity, provocation, and self-defense,
which can reach fever pitch in such cases as the substantive defenses made
available to battered wives. But no one would defend the proposition
that killing is not wrongful because the accused did not like the color
of his victim's eyes, or thought that anyone who did not like his mother
deserved to die. It is on just these rudimentary areas of agreement that
the survival of social order depends, not on the subtle variations in the
established defenses that take some homicides out of the class of murder. Ordinary language includes the terms "excuse" and "justification"
(or *Entschuldigen*—escape from guilt; and *Rechtfertigen*—to make right
what is prima facie wrong) for good reason: they mark out the corrections
needed to the original but overbroad proposition that killing is wrongful.
But no legal system recognizes anything close to complete plasticity in the
particular excuses and justifications admitted into the system.

The proof of this position is, moreover, in the eating. The Nazi propaganda never took exception to the basic principles of social coordination

that Posner disparages. Rather, they made the malicious factual assertion that mass deprivation of Jewish rights and Jewish lives was appropriate because the Jews themselves were bloodsuckers and, worse, *deserved* imprisonment and death because they had not followed the rules demanded of, and complied with, by all right-standing Germans. It was the false racist element about human conduct that converted traditional morality into an instrument of mass destruction. To defend the Nazis one has to adopt a factual skepticism that makes truth as arbitrary as moral propositions, which, alas, Holmes, the philosopher, was prepared to do when he wrote that "moral preferences are more or less arbitrary. . . . Do you like sugar in your coffee or don't you? . . . So as to truth."[54]

But all of this falls by the wayside when one looks closely on a comparative basis at the principles of law that govern most civil societies, including Germany. For example, we can recognize the many variations in family organization, evolution in the status of women. Yet at no point do we see the level of ostensible variation that Posner finds in universal laws. It is quite clear that random violence cannot be tolerated in a family no matter what the relative positions of its members. But what is quite striking about comparative law generally is how *little* difference one can find in legal principles that govern the relationships between strangers.

This convergence does not originate in high theory. It comes from the brute necessities of human life. H. L. A. Hart referred to just these conditions when he gave his account of the *minimum content of natural law,* which was lifted, as he acknowledged straight from Hobbes and Hume.[55] Individuals start in positions of vulnerability. Yet it is not possible for each person to contract with all others to renounce the use of force. But owing to their approximate equality in strength, no one person could expect to prevail against a coalition of three or four determined rivals. Yet by the same token the limited forms of human altruism allow cooperative arrangements to develop that reduce the reliance on force and induce individuals to rely on mutual exchange as a way to overcome scarcity. And so we get the principles of autonomy, property, contract, and tort. The only mistake in Hart's analysis is to call the commitments that flow from this version of human nature "minimal." Quite the opposite, once these basic postulates are in place, they effectively constrain the nature of the debate that follows. The next chapter tries to show the way in which minimum principles expand by increments to fill the social space.

4 Moral Incrementalism

Successive Approximations

IT IS ONE THING TO ATTACK MORAL RELATIVISM and moral skepticism in their protean forms. It is quite another to undertake the constructive task of figuring out how to put the system back together again. In this chapter I begin that inquiry. I hope to show in the first section how a system of successive approximations of use in other contexts allows us to hone in on the right conclusion by a step-by-step process that is consistent the general consequentialist agenda. I then apply that method to various issues of liability both in easy cases of liability to strangers and in the more complex situations arising out of cases of necessity and rescue including Judith Jarvis Thomson's famous "trolley problem." I then conclude with a brief discussion of the abortion matter. It is not possible to generate a comprehensive set of rules in one fell swoop. But it is possible to articulate that set in careful stages.

One of the recurrent tensions in moral theory is the reconciliation of ordinary intuitions, often cast in terms of fairness, with more formal rules and procedures. Philosophers, linguists, and lawyers have made, I believe, too much out of the differences among them, while ignoring the key way in which they reinforce each other. In my view, the best way to find one's bearings on moral questions is to begin with ordinary discourse. Ordinary language philosophy, as such, had its vogue in the 1950s, when it was associated in philosophy most famously with the work of J. L. Austin,[1] whose approach was carried over into law, in part, by his colleague, H. L. A. Hart.[2] The deficiencies of ordinary language philosophy, chiefly in its lack of theoretical unity and ambition, have led many to reject it in favor of a more scientific and systematic approach—first to language and morals, and then to its legal outcroppings.[3]

I believe, however, that the ordinary and the systematic elements of ordinary language reinforce each other, and the object of this chapter is to show how they function together. Ordinary language gives us the basic grammatical structures, whose key terms are "ordinarily," "as a general rule," "unless," and "except for." These terms have more or less precise analogies in the legal system that operates by presumptions whereby the plaintiff states a cause of action, or a prima facie case, and then the defendant seeks to introduce, as ordinary language has it, some "excuse" (literally, to get out of culpability) or "justification" (literally, to make right what is prima facie wrong).

The method holds out much promise of success even though it offers no tidy, universal solution to the hardest of cases. It is important to do a good job in the common cases for which we can identify both better and worse answers. It is vital that we insulate the good work we can do in 99.9 percent of the real cases from the perplexities that dominate the other 0.1 percent. The common law system of presumptions allows one to keep the hard cases in perspective, because it first directs our attention to the easiest cases of aggression and promise breaking that lie at the heart of any system of rights and wrongs. That system of successive approximation, outlined above, is run by a powerful intellectual engine, and, ironically, it is one that has been picked up but not exploited in the philosophical literature, under the guise of prima facie duties.[4] Yet by the same token, it yields in most cases progressions that are tolerably simple so that they can be communicated to and internalized by huge numbers of individuals simultaneously.[5]

This widespread use of presumptions, moreover, exhibits uncanny parallels to a strategy that is well known and frequently used in mathematics and the physical sciences. Often it is quite difficult to get a formal solution to a complex expression—for example, to find the roots of a complex polynomial that cannot be factored. In these cases it is often best to proceed by approximation, using, say, Newton's rule to get ever better successive approximations of the solution. One general question asks just how good are these systems of approximation, or stated otherwise, just how quickly does successive application of Newton's rule lead to an accurate approximation of the needed root. People who think that the world is full of imperfections and confusion might assume that convergence is a slow and arduous process, in which the idiosyncratic elements dominate the landscape. But Newton's rule points to the opposite conclusion, insofar as most approximations converge quite rapidly on the correct solution. The same is often true of most convergent infinite series for which there is no exact rational equivalent. Consider an approximation for

$$e = 1 + 1/1! + 1/2! + 1/3! + \ldots + 1/n! \, .$$

We reach an answer that deviates from the true answer by less than one part in a billion when we set n equal to 12.[6] Legal approximation is less dramatic, but still moves with great rapidity. The objective is to maximize social welfare (in my view, generally under Paretian standards), which is no mean feat to accomplish in the abstract. So we attack that problem by approximation, and within a few iterations reach a sensible result.

The simplest way to do this is to begin with the easy cases of disputes that arise in the course of ordinary life. The right way to understand moral behavior and to do moral philosophy is by beginning with the most routine and boring transactions to figure out why they work as well as they do. Who enters these transactions? Whom do they pair up with and why? What is their source of gain? Of risk? Only when these are understood should we tackle the difficult marginal cases that are tested in the crucible of litigation. It is a mistake to begin by looking at extreme cases, notwithstanding the inveterate philosophical inclination to attack the system of social convention at its weak point before its inner strengths are appreciated. We should avoid the temptation to start with lifeboat, desert island, and Nazi examples to evaluate the regime of individual autonomy, private property, and voluntary exchange. The grim outcomes in these hard cases come as no surprise, for the constraints of scarcity are binding against all forms of moral ingenuity. Of course, we should expect that something has to give when ten people try to squeeze onto a lifeboat that will capsize if it holds more than six. Who would want to determine who should survive and why? Does anyone have any sympathy for the first to come upon a water hole in the desert who wants to exclude all those who come a minute later? It is on to the easy cases.

Easy Cases: The Morality of Everyday Life

This general framework still leaves open the question of how ordinary people learn to articulate and apply moral principles. The answer to that question does not lie in some grand exhortation of moral philosophy from on high, for this sounds preachy and fails to communicate any experience from the trenches. Rather, the source of moral wisdom often comes from repeated, ordinary interactions between individuals, who often do not stop to reflect on the judgments they make. That result is common enough because for the most part day-to-day moral disputes with family, friends, and coworkers take place in a spirit of amity, so that people are willing to admit that they were wrong. The key, therefore, to understanding the strength of a moral principle rests in large measure on its tacit acceptance in ordinary discussions. The articulation of that principle becomes far sharper when people disagree. C. S. Lewis seizes on this fact of life to begin his defense of natural law:

Every one has heard people quarreling. Sometimes it sounds funny and sometimes it sounds merely unpleasant; but however it sounds, I believe we can learn something very important from listening to the kind of things they say. They say things like this: "That's my seat, I was there first"—"Leave him alone, he isn't doing you any harm"—"Why should you shove in first?"—"Give me a bit of your orange, I gave you a bit of mine"—"How'd you like it if anyone did the same to you"—"Come on, you promised."[7]

Lewis, of course, was not a lawyer, but a classical and literary scholar, and a Christian apologist to boot. But his arguments show an unerring instinct for evaluating these transactions. First, note what he *leaves out* of the analysis. There is no talk here that some people may be offended because they don't like the behavior of one of the protagonists to the dispute. It hardly matters that A is offended that I asked for my seat back, while B would have been offended if I had not asked. Everyone has some response to what other people do, but these are strictly second-order effects. The right response is to ignore all these sentiments one way or the other, on the ground that they are so numerous as to wash out in the aggregate. Take any other view, and we could never decide whether one outcome represented a social improvement over another, for it would only take the disapproval of a single individual to make the entire matter indeterminate. The legal system has always taken just that view. The offense to (some) bystanders was, to use the Roman phrase, *damnum absque iniuria*—harm without legal injury. The point is not just isolated double-talk. It is designed to identify who lacks "standing" to protest the outcome of a transaction in which they have not participated.

That diversion to one side, the analysis rightly concentrates on the parties to the dispute. Here Lewis's examples show the power of the rules that underlie these simple exchanges. Thus his first example—"That's my seat, I was there first"—is a direct appeal to the principle of first possession, on which so much of the system of private property depends. His second—"he isn't doing you any harm"—suggests that the transaction is one that does not fit within the nascent tort law: "no harm, no foul," to quote that noted Laker philosopher, the late Chick Hearn. Someone else might be able to protest his actions, but not you since he is not doing *you* any harm. "Come on, you promised" ushers in the law of contract. Lewis's most difficult example—"a bit of your orange"—shows the critical place of reciprocity in ordinary discourse, without coming to grips with the question of whether there was some prior implied understanding between the parties that sharing in the first instance would either lead to, let alone require, sharing later, which turns out to be the single most vexing issue in the law of restitution. And the appeal to the Golden Rule, of course, is a way to constrain individual excesses by invoking the principle "turnabout is fair play," a principle with real tenacity in constitutional law. One paragraph of down-to-earth good sense gets us started into four of the major branches of law: property, tort, contract, and restitution. It also contains some of the key insights that underlie the use of incentive compatible arguments—the only way you can do best by yourself is to do best by everyone else—in human affairs generally.

But, of course, these principles are guides, not absolutes, and Lewis is aware of that as well. The moment he finishes with his bits of unexceptionable imaginary dialogue he reaches the obvious conclusion that the dialogue makes sense only because both sides to the disagreement share some implicit standard of judgment and evaluation. "And the other man very seldom replies, 'To hell with your standard.' Nearly always he tries to make out that what he has been doing doesn't really go against the standard, or if it does, there is some special excuse."[8]

Lewis does not go into the nature of the excuses that could be offered, but, once again, he makes an appeal to the practice of successive approximations that are ingrained in ordinary discourse. But it is easy to make good on his omission if we follow each of the cases down its initial path. The question of why the promise was not kept could turn on the fact that circumstances had so changed that it was impossible for me to fulfill the promise even if I wanted to, or I hit you because you had attacked me first and the like. The technical way of describing these connections is that the prima facie charge of liability is *defeasible* on a showing of the appropriate justification or excuse. The commonsense way of grasping the same point is that moral reasoning proceeds by successive approximations, starting from sensible principles and moving to counterexamples, which are always available to round out the system, but not to falsify its initial premise.

The achievement is impressive. Without any direct knowledge of the rules of pleading, Lewis has adopted the same strategy for smoking out these excuses and justifications that are used by all civil and common law systems.[9] It begins, of course, with the prima facie case, which often sounds just as Lewis would have it: you did not keep your promise, you hit me, or you took my property. Then the question is what do those justifications and excuses look like. Here the skeptical argument could be that the consensus that one has about the structure of the prima facie case dissolves when one looks for the matching set of excuses or justifications. So, if we define murder as the "wrongful" or the "unjustified or unexcused" killing of another human being, we have not solved our difficulties; we just fobbed off our difficulties to the back end of the analysis.

Exactly the same use of presumptions surface in the more academic work of the intuitionist philosophers, such as W. D. Ross. His influential philosophical work *The Right and the Good* develops the theory of prima facie duties, which, under a general theory of ethical intuitionism, echoes the starting points of the common law theory.[10] Thus Ross observes:

> (1) Some duties rest on previous acts of my own. These duties seem to include two kinds (a) those resting on a promise or what may fairly be called an implicit promise, such as the implicit undertaking not to tell lies which seems to be implied in the act of entering into conversation . . . (b) Those resting on a previous wrongful act. These may be called duties of reparation. Some duties rest on previous acts of other men, i.e. services done by them to me. These may be loosely described as the duties of gratitude.[11]

To these Ross quickly adds duties of beneficence, which rest neither on promising nor correcting wrongful acts. At points, Ross does not quite have the right terminology. "Restitution" is better than "gratitude," for example. But again his position closely tracks that of Lewis, and picks up the law of contract, misrepresentation, tort, and restitution in short order. In calling these prima facie duties, moreover, Ross recognizes them to be subject to elaboration and qualification, even though he is at a loss, apart from an urgent consideration of the relevant choices, as to how those exceptions and qualifications should be crafted. Unfortunately, Ross does not quite explain the functional underpinnings of his intuitions, since questions of standing and enforcement are not etched into his working vocabulary.

In taking this sensible position, Ross seeks to distance himself on the one side from the absolute duties (truth telling and promise keeping, for example) championed by Kant[12] and on the other from "ideal utilitarianism," which he associates with the views of G. E. Moore. The ideal utilitarian declines to organize duties by specific relationships, such as creditor and debtor, buyer and seller, or husband and wife, but instead goes overboard in the opposite direction by reducing (in ways that portend modern efficiency language) all moral inquiry to a single question: "all 'conflicts of duties' should be resolved by asking 'by which action will most good be produced?' "[13]

The appeal to prima facie duties is an effort to split the difference between the two positions. Kantian absolutism fails because of its rigidity.

Yes, there is a general duty not to lie; no, it is not wrong to lie in order to prevent a murderer from discovering the location of your hidden children. In Ross's view, the ideal utilitarian program fails as well because it overlooks the "highly personal character of duty,"[14] by which is meant that as a general matter it is important first to be just in specific relationships before one is generous to strangers who have no special claim on one's time or resources.

At the particular level Ross is no doubt correct. The only way in which the law has been able to achieve an intelligent account of personal duties is through a contract law that has two components. The first is a general part that concerns the rules of offer and acceptance, principles of interpretation, and rules dealing with such factors as fraud, incompetence, and mistake. The second is an overall concern for particular relationships, such as buyer and seller or husband and wife, for which the law offers a set of relation-specific default terms (the standard order between payment and performance, for example) that individuals can then (in a highly personal way) vary by agreement in accordance with their own needs.

What is critical to note, however, is that the relatively strict priority of contractual duties over duties of benevolence is, in truth, more consistent with the general utilitarian program than Ross understood. Duties of benevolence are "imperfect" in the sense that they do not depend on any special prior relationships between parties. Anyone can be benevolent to anyone else; and anyone discharges any (moral) duty of benevolence by helping someone in need. It does not matter much who is helped. Mr. A. cannot sue Ms. B. for want of benevolence. In a systematic sense, therefore, duties of benevolence generally should take a backseat to specific undertakings, so that one first pays debts before making charitable contributions. Those contractual undertakings when performed yield on average higher levels of wealth, which in turn make possible higher level of benevolence. Yet all benefit from the improvement in lending relationships. It is only therefore in those cases of immediate necessity, when, for example you are the only person who can save a stranger in imminent peril of death, that it becomes proper to be late for a business meeting. But even in these cases most contractual undertakings recognize a set of implied but persistent exceptions to the strict performance of contractual duties. Yet even here, those duties may be deferred or postponed, though usually some form of substitute performance is required. The method of presumptions thus becomes the key for making manageable what would otherwise be inordinately complex utilitarian calculations.

Lewis and Ross thus invoke different philosophical styles to reach the same basic point about the dominance of presumptions in the organization of daily life. Yet to the skeptic, their dependence on a prima facie case will be dismissed as a dodge. Standing alone, it does not tell us why these and not other prima facie cases should be treated as valid; nor does it give us any clue as to what counts as an excuse or justification. Without strong techniques, we shall not be able to navigate very far toward the kinds of midlevel issues that occupy so much of the law of tort, property, and contract. And in the end we will be able get that guidance only from the, broadly speaking, utilitarian or consequentialist theories that Lewis, and especially Ross, seek to displace from the analysis.

Their results, but not their methods, will turn out to be far more robust if, in fact, the intuitive writers have rightly identified the conduct that counts as prima facie wrongs. For starters, on this issue they can escape the skeptical argument that these classifications are, at best, arbitrary. To see why, compare the analysis of killing to an improbable parallel argument about smiles. Suppose we wanted to demonstrate that smiling, like killing, is presumptively wrong. Although most people immediately would regard that prescription as slightly batty, a bit more reflection would indicate that there are indeed cases where it is inappropriate to smile, at a funeral for example; but these would be regarded as situation-specific rules, not general propositions. Stated otherwise, the conduct here is prima facie proper. In the absence of some definite context, I do not have to justify to anybody my decision to smile when I awake in the morning. It is a rather different task to justify killing as opposed to smiling, which is why the inquiry as to the classical definitions of murder, rape, or theft takes the form of counting them as *unlawful* killings, sexual relations, or takings. What's going on with these definitions is really as follows: presumptively, there is a close enough connection between generating some bad social consequences and killing another individual that, for this particular action, we're going to require you to offer some powerful reason why this killing is right. We will not allow you to treat that action as a part of the general liberty in human action open to all persons, for which no further explanation is required. And parallel arguments are made for rape and theft, although treatment may not be uniform: consent does not loom large in murder cases, but it is critical in rape and some theft cases.

Now why do we make these distinctions? Again, a little armchair economics makes them intelligible. When most people smile, they please themselves, and probably other individuals as well. ("When you smile, the whole world smiles with you . . . When you're down, oh how it brings on the rain . . ." as the old song goes.) So owing to the *positive* externalities that smiling generates, it is very difficult to isolate some deep conflict of interest between the individual who smiles and the rest of the world. Hence the presumption is in favor of liberty, subject to narrow exceptions. And even here the harm in question is sufficiently ephemeral that any sanctions for inappropriate smiling are likely to be social, not legal.

To kill, rape, maim, or steal, however, is to engage in actions whereby one person's gain comes at the price of somebody else's loss; for that invasion, some urgent explanation is required, lest the conduct replicate itself without end. It is not, however, impossible to think of explanations that do carry weight, and these are not ad hoc, but are linked to the initial concern with the preservation and advancement of human life. Self-defense is perhaps the most obvious one. But it is not the only one: capital punishment is not murder so long as the state sanctions killing as a punishment for some heinous crimes. What the definition of murder invites us to do is to argue through each of these purported justifications in ways that respect the initial impulse to call certain kinds of conduct presumptively wrong.

Within this framework, we have to be aware of leaping over some philosophical precipice by conjuring up fantastic justifications for killing, such as those that hold it is all right to kill other individuals who make you miserable precisely because they are happy. It is a testimony to common sense that, even with all the weirdness in human history, we have never allowed our discourse to descend to such pitiful levels. We have quite enough on our hands to deal with contested propositions that do matter. Normally, consent is not a defense to murder; but in many end-of-life situations, however, respectable arguments could be made on behalf of the practice for persons in desperate pain and with no possibility of recovery from some terminal affliction. The definition of murder does not solve all these hard cases, but it does constrain the course of our inquiry, and in so doing leaves the Nazi defenseless against the indictments lodged against him. It serves as a useful guide by generating a set of successive approximations, which reduce the level of confusion and ambiguity in ordinary life.

Note again the ingenious method. The customary definitions isolate the types of conduct that require further scrutiny. Within the confines of a solid moral theory, no single proposition will answer any and all questions. To the extent that our definitions provide us with workable presumptions, they offer us insight into how a decent system of moral philosophy works. It is not a matter of pure deduction. It is not a matter of pure definition. It is a matter of successive approximations to some greater understanding of right and wrong. If certain actions were taken in self-defense, it is proper to ask whether you exceeded the justification by using excessive force. Even then, you might be free to argue that you are entitled to the benefit of the doubt: perfection under stress is impossible, so the risk of too much force is preferable to that of too little, unless, of course, you were simply taking advantage of a crisis situation to wreak long-standing vengeance on another individual.

This system of presumptions as an organizing principle does not appear even as a distant shadow on Richard Posner's bleak landscape. He thus misses utterly the ways in which we enrich the analysis without falling prey to deductive absurdities on the one had or moral boorishness on the other. This method thus generates greater richness in analysis. The complexities it reveals tend to be restricted to fewer and fewer cases, which means that most practical matters can be resolved even when some theoretical loose ends remain untied. The ability to dispose of simple cases in this system does not open the door to mass indeterminacy. To the contrary, it leads to lots of dead ends for those hapless or devious souls who wish to manufacture ingenious excuses on their own behalf. If you insert your knife between the shoulder blades of some stranger walking down the street, you're not going to be able to argue self-defense, voluntary euthanasia, capital punishment, or lack of parental discipline. You are not going to be able to argue that the sentence should be reduced because you snuck up on him from behind. You are going to be charged, and convicted, for murder. And the same applies to those, rightly called "terrorists," who commandeer commercial jets and then fly them into high towers. Pressed with the horror of a bin Laden, pleas of moral relativism, even in its most constrained form, rightly fall on deaf ears. Even his ardent defenders much prefer to blame the incident on Israelis or mountain militiamen rather than seek to justify it in its own terms as punishment for the new crime of "American arrogance."

One sign of the power of this presumptive method is that it is not a newly found invention of modern lawyers or philosophers. It has been in common use in other legal systems that bear scant relationship to our own. Once again, comparative law provides a useful laboratory. Roman law is quite different from our own on many issues: at the extremes of family life and political constitution Imperial (and Republican) Rome differed markedly from our own society. But what is truly astonishing is that it anticipated the method of successive approximations, the language of excuse and justification, to reach convergence in their treatment of key questions of liability.[15] The terms of legal discourse are the same in their system as in ours; and, more impressively perhaps, the pressure points and confusions arise in identical places as in our own. In both the Roman and English systems the fault lines manifest themselves in the same way in the same type of cases. The reasons have more to do with the unavoidable difficulty in sorting out the basic building blocks of a generalized system of responsibility, and less to do with the localized conditions of social life found in one culture or another. Those are simply not random occurrences. They stem from the clear point that so long as the usual principles of physics and biology apply across the world, then some legal responses will be similarly broad. All this is not to say that a serious discussion of moral thought has to echo Blackstone's sentiments that law in its largest signification covers both natural and human laws.[16] Nor is it a question of whether the same rigor that Newton brought to the universal laws of gravitation could be carried over to legal studies.[17] The question is just how well the system of improvement by increments works to reach some stable resting point.

One key element has to do with the basis of liability in tort. For this issue, the major possibilities present themselves in all systems. Starting with the most culpable forms of conduct, a defendant could be held liable for harms intentionally caused. Then liability could turn on recklessness or negligence—the failure to exercise reasonable care under the circumstances. Finally, liability could be strict; the defendant is responsible (prima facie) for whatever harm he has caused even though he has not intended the adverse consequences and exercised all reasonable care to prevent its occurrence. There is no legal system of which I am aware that reverses the rank order of responsibility. For example, none finds it proper to hold someone presumptively liable for negligence and wholly exonerate him for a deliberate harm. But every legal system has the parallel difficulties in deciding which legal standard should be used in what circumstances and why.

Part of the difficulty comes with language. It is easy to require that a defendant should be blameworthy—"*culpa*" in Latin or "culpability" in English.[18] But blame is ambiguous in both languages. It could either mean that one is prima facie to blame for what he has done, subject to excuses and justifications, or that blame can only be charged to persons who have acted with negligence. The former relies exclusively on a system of presumptions to carry the day while the latter muddies the water by mixing a system of presumptions (that is, contributory negligence is a defense to negligence) with global appeals to reasonableness that tend to suppress the formal structure of the system. The conceptual issues, moreover, do not get quickly sorted out because as a first approximation the overall economic consequences of negligence and strict liability appear to be relatively close: both rules induce actors to take only cost-justified precautions against harm.[19] The choice of rules has, moreover, no obvious distributional consequences; from behind the veil of ignorance, no knows whether he is likely to be a plaintiff or a defendant in any chance interaction. The differences between them therefore extend only to second-order matters, dealing with the relative cost of administering the rules.

Moral incrementalism is also evident in the treatment of the requirements of causation: Which harms are too "remote" to be linked up to the defendant? In so-called philosophical discourse, it is all too easy to insist that the "but for" offers the correct account of causation.[20] "But for the negligence (or other wrongful conduct) of the defendant, the plaintiff would never have been injured." At this point the effort to develop a comprehensive definition of causation quickly veers off into an abstruse discussion about the role of "necessary" and "sufficient" conditions of a particular harm. The exercise starts to look more like one of logic and less like one intended to address concrete disputes.

The historical evolution of the doctrine of causation started from the exact opposite pole. Instead of invoking an arcane theory that required the solution of some complex general equilibrium, the cases all began with the defendant's direct use of force against the person and property of the plaintiff: the defendant poked out the plaintiff's eye, or broke her vase. These involve simple transitive verbs (which are used to organize ordinary experience) that have the defendant as their subject and the plaintiff as their object. This stark opposition follows a set of physical laws that are uniform in all systems and underlie the needed legal judgments. The harder cases of "indirect" causation come when some human action or natural event intervenes between the action of the defendant and the harm suffered by the plaintiff: dropping a log in the road over which the plaintiff trips, or giving the plaintiff a poison that she drinks in ignorance of its harmful qualities, or storing water in a reservoir that empties when its bottom gives way. Again the marginal cases are more or less the same in all legal systems. The defendant could escape liability where someone else bombs his reservoir, or where a huge natural disaster causes its sides to crumble. But simple leakage brought on by weight is a continuation of the causal chain set in motion by the original actions.[21] The process of incremental reasoning leads to a safe landing place. The difficulty in resolving the hard intermediate cases is inverse to the social importance of their resolution.[22]

Once the prima facie case is established, excuses (for accidental) and justifications (for deliberate) harms must be included. All legal systems necessarily accept some version of the contributory negligence and assumption of risk defenses, although there is some variation as to what kinds of conduct fall into each of these classes. A strict liability rule may well apply to harms inflicted on strangers, but a trespassing plaintiff will normally be forced to bear the risk of any accidental harm he suffers while trespassing.[23] Yet the balance of advantage shifts back to the plaintiff when the defendant's attack on the plaintiff's person or property was deliberate unless the defendant can *justify* the deliberate infliction of harm. At this point the approximations continue, for self-defense does not justify the use of excessive force. Yet by the same token, such force could be *excused* if the defendant, owing to his personal frailties, had done all within his power to avoid the harms in question.[24]

The delicate minuet of plusses and minuses in difficult cases with low frequency of occurrence should not be allowed, however, to obscure the fundamental point that easy cases dominate in practice. For instance, all legal systems impose liability in the common case of a careless defendant harming an innocent plaintiff. Indeed, the more restrictive negligence rule is often championed by *plaintiffs*, who insist on the opportunity of skirting the moral qualms about strict liability by showing that the defendant both caused the harm *and* could have avoided it with reasonable care, which they can do most of the time. The "happy" circumstance is that most harms have negligence in their pedigree. It is precisely because the hard cases—where causation is present but negligence is absent—are infrequent that the intuitions about them tend to break down in exactly the same place in all legal systems. It should come as no surprise, therefore, that finding which of these rules is an "efficient" solution to the overall problem of minimizing the costs of accidents is no easy task because the equities are so close. Once small differences in terminology are stripped away, it becomes relatively easy for lawyers in one system to swap notes with their peers in another system precisely because the set of problems they face, and menu of possible solutions, converge so powerfully. None of this would be remotely possible if differences in locale and time had anything like the centrifugal force that moral relativists attribute to them.

So how did the convergence in the choice of legal rules take place? One possibility is that the Roman rules were continuously incorporated into modern ones by English judges who had access to Roman materials.

The better explanation appears to be that the actions for trespass were introduced by the Crown in order to control the private use of force that was a danger to everyone's person and possessions.[25] But if differences in time, locale, and culture matter, then how did the tort doctrines of ancient Rome, warts and all, find a friendly reception in England and in the American colonies? So—let us never forget—did the German Civil Code of 1900, which drew heavily on Roman materials, find a new home in Japan. The only plausible explanation is that these rules resonated with the same "rudimentary" sense of justice found in all cultures. Why doubt that? The rules of physics are the same across time and space, and these determine what kind of conduct is likely to result in the use of force and to cause harm. The rudimentary need for cooperation is the same in all cultures and is much facilitated by a law of contract, as well as the full network of informal obligations.

Alternatively, one could assume that independent creation, not reception, explains how the same (kind of) tree grew not twice but multiple times, and in different soil. But why did the tree grow in the same shape? Again the same answer makes sense. It is the older natural law principle that says the fundamental needs for human flourishing are sufficiently uniform across societies that any fundamental repudiation from the rules of autonomy, property, promising, and harm would lead to the disintegration of society, just as happened in Nazi Germany.

This point, about the sources and magnitudes of differences within and across legal systems, has been made with great force by Saul Levmore in his study of diversity and uniformity in ancient legal systems.[26] Whenever social survival is at stake, we find extensive unity within and across legal systems. No society treats theft as a creative form of self-expression, or treats innocent conversion with the same severity as a deliberate theft. But, by the same token, on questions where the equities are genuinely uncertain it is possible to find as much diversity of views within societies as it is between them. T takes property from O, which T then sells to B who is ignorant of the theft. There is no society that holds that the thief is not answerable to the owner or the buyer as the case may be. He cannot keep either the property or the proceeds of sale.

The contest between the original owner and the innocent purchaser of the goods or land is, everywhere, far closer. So here we find immense differences of opinion within and across cultures as to whether the original owner should be able to recover his property from the bona fide purchaser. The owner asserts the obvious (libertarian) proposition that no one should be required to lose his property, real or personal, without his consent unless he has committed some wrong. The buyer insists that it is cheaper for the owner to take precautions against misbehavior of his bailee, whom he entrusted with the goods, and should therefore bear the loss. It is also said with somewhat less conviction that it is easier for an owner to prevent theft of goods than it is for buyers to examine the pedigree of title. In most commercial markets, traders are sometimes buyers and sometimes sellers, so that all of them would prefer, from behind a veil of ignorance, that rule which, in the long run, enhanced the security of transactions, even if it disregarded the ordinary rules of property and autonomy. It is not surprising, therefore, that the third party often wins against the original owner, especially in cases of bailed goods. That impulse should not be regarded as a repudiation of the rudimentary natural law norms. Rather it is best understood as a rough-and-ready application of the general rules of forced exchanges, coupled with implicit-in-kind compensation. Each person gives up his right to recover property from innocent purchasers in exchange for the like-immunity when he assumes that role, which is today the dominant rule for checks and other negotiable instruments,[27] as well as for goods,[28] at least in the absence of a system of public recordation, as with land, that goes a long way to cut off the risk of double dealing at its root.

Hard Cases: Lifeboats and Desert Islands

Moral incrementalism insists that the world is best analyzed by first understanding the easy, but frequent, cases that dominate social life. The footholds from the easier cases make it possible to tackle the more difficult cases, virtually all of which revolve around some theme of necessity—the life and death situations where people try desperately to save themselves even at the expense of others. Most people, fortunately, have never had to face cases of this sort. Although the waters are treacherous, it is necessary to wade in.

Private Necessity

Start with the classic illustration of private necessity. I own a dock and you are caught out at sea in a small boat during a severe storm. You may have even been careless and not looked at the sky. When the weather turns bad, you come to my dock and say, "I have to moor here or I will die and my family will die with me." And I turn to you and say in reply, "This is my dock, I have the right to exclude at will, so if you want the moor, forfeit your boat and 20 percent of your future lifetime earnings." My calculation is that you will be better off because you survive, and I will be better off because the dock is worth a tiny fraction of the value of the boat and a slice of your future earnings. So why not enforce a deal that leaves both sides better off?

That outcome leaves everyone with a pit in his stomach. In order to hold you to that bargain the law would have to overlook the background conditions of necessity and focus exclusively on the short-term mutual gain. The case does not look like a supermarket purchase because of the absence of choice of alternative places to do business. At this point, the *wrong* impulse is to argue that the illustration discredits the principles of voluntary exchange, and thus undercuts the market as a whole. The more accurate rendering stresses the holdout risk created by conditions of necessity, which then *reverses* all the standard presumptions about ownership in order to obtain a better fit with both our moral intuitions and social objectives. The owner of the dock normally has the right to exclude others from its use. But that right of exclusion is lost in the cases of necessity, even when the stranger's use could cause some incidental damage to the dock. The owner who casts away the stranger in need can be sued for the harm that follows;[29] indeed, the outsider can use force in self-defense in order to wrest control of the property from its true owner. But this reversal of roles lasts only so long as the condition of necessity lasts. When it is over, the property must be returned along with payment for any needed repairs and perhaps some modest rental fee.

Litigation over necessity arises but infrequently. The tradition of maritime rescue, for example, is so strong that help is routinely extended without regard to legal rules. But these principles do matter in commercial contexts, such as the law of salvage.[30] In the classic nineteenth-century decision of *Post v. Jones,*[31] the Supreme Court refused to enforce contracts against the owner of a whaling ship, the *Richmond,* stranded at sea with a full load of oil. The Court stated that an agreement, formed "under such circumstances, where the master of the *Richmond* was hopeless, helpless, and passive—where there was no market, no money, and no competition where one party had absolute power, and the other no choice but submission where the vendor must take what is offered or get nothing—is a transaction which has no characteristic of a valid contract."[32] All this was not meant to shut salvage operators out of the market, for "[c]ourts of admiralty will enforce contracts made for salvage service and salvage compensation, where the salvor has not taken advantage of his power to make an unreasonable bargain,"[33] or, in circumstances of imminent peril, in which bargaining is impossible, award "liberal" compensation for any services so rendered.[34] In essence, the salvors receive the competitive rate for saving the oil, with due allowance for risk, so that they are better off with the standard deal imposed by the legal rule than by sailing away from the situation.

The intuition behind such cases rests explicitly on the ordinary condemnation of "taking advantage of someone who is over a barrel"—that is, a position in which he can get neither his hands nor his feet on the ground. *Post* thus highlights the recurrent tension in ordinary morality when the language of advantage-taking clashes with the general prohibitions on force and fraud against the person or property of another. Putting the two points together exposes the deep need for moral theory to organize social practices and institutions to minimize the sum of these dangers simultaneously. Simply stopping aggression may satisfy the consistent libertarian, but it also allows the dockowner to leave the sailor to drown unless the latter forfeits his life earnings, or forces the ship stranded at sea to sell its cargo for a song. The alternative solution defangs the dockowner and the salvor, while allowing them competitive returns on their investment.

The Duty to Rescue

The next type of hard cases involves the parable of the Good Samaritan. Standing alone, you see another drowning but do not throw an available lifeline that might easily save her.[35] The example precludes the multiple possibilities of evasion: you have done nothing to cause the initial position of peril; you have no special relationship to the drowning person, be it as parent, guardian, partner, or friend; you do not face any exposure to risk; no extensive time or labor are needed; you are not required to sacrifice or use your own property; and no one else is around to pick up the slack if you turn away.

The libertarian norms against force and fraud do not require any assistance to persons in peril. Such assistance may be freely offered but never required.[36] This norm makes sense over a broad range of cases, for people are normally able to handle scrapes themselves. But once the costs of self-help spike, and the costs of help plummet, does the example from the private necessity cases entail reversing the general rule and mandating the aid, as many have urged?[37] This new duty to rescue could be defended by noting that others are affected if a helpless person is allowed to die, which is one of the reasons so many voluntary rescues take place at all.[38] This limited duty might also be defended by appeal to the just compensation principle: each of us is better off *ex ante* if everyone were subject to a duty of easy rescue, enforceable by tort damages or criminal sanctions.

The answer to the question posed above is probably not. In the private necessity case, what is demanded of the property owner is noninterference. He need only stand aside, but he cannot be made to assist. The imposition is smaller. In addition, are we confident that imposing legal duties to rescue increases rescue, or does it only lead people to retreat from the scene, lest they be held liable? Why impose the duty to rescue in some narrow class of actions where rescues are likely to take place anyhow? Better is to insist that the rescuer is subject to a moral duty but to no legal duty. The potential gains from rescue justify the social condemnation but not the use of legal compulsion. After all, right now the balance looks about right: forest fires, floods, children down wells—all evoke tremendous outpourings of organized assistance even when the chances of success are tiny relative to the costs involved. Whatever the tragedies of September 11, 2001, the willingness of people, both in uniform and as ordinary citizens, to step forward in a time of crisis was not one of them. Indeed, sometimes the real problem may be too many failed heroic rescues that were not cost justified to begin with.[39] When Catherine Genovese was stabbed to death in March 1964 as thirty-eight witnesses watched, without so much as making a single phone call among them, there is a reason for deep community self-reflection, not for altering the rule.[40] If anything, use the carrot instead of the stick, by allowing those few hardy folks who actually care about the compensation to recover any out-of-pocket expenses. In the end, therefore, it is not surprising that the law remains stubbornly close to its common law origins.

The Trolley Problem

This combined analysis of necessity and rescue facilitates the treatment of other difficult cases. Judith Jarvis Thomson, for example, has written ingeniously about what Philippa Foot terms the "trolley problem."[41] You, the driver of a trolley, while coming around the bend in the road, spot five workmen on the tracks before you at the bottom on a steep incline. Your brakes unexpectedly fail and you now have to decide whether to turn off to a side track, where only a single man is working. Is it "morally permissible" for you to turn and kill the one man to save five? Everyone, she concludes, would regard the saving of four lives on net as morally permissible. Yet by the same token—and here is the catch—no one would regard it as permissible for you, as a truly great surgeon, to dismember the body of one of your patients in order to use his organs to save the lives of five other needy individuals. Same ratios: What is the difference? Does the distinction between killing and letting die help explain the overall solution?

The method of presumptions helps to unpack these problems. Rather than taking one variation in isolation, it is best to sharpen the inquiry by asking not just about "permissible conduct," but also about tort liability. First question: Are you prima facie liable for the death of the five men if you continue to drive down the steep incline? Thomson tries to give you an out by noting that the brakes suddenly failed without warning. But under a strict liability rule, the loss falls on you anyway.

Now what happens should you turn the trolley onto the side track? At first blush, this makes matters worse because the harm is not just accidental, but deliberate. Yet even as a moral matter, your choice should be justified by the saving of the lives of five innocent people. If the objective is to minimize human suffering, you have no parallel justification for the five people who die if you keep the trolley on its initial course. After all, no one likes the thought of killing even one person, but if the six workmen had been polled *ex ante,* each of them would have consented to a rule that would have increased his chances of survival from 16.67 percent to 83.33 percent. So you should be allowed, and perhaps required, to direct the trolley onto the side track. But will you do so? It's not so obvious. Thomson does not broach the *ex ante* question of whether the law gives you as the trolley driver an incentive to make the right choice. Suppose you were *not* liable for the accidental death of the five workmen if you continued on your way. Now it becomes *necessary* to spare you from liability for the death of the single workman as well, for otherwise it would be better *for you* to hold the trolley to its course, notwithstanding that (net) four individuals could have been saved by turning. That combination of outcomes would introduce a wedge between private and social costs: you must pay for one death even though you have saved on net four lives. Finding liability in *neither* case thus eliminates that perverse incentive but introduces still other complications. First, this "no-liability" solution reduces your incentive to maintain and inspect the trolley prior to the moment of crisis; and second, it leaves you with no strong incentive to deviate from the original course, which is not only permissible but also preferable. Only holding you liable *either* way gets the right solution. It gives you both the incentive to turn at the moment of crisis, and to maintain the trolley to avoid the calamity in the first place.

Now, as Thomson asks, suppose that you are unable to divert the trolley to the side track, but that some bystander can switch a lever that will redirect is course. Here the private necessity problem is married to the

Good Samaritan dilemma. What liability should attach to the bystander? In principle, we would like for the bystander to throw the switch. But since she did not drive the trolley, she is not prima facie liable for the death of the five if she does not intervene. But if she is held responsible for switching its track, then we introduce a fresh set of perverse incentives: the woman who saves four individuals finds herself worse off for her good deed by having to bear the costs of the one who died. We should therefore excuse the bystander if she throws the switch, and hope that she does so. Unfortunately, there is no easy way to *pay* the bystander to throw the switch. The law cannot guarantee the right result, but it can improve the odds.

At long last, this detailed analysis helps lay bare the strong differences between the trolley case and the physician case, which turns on the *ex ante* incentives on the conduct of patients and road workers respectively. The latter will like a strict liability solution because it minimizes their losses. In contrast, patients will flee in horror from the best of physicians if they think that they could be dismembered during an ordinary office visit. They will shift their allegiance to lesser surgeons who promise greater security of their person. At the same time, the supply of organs could be expanded, in ways that it has not, by relaxing the rules on sales of live or cadaveric organs, which would help ameliorate today's severe shortages.[42] The conduct of the physician cannot be justified in the same fashion of the trolley driver. The patient dissection of the issue through the method of presumptions does its advertised task of structuring the inquiry in ways that lead to the convergence between ordinary intuitions and the general prescriptions of a consequentialist system.

Abortion and Infanticide

This same method can, I believe, be carried over to other difficult areas as well. Here I deal only briefly with abortion, infanticide, and stem cell research. Start with abortion or with infanticide. The initial question is whether it falls within the prima facie case of killing another human being. Right here there is a discontinuous choice to be made over the status of the fertilized embryo: Does it count as a life because of its potential for growth to a human being in the ordinary course of nature; or does it count as a gob of undifferentiated cells that have no pattern? The issue is of enormous consequence, because if the former judgment is treated as accurate, then we have a prima facie wrong that cries out for justification. Even under the narrowest version of the harm principle, the killing of another person counts as harm.[43] But if there is no person involved, then we have the exercise of an ordinary liberty that needs no special justification at all. In my view, the former position has always been the more defensible because I can see no moment in the generative process, either prior or subsequent to fertilization, that counts as a sharper line between organic matter and human life: the only truly discontinuous moment in the process is that of conception. That said, however, the sources of disagreement as to the overall outcome are evident even within the libertarian camp. We can easily think of organizations of "libertarians for choice," and "libertarians for life." Clearly, the on/off nature of this initial characterization prevents any easy compromise between the warring factions: using either trimesters or viability as the test for personhood does not obviate the difficulty of explaining why any individual should stop what is, in the ordinary course of events, an inexorable march to personhood.

Yet for these purposes, I do not want to argue the question of who, what, or when counts as a person. Instead it is useful to shift to the other side of the debate, which assumes that a prima facie wrong has taken place and then asks for the excuses or justifications that might be offered on its behalf. On this score, the strongest justification is that the abortion is done to protect the life or bodily health of the mother: self-defense is invoked against an aggressor who is incapable of forming any intention at all, just as it may be invoked against a madman. Other potential justifications come closer to the line, such as allowing abortion in cases of rape or incest, even though neither is the fault of the person (by assumption, remember) asked to forfeit his life. The clear implication here is that there are certain burdens that no person can even demand of his or her mother. Needless to say, many women would recoil from this option even if allowed to exercise it under law.

Next on the list comes abortion for seriously defective infants. That justification tracks the similar, if covert, practice of infanticide for newborns with serious birth defects, which long predates the modern abortion controversy. The difference here is that infanticide is done with more knowledge of the ultimate condition at childbirth and can be disguised more easily as a futile effort to save a newborn child that could not make it on its own. Abortion makes the use of that justification far more dangerous because it is invoked before the defective condition manifests itself. Yet I am drawn to this justification nonetheless, if only because it seems clear that most couples who have struggled with infertility will abort if they learn that a child has serious birth defects, notwithstanding the enormous lengths they went to in order to secure conception. At this point, we are still a long way from the more radical claim for abortion at will.

One possible way to achieve that argument is to make the claim that prohibition on abortion has been simply a device used by males to keep women in subordinate positions. Or is it that conferring a right to abortion forms part of a plot to increase men's opportunities for casual sex by reducing its costs to women? It does not help to reclassify restrictions on abortion as a form of sex discrimination. Let us assume that the antidiscrimination principle has an important role to play in dealing with the use of public force. But the antidiscrimination principle is no more absolute than the right of private property. Even if we assume its application, we can justify an exception to it by appealing to the public need to protect human life.

The question, then, arises whether other forms of justification could prop up the defense for a woman's asserted right to abortion on demand. One line of argument stems from the fact that the fetus places special burdens on the mother, burdens that one person should not have to shoulder for the benefit of another. In one sense the point is ironic because of its implicit appeal to the common law rule that denies any obligation to rescue a stranger.

Just that argument has been pursued with uncommon ingenuity by Judith Jarvis Thomson, who also gave us the trolley problem.[44] As befits her philosophical boldness, Thomson elected to attack the pro-life forces in the abortion debate on their own grounds. Let us concede, she suggests, that the unborn fetus is a person and thus presumptively entitled to some protection. Even so, she works to *justify* the mother's decision by comparing her situation to that of a woman who has been hooked up by an elaborate pump to a famous (male) violinist in the dark of night by the Society of Music Lovers because she is the only person, conclusively determined, whose blood type is compatible with the violinist. Disconnecting this violinist is to her mind perfectly proper, even if it kills him. Abortion, she claims, is no different. Killing it may be, but justified it is nonetheless.

This example works off the necessity theme that dominated the trolley problem. But it is so wholly contrived that there is every good reason to fight the hypothetical. Left unexplained is why only *one* person in the world has the right kind of blood, and why no transfusion will do the job, even if that is the case. It is perhaps suggestive that something is amiss in that her example runs counter to the universal practice in organ transplantations, which is preoccupied with the fear of coercion against organ donors in situations that do not come within light years of her hypothetical situation: hence the common fear that doctors will kill young patients to capture their healthy organs before they decay. But what is so utterly mystifying about the example is the idea that this impossible scenario should be used to organize our thoughts on how to treat something, pregnancy, through which all of us have gone (at least for the first half of the process). The trolley example strikes a chord because people have been in that situation or are able to imagine how it comes about at most inopportune times. But the violinist case is a fantastic chimera with no natural referent. Our basic human instinct is to treat external invasions as the worst offenses against our persons. Breaking bones and drawing blood are so much the sign of death that we need anesthesia to neutralize the pain even when we know that the actions, for example, surgery, are undertaken for our benefit. Nature has well endowed us with a strong instinct for bodily integrity from external agencies that makes us all recoil at the thought of this involuntary hookup.

Yet pregnancy is the source of life, not the harbinger of death. As the old natural law philosophers said, no species, including the human race, could have survived unless women were conditioned to want to endure the risks and burdens of pregnancy. Thomson's example treats natural birth on a par with external invasion, and thus seeks to carry the revulsion toward the one over to the other. It cannot work. Our entire psychology is geared to preserve the independence of the person from external assault. But it is hardly geared to prevent the normal biological processes of pregnancy on which the survival of the species depend. In principle, it might be still possible to find some justification for abortion on demand. The fetus surely lives off the mother, and could be called a parasite. But here again there is a clever effort to play off the Good Samaritan rule, which talks about no duties to rescue *strangers* from abject necessity, which the unborn child is not. The utter dependence of the infant on the mother points to an increased duty of care, not to an increased right to repel or abandon another person.

Why, then, the defense of the abortion right? Perhaps it is for more pragmatic reasons. Most simply, state intervention is far more costly against abortion than against infanticide, when children are already within the care of hospitals, physicians, and other family members. Birth also negates any claim that the continued life of the child eats away at the innards of the mother. But in fact the real reason may well be that whatever the risk that abortion holds to the child, it poses no risk to other individuals and their children. People who have doubts about the ontological status of the embryo would all look horrified at any doctor who sought to perform an abortion on a woman against her will. And the offense would not be just to the mother, but also to the embryo whose life chances were ended at that moment. But the ordinary defense of abortion gives only the mother the right to terminate her own pregnancy. Unlike other killings, abortions do not send any ripple of uncertainty through the community by people who fear that they will be next. Its compartmentalized nature removes one powerful externality from the practice, and in the end that, for some people, is enough to tip the balance in favor of a practice that reduces the public burden of paying for the upkeep and education of unwanted children. We have moved a long way from traditional justifications.

Yet what about stem cell research that uses fertilized embryos that otherwise would slowly disintegrate even in cold storage? Here the ironies are multiple. In one sense, pro-life persons welcome in vitro fertilization because it helps barren couples to create new life. But the "excess" embryos will not in the ordinary course of events become life when they are stored in freezers. So here, what is the potential life that is being saved? In my own view, the physical isolation of the cells means that they look less like a future person and more like a clump of cells. The line between embryos that are within the mother and those that are not seems clear enough, and some additional rule could be made to punish the creation of embryos solely for the purpose of research should that be necessary to prevent certain kinds of perverse behavior. On balance, the potential benefits of this treatment are large enough to justify this practice.

But no matter how one thinks about this case, we can be confident of at least one thing. The method of presumptions works better in those cases that do arise in ordinary life, close to the sources of everyday experience. That these do not solve all questions is surely no surprise. That it solves many hard questions is, I think, enough to reject any global claims of moral skepticism or moral relevance. One attack on the possibility of a coherent system of laws and morals can be deflected. But others lurk nearby. The next chapter takes on the conceptual challenges to the possibility of the coherent version of individual liberty and state control articulated in chapter 2.

5 Conceptual Skepticism

Linguistic Chaos?

A SECOND SET OF OBJECTIONS to the traditional liberal order revolves around not moral but conceptual considerations. By any account, the basic tools of legal and moral theory center around a few key concepts that are common in ordinary language: autonomy, property, causation, voluntary, necessity, and the like. These terms take an enormous pounding once they become the fulcrum for legal decisions.[1] Difficult fact patterns inevitably create puzzles in individual cases. A line of cases develops in erratic fashion as judges seek to tie up loose ends. Some interested parties have every incentive to muddy the water when the established rules cut against their position. No single person controls the process of legal decisionmaking, which lurches down an uncertain path. The preoccupation with hard marginal cases tends to obscure the agreement over the easier cases that arise, as usual, with much higher frequency.

Everyone knows, for example, what the word "possession" means in ordinary English. We use the term—or its near equivalents, such as "occupation"—many times each day with little reflection and great accuracy. But it is less apparent that it is also a term that carries consequences with it. Possession often serves as a "standing" rule that decides *who* gets the right to complain about certain changes in the external world: the possessor of property, but no other, may be entitled to forcibly remove those who enter the land, or bring actions to protect the land from nuisances. On the flip side, he may be targeted for liability to those injured by some concealed, dangerous condition. Our conceptual grasp of the term is quickly tested as we move from unitary to divided control.[2] Who is in possession of a house held in joint tenancy when one of the owners is out shopping while the other remains at home? Does possession rest on the weekend guest when the owner is out of town? But on conceptual as well as moral matters, too much can be made of the role of marginal cases in assessing general theories. It is one thing to recognize that all critical terms cover cases that fall outside the core meaning of any term. It is quite another thing to insist that all important terms are subject to incurable ambiguity that destroys their utility for everyday use or analytical work.

The objection has no political direction because it does not allow or compel us to differentiate among legal theories. Any set of terms, regardless of its moral resonance, is subject to the same set of conceptual difficulties, which can be met by the same type of corrective measures. To return to possession, it is possible to emend the standard definitions to handle some recurrent questions: both joint owners share possession of the property unless the one party in, as it is said, "actual" possession "ousts" the other. The weekend guest is not treated—a legal fiction starts to creep in here—as the party in possession with respect to damage to real property because he has no permanent interest in that property. Lawyers instinctively know the source of the problem: tie the ability to sue to the loss of possession only, and the concept will have to be altered to generate rules that make sense. Folks out of possession (like the owner in the previous example) will be regarded as in "constructive possession" of the property, where the first word signals that the system has made marginal adjustments in its conceptual frame in order to effectuate its smoother operation.[3] But there is no defect of understanding or comprehension here. Rather, like the tailor who adjusts a suit after it is purchased, these emendations (which are apparent to all) help fine-tune the operation of the system, here on the critical idea of who has standing to sue. The use of the clear signaling word like "constructive" is a strong sign that everyone knows just what is happening and why. That conclusion then generalizes to similar situations of joint control and gradually expands in orderly fashion our understanding of the governing legal principles.

The attack on the general coherence of the classical legal system does not, however, accept the incremental improvement that comes from resolving novel cases in light of the undisputed ones. Rather, as a parallel to Holmes's extreme moral skepticism, it argues that the defects in terminology and logic send an entire legal edifice crumbling to the ground. In this context, it is no simple coincidence that the most ardent exponents of terminological skepticism are also the most indefatigable critics of laissez-faire economics and the legal rules that undergird it.

It is of course possible to attack laissez-faire on the grounds that it does not produce the desirable consequences for human welfare claimed for it. Indeed, the earlier defenses of socialism often rested on the explicit economic assertion that a well-oiled socialist system could outperform capitalism by subjecting key investment decisions to state approval and review.[4] These empirical attacks on laissez-faire have fallen into disarray with the economic failure of moderate socialist regimes, such as that instituted in Britain in the first half of the twentieth century, and their more extreme forms in the Soviet Union and its eastern satellites before the 1989 breakup of the older communist empire.

Two forms of attack now survive. One of these, the attack on the behavioral assumptions behind the economic models, is the subject of chapters 8 and 9. This chapter takes on a more philosophical cast by addressing criticisms that seek to demonstrate the conceptual incoherence of laissez-faire. The arguments in question have been assayed by many writers, but for ease of exposition I concentrate on three examples of that criticism: the writings of lawyer-economist Robert Lee Hale; the contrast in the conceptions of security found in Franklin Roosevelt's Economic Bill of Rights and F. A. Hayek's *Road to Serfdom,* both published in 1944; and the political philosopher G. A. Cohen. Hale wrote in the first half of the twentieth century, but his influence continues to this day and, if anything, seems to be on the increase. In the words of his recent intellectual biographer, Barbara Fried, Hale's key objectives were to show that laissez-faire crashed and burned because it rested on the "empty ideas" of "liberty" and "property."[5] Hayek and Roosevelt need no introduction. Cohen continues the philosophical attack in a more modern vein. In my view, all these criticisms of the traditional synthesis fail.

Liberty and Coercion

Classical liberalism requires us to maintain the distinction between liberty and coercion, to advance the former while constraining the latter. Unless we can hew to the line, it becomes impossible to give any coherent account of freedom of contract on which the overall system rests. The earliest conceptual counterattack on the viability of this conviction was undertaken by Robert Lee Hale, a leading member of the first law and economics movement, who did most of his legal work between 1920 and 1950. Intellectually, he was one of the most influential defenders of the Progressive movement, whose agenda included more extensive regulation of the economy, including the employment relation.[6] It is therefore no surprise that Hale was a strong proponent of the Wagner Act, which introduced collective bargaining into labor relations, as well as such hardy standbys as maximum hour and minimum wage laws that had been under constant judicial attack before the Supreme Court's constitutional revolution of 1937. The key opposition to these various forms of regulation rested on the constitutional primacy of liberty of contract.

Hale's arguments are perfectly general. He attacks this idea of liberty by noting its dependence on a vision of voluntary transactions, which is parasitic on a sound account of coercion, which, as everyone concedes, undermines the voluntariness of those transactions. Now, everyone agrees that the idea of coercion includes the use and threat of force to procure another's consent to the surrender of her property.[7] The usual case is where a robber gives his victim a choice between her money and her life, and she chooses, quite properly, to surrender the former to preserve the latter. This simple example shows that the use of coercion is not negated simply by the presence of victim's choice but is rather defined by the set of choices that remain available. Threats only work if people have the capacity to yield to them. The robber thus creates for his victim a constrained choice set, and she, in turn, chooses that alternative that leaves her better off. The reason we conclude that she is put to an *unacceptable* choice is that she initially has rights to *both* her money and her life, so that the thief has forced her to surrender one thing that is hers as of right in order to keep another, when in fact she is entitled to both. When faced with the external threat she will act rationally to minimize its sting, but her ability to minimize the peril hardly justifies its initial imposition. The idea of coercion, therefore, is not negated by the presence of choice. Its full explication must be done against the background of a specific theory of rights, which in this case ordinary understandings of autonomy supply.

Hale's distinctive contribution to this debate is not to defend the robber but to indict the capitalist. The usual laissez-faire defense of ordinary contracts depends on the clear line between voluntary and coercive transactions. For Hale, this line is not defensible because coercion cannot be limited to the traditional forms of duress recognized by the common law and other legal systems. Instead, coercion covers any particular move by one person that leaves someone else worse off in consequence. Let the state decide to protect one person's home from destruction by others, and it has engaged in coercion—here against the potential marauders—just as if it had ripped that house down or allowed some nonowner to destroy that property or take it for his own use. Conceptually, *no* assignment of rights is able to negate either the frequent use or threat of coercive action. Laissez-faire thus comes apart at the seams, not because of its empirical shortcomings, but owing to its conceptual incoherence. Its chosen criterion of evaluation requires the minimization of coercion—an impossible task, Hale concludes, given the ubiquity of coercion in social life.

To make matters worse, mutual agreements are powerless to reduce the pervasive levels of social coercion because these agreements themselves are necessarily tainted by the coercion they are asked to eliminate.

For example, a worker who does not accept an employer's terms is forced to do without the wages the employer would pay.[8] Coercion is so deeply embedded in all human arrangements that the only question worth asking is what form of coercion we prefer and why. Hale explains his views as follows:

> If the non-owner works for anyone, it is for the purpose of warding off the threat of at least one owner of money to withhold that money from him (with the help of the law). Suppose, now, the worker were to refuse to yield to the coercion of any employer, but were to choose instead to remain under the legal duty to abstain from the use of any of the money which anyone owns. He must eat. While there is no law against eating in the abstract, there is a law which forbids him to eat any of the food which actually exists in the community—and that law is the law of property. It can be lifted as to any specific food at the discretion of its owner, but if the owners unanimously refuse to lift the prohibition, the non-owner will starve unless he can himself produce food. And there is every likelihood that the owners will be unanimous in refusing, if he has no money. There is no law to compel them to part with their food for nothing. Unless, then, the non-owner can produce his own food, the law compels him to starve if he has no wages, and compels him to go without wages unless he obeys the behest of some employer. It is the law that coerces him into wage-work under penalty of starvation—unless he can produce food.

So there we have it. Private coercion is elevated to the status of an unavoidable necessity; the only issue left on the table is the brute political choice of who gets coerced by whom and for what reason. Hale himself acknowledged that the social position is not quite so bleak and one-sided as it appears, for the worker is also able to coerce the employer by refusing to accept work unless the wages meet his approval.[9] Parallel arguments could be made, of course, about the fragility of all dyadic relationships: landlords and tenants, merchants and consumers, or physicians and patients. But that one concession to Hale's definitional ploy gives away the game. Coercion becomes an inescapable fact of life practiced by all customers who decide to take their business elsewhere. The condemnation once reserved for robbers and ruffians can now be applied to every decision of market actors under a constraint of scarcity, which is to say, to any decision at all.

What then does Hale gain from his serpentine maneuver? It is surely not some improved understanding of the operation of labor, housing, product, or service markets. Quite the opposite, Hale blurs the important distinction between monopoly and competitive markets by writing as though the "unanimous consent" of the owners (in not dealing with prospective employees) has been reached by collective decision, which surely hints at the monopoly practices that most advocates of laissez-faire, on Hale's own admission, think it proper to restrain. In effect, Hale is saying that competitive markets are so constituted that they embody necessarily coercive arrangements. But that ostensible coercion equivalent is a far cry from the work camps of Stalin.

One way to see the error of Hale's argument is to ask who is coercing whom in any particular negotiation. When a worker does not get a job, he has either received no satisfactory offer or has been turned down by all the firms to which he has applied. To which firm do we attach our disapprobation and why? When a manufacturer is unable to sell any of its wares, which of the millions of its potential customers is guilty of coercion and why? Surely a firm is not improperly coercive because it does not hire every applicant for a given position. Nor are consumers coercive when they do not purchase unlimited quantities of every different brand of breakfast cereal. So long as scarcity is a constraint on human behavior, then it is just wrong for Hale, or anyone else, to treat ordinary refusals to deal as tantamount to the use of force. Hale's all-encompassing definition of "coercion" robs the term of both its analytical use and its moral opprobrium.

Nor is there anything troublesome about the market outcomes he posits. It is inevitable for people to have to choose what to buy and sell, where to work, and whom to hire. The mere fact of scarcity requires some level of choice. The insistent demand for higher living standards leads to the division of labor and specialization within the market. But it is not inevitable that people kill, rob, or steal: millions of people have lived productive and happy lives without once committing trespasses or extortion against their neighbors. Confusion is only sowed when the term "coercion" is applied indiscriminately to these two disparate situations. Indeed, to brand all market transactions as coercive deprives that term of its much needed sting for transactions that are tainted by aggression and force. Naturally, there are wrinkles. The two situations—the use of force and the refusal to deal—show some useful adjacencies only when a *single* supplier controls a given good or service, as with public utilities or common carriers. But in ordinary competitive markets, we are all better off in the long run ignoring the inconveniences and frustrations of failing to achieve our personal objectives in individual transactions, rather than turning them into legal grievances remedied by the coercive power of the state.

Although Hale never quite makes this concession, his recent defender, Fried, is forced to do so in the end. To be sure, she starts with high praise for Hale: "Hale's critical work endures as among the best examples of the Realist and institutionalist tradition, casting the nature of legal rights and private economic relations in a new and significantly different light."[10] But when the rubber meets the road, she has to conclude, limply: "There remains a difference, after all, between pointing a gun at another's head and demanding 'Your money or your life,' and threatening to withhold bread from a starving person unless she consents to pay the market price."[11] Hale's philosophical critique of coercion fails at a conceptual level because it sweeps too much under the carpet. The critical fault lines in the debate are two: that between coercion and refusals to deal on the one hand, and that between refusals to deal in a competitive versus a monopoly situation on the other. The substantive debate only begins after the conceptual underbrush is cleared away. Hale cannot win that debate unless he first demonstrates how centralized control over labor markets outperforms competitive markets in the overall levels of satisfaction supplied to their participants. Yet that substantive task is outside his self-described mission.

Security, Protection, and Competition

The mistakes that Hale makes about coercion do not appear in isolation, for they lead to a similar inversion of other critical terms in the classical liberal lexicon, such as "protection" and "security." As before, the basic strategy remains the same: terms with narrow, focused meanings are "generalized" in ways that end up embracing their opposites.

The protection of person and property from the use of force states one of the prime tenets of laissez-faire and the theory of limited government. In dealing with the virtues of protection, however, it is critical to ask "Protection against what?" The classical liberal answer is: against force and fraud. But from the vantage point of the party who claims to be hurt or injured, "protection" can easily be expanded to justify protective tariffs against ruinous foreign competition, to create legal barriers, such as licenses, to entry to protect established firms from their upstart rivals, or to organize state-sponsored national cartels. Originally, protection assured individuals who acquired and improved property that no one else could snatch away the fruits of their labor. Who would sow, writers like Blackstone have long asked, if they could not also reap? The mismatch of private and social incentives from the denial of property protection is too plain to deny.

The common law cases set themselves four-square against "unfair competition," but they were always careful to prevent an expansion of adjective from swallowing the noun. The paradigmatic case of unfair competition involves the defendant's use of force to prevent potential customers from doing business with the plaintiff.[12] Any individual customer has little incentive to bear the cost of suit if he can shift his business elsewhere, and large numbers of independent individuals cannot be counted on to organize themselves to protect their prospective relations with the plaintiff. So the aggrieved trader is allowed to sue for the loss of his relational interest from the defendant's forcible interference even if the individual customers choose not to sue on their own right.

The same approach applies to a defendant's use of fraud to upset the relationship between a plaintiff and third parties. Any fraud by D to T about P is both a wrong against T (who is deceived) and P (who in consequence is passed over). T might not sue because it is easier for her to shift her business elsewhere.[13] But P will have an action for defamation against D. The injury to P's reputation is not just an abstract appreciation of the esteem from the world at large or from some segment of it. Rather, the damages function chiefly as a shorthand composite of the thousands of anticipated interactions that are dashed or altered by D's false statements "of and concerning" P. The statement that P cheats his trading partners not only damages P's psyche, but also deters some unknown T from dealing with him. Of course, it is easier for T to resist fraud than force, but that hardly constitutes a reason to disallow suits for fraud or defamation.

Yet once we move beyond force and fraud, the word "unfair" carries no discernible content, which is why the common law refused to expand its scope of protection to treat predatory pricing as a generalization of the tort of defamation or interference with prospective advantage.[14] Any recognition of that supposed tort converts the common law from a protector of competitive markets into its dreaded opponent. What loses, however, as a private law claim often emerges victorious in the political arena. Protective tariffs (especially those for infant industries) and restrictive entry regulation are billed as protection against "ruinous" competition, but in practice they operate as a state-sanctioned form of interference with prospective advantage by insulating inefficient firms from their more efficient competitors. Lost in the shuffle are the unhappy customers, who *by state force* are precluded from doing business with their preferred trading partners. The legal regime flips over by the false generalization of the idea of protection. Now claims for protection against coercion are everywhere. The language of classical liberalism is thus pressed into service of its opposition.

A similar approach has taken its toll on the social idea of individual "security," which is yet another main pillar of classical liberal theory. Here the discussion dovetails nicely with the debate between the oft-canvassed negative and positive rights. Under the classical conceptions, the longing for personal security was well stated by Hobbes: "And therefore, as long as this natural right of every man to every thing endureth, there can be no security to any man, how strong or wise soever he be, of living out the time, which nature ordinarily alloweth men to live."[15] Blackstone stated the legal antidote with his usual clarity: "The right of personal security consists in a person's legal and uninterrupted enjoyment of his life, his limbs, his body, his health, and his reputation."[16] Shortly thereafter, he makes his meaning still clearer: "Besides those limbs and members that may be necessary to man, in order to defend himself or annoy his enemy, the rest of his person or body is also entitled by the same natural right to security from the corporal insults of menaces, assaults, beating and wounding; though such insults amount not to destruction of life or member."[17]

Conceptually, then, the idea of security was thus linked closely to the threat or use of force by another individual. But like coercion and protection, modern discourse threatens to turn this term on its head. We can take it as a given that any individual in isolation would like to have security against the vicissitudes of life, of which illness and natural catastrophe are the most common. The farmer who plants his crops wants to secure his profit from sale. Individual retirees seek financial security against the ravages of old age. All of us seek security against the downsides of bad health. Hence, in short order we find crop support programs, the Social Security Act of 1935, and ex-President and now Senator Clinton's adroitly named (if abortive) Health Security Act that went down in flames in 1994. The choice of names for the latter two initiatives is not an accident, for both consciously evoke the ideal of security, knowing that it is a strong word with few, if any, negative connotations in public life or political theory. Security is the ultimate defensive virtue for everyone.

This transformation of language is neatly captured by a pair of strange bedfellows writing at the end of World War II. I refer here to Franklin Roosevelt's 1944 message to Congress proposing an Economic Bill of Rights,[18] and to chapter 9 of Hayek's famous *Road to Serfdom,* fittingly entitled "Security and Freedom." Roosevelt's proposal consciously apes the traditional classical liberal line:

The one supreme objective for the future, which we discussed for each nation individually, and for all the United Nations, can be summed up in one word: Security.

And that means not only physical security that provides safety from attacks by aggressors. It means also economic security, social security, moral security—in a family of nations.[19]

Lest the message be misunderstood, Roosevelt hammers his theme home:

We have come to a clear realization of the fact that true individual freedom cannot exist without economic security and independence. "Necessitous men are not free men." People who are hungry and out of a job are the stuff of which dictatorships are made.

In our day these economic truths have become accepted as self-evident. We have accepted, so to speak, a second Bill of Rights under which a new basis of security and prosperity can be established for all-regardless of station, race or creed.

Among these are:

The right to a useful and remunerative job in the industries or shops or farms or mines of the nation;

The right to earn enough to provide adequate food and clothing and recreation;

The right of every farmer to raise and sell his products at a return which will give him and his family a decent living;

The right of every business man, large and small, to trade in an atmosphere of freedom from unfair competition and domination by monopolies at home or abroad;

The right of every family to a decent home;

The right to adequate medical care and the opportunity to achieve and enjoy good health;

The right to adequate protection from the economic fears of old age, sickness, accident and unemployment;

The right to a good education.[20]

Roosevelt's new Bill of Rights rests on a conscious imitation of the classical liberal position. The 1776 Declaration of Independence boldly proclaims: "We hold these truths to be self-evident, that all men are created equal, that they are endowed by their Creator with certain unalienable Rights, that among these are Life, Liberty and the pursuit of happiness." By 1944, Roosevelt could declare that certain "economic truths have become accepted as self-evident." His implicit conclusion is that the incorporation of these positive rights (freedom for) into the legal pantheon will not displace the older negative rights (freedom from) on which they build. Yet his remarks contain not a single mention of either the correlative duties that additional security imposes on, for example, employers or landlords, or the taxes they require, or the economic dislocations they impose.

Hayek echoes some of the same themes, but with far more analytical detachment. He begins by noting that the word "security" is used in two senses, one "limited" and attainable, the other "absolute" and unattainable: "first, security against severe physical privation, the certainty of a given minimum of sustenance for all; and second, the security of a given standard of life, or of the relative position which one person or group enjoys compared with others; or, as we may put it briefly, the security of minimum income and the security of the particular income a person is thought to deserve."[21] What is striking about Hayek's position is that *neither* of his two senses of security refers to the protection that the state supplies against external aggression, independent of the wealth of its citizens. In contrast to both Hobbes and Blackstone, both of Hayek's conceptions involve some level of financial support that the state, impersonally conceived, will grant to all of its citizens. The choice is between universal minimum security of resources and some higher level of personal security that depends on past earnings instead of basic needs.

Putting aside delicate questions at the margin, Hayek opts for the former definition: "There is no reason why in a society which has reached the general level of wealth which ours has attained the first kind of security should not be guaranteed to all without endangering general freedom."[22] He then concludes in ways that echo Roosevelt's rhetoric that on matters of "sickness and accident" "the case for state's helping to organize a comprehensive system of social insurance is very strong."[23]

Hayek therefore directs his fire toward the second kind of security that preserves for each group in society their relative position of wealth, notwithstanding changes in demand and technology. Blacksmiths as a group are not entitled after the rise of the automobile to the same income they had fifty years before. In Hayek's view, the effort to preserve the absolute position of any group against economic fluctuations introduces price and wage rigidities that undercut the possibility of rational individual behavior in a competitive economy. But if the system of entry and exit is left open, fortunes can rise and fall, so long as group members remain above that critical social minimum. Because Hayek does not think that overall social output will diminish, he regards limited security from need as a proper object of government effort. Hayek departs from Roosevelt on minimum prices for farm support. But his definition of security is far broader than that found either in Hobbes or Blackstone. The upshot is a powerful consensus: both Left and Right endorse some ideal mix between a competitive economy and a system of minimum welfare rights.

That influence, particularly Roosevelt's, has worked itself forward in time. The International Covenant on Economic and Social Rights borrows copiously from the list of rights that Roosevelt articulated.[24] Even within the United States and other Western democracies, much modern scholarship has sought to redefine the scope of constitutional and administrative law to incorporate this broader account for security of all.[25] Yet the political and intellectual success of a new vision of security invites a comparison with the older view. In that earlier system, the general protection of security, like the mutual renunciation of force, was a positive-sum game. Each person was forced to abandon the right to attack other individuals but received in return security against like attack. The net level of uncertainty in society was thereby diminished so that the overall prosperity of all was advanced, without there being any special favor to one group relative to another.

In comparison, the newer forms of security do not have such benign global consequences. The only way to increase the security of farmers is to reduce the security of others. As Hayek perceptively notes: "With every grant of complete security to one group the insecurity of the rest necessarily increases. If you guarantee to some a fixed part of a variable cake, the share left to the rest is bound to fluctuate proportionally more than the size of the whole."[26] The economic principles of leverage thus work to explain why greater stability for some necessarily implies greater instability for others. Assume that farmers are guaranteed 20 units of wealth in a society whose overall wealth could vary from 100 to 200. Now these people face no risk when wealth moves from one level to another. But let total wealth move from 100 to 200, and other individuals find that the volatility of their wealth is not twofold but 2.25-fold (80 to 180). The purported immunity from risk for one group therefore necessarily increases risk for the rest.

In reality, however, the situation is still worse because the amount of resources devoted to any activity is not fixed, but depends in part on the rate of return from the designated activity. The fixed minimum rate of return to agriculture thus operates as a kind of state-insurance policy against the risk of loss, which will induce farmers to undertake unnecessarily risky investments precisely because some other group is forced to bear a risk for which it has received no premium. With fewer resources available, they will have to cut back the level of their own investments. In sum, the overall attractiveness of investments will shrink so that the expected social yield will drop from 100 to 200 to some lower range, say 90 to 195, with a lower median and a higher volatility. What looks, therefore, in the first instance to be a step for universal security is exactly the opposite: a decrease in expected productivity and a lower level of security for all.

The striking feature about Hayek's position, however, lies in his failure to see its application to the modern affection for guaranteed protections against natural catastrophe or personal sickness or disease. Let the state supply insurance against floods and earthquakes, and the private market for those goods will be crowded out, often with catastrophic effects.[27] Hayek writes as though these markets are free of moral hazard when he describes these losses as "disasters against which the individual can neither attempt to guard himself nor make provision for the consequences."[28] Not so: once the state provides insurance at below market rates (or worse, bails people out without requiring any insurance from them at all), it invites the moral hazard and adverse selection that undermines the sensible allocation decisions of a centralized economy. Individuals are encouraged to build their homes in areas exposed to high risks of floods, hurricanes, and earthquakes. When governments resist paying for these subsidies directly, they find ways to burden private insurance companies with the systematic losses associated with assigned risk pools. One common strategy is to forbid companies to exit markets in which the premiums are set too low, as Florida did after Hurricane Andrew.[29]

The same point can be made about social security, which works wonders for those who joined the program earlier and whose income today is guaranteed against major fluctuations. But the taxes needed to fund the program place at ever greater risk the next generation of workers who are required to foot the bill. It is not surprising, therefore, that the rates of returns that workers receive under this program systematically drop with time, so that for those workers born in the 1890s (who collected soon after the introduction of the program), the effective rate of return was, probably, around 10 percent; for those born in 1915, the average real rate of return was about 5.5 percent, only to drop to 3.25 percent for those born in 1930; the rates of return continued to drop so that those born in the 1955–59 period, for example, can expect little more than a

1 percent real return, while those born between 1995 and 1999 will eke out a barely positive return of around 0.2 percent.[30]

Sixty years after Hayek's analysis, the new battleground for security was the ill-fated Health Security Act of 1994.[31] One reason why the proposal failed was that it could not generate increased security to all individuals simultaneously, even though it could impoverish them all simultaneously. Politically, the group most opposed to the passage of the act turned out to be senior citizens on Medicare, who recognized that their preferred position was threatened by any effort to extend guarantees to all citizens.

A more limited intervention can also have profound effects. We can have entry and exit of firms into labor markets, but so long as all workers are entitled to receive Medicare protection at age sixty-five, competition over one important component of retirement benefits is effectively curtailed by the state monopoly in critical contract terms. Similarly, the same pattern of intergenerational transfers is an outgrowth of the recent amendments to the age discrimination laws that eliminate mandatory retirement by contract for (among others) university professors. Here again, the additional security that is conferred on senior employees comes out of the hide of younger generations. In academic terms, senior faculty get to keep their positions, their pensions, and their salaries while many younger faculty members scramble to fill folding chairs that, as their name suggests, offer no job security at all.

Monopoly as Coercion

A grand philosophical critique, then, has brought forth a mouse. So long as we want to maintain the distinctions between freedom and coercion, the conceptual tools to do so are at our disposal. Nonetheless, it would be a mistake to assume that the principle of freedom is so powerful that it brooks no limitation, or that the notion of coercion is so heavily tied to the use or threat of force that it has no other independent meaning. To be sure, commentators like Hale are incorrect when they treat the ordinary refusal to deal as a form of coercion between strangers. Indeed, within the stark libertarian framework, any refusal to deal is legitimate precisely because it does not involve the use of force or fraud. But within the more extended classical liberal framework, context becomes key, so the refusal to deal when practiced by a monopolist brings forth a very different response. One real cost of Hale's sweeping attack on refusals to deal is that it dulls our awareness of such refusals in cases of monopoly power. In ordinary contexts, the absolute right to exclude other individuals creates the legal regime on which the functioning of all competitive markets depends. In contrast, we can force a common carrier or a public utility to do business with us to overcome its "coercive" power. But this ostensible equivalence between coercion and monopoly power is productive of vice as well as virtue.

Ideally, the optimal level of coercion (that is, the threat or use of force) by one individual against another is zero. The only concessions that we make to this ideal rest on our practical inability to create any fail-safe social institutions. To ferret out and prevent all forms of mischief under conditions of uncertainty is to spread the net too wide. So we have to gear up with remedies that cut too broadly too soon, or content ourselves with those whose relief comes too little and too late.[32] The troubled choice between injunctions and licenses before the fact and damages and fines after the fact always takes place against the backdrop of two kinds of error: stopping lawful acts that should go forward or allowing unlawful acts that should be stopped. Yet with all the uncertainty over the right mix of remedies, no skeptic has yet defended the bright idea that the right way to curb coercion is to compensate individuals whose (Hobbesian) liberties—the unfettered use of their physical capacity to coerce others— we curtail. The follow-on effects will be disastrous, as eager, if perverse, individuals would line up round the block in order to be bought off from threats that they should never have made in the first place.

The use of the term "coercion" in connection with monopoly behavior provokes the opposite response. Here, the risk of follow-on mischief no longer applies. Shutting down the activity altogether is no part of the social plan, because we all need the services that the monopolist provides. Nor can we sensibly break that particular monopoly in two or more parts (so as to create a competitive industry) because the parts of the network when separated work less efficiently than when managed as a unified whole: natural monopolies receive their name for declining marginal cost industries where it is cheaper for one party to supply the market than for any larger number of firms. To speak in this context of "coercive" behavior is not to speak of activities that are wrong in themselves. It is rather the more modest inquiry of whether it makes sense to limit the pricing and sales strategies available to the monopolist endowed with legal protection or natural advantage.

The awareness of this difference has long been evident at common law, whose basic rule, as announced in *Allnut v. Inglis,* denied the monopolist the absolute right to exclude by requiring him to supply his goods or services, not at whatever price he could fetch, but only at reasonable prices.[33] That judicial inquiry into price may be easy when an ordinary business is granted a state monopoly for some public reason: in *Allnut*, a warehouse was designated by the Crown for storage of imported goods destined for reshipment abroad free of all local custom duties. But establishing prices is much harder where the defendant operates a vast gas, electrical, or telephone network that, no matter how we tug at it, cannot operate if broken up into competitive components. In this context, zero coercion no longer is an intelligible ideal; rather, the task is to secure just compensation to the network owner (that is, the competitive rate of return needed to induce them into the line of business in the first place)—no more and no less. Branding the use of monopoly power as coercive looks to offer an easy path to justify state regulation, but the choice of words only obscures relevant inquiries into institutional design. The task here is not to stop the operation of the network in its tracks, but to make its behavior approximate that of the competitive firm.

In an odd sense, therefore, the recognition that both states and private parties may have monopoly power introduces a parity between them. In light of their overlapping structures, neither the state nor the market has a monopoly on virtue or vice. Just as there are private monopolies that operate under legislative supervision, so political monopolies should, in principle, operate under constitutional supervision. Within a federal system it is easy to identify multiple sources of coercion. The national government is the sole monopolist with respect to activities that fall within its jurisdiction. In addition, each state can act as a monopolist with local activities committed to its care, such as land use regulation; perhaps more ominously, each state can act as a monopolist with respect to private network activities—rails and communications come first to mind—that operate across state lines. In analyzing these government activities, it is tempting to condemn them with the convenient label of "coercion," which now covers a number of disparate sins. Hale, who had a knack for seeing common problems in distant places, took just this attitude. In writing about the use of state power,[34] he took the position that just about any condition that the government attached to the use of the public roads, the grant of a license, or the exemption of a tax was coercive.

But once again his dubious conceptual framework precluded him from sufficiently differentiating between the various cases. Initially, and trivially, no one doubts that the state can engage in garden-variety coercion, like ordinary individuals, but with greater force available: pay this fine or we shall throw you into jail. And no one doubts that such coercion is justifiable when applied to individuals who have broken some proper law, such as those relating to theft, pollution, or taxation. But in many cases the government does not use force to counter force, but rather imposes conditions on individuals who wish to use various public facilities for private advantage.

Consider the following examples. The public highways system forms a state-run network that shares many features with private railroads or private phone companies. Now suppose that the government is treated as the absolute owner of these facilities, so that it can say to any private citizen: "Look, we will make the following bargain that will leave both sides better off. You can use our system of roads, but you must agree not to speak out in protest against any present government policies."[35] The logic of mutual benefit is written across the face of this transaction. An ordinary individual will be left housebound and penniless without access to public roads for the goods and services needed to survive. The sacrifice of political protest rights normally counts for very little in the lives of most unbenighted citizens for whom politics is a chore rather than an opportunity. This transaction securing entry is thus a win-win transaction in some short-run view. But it is a catastrophe for the stability of democratic institutions. Seriatim, the voluntary release of these small individual benefits solidifies and entrenches the power of dominant political factions. Global negatives thus overwhelm local gains. But this fiasco is avoided if the state is subjected to the same rules that apply to private common carriers: all customers have presumptive access to the network at reasonable prices that can be lost only by individual misbehavior. If the public utility cannot condition service on the surrender of its customers' rights to participate in politics, then neither can the state.

Now compare the bargain of access-for-speech with a second transaction. Suppose the state says to all individuals: "If you wish to use the public roads, you have to agree to obey the rules of the road and consent to suit against you arising out of any accident within this state." Here we have a win-win transaction if the rules of the road prevent collisions, and the use of tort actions provides both deterrence against dangerous driving and compensation for its victims. At a formal level, this transaction also looks to have the same win-win characteristics as the first one, but it passes the test that the first transaction flunks and has rightly been upheld.[36]

What, then, accounts for the difference between these two?[37] The magic element cannot be found in the short-term consequences of the respective transactions: both are win-win as between the immediate parties. Yet once we recall that the state has a monopoly of the road system, then our intuitions should be sensitive to the proper and improper uses of that power. Like the ordinary common carrier, the state cannot impose whatever price it wants on the traffic, but must charge only a reasonable price. That price in turn contains not only financial charges (tolls for highway services, gasoline taxes, and the like), but also in-kind conditions. The proper approach in each case, therefore, is to carry over to the public law the identical tests that are imposed on private common carriers. Considered most broadly, do these transactions advance any long-term conception of social welfare? It is easy to see that any rule that requires conformity to rules of the road, and that calls for local adjudication of claims, will achieve that end by encouraging efficient use of a common resource to which all have access but over which none has total control. No matter how many times we multiply the effect of the rule, its consequences remain benevolent because they help ever-larger numbers of users coordinate their behavior within the unified network. Stated otherwise, once these conditions are imposed, all users of the road can compete with each other on even terms in ordinary product and service markets. The restrictions in question, therefore, facilitate the operation of competitive markets that run on top of their monopolistic state elements. Public and private monopolies are thus governed by the same set of legal institutions, so that the choice between them should depend on their relative levels of performance.

Thus far I have spoken only of two polar cases: illicit restrictions on speech and the imposition of needed safety regulations. But in many cases government motives are mixed. The state could impose rules that limit the carriage of toxic substances on public roads unless these are contained in certain types of trucks. Is this an effort to prevent low-tech firms from competing with high-tech rivals? Or is there is a genuine safety risk that requires this restriction in question? As with the earlier discussion of the difference between "labor" and "health" statutes under the police power,[38] the question becomes one of balancing, on which some cases will be close to the line. But that melancholy fact should not blind us to the proposition that some cases are easy as well. It seems clear, for example, that a rule that prevented a private carrier (one that carries only the goods of its owner) from entering public highways unless it agreed to be regulated as a common carrier has no safety implications and was accordingly struck down on a proper assessment of its illicit objective. Speaking of this regime, Justice Sutherland wrote: "Its primary purpose evidently is to protect the business of those who are common carriers in fact by controlling competitive conditions. Protection or conservation of the highways is not involved."[39] The decision thus thwarted the state's effort to extend its network monopoly over highways to the composition of the traffic.

The same types of considerations apply when the conflicts are not between the government and the citizen in a single jurisdiction but between the citizen of one state and the government of a second. Where the two states are totally separate, the usual strong rule of exclusion applies, so that the citizen can gain entry to a state not his own only on terms that meet their joint consent. The resulting holdout problems between the sovereign of one state and the citizen of another (or the firm organized under its laws) can become titanic in the face of retaliation, as when two autonomous nations squabble over the landing rights for airlines that travel between them. A system of federalism, however, is best understood as curbing the unbridled power of states vis-à-vis citizens of other states. The absolute sovereign right to exclude is muted, and in its place is imposed a rule that prohibits the state from discriminating against the outsiders for the benefit of its own citizens.[40] The obvious parallel is again the nondiscrimination rules imposed on common carriers and public utilities, which are intended to prevent exploitation of their monopoly power by banning discriminating against customers receiving the same class of service.

Last, monopoly power could be exercised by the federal government in its efforts to "leverage" control over the internal affairs of the states. This was of great importance before the 1937 constitutional revolution that (mistakenly in my view) ceded under the Commerce Clause ("Congress shall have the power to regulate commerce . . . among the several states") virtually comprehensive power to the national government to regulate any and all productive activities, no matter how local.[41] But prior to 1937, Congress's power to regulate commerce was largely restricted to the control over the instrumentalities of interstate commerce (the rails, telephones, and highways). In this bygone era, a key question was whether Congress's admitted control over transportation networks allowed it to impose conditions on local firms such that they could only ship their goods into interstate commerce if they agreed to abandon the use of child labor in any of their operations. The nature of the *quid pro quo* is clear: the ability to gain access to out-of-state markets is so critical to most firms that they would gladly conform their use of child labor (or anything else) to federal mandates in order to reach national or international markets. But why should they be put to that choice at all when the use of monopoly power essentially undoes the distribution of power between state and national governments under the original federal plan? The law was thus properly struck down even though the regulation was only on the goods after they entered the stream of interstate commerce itself.[42]

Property as a Creation of the State

The above discussion of the relationship between liberty and coercion shows that both elements of the classical liberal synthesis resist the deconstructive attacks on their internal integrity. The classical liberal synthesis, of course, yokes the protection of liberty with that of property. Hale seeks to bring down the second side of this synthesis by showing that the idea of property is as empty as that as liberty. But his line of attack differs in some important ways. Initially, it is very difficult for anyone to accept that all aspects of individual liberty should be regarded simply as forms of state largesse. No matter how many refutations of natural law are advanced, ordinary people do not regard their entitlement to exclusive physical control over their own bodies as dependent on official favor. They would brand as unjust, for example, laws that give (all or some) men free access to women's bodies without their consent. They might be hesitant in their answer to the lawyer's query of whether a liberty or property interest is at stake. But why worry whether we speak here of the liberty of action and choice or of the exclusive right to one's own person? The two are so rapidly intertwined that in practice everyone draws, by conduct as by word, the prosaic inference that actual bodily control over one's person stems from (and carries with it) the—dare one say it?—natural right of control over one's body. This theme has worked its way into modern constitutional law. Even as judges have trimmed the protection for freedom of contract within the economic sphere, they have simultaneously expanded the constitutional right of privacy for "intimate" personal associations, which are thought to lie beyond the power of the state to regulate.[43]

Property rights in external things evokes a very different response. It covers a bewildering array of resources—land, chattels, water, oil and gas, air, intellectual property, privacy—that seem to cry out for different legal regimes, some of which (such as copyrights and patents) do not lend themselves to any easy natural rights interpretation: Just how long should copyright or patent protection run?[44] Even when confined to tangible property, there is no necessary physical connection that binds a person to his clothes or his house as it binds a person to his own body. Somewhere along the line some action must be taken to link discrete individuals to things external to themselves. The common law rule—first possession of land and unowned things established ownership in them—

relied on a bottoms-up theory for land and movable property. In the initial position, we could find families, clans, and tribes, but no state with permanent organized control over extensive territories. It would have been incongruous to speak of an organized political collectivity, divorced from extended blood relations, that held things in common.

In this early environment, individuals acquired property by taking it, and then entered into a political compact under which they surrendered part of what they owned in exchange for greater security for the remaining portion. Even if that contract was "social" and "hypothetical," instead of "individual" and "actual," the thrust of the legal theory was to limit the form and extent of state control over private property: the state gave back to each person security that was worth more to them than the property (and liberty of action) they were required to surrender in order to secure its maintenance, typically in the form of a proportionate tax. But for Hale, as for so many other realists, this bottoms-up approach was simply wrong. Now the state is posited with initial ownership of all land and other scarce resources, so that individuals obtain what they own on grants from the state, subject to whatever conditions, express or implied, the government wishes to attach to them either at the time of the initial grant or, more ominously, on the strength of some general reservation of rights, at any time thereafter. The attached conditions could include regulation on private rights to use and dispose of land or other resources. The sole question that one has to ask is what kinds of restrictions we wish to impose, then—presto!—these are all in place.

In principle that result could work. The state in question could have perfect knowledge of the consequences of its own action and be motivated only by the desire to advance the welfare of all its citizens. In so doing, it (or its chief architects) could design a system of private property that it could not remove at its mere demand. Indeed, if the classical liberal synthesis were correct, then it should be obliged to create just these institutions so that the limitations on government would come from above instead of below.

But the effort to create the "myth of ownership"[45] is undertaken precisely because of the belief that governments should determine both resource allocation and income distribution. Necessarily lost in this modern shuffle, however, is the older idea of private property serving as a bulwark of protection against excessive state power, not only for ordinary individuals, but also for those who are politically isolated. Once that earlier, Lockean conception is abandoned, the state no longer has to *justify* the restrictions it imposes. State power becomes predominant; individual titles are all held on sufferance of state control. The Lockean view that the state is formed to protect the property of its members is necessarily turned on its head, for the state is now under a duty only to protect those forms of property it chooses to create, and then only to the extent it deems them worthy of protection. The state giveth; the state taketh away; blessed be the name of the state. Whatever system of land use or environmental controls that the state wishes to impose simply "inheres" as limitations on the title already created.[46] The question of compensation for loss of use becomes a matter of politics and never a matter of principle, as "implied state reservations" can rip out the heart of any grant or original title. Wholly apart from any constitutional considerations (more on this later), the theory of property cannot be regarded as malleable as Hale would have it be. Once again, the attack on laissez-faire fails insofar as it rests on the ostensible conceptual incoherence of its underlying principles.

Cohen on Nozick

In more recent times, the attacks on the coherence of notions of liberty and property have been advanced by G. A. Cohen in his influential volume titled *Self-Ownership, Freedom and Equality*,[47] which was written largely in response to the libertarian theories espoused in Robert Nozick's classic work *Anarchy, State, and Utopia*.[48] The core of Nozick's position is contained in his unacknowledged recreation of the common law rules of property, contract, and tort. Nozick starts with a somewhat imprecise assumption of individual self-ownership that is then used to reduce things in nature to private ownership. Thereafter, the state protects the entitlements so obtained from the force and aggression of other individuals and allows for their voluntary exchange, such that an individual with good title in a given resource is allowed to transfer that title, by sale or gift, to another individual or group of individuals. One clear implication of this theory is that large inequalities of wealth can result from differences in original human endowments (given the self-ownership assumption) or from the lumpy and unequal distribution obtained when unowned things are reduced to private possession. The point has been well understood by judges operating in the libertarian tradition. Thus Justice Pitney in *Coppage v. Kansas* predates Nozick when he writes: "It being self-evident that, unless all things are held in common, some persons must have more property than others, it is from the nature of things impossible to uphold freedom of contract and the right of private property without at the same time recognizing as legitimate those inequalities of fortune that are the necessary result of the exercise of those rights."[49]

Nozick illustrates how these natural differences can easily be magnified through voluntary exchange in his fabled example of how Wilt Chamberlain becomes rich, even in a world in which all start with equal money endowments: each fan who agrees to watch him play parts with some small sum of money, which in the end aggregates to very large sums indeed.[50] Since each of the individual transfers are legitimate, then so too is the final state of affairs generated under Nozick's "entitlement theory," which finds legitimacy in the pedigree of title to wealth, not its ultimate distribution.

In working through his position, Nozick does not take a consequentialist view of these transactions. He thus glides over the point most critical to efficiency-oriented writers, namely, that each voluntary transaction is a positive-sum game that enhances the overall level of wealth. The magnitude of these gains, moreover, is amplified because of the recursive nature of transactions. The law imposes no external limitations on the number of times that individual entitlements can be resold; nor does it prevent the subject matter of those entitlements from being altered or repackaged before sale. At root, the only limitations on the operation of the system are those internal to it. Certain goods will eventually be consumed, and thus withdrawn from the system as a whole. Alternatively, the level of transaction costs may exceed the gains from certain transfers so that practical limitations will preclude further exchange. But the system has a level of decentralized direction that makes it both unnecessary and impolitic, as Nozick forcefully argues, to insist in advance that certain final "patterns" emerge from these transactions in order to legitimate the overall process. Not having to decide what these patterns should be frees up the system for a higher velocity of transactions and reduces the incentives to consume resources before they are taken for redistribution. So long, therefore, as the process is sound, the outcome is sound. This theory looks to the standard set of contractual vices in deciding which individual transactions are blocked: fraud, duress, undue influence, and the like—none of which depend ultimately on the substantive terms of the transaction or on the relative wealth of the parties to it.[51]

Even after these most considerable virtues are acknowledged, there are, in my view, profound gaps in Nozick's theory of entitlement that stem from his failure to explicitly acknowledge and incorporate the functional roots of his system. It is the case that any system of property looks backward to determine the "chain of title" that gives rise to present holdings. But this is not because of any fetish with the past but chiefly from the profound sense that stability in transactions is necessary for sensible

forward-looking planning. One need only look at the profound social dislocations that occur whenever current titles come under systematic attack,
whether because of a belated claim of aboriginal title for lands that were
thought to be held free and clear (as in Australia, Canada, New Zealand,
or the United States) or because of the widespread plunder in Nazi Germany and the Eastern European countries under the control of the Soviet
Union. No one will lend, buy, or insure titles that are not marketable, so
that ongoing economic activity grinds to an unhappy halt.

It hardly follows, however, in any functional sense that preserving the
chain of title dominates all competing concerns. More specifically, Nozick
dabbles with the question of what might happen if, say, one individual
buys up all the drinking water in the world.[52] But he never takes the next
step to address coherently the refusal at common law to enforce contracts in restraint of trade.[53] These cartel arrangements are embodied in
transfers that satisfy Nozick's rule of justice, but their adverse effects on
social welfare, by restricting output and raising price, lead to the strong
condemnation that they received at common law, which refused to treat
them like ordinary contracts of sale.[54] The exact rules governing these
alliances among sellers are complicated, given the tendency of firms to
press to the limit of the law. For example, although the basic rule renders
the sharing of information presumptively illegal,[55] an exception has been
carved out where the effects of cooperation between business rivals are
positive on third parties.[56]

The continued vitality of this body of law shows the ultimately consequentialist nature of the overall system, which distinguishes between ordinary contracts for sale and services, as when Wilt Chamberlain played
basketball, and collusion (or transfers of property) among firms in an
industry that usually, but not universally, have negative allocative effects.
The exact remedy for contracts in restraint of trade presents delicate questions that have vexed the antitrust law from the playing cards monopoly
of the seventeenth century to the Microsoft antitrust action at the end of
the second millennium. The reason is that the error costs are high even
for the best approach. The simple remedy of refusing to enforce such contracts provides cheap but limited protection: parties can, and often will,
cheat on their cartel arrangements, and if they do the law will not stand
in their way. But if they do not, or do not do so immediately, then the
subsequent misallocations must be endured. The allowance of full-scale
damage actions by injured consumers is a far more complicated affair
that exuberant governments are likely to overuse when principled inac-
tion should be preferred. Here, as everywhere else, the trade-off is hard to

master.[57] But only a consistent consequentialist theory offers any explanation as to why the entire evaluative enterprise should be undertaken in the first place. Under the Nozick theory, a contract to divide markets or rig prices—transactions that are, or at least close to, per se illegal under the antitrust laws—are valid contracts that, irrespective of their content, should be enforced like any others.

The upshot is that Nozick's rule of justice in transfer represents a strong intuitive appreciation of the first round of substantive rules for a comprehensive theory of individual rights and state power. But the strong intuitions he expresses in his opening salvo—"Individuals have rights, and there are things no person or group may do to them (without violating their rights)"[58]—lack the theoretical underpinnings to protect them against potent counterexamples from nonsocialist critics. No matter what one says, the object of the antitrust laws is not the creation of some massive system of redistribution. It is the prevention of untoward industrial practices, which when proscribed on a uniform basis, has the potential to improve the average advantage of all members of society, at least in a state of nature when none of them has formed alliances and combinations that run afoul of any sensible version of the antitrust law.

Given the weaknesses of his system, it seems clear that Nozick's epic achievement should not escape a fair bit of criticism. But what is equally interesting is that for all Cohen's Marxist leanings—his book is published in the Cambridge University series on Marxism and social theory—he faults Nozick for conceptual weaknesses that suffer from many of the defects associated with Hale's critique of traditional laissez-faire economics. Cohen quotes from Hale with approval,[59] but never addresses the important limitations on libertarian property rights that need to be incorporated into any general theory. Instead, Cohen's basic strategy is to trap the libertarian by showing that his commitment to a system of self-ownership leads him to embrace a largely egalitarian distribution of resources.

His first point, vintage Hale, is that any conception of private property is inconsistent with a generalized notion of individual freedom. Freedom, in a good Hobbesian sense, means that I have the right to do what I like.[60] Property gives you the right to limit my freedom by keeping me off your land. When I want to pitch a tent on your land, the state interferes with my freedom by using force to back your claim.[61] "The banal truth is that, if the state prevents me from doing something that I want to do, then it places a restriction on my freedom."[62] The same could be said of murder and rape, but in all cases, so it appears, the answer is the same: any limitation on human action is a limitation on human freedom.

In some sense this argument is so counterintuitive that it leads nowhere, for it is difficult to think historically of any regime that prizes individual freedom without also protecting private property. Indeed, two books, both suspicious of government power and bearing the identical title *Property and Freedom,* have been published in recent years.[63] But let us assume that in a state of nature the baseline condition is that each person has the perfect freedom to do whatever he wants with his body, so that any system of (exclusive) private property is regarded as a limitation on the natural liberty of all individuals. That situation might prove embarrassing to anyone who thought that the initial position was impervious to improvement by conscious state action. But it has no force against a rule that allows (in high-transaction-costs settings) the state to force a set of exchanges wherein each citizen surrenders some of his natural liberties in exchange for the (like) surrender of liberties by others.

At this point, it takes only a little imagination to reach the conclusion that defining liberty in a more constrained and more socially recognizable way—that is, to do what one wills without using force or fraud against another—is, as an empirical matter, as close to a Paretian improvement as we are likely to find in the real world. So this revised definition of liberty, more Lockean and less Hobbesian, becomes the new baseline against which all further transformations of the legal order should be judged. Thus, we have little reason to fear a translation from this set of rights to an impure libertarian system in which proportionate taxation is used to fund the system of laws needed to secure the initial rights. The hard question is whether the transformation yields in security more than it deprives in liberty and property—a question that cannot be answered in the negative by anyone who thinks the ideal of limited government does not give the state enough to do.

Once this point is established, accepting state power to impose Paretian improvements has this critical conceptual advantage: the choice of initial baselines matters less than first meets the eye. If distribution A is Pareto superior to distribution B, then if A is in place, B cannot displace it; but if B is in place, then (if transaction costs are low enough) A can displace it. A constrained definition of liberty, consistent with the protection of property, thus dominates, no matter what form of liberty is protected by the perceived initial baseline. In this world, it becomes more important to reduce transaction costs than to insist on the one, correct definition for the state of nature. Any consistent, general definition should do in a conceptual world where hypothetical transformations can be introduced at zero cost.

Cohen, however, is not content to attack the initial definition of liberty on which Nozick (and every legal system) relies. He also attacks both the rules of acquisition of property and those governing its transfer. Thus one of his most famous examples involves the parable of Able and Infirm, each of whom is treated as a self-owner, but who together are stipulated to own the world jointly.[64] For Cohen, the point of this example is to show that Infirm's holdout position over material resources deprives Able of any bargaining advantage that he might have with respect to these material resources. (Presumably Able could not even stand on this earth without Infirm's consent.) The upshot, Cohen claims, is that Able must split the proceeds roughly equally with Infirm—a far cry from the outcome in a Lockean world. Individual self-ownership, Cohen concludes, is consistent with egalitarianism and offers no special justification for any Lockean inequality.

Yet this is a case where the choice of examples reveals more about an author's philosophical preconceptions than about real-world complications. Desert island hypotheticals, criticized generally in chapter 4, should not blind us to the fact that it makes no sense to speak of regimes of "property rights" in a world with only two people. The great practical advantage of private property is that it requires all individuals but one to forbear from the use of a single plot of land, thereby giving the owner the opportunity to put it to productive use without having first to transact with thousands (or millions) of unnamed individuals who would otherwise have equal claims over that land. The clear transactional advantages of private property are unintelligible when (in defiance of all principles of evolution) we begin the analysis with a world (or even some remote island) populated by only two people. No matter what the original allocation of ownership, the two will surely have to bargain and cooperate with each other, or both might perish from either starvation or boredom. Without other sources of companionship, their incentives to act cooperatively are likely to be great, but, if not, there is no neutral third party to whom they can appeal if they fail to agree on some division of the whole. So why worry about this example in developing a comprehensive legal regime?

Suppose, however, that we put all mundane questions of realism and enforcement to one side. The next question is: How does one defend Cohen's working assumption that all natural assets are owned jointly? The alternative position—one adopted by virtually every legal system, ancient or modern—is that land in a state of nature is unowned and thus acquired by initial occupation.[65] Under this rule of occupation, Able gains an enormous advantage over Infirm (as Diligent gains over Lazy in similar circumstances) because Able's greater energy will usually allow him to occupy and develop larger and better portions of land without Infirm's cooperation. The first possession rule, by knocking out the implicit holdout advantage created by joint ownership, thus nicely puts land into use more quickly than would otherwise be the case. That advantage may seem small in a two-person world, but it increases as the population base increases. This point was not lost on Locke, who noted that in the state of nature everyone would starve if each had to gain the consent of all others before occupying or cultivating any portion of the land.[66]

Yet let us suppose that in the two-person world we do have joint initial ownership, as Cohen stipulates. Within a pure libertarian world (one governed by only the first four rules of autonomy, first possession, contract, and tort), Able can gain access to nature's riches only by sharing them with Infirm. But once we allow forced exchanges with compensation, it no longer follows that mutual consent is the only possible way to dissolve the original joint ownership, just as it is no longer the only way to obtain a divorce. A suit for partition of the property (or sale with a division of proceeds) allows one person to break from the other under narrow conditions of necessity in order to overcome just this kind of holdout problem. With partition, Able may now claim half (by value) the island as his own, and leave unlucky Infirm to his own devices—a solution that could well generate more for him than a rule that assigns ownership to the first possessor, under which Infirm will acquire very little. At this point, Infirm will have to enter into cooperative ventures with Able, a task more difficult in a two-person world than one with thousands of people, where competitive conditions make contracts for wage labor (or the sale of real estate to third parties) quite easy even for infirm individuals. Or stated otherwise as we move from two people to large numbers of people, the holdout problems in coordination games that require unanimous consent get progressively more difficult, while bilateral contracts (for the exchange of labor or land) become progressively easier to organize.

These variations on joint ownership cannot, I think, be easily dismissed as lawyers' musings. All societies have rules that deal with joint ownership of private property, and while these differ in their details, none allows any one owner to bar the use of the jointly owned property by others. Rather, all systems have rules that allow for joint occupation of the premises, or allow one owner to either force a partition of the land or (in a world with more than two people) to put the property up for sale and divide the proceeds among its joint owners.[67]

The legal rules governing these divisions necessarily take into account the exact situation that Cohen contemplates: initial joint ownership of an asset that one but not the other co-owner then improves by labor. The usual solution is to award the party the reasonable value of his labor (which could not be determined in a two-party world because the labor could not be priced in the absence of a market). Thereafter, the proceeds of sale can be divided in accordance with the appreciation (or depreciation) of the underlying asset. The holdout problem is avoided: the asset is usefully redeployed without any implicit wealth redistribution between the parties. All blockades are broken.

In some cases, however, the partition of property leads not to the elimination of blockades and holdout problems, but to their creation. In these instances, the creation of the maintenance of a common may be preferred because of its overall social effects. Waterways, fisheries, beaches, oil and gas pools, communication and transportation networks, and public utilities are all mixtures of common and private property. As noted earlier, a complete theory of property has to explain why water is subject to common ownership (so that dams cannot block rivers, even though some water can be removed from rivers for farming); why public utilities have duties to serve their customers at reasonable rates, but are protected against confiscatory rate regulation; why infrastructure is financed by certain kinds of special assessments; and why some agrarian lands are held in common for some seasons of the year and privately operated in the others.

Cohen also extends his attack to the basic rules of transfer. But that critique does not criticize those voluntary transfers that tend toward monopoly. Rather, he identifies certain indefensible distributions of property that are not brought about by any illicit transfer. His chief target involves a transfer made by mistake—a problem long handled by the common law rules of restitution. He thus posits a situation in which my justly held rolling pin rolls out the door into your house, where you use it, thinking that it is one of your own.[68] Your use of the thing is improper (but only against the owner, not against third parties, a detail of relative title that Cohen does not discuss), even though you have not committed any improper act. In this situation, the obvious libertarian response is that you must return the thing to me once I demand it from you: since the transfer is not properly sanctioned, it should be undone, just as money paid over by mistake (as to the wrong person) must be returned.

This simplest cases of mistaken transfers, once understood as a discrete category, should launch us into a discussion of its complex variations. Suppose that you damage the rolling pin in ordinary use. Is there liability for the harm, given the innocent conversion of the thing? Probably not, at least if you were not negligent in its use. Or suppose that you repair the pin. Can you recover the value of your labor once it is returned? Probably yes, at least if the repairs were done in ignorance of ownership. But even then, recovery is limited to the lower of the cost of repairs or their value to the original owner. Or suppose that the pin was shaved down and incorporated into the walls of your play pen. Once specific restoration is impossible, then provision of a substitute or payment of cash becomes appropriate. Speaking more generally, in all cases where the mistaken transfer is not obviously reversible, the problem cannot be solved within the simple libertarian framework. Instead the transfer either of the thing or some portion of it or of the labor used to improve it is, of necessity, approved in exchange for just compensation in cash to the former owner. Within this framework, the Roman (and common) law developed extensive rules to decide who would keep the thing and who would receive just compensation when the labor of A was mixed with the material of B.[69] The basic rules usually seek to assign the ownership of the resource to the party who made the distinctive investment in it, such that the sculptor keeps the marble, whose owner receives either a substitute slab of marble of equal quality or its value. After the fact the transaction is treated as though the sculptor had borrowed or purchased the marble slab from its owner in a consensual transaction. The common variations thus have straightforward solutions. The intractable variations are too infrequent to matter socially.

In a word, Cohen is right to think that the mistake cases are difficult to fit within a pure libertarian theory. But he is wrong to think that the needed adjustments require some fundamental repudiation of its central insights, which survive within more powerful theory that incorporates a regime of forced exchanges. But this regime offers no protection to any person who seeks to sidestep the system of ownership by converting the property of another to his own use *knowing* that it is owned by another. That willful converter is required to return the thing forthwith and to forfeit any value that he added to the thing by his own labor. The only cases of involuntary transfer that require these delicate adjustments of ownership and the making of side payments are those of honest mistake. Happily, once it becomes easier to keep track of both property and labor, there are fewer occasions in which the law of restitution is needed to sort these mistakes out. It is erroneous to assume that conveyancing anomalies undermine the presumptive force of the rules regulating justice in transfer or point the way to some egalitarian social order.

In sum, Cohen's pattern of argument takes the common form: reveal some chinks in the stripped-down libertarian rules of acquisition and transfer, and then conclude that it discredits any system that recognizes the presumptive force of voluntary transfer. But those arguments do not work against any system that prizes voluntary exchange but goes beyond it to take into account third party effects (as with the antitrust laws) and cases of mistaken transfer (as with the laws of restitution and just compensation). These sensible extensions respond to the conceptual shortfalls of the pure libertarian system but do not justify any more comprehensive system of redistribution, let alone one that leads to egalitarian outcomes. The case for egalitarianism has to be made on its own substantive terms, and that task cannot be discharged on conceptual grounds alone.

6

A Preference for Preferences

A Roadmap through Preferences

IN CHAPTERS 3–5, I have defended my basic model of legal entitlements against the charges of moral relativism and conceptual incoherence. This chapter addresses a third attack on the system, which criticizes the idea of "preference" as a crude and unsuitable tool for understanding and organizing human behavior. The issue is clearly relevant to the overall inquiry because of the basic naturalist effort to link preferences (or desires or wants) to a workable social welfare function. Should these preferences turn out to possess properties that render them unstable, slippery, or infirm, then they can hardly serve as the foundation for any comprehensive social system—even if it leaves in doubt what notion should be substituted in its place.

The initial section of this chapter investigates why preferences play such a large role in the overall design of any legal system. Thereafter it examines the various ways in which the use of preferences is thought to be problematic or uncertain. More specifically, it is useful to isolate six variations on the basic theme. The first is the charge that individuals have "adaptive" preferences, whereby the utility that they attach to some given outcome is said to turn on whether they are able to obtain it. People are said to adapt their preferences to take into account the limits of their possibilities. Second, it is often said that some individuals' choices do not satisfy the minimum condition for rationality, namely that of transitivity, which requires that if A prefers x to y, and y to z, then he must perforce prefer x to z. Third, the set of choices that individuals have to make are held "incommensurate" with each other, so that no common metric may be found for people to evaluate the trade-offs that the classical legal theory presupposes. Fourth, the use of preferences often but incorrectly posits consistent individual preferences over time, without taking into account the changes of personal identity or circumstances that could undermine this position: we are not those persons that we were. Fifth, it is claimed that the reliance on individual preferences fails to consider the difficulty in working a sensible coordination of preference across individuals, as found in the standard Prisoner's Dilemma game. Sixth, the traditional reliance on "revealed preferences" is said to falsely assume that the observed individual choices accurately mirror the internal and subjective preferences of the persons who make them. Unfortunately, the argument continues, the idea of preference glides over and simplifies the complex set of emotions and drives that lead to, and sometimes contaminate, individual choice and judgment in many human situations.

Why Preferences?

Classical legal theory is built on certain key assumptions about the regularity of human behavior for two major reasons. The first, directed toward accounts of legal and moral responsibility, is that these make it possible to assign both credit and blame to individuals for their own actions. On this point, there is a clear connection between the views one takes on human action and the views one takes on individual rights and duties within the political order. Thus, when Locke writes on the meaning of human personality he hones in at undue length on the sensible point that continuous consciousness is the hallmark of personal identity.[1] Shortly thereafter, he concludes that only that continuous sense of personality allows the individual to be the proper object of reward and punishment today for actions undertaken previously.[2] What good would it do, for deterrence or retribution, if the law were to inflict punishment on some person (that is, sensible body) if the conscious agent that directed its actions had migrated to some other physical vessel? Indeed, what would the world look like if the naïve account of human behavior were systematically wrong? One shudders.

Second, these assumptions about rational behavior allow the orderly inference from judgments about individual preferences and behavior to judgments about social states of affairs. Why, if individual choices are disjointed or chaotic, should we have confidence in any social judgments that flow from any aggregation of these individual preferences? One hallmark of standard economic and legal theory is methodological individualism, in which all statements about the welfare of complex organization—corporations, partnerships, unions, states—are at bottom statements about the behavior of and relationships among the people that compose them. Social utility does not hover over individuals or societies like some disembodied being. Rather, a systematic evaluation of the consequences of certain rules on the individuals in these collectivities is needed to develop any judgment about alternative social states.

Working that task requires a coherent account of preferences. More specifically, notwithstanding the differences between the stringent standard of Pareto superiority or the somewhat more forgiving Kaldor-Hicks standard,[3] both theories allow for, indeed require, social judgments to be made in light of individual desires and preferences. The basic point of this theory is to allow the aggregation of preferences across individuals without running into insuperable problems of interpersonal comparisons of utility. If, however, individuals' desires and preferences are unstable and erratic, then this entire system of valuation quickly dissolves. Both the Pareto and the Kaldor-Hicks standard fall to this single objection.

In order to steer clear of these unfortunate tangles, Gary Becker has incorporated the traditional commonsense accounts of human preferences into his basic economic model: "[A]ll human behavior can be viewed as involving participants who [1] maximize their utility [2] from a stable set of preferences and [3] accumulate an optimal amount of information and other inputs in a variety of markets."[4] That position does not commit one to the indefensible position that once someone prefers steak, he always prefers steak. Rather, "the preferences that are assumed to be stable do not refer to market goods and services, like oranges, automobiles, or medical care, but to underlying objects of choice that are produced by each household using market goods and services, their own time, and other inputs. These underlying preferences are defined over fundamental aspects of life, such as health, prestige, sensual pleasure, benevolence or envy, that do not always bear a stable relation to market goods and services."[5]

One possible reading of this position is that it adopts a "thin" model of preferences, such that one cannot draw any inferences about what goods are liked without some further specification of "the underlying objects of choice." For if these are left completely untethered, then it becomes unclear how the analysis moves from a description of overt preferences in the market for goods and services to an understanding of the deeper preferences that drive them. But there is no reason to accept that view because it is possible to link those deeper preferences to the necessities of survival and reproduction that are so central to evolutionary biology. In that context, the stability of preferences is not some extra like whitewall tires or fancy trim. Rather, stability of preferences over time counts as the one key element for making sure that the cycle of life can repeat from one generation to another. Let parents waver in the protection of their young, and the ravages of natural selection will quickly result in their demise in competition with other creatures better able to keep their heads, hearts, and hands together over the long haul. Indeed, for so much of the history of human life the idea of "preference" does seem inapposite, not because of humans' instability, but because of the need for quick action to meet the fixed imperatives for survival faced by all living creatures. The need to breathe; the need for food; the need for flight. The emotional states that induce these necessary behaviors—the fear, the hunger, the rage—are not creatures of conscious choice, which could easily prove to be too slow and uncertain for the occasion. Rather, they are hard-wired responses that conscious choice can override only with extreme difficulty, if at all: in cases of dire emergency speed beats judgment.[6] Anyone, no matter how primed for the occasion, will jump back when a rattlesnake strikes, even if they know for certain it is housed in a sturdy glass container.[7]

How human (or animal) behaviors are constituted takes into account the costs of error in response to any lethal attack. Leaping away from an attack that never comes is a small cost relative to the failure to respond to the attack that does come. So the dominant strategy is to react first as if the attack were real and to reflect about one's good fortune later if it is not. So long as one choice dominates, it is inefficient to leave the associated behavior to conscious, but plodding, faculties. Higher error rates are tolerable in other settings, where the gains from planning and reflection allow for levels of achievement that no preprogrammed instinctive response could hope to duplicate.

The intersection of these two spheres of human behavior, conscious and instinctive, is not seamless. It surely makes sense for evolution to have added the higher cognitive powers atop the more primitive human infrastructure. But the juxtaposition of two inconsistent forms of behavior necessarily creates some tension along the boundary, tension that doubtless manifests itself in odd forms of behavior in some particular settings. It also suggests that human capacities will not conform to any stripped-down rational choice model for the simple reason that the evolution of the human brain did not start with a comprehensive organization, but rather developed highly specific responses to particular needs, which explains why, as the cognitive psychologists love to remind us, most untrained individuals always trip up over simple questions of probability theory—at least until coached.[8]

Whatever these deficiencies might be in the patchwork creation of human intelligence, the offsetting gains from having two interlocking systems are enormous. To require conscious thought to regulate breathing is suicidal; to allow unconscious thought to block the emergence of the higher powers of calculation and speech puts the kibosh on all distinctive human behavior. But it is important to keep any marginal anomalies in perspective. Their presence hardly shows that human beings have unstable preferences. It only shows that evolution, which can only work with what was there before, does not create perfect human beings even with the powerful pressures of natural selection. Where one goes depends in large measure on where one has been.

It is quite striking that most of the objections against classical liberalism do not come from a reinterpretation of the biological evidence, but rest instead on a variety of hypothetical conundrums that do more to raise possibilities than to make any concrete descriptive statements about how human behavior works. In dealing with these multiple objections to the classical theory, I take one of two tacks, or sometimes both. The first is to argue that the concerns that are raised are overblown (as is the case, for example, with adaptive preferences or incommensurability) relative to the problems that every social (and legal) system must cope with: the need to control force and fraud, to secure coordination for certain collective projects, and to prevent the evils of faction and strategic behavior. The second is to recognize that the descriptive claims have some indisputable truth (as with claims of limited altruism and rationality), only to insist that these behavioral corrections to the naïve theory of rational self-interest *strengthen* the model of rights and duties developed in chapter 2. Either way, the set of complexities that are introduced do not require a movement toward greater government regulation, let alone to some form of socialism. We have to learn to live with ambiguity. We do not have to revolutionize social institutions to do it.

Adaptive Preferences

The phenomenon of adaptive preferences—"the adjustment of wants to possibilities"—is said to offer one reason why the standard theories of utilitarian calculation will not work to describe human behavior.[9] The nature of the fundamental difficulty that adaptive preferences is said to pose to all forms of utilitarian behavior is set out by Jon Elster as follows:

> [W]hy should individual want satisfaction be the criterion of justice and
> social choice when individual wants themselves may be shaped by a process
> that preempts the choice? And, in particular, why should the choice between
> feasible options take account of individual preferences if people tend to ad-
> just their aspirations to their possibilities? For the utilitarian, there would
> be no welfare loss if the fox were excluded from consumption of the grapes,
> since he thought them sour anyway. But of course the cause of his holding
> the grapes to be sour was his conviction that he would be excluded from

consumption of them, and then it is difficult to justify the allocation by reference to his preferences.[10]

Having set out this basic position, Elster is careful to distinguish this view of adaptive preferences from other common phenomenon that are more easily explained with the traditional rational choice framework, most notably "preference change through learning and experience."[11] Indeed, it could hardly be otherwise. Individuals are constantly exposed to new information, no matter what their set of past choices, and it would be odd in the extreme for them to ignore what they have learned, even if they did not seek to learn it in the first place. It is always sensible to update one's estimation of the world based on new information; the only question is how fast and reliable that process can take place.

The tale about sour grapes, however, is said not to fall into that category, for the fox receives no new information about the grapes that he is unable to eat; yet he is said to conclude that they were not worth eating in the first place. We thus have the apparent paradox of grapes that receive high value if obtained, but only low value if they are not. How can one decide whether having the grapes is good or bad if their value depends on the fate of the fox's quest? One possible answer to this query is to allow a simple expected utility calculation that takes into account alternate states of the world—one in which the grapes could be got at and eaten, the other in which they could not—for each of which it assigns the grapes different values depending on whether they are consumed. That split-mind preserves the appearance of expected utility calculation but forces the entire exercise into modes that have no intuitive appeal. The difficulty here lies not with the decision procedure for dealing with adaptive preferences, but with the supposition that preferences are ever formed along these lines. On this point it is best to be careful. The origin of the position is said to go back to one of Aesop's fables—"The Fox and the Grapes."[12] That fable is short, but properly read its greatness does not so much as hint of the psychological problem that it is said to introduce. It reads in its entirety as follows:

> A famished Fox saw clusters of ripe Grapes hanging from a trellised vine. She resorted to all her tricks to get at them, but worried herself in vain, for she could not reach them. At last she turned away, beguiling herself of her disappointment and saying: "The grapes are sour, and not as ripe as I thought."

The first point to note is that Aesop tells us early on that the grapes were as a matter of fact ripe. Within the traditional naturalist universe, that description scarcely requires extended comment. These grapes are firm, juicy, and full of flavor with the high nutritious content that foxes crave. There is no need for a complex evolutionary story here. The fox acts in a rational manner to get the grapes, but she is unable to do so. We are not told explicitly whether her initial efforts to reach the grapes were well advised given their distance from the ground, or indeed any other circumstance, but the fact that she "resorted to all her tricks" does not suggest a fox that was, so to speak, off on a wild goose chase. But we do know that the fox gives up the quest and refuses to continue to expend further good energy on an unattainable result, a rational response. She then rationalizes her failure by saying that these grapes are sour anyway, which leaves it open why she tried so hard to get them in the first place.

Only the most literal and wooden reading of the story dovetails with Elster's account of adaptive preferences, which makes it appear that the fox no longer thinks the grapes are ripe, or that, less plausibly, if ripe, are no longer valued as objects. The whole point of the tale is that *nothing* has changed about either the grapes or the fox's evaluation of them, much less her freestanding preference for eating ripe grapes. The psychological subtlety of this brief tale lies in the fox's failed effort at self-deception as a way to soften her disappointment at not getting what she so desperately wants. It is an effort to maintain personal equilibrium in the face of evident defeat. The story pays homage to the stubbornness of preferences, not their adaptive nature. When people to this day shout "Sour grapes!" no one thinks of adaptive preferences. Everyone understands that the phrase is used to describe people who talk down (or bad mouth) the unattained object of their desire in order to minimize their loss. The image gains its poignancy precisely because it shows the extent to which people will go to cover their signs of hurt and defeat, both to themselves (recall the fox is alone) and to others. But let those grapes be blown from the tree and placed at the feet the fox, and she will gobble them up with the greatest of glee. She could not survive a cold winter acting on the strength of adaptive preferences.

The question, then, is what should be made of this account of adaptive preferences in our understanding of choice and behavior. Elster speculates that it renders more complex traditional accounts of autonomy and freedom, precisely because possibilities now reshape desires. He first quotes a passage in which Isaiah Berlin rejects any program to make freedom depend on desire: "If degrees of freedom were a function of the satisfaction of desires, I could increase freedom as effectively by eliminating desires as by satisfying them; I could render men (including myself) free by conditioning them to losing the original desire which I have decided not to satisfy."[13] Elster seeks cautiously to rehabilitate the position that Berlin debunks by suggesting that freedom is served when people are able to condition themselves to want only what they are able to get.

Two strategic possibilities cast doubt on that program. First, other people will try to persuade them to shrink their desires in order to get them to shrink their rights. Second, some people will inflate their desires in order to expand their rights through the political process. People should adjust their expectations to meet circumstances, but only in the context of a coherent framework of rights. Berlin's observation has to be right, for otherwise no account of rights could be stable if an intense set of desires adds to the rights of self-interested individuals. The incentives for perverse behavior are too great.

Nor does the concept of adaptive preferences come into its own in any empirical setting. Elster offers us the "conjectural" example of an individual who, while a free civilian, ranks his preferences thusly: free individual, camp prisoner, camp guard.[14] But once in prison, he now prefers to be a camp guard to a prisoner. Perhaps so, but the obvious explanation for this is the one that Elster has already ruled out. Being a prisoner makes him aware of the hardship he faces so he updates his preferences on the strength of new information, just as rational choice theory would have it. His second example fares no better. There are, as he acknowledges, lots of complexities to explain the migration of people during the industrial revolution from country to city and often back again.[15] But once the obvious pieces of the puzzle are put into place, it is not clear what adaptive preferences add to the overall mix. Explanations that talk about the relative costs (including the risk of death from external causes) of living in the two settings help explain the net flows in one direction or another, even if they do not explain the discrete motivations of particular individuals. People leave the farm because farming is both dangerous and lonely; they return to the farm when unemployment and disease rise in urban settings. Their movements may be hastened in one direction or the other by policies that drive them off the land or out of cities. The explanations take into account multiple causes, and any social account works in the aggregate and can easily miss decisive concerns that control in individual case. Yet the rates of change do not depend on the detailed psychological portraits of particular individuals, nor on peculiar elements of individual experiences (a parent injured at home, a desire to marry, and so on).

The tortured introduction of adaptive preferences into the discussion suggests the lack of both conceptual coherence and empirical grounding. Nonetheless an appeal to these preferences offers no reason to depart from the traditional accounts of individual behavior, generally rational and self-interested, which undergirds the classical liberal conception of the relationship between the individual and the state. Nonetheless, it seems clear that this idea lives on in the legal literature where the argument takes the form that the mere official expression of a legal sentiment in legislation will be sufficient to alter the preference sets that individuals have toward the subject of the legislation. It is said, for example, that the decisions in *Brown v. Board of Education*[16] and the passage of the Civil Rights Act of 1964 might have gone a long way to legitimate a public consensus against racial discrimination in public accommodations and employment; or that public antismoking campaigns can persuade impressionable youths to change their basic preference structures.[17]

Treated as a positive matter, the claim founders on empirical difficulties. It is of course true that the *content* of a case or a statute may persuade people of its soundness—this is true for all statements. So too the coercive effect of a statute or common law decision will change behavior by raising the costs of some form of conduct and lowering it for others. But it hardly follows that the mere fact of the passage of a statute or the publication of a decision, divorced from these consequences, is sufficient to change attitudes or preferences. The legal decisions to eliminate discrimination in public life were met not with changed preferences among the diehards, but with resignation by some and massive resistance by others. Campaigns to decry the hazards of smoking sometimes facilitate a fashionable form of rebellion against parents and other authority figures.

The point is made with some clarity by the recent Dutch legislation that legalizes prostitution and renames prostitutes "sex workers."[18] Two points already seem clear about the legislation. First, the change in the name does nothing to legitimize the activity in the eyes of ordinary people. The taboo remains, for "Legalization does not mean acceptance." Prostitutes still find it difficult to get credit and insurance from ordinary sources who fear the impact on their reputation, and the business of prostitution is still regarded as falling at the edges of social life. Nor should there be any surprise in this. No matter what the name, prostitution continues to have sordid connotations and connections. It is linked with lust, not love; customers demand that it be conducted in relative secrecy; in many cases it is thought to undermine marriages and carries with it the risk of sexually transmitted diseases. None of this changes with cosmetic alteration of its name or the legalization of its practice. People's views of legislators may well change, but it is likely that they will continue to think of prostitution afterward pretty much they way they did before. It is perfectly coherent to be in favor of the legalization of a practice that most people want as little to do with as possible.

By the same token, we should not overlook the familiar effects of mandated changes in legal status. Outside the law it is possible to operate under a veil of anonymity, even from one's own spouse and children. But once practices are made legal they are exposed to taxation, regulation, inspection, and public disclosure, which raise the cost of doing business and may well drive elements of the practice further underground, into more dangerous territory. All this seems to have happened with the Dutch experience, for one effect of the law has been to reduce the use of brothels, a protected environment, and to force the trade into ordinary hotels, under the protection of pimps. Sadly, the law of unintended consequences holds for social legislation as well. In principle, there might be some pure adaptive effect, but so long as all regulation changes, up or down, the set of sanctions on the target behavior, these will never be isolated. As a descriptive matter, it looks to be a losing strategy to stress adaptive preferences when they are swamped by more potent and more familiar effects.

Nor, as a normative matter, should we be distressed with the failures to inculcate preference changes through public legislation. Private persuasion still remains a viable option, and individuals can easily learn from their mistakes and update their prior beliefs on the basis of new information in the old rational choice way. Social change does not depend only on government, but can be stoked by ordinary changes in technology and price, backed by a willingness to market the changes in question. These changes can be either slow or rapid, depending on the level of support they receive from the independent decisions of lots of autonomous individuals. These changes do take place on all matters of social morality. Think only of the sanitized television sit-com of the 1950s (where mom and dad always slept in separate beds) in relation to contemporary programs depicting fast-paced singles talking of their sexual exploits. The difference between the two reflects changes in social preferences to which millions contributed, but no one person or group controlled. For its part, regulation had powerful but indirect effects. The rise of cable undermined the dominance of network television and permitted *Sex and the City* and *The Sopranos* to make it on HBO.

Indeed, we should be relieved that campaigns of public education fail. Education to some is indoctrination to others; and no matter what the substantive cause, the risk of an organized state monopoly in the realm of ideas is far greater than the risk that some people have stubborn or unreflective preferences—so long as they cannot impose their will on others by force. We should, moreover, breathe a collective sigh of relief at the impotence of governments to shape preferences by the passage of new laws. Should the mere passage of Jim Crow laws legitimate the practices of racial segregation? Should women before suffrage rejoice in their denial of the vote? Once the state is no longer neutral with respect to preferences, it can intervene on the side of the bad guys just as easily as on the side of the good. The relative immunity of preference formation from state legitimation protects basic liberties at least as often as it offends them.

Mistaken Preferences

The idea of adaptive preferences is closely allied with the problem of mistaken preferences. In its narrowest sense, the problem is not subversive of the standard liberal order. Rather, it only refers to the fact that people often say one thing when they intend another. In light of these errors, the question often arises in the contractual setting as to who should bear the risk of this miscommunication. Here the initial premise is that the law defines a contract as "a *manifestation* of an intention to act or refrain from acting in a specified way, so made as to justify a promisee in understanding that a commitment has been made."[19] The use of the term "manifestation" conveys that in the first instance the risk of error falls on the person who makes it. That rule encourages the reliance that other people can place on the spoken word and thereby reduces the chance of error in the first place. Occasionally, in those cases when the person who receives the communication is aware of the error, then the risk of that mistake will fall on him. Thus, if A says he offers his horse for sale when he wishes to sell his cow, and B knows of that error when he accepts the offer, they are bound for the sale of the cow, not the horse, consistent with their joint subjective intentions.[20] B could have revealed the confusion and thus protected his own interest.

In some cases, however, the analysis of revealed preferences is designed to address more than the occasional cases of mistake in the expression of a preference. In ways that parallel the discussion of adaptive preferences, the question arises whether unrevealed preferences should count even for market actors who make no slip between tongue and lip. Cass Sunstein states the point forcefully:

> In its standard form, a preference is supposed to be something that lies behind choices and that is more abstract and general than choices are. But what lies behind choices is not a thing but an unruly amalgam of things—

aspirations, tastes, physical states, responses to existing roles and norms, values, judgments, emotions, drives, beliefs, whims. The interaction of these forces will produce outcomes of a particular sort in accordance with the particular context. Hence we might say that *preferences are constructed, rather than elicited, by social situations,* in the sense that they are very much a function of the setting and the prevailing social norms.[21]

The italicized conclusion does not follow, however, from the previous descriptive account, for while roles and norms have powerful social origins, emotions, drives, and physical states, their biological constraints tend to resist the forces of socialization. It is, therefore, a mistake to conclude that preferences are "socially constructed," that is, sufficiently malleable to yield to systematic reformation. As noted earlier, individuals should, and do, update their preferences on the strength of new information. But from that it hardly follows that the complex origins of individual behavior give the state an open invitation to intervene to change the "social meaning," as it is sometimes called, of individual behaviors. Perhaps some people smoke only because their peers do.[22] But that hardly precludes the possibility that other people smoke because they like its taste, even in the solitude of their own homes. And it overlooks, ironically, the huge social pressures that work to encourage quitting. Anyone who disapproves of smoking (as I do) is free to argue with smokers that their conduct could lead to their own demise, and individual owners can express their preferences by excluding smokers from their premises, which happens every time a hotel designates certain floors as nonsmoking. Perhaps certain individuals form the wrong stereotypes about women, blacks, or homosexuals. If so, then those who find these characterizations offensive are free to argue against them. It has been an invitation often accepted. Yet it is just here that one can detect the dangerous undercurrents of Sunstein's preoccupation with reforming or ignoring dubious preferences. All of the bad preferences are associated with the political positions or personal behaviors of which he disapproves. His article contains no mention of the unruly forces that shape the minds of socialists, feminists, civil rights activists, or liberal democrats. We should all beware of basing a general theory on the operation of preferences by thinking as suspect only the preferences of privileged individuals whose conduct is said to marginalize and subordinate others.

The net effect of this position, however, is to use the ostensibly neutral doctrine of preference formation to support one side of contentious political issues. That effort should be strongly resisted. So long as the social critics fall prey to the same unruly amalgam of influences as the rest of us, then they should be as uneasy about their own judgments as they ask the rest of us to be about ours. A divided society will never have a sensible social debate if one side is never forced to take the risk that it will be proved wrong. If deformed preferences can influence the smoker, then they can influence the antismoking activist. If they can upset the judgment of the misogynist, then they can distort the judgment of the feminist, radical or otherwise.

Lest we lose sight of the ultimate issue of the scope of law, any complex multidimensional account of preference formation, uniformly applied, does nothing in itself to justify state power to ban or require certain practices that might otherwise be left to individual choice. Nor does it justify the use of more subtle actions designed to alter preferences by changing the social environment in which these are expressed. One example that neatly sets out the conflict between the two positions was the recent decision of the U.S. Post Office to touch up the portrait of Jackson Pollock used on the then new thirty-three-cent stamp to remove the Camel cigarette that habitually dangled from his lip.[23] For the sake of argument, assume that Pollock's estate consented to the change in the picture out of a burst of high-minded social conscience, so that there is no unauthorized use of Pollock's name or likeness. It seems improper to say that this practice is justified because it will lead impressionable youth to believe that clean living and artistic genius go well together. The stamp is a crude government fraud designed to deny the common belief that smoking releases creative energy. It cuts against the belief that free and independent individuals have within themselves the capacity to make judgments as to how to lead their own lives.

So what, then, might the government do? One possibility is to publish Pollock with the cigarette and then to urge individuals to abandon this practice by noting how his unstable life may well have contributed to his untimely demise. Yet here we have the government seeking to lobby one side of the issue, and doing so with revenues collected from individuals who may well take quite the opposite view of the matter. The standard doctrines against "compelled speech" generally prohibit the state from setting up legal arrangements that force one group of individuals to subsidize speech for causes in which they do not believe or indeed oppose.[24] Why then use federal power to support one side of a contested issue when it is possible to use stamps that picture birds and flowers, or even presidents, but that do not commit the state to one side or another in the political debate? Ideally, once the government decides to honor artists, then it should have to rank them by their artistic merit and reproduce them in their characteristic poses. I suspect that the administrative problems preclude judicial intervention on this porous standard. But even if the Post Office's revised version of the Pollock stamp escapes legal censure, it blurs the line between history and propaganda. The moment that the state has power to cure suspect preferences, the risk of state monopoly on matters of thought looms large: recall again the history of Jim Crow. The risk of legislative capture is so great that we should never start down that collective road: let private parties launch their own campaigns to rid the nation of untoward preferences and practices. The state should confine itself to the antifraud mission, no matter who speaks or for what end.

Intransitive Preferences

The theory of rational behavior also runs into criticism on the ground that preferences are not transitive. Transitive preferences are needed to order human behavior. Thus, it seems to be a minimum condition for rational conduct that where A prefers x to y, and y to z, he also prefers x to z.[25] From this it follows that if A is observed to have taken x when y is available, then he cannot also reveal a preference for y over x.[26] Similarly, if A prefers x to y, then the introduction of some third choice, z, should not lead to a reversal in the initial preference ordering between x and y, for if it did, then we achieve the result that the transitivity axiom prohibits, namely, that A in one breath prefers x to y only in the next to prefer y to x, given that his order is now y > z > x.[27]

Initially, it would be very odd to think that this cluster of propositions played an important part in ordinary life, for if preferences were allowed to cycle through the various permutations then all choices would be deeply arbitrary and manifestly unstable, if they could be made at all. Indeed, it seems clear that individuals who act on intransitive preferences are condemned to poverty. If y is preferred to z, then A should pay something to get from z to y; and likewise from y to x. But once at x, then A should pay something to return to z, where the cycle can begin again with A poorer than before.[28]

Even so, efforts are often made to identify this form of instability. As is so often in this area, the illustrations are both elegant and imaginative. One prosaic example assumes that someone is offered fruit at a dinner party.[29] The initial choice is between a small apple and an orange, in which case the guest would prefer the orange. But if offered a large apple and an orange, she would choose to take the large apple. Alas, once given the straight up choice between the large and small apple, she might violate the rules of transitivity and choose the smaller apple to the larger one, say out of a concern for general etiquette. The question is whether this hypothetical sequence of behaviors, if observed, undermines the intransitivity of preferences.

Clearly not—for context matters, so that what is at stake is not only what one wants but how one is perceived by others in a public setting, and must therefore be seen to leave something from this regulated commons for other guests. The example recalls the impact of the Lockean proviso— "as much again and as good"—which, if strictly applied, would imply that no one could eat anything. The implicit social norm thus allocates one piece of fruit to each guest, at least in the simplest case where there are n pieces of fruit and n guests. This informal commonsense crops up in countless settings, and typically the problem is solved by coupling a first possession rule with a limitation on the size of the initial take. When a group of individuals comes to a table without assigned seating, the first possession rule may let each person take any seat as yet unoccupied. It may be appropriate at as well to save an adjacent seat for one's spouse or friend. But no one has the option to sit on one chair and to place his feet on the next, requiring the last guest to stand throughout the entire meal.

With all this said, contretemps over the three pieces of fruit may be more subtle than this: the first guest may decide to trade off desired consumption for desired prestige by taking a smaller piece to appear generous, or at least not greedy, in the eyes of other guests. But once both dimensions of the choice are made explicit, then any concern with intransitive preferences disappears. The guest could, for example, give a value of 10 to the large apple, 8 to the orange, and 6 to the small apple. But when the three are presented at one time, she could assign a social weight of 10 to being seen taking the small apple, 4 to being seen taking the orange, and 2 to being seen taking the large apple. By simple addition, a value of 16 for the small apple trumps the 12 assigned to either the large apple or the orange. Of course these numbers are arbitrary, but hardly implausible. No fatal discontinuity in preferences here.

An alternative explanation for this switching behavior could rely solely on imperfect information. An isolated guest of average appetite might not know whether to eat a large or small apple. But the addition of a third alternative gives her a focal point that informs her choice and thus reverses her ranking. Thus, A may choose the smaller apple when only two apples are present. But add a still larger apple to the table and she switches from the smallest to what once was the larger apple but is now the middle-sized apple. The new information tells her as an eater with an average appetite to change her choice. For this example to make sense, that third choice should not be just an experimental contrivance. In order to supply the needed reference point for her decision, it should reflect the real demands that others have for its consumption. Yet once it does, then the ostensible puzzle disappears.

The importance of context is also critical in evaluating the legal implications of these ostensible reversals. In one experiment Mark Kelman, Yuval Rottenstreich, and Amos Tversky examine how ordinary individuals (and potential jurors) classify homicides.[30] A description is given of a homicide in which a woman kills her husband by poisoning, and then seeks to mislead the police as to the cause of death. Matters are further confused because there is evidence that the defendant believed that the decedent had sought to molest her seventeen-year-old daughter—his stepdaughter. Cutting in the opposite direction is evidence that she stood to inherit a substantial sum of money from his death. The tale was told to three different groups of individuals, under three different legal regimes, with these verdicts:

	Percentage Choosing		
	Manslaughter	Murder	Murder with Special Circumstances
Group 1	47	53	—
Group 2	19	39	42
Group 3	52	48	—

For Group 1, there were only two offenses, murder and manslaughter; 47 percent chose manslaughter and 53 percent chose murder. But Group 2 was instructed as well on a more severe category—murder with special circumstances—that covered cases of killing for financial gain and that depicted the use of poison as exceptionally heinous, manifesting exceptional depravity. Sure enough, the number of individuals who chose manslaughter plummeted to 19 percent, with 39 percent of the remainder choosing murder and 42 percent choosing murder with special circumstances.

One obvious inference is that the introduction of the third alternative led some people in Group 2 to switch their judgment from manslaughter to murder, so that the choice between them was now dependent on a third variable. That would be correct if the three choices here were invariant with context, as is the case when a large apple is added to a plate on which sit a small apple and an orange. But in this case the conclusion does not follow because the *content* of each choice does change with the additional information. The results square with how we should expect and want conscientious jurors to act when preference reversals play no role in their behavior.

The basic point is that the *meaning* of these offenses depends not on words in isolation, but on their legal context. The initial two-part classification suggests an uneasy break between manslaughter and murder, where the two crimes cover the entire domain. Because the words themselves do not draw the needed line, these individuals must do so themselves. Say ordinary individuals array homicides on an implicit scale from 1 to 100, and most individuals draw the line between the two offenses at 50. That mode of thought would lead to what was observed in the first trial. What remains is some disagreement as to where the line should be drawn, and some disagreement on which side of that (moving) line the case falls. The upshot is an even split.

Now once the category of murder with special circumstances is introduced in the second example, that space from 1 to 100 has to be divided into three categories. At this point, someone whose judgment hovers about the middle would find it harder to defend a judgment of manslaughter, and easier to move to murder, now that the cut-off points have changed. In and of itself, that shift might lead most individuals to place this case in the middle category of murder. But the special circumstance instruction does more than take murder into the middle category. It also tells what elements bump a homicide into the most serious category—poisoning for financial gain—without allowing mitigation for the provocation of having been upset at the prospect that the victim had molested her daughter. What is at stake, therefore, is not simply a change in private preferences, but first a change in legal meaning and next in the legal rules used to identify implicating and exculpating factors. It is no longer permissible to regard poisoning as no worse than killing with a deadly weapon, or killing for greed as no worse than killing for hatred.

The authors tried, commendably, to control for these variables with the third group, which was told of the requirements for special circumstances murder but told further that it was not part of their law. That group gravitated back to the behavior of Group 1, with 52 percent finding manslaughter and 48 percent manslaughter. It could well be that the rejection of the special circumstances doctrine communicated to the jury the view that the state affirmatively did not regard either poisoning and greed as an aggravating circumstance, so that, paradoxically, this crime would now be seen, at the margin, as less severe than in the first case, when that question was at least left open. The entire pattern looks more like individuals trying to understand what the law requires. It does not look like a form of psychological preference reversal. Instructing juries in a criminal case is no simple matter, but here the lesson these experiments teach is that jury instructions matter and that these should be framed with as much simplicity and precision as possible—an objective that makes sense no matter how preferences are formed.

Incommensurable Preferences

The ranking of preferences proves from yet another perspective: the moment that two elements must be compared in order to make a choice, it is frequently claimed that the *incommensurable* nature of the choice precludes the reliance on the transitivity axiom. The basic point is that the rank ordering of any set of preferences requires that they be reduced to a single measure so that various elements can be compared and contrasted. But once it is determined that the relevant choices lie in different domains, then these relationships do not hold. Thus it is said that "A and B are incommensurate if it is neither true that one is better than the other nor true that they are of equal value."[31] If that is so, then it becomes difficult to make the kinds of informal adjustments that I suggested in the matter of the fruit: trade off one kind of good (appetite) against another (social standing). It is not that all choices are precluded. In a world in which matters of etiquette played no role, for example, we could assume that someone would prefer a dozen apples to one apple, because if worse came to worst he could trade or sell eleven of them in order to purchase something else of value, even if he could only consume one. But let the choice be made over two variables that inhabit two separate ranges, then the simple rank ordering is no longer possible. The decisionmaking process becomes ever messier and less satisfactory with compound choices that require judgments that involve three or more domains at the same time. Sometimes the point is elevated to the level of a Kantian imperative, where the problem of incommensurability is presented in only two dimensions. "In the kingdom of ends everything has either a price or a dignity. Whatever has price can be replaced by something else as its equivalent; . . . whatever is above all price, and therefore admits of no equivalent, has a dignity."[32]

The initial point of the response goes to the familiar question: Suppose that all this complex psychology supplied an accurate portrait of the individual mind? People who are faced with the choice between work and leisure, or love and money, or playing basketball and practicing the piano simply could make the needed comparisons between alternatives. Clearly, we do observe them making frequent decisions over lots of complex choices no matter how flawed their decision process turns out to be. So the question that then arises is what, if anything, could a third party regulator do to improve the quality of these decisions. He faces all the problems of incommensurability in deciding whether the hypothetical decisionmaker should eat or sleep. In addition, he suffers from the insuperable disadvantage of not being privy to the any of the subjective information that each person brings in making his own choices. Legal intervention costs money; legal intervention opens up new avenues for abuse, including totalitarian excesses by government officials who seek to determine preferences on personal matters.

The conclusion seems clear. Let people be as conflicted and indecisive as this portrait of human behavior suggests and, when all is said and done, *nothing* moves the appropriate boundary between private choice and state action. It may well be, apropos the discussion of prostitution, that cash payment is inappropriate in certain situations: spouses should not use cash payments whenever they have been inconsiderate to each other; the neglect of an important social engagement with a friend is better met with not with cash, but with a sincere letter of apology accompanied by a dozen roses. All of this can be granted. But even if intimate and business obligations are experienced in different ways, it hardly follows that the boundary between them should be policed by the law, which in this context is likely to have a strongly counterproductive effect. It would be foolish, for example, to ban prenuptial agreements on the ground that romance and business fall into separate domains. It is best to let the parties sort out matters as they see fit. Here, as in so many other areas, the introduction of legal compulsion does nothing to sort out the mix but only complicates matters. If cash payments are utterly inappropriate in certain settings, then paradoxically something is *lost* by prohibiting them to be made. Under the old regime, in the right circumstances the decision not to offer or use cash could be regarded as a sign of social savvy. But that possibility of informed sorting is eliminated when the cash option is banned by law. To mandate good deeds makes it impossible to achieve the right result by making it uncertain that good will and personal thoughtfulness lie behind the particular act.

There is, however, no reason to credit the psychological paralysis implicit in this account of incommensurability. Individuals in the course of their lives reduce all components of choice to a single metric (which is why we call this problem one of incommensurability), and then decide which path maximizes the goals that they wish to achieve. The one candidate most worthy of consideration for this exalted state is that of "utility," which becomes a convenient placeholder for all forms of subjective satisfaction, no matter how differently these are experienced as psychological states.

In making this observation it is important to keep kindred conceptions distinct. In particular, wealth is not the metric people use to place value on the decisions they make with their own lives. Indeed, they are quite happy to trade away wealth for happiness. Over some domains, to be sure, people will seek to make as much wealth as possible, not as a good in itself, but as a means to obtaining a higher level of subjective satisfaction. Wealth thus becomes one standard medium through which to pursue utility. In those cases in which people believe that more wealth is a bad—or more commonly, bad for their children—they may follow in the footsteps of Andrew Carnegie and Bill Gates and give all or most of it away to a charitable foundation that bears their own name.

In light of these preliminaries, no special legal difficulties are posed for matters of individual choice: each person moves back and forth across the domains of wealth and utility as he or she pleases. Thus the strong utilitarian does not imagine that people suffer fits of paralysis when required to compare goods in different social domains of their social lives. In this context, moreover, "goods" does not refer only to commodities or other exchangeable things of value; the term also refers to relationships, experiences, and the intangibles of self-esteem and self-respect, to love and affection—all the stuff that "money cannot buy." The basic problem is to chart a path among these alternatives when the constraints of scarcity—measured in dollars, time, or emotional energy—make it impossible to satisfy all wants (or needs) simultaneously.

Abstractly, this task sounds formidable, but the apparent ease with which most choices, even choices across separate domains, are made in practice should offer some comfort. By ordinary observation, most people do not regret most decisions they make: a mother may stay an extra hour at work even though she will have to miss her ten-year-old's band concert, or she may come home early from a trip out of town to attend that same concert. To act, she has to decide whether on this occasion the family engagement is more important than the business engagement. It is not always the simplest of things to do, and people often resort to readily made presumptions to help order their choices. We tend to favor family events that take place after working hours, and business events that take place during working hours. But we also have rules that allow the schedules to be altered (perhaps, with compensating time supplied to the employer) to take into account the milestone of a wedding, a bar mitzvah, or baptism. Over the long haul, the great puzzle is not why these choices are thought hard in the abstract, but why routinely they turn out to be so easy to make in the concrete.

The key, I think, to making (and understanding) these decisions is to avoid thinking in terms of categorical judgments used to usher in the incommensurability debate: it is hopeless to ask categorically whether we value family more than professional attainments, or a pristine environment more than a warm and safe home. Typically, we value both, so our key decision is never made in the abstract, but always at the margin. When the question is posed grandly, as family versus work, or environmental versus home, it is as though we are allowed to choose between only two points on the private indifference curve, $(1, 0)$ or $(0, 1)$, without having the luxury of any intermediate solutions. In practice, however, we are usually at some point closer to the middle of the range. At that point our task is to adjust the balance to take into account external changes in the overall state of affairs. That choice may be close because we were already in equilibrium. But we usually make some improvement by updating an earlier allocation. With lots of decisions, we can be confident in the overall process even if we remain uneasy about close decisions in individual cases. Here, these cases may well be wrong, but so what? The marginal decisions have the desirable property of being both more difficult and less important.

This model also explains why some stark choices become very difficult to make. Suppose our choice is not whether to come home from work an hour early for a birthday party, but whether to go overseas for six months to secure large financial rewards or professional advancement, which can be used to improve the position of the family back home. With *lumpy* choices, we start to face situations that verge on the difficult $(1, 0)$ versus $(0, 1)$ choices, with high costs both ways. But we do not need any fancy theory of incommensurability to explain why these choices are hard. Discontinuous choices within the family domain (deciding whether to attend the graduation of my son or my daughter, or at the limit of such choices, having to choose as Sophie did between the survival of her son or her daughter) are just as difficult as discontinuous choices across domains (deciding whether to attend the key business retreat or my daughter's graduation), as are difficulties within the business domain (choosing to capitulate or fight a strike). Discontinuity, not incommensurability, is the culprit.

The same point can be made from another direction: Just how many separate domains are there over which choices are incommensurate? Do we have only two domains, one with intimate personal relationships and the second with business relationships; or are these categories endlessly fragmented to take into account the different relationships we have with spouses, children, cousins, friends, partners, and strangers? If so, what prevents the ultimate fragmentation and disintegration of any comparisons between any pair of alternatives? The world will become disconnected in ways that once again do violence to ordinary perceptions of how people think and relate to each other. It is far easier to think of uncertainty and discontinuity as the driving variables, which can be of greater or lesser force, than it is to postulate some large, but arbitrary, number of separate domains of incommensurate choices.

The defenders of incommensurability do not only insist on hard lines between the separate domains for choice. They often claim that it is odd, if not perverse, to seek to make certain kinds of comparisons. Consider the familiar example offered by Joseph Raz and embellished by Margaret Radin, which posits that a man has been offered a job in some distant city which will pay one hundred thousand dollars more per year than his current position.[33] Taking the job, however, means that he will have to live separate from his spouse. Raz's question is whether his decision to take the job should be regarded as a judgment on his part that he prefers one hundred thousand dollars to living with his spouse. Raz finds this conclusion odd, and sees the culprit in the pretense that these two halves of the choice are commensurate with each other. Yet his conclusion in itself seems odd, because he leaves us with no explanation as to how that choice was or should have been made. The better explanation for the apparent anomaly is that our man did not make this choice by himself, but first consulted with his spouse so that their joint decision may well have been that it was "worth it" to sacrifice the companionship for the cash.

So understood, Raz's major mistake lay in his improper specification of the relevant utility functions of both husband and wife. The individual self-interest of the arm's-length transaction gave way to the *interdependent utility functions* of the couple, whereby his utility is positively or negatively influenced by her well-being and vice versa. The right question is not whether the husband values the one hundred thousand dollars more than he values his spouse. It is whether the husband *and* the wife as a team valued, after deliberation, the extra money more than their living together. Raz makes it appear that the husband will spend it all on himself when it is more likely that he will spend on a new house or college tuition for the children. It is too easy to parlay suspicions about misguided egotism into a mistaken finding of incommensurability. Nothing about the calculus of utility binds it to an unwavering view of individual self-interest, which on biological and psychological grounds seems false to the fundamental facts of human experience.

Intertemporal Preferences

Another attack on the utility of individual preferences stresses their temporal instability. At one level, it seems a truism to claim that individual tastes evolve with time. After all, the evolution of preferences should be expected on the strength of new information. In some cases, however, it looks as though other factors can impair judgment. Here the issues could emerge in both the short and the long run.

Turning to the short run first, some recent experimental evidence suggests the existence of a so-called projection bias,[34] by which today's decisions badly predict tomorrow's desires. Individuals who choose summer vacation plans in the dead of winter are likely to pick places that are too warm because they project their present freezing self in some warmer time. Hungry people before lunch will order too much food for their evening meal because, one supposes, their eyes are larger than their stomachs.

Surely these biases do exist, but what should be done to counter them? One possibility is to introduce cooling-off periods to allow individuals who buy in haste to repent before the harm is done. But here again there are multiple complications with this proposal. One danger is that rules of this sort cannot be drafted so as to apply exclusively to the people who suffer from this bias. Some individuals therefore can take advantage of the cooling-off period as a free option that allows them to decide later whether to take the goods. The seller thus finds that the costs of these aborted transactions must be loaded onto those consumers who are happy with their initial choices, the better to preserve the options of the opportunistic few.

Alternatively, some of these options turn out to be of no value to anyone, and thus become a cost of business without any offsetting benefit. I have done no empirical research on this question, but I did ask the pointed question of my mortgage broker whether any of her customers had ever backed out of a mortgage deal during the mandatory cooling-off period, to which her answer was no. The usual frustration, if any, was from the added wait for the funds. Obviously, this casual empiricism is subject to the objection that the results could easily be different in other segments of the market. But if so, then a sensible lender could gain market share by offering his potential borrowers this option, without the statute. If that option is not provided in any unregulated markets, then it appears that biases of this sort are more likely to occur in personal settings, where they are notoriously difficult to regulate. In the end, it is best for everyone to act the maxim: to be forewarned is to be forearmed. Surely it is better for each person to learn these truths about themselves at home than to require warnings at travel agencies and supermarkets on how present background conditions can contaminate choice.

The question of altered preferences assumes a more philosophical hue in dealing with the long run. Here it is common to expect that the desirability of activities may, but need not, alter with age. Some youthful pastimes will not make it past middle age: some hobbies are taken up only after forty. That prosaic point can be made in more dramatic (and more mischievous) fashion by claiming that Epstein today is a different person from Epstein a generation from now. But that psychological claim of discontinuity is again said to supply the opening wedge for state intervention. Let two persons (or at least personas) inhabit the same body over two different times. What is to prevent the younger person, in possession of his body, from doing in his future twin? The clear implication could well be that compulsory savings plans are required to prevent the younger self engaging in systematic neglect of the older and different self some years later.[35] From that observation it is only a short leap to the defense of a state-mandated system of social security or old-age pensions, which then invites all the problems of factional squabbling and systematic underfunding that currently plague the system for perfectly obvious public choice reasons, none of which disappear under this refined view of human personality.

Even with pensions and social security, the public debate is devoid of any reference to clever theories of multiple personalities. Speaking English once again, each of us keeps his own individual retirement accounts and private pension plans. The only other persons for whom I save are not another version of myself but the other members of my immediate family. No one suggests that we randomly pool future persons so that I save for the future person of John Doe who in turn saves for Richard Roe. Any coherent theory of rights and duties has, by definition, to be good over time, and it will work, as noted, only from the Lockean insight of continuous conscious identity as the defining feature of the individual person. (No, sleep does not destroy personal identity.) Unless this conception of personal identity holds firm, I do not have to worry only about the coordination of two people but potentially of an infinite array of them measured in time slices of arbitrary length, none of whom knows anything about the ones to come or cares about the ones just past. No one worries about long-term friends or personal reputations; no one ever bothers to travel to a college reunion with a group of reconstituted strangers; no person ever grieves over the loss of a loved one. The level of personal disintegration is a one-way ticket to the psychological funny farm. It is not a description of an integrated person.

Any workable approach to human nature takes more prosaic lines. Most of us worry about our futures and take steps to protect against the time when we are unable to provide for ourselves. We know, of course, that our preferences might change, but we also know that they will tend to change in predictable ways. I have no doubt that in retirement I shall continue to like to play the piano, read "Science Tuesday" in the *New York Times,* and fume over its editorials on welfare rights or gender equality. I am confident that I shall continue to like Mozart, Gershwin, and the Beatles, and shun rap and atonal music. The intensities may change; some new hobby or activity may enter my life, but what of it? It is not as though I have provided for the future only with a stock of CDs. Most people save large portions of their money in cash or other liquid assets precisely because that form of wealth reduces the burdens on their knowledge of future events. The wealth is good insurance against all contingencies and thus supplies some flexibility in the light of changed circumstances— although even here the prospect of a major personality transformation rates a lot lower in my book than the risk of incapacity or the changing fortunes of one's spouse, children, or friends. But it is a sign of how much we think we know our preferences that people invest in second homes in the dunes and equip them with the kinds of appliances and features that will enhance their future lives. All this makes sense only if each person is one person even over time. Rest assured, just about everyone is.

7 Metapreferences, Relative Preferences, and the Prisoner's Dilemma Game

Complex Preferences

THE DETAILED EXAMINATION OF PREFERENCES in chapter 6 looked at preferences from the inside out. These modern theories of preference formation all seek to undermine two propositions: first, that individuals have some sense of what they desire, and, second, that they are able to act in a consistent fashion to obtain more of what they want, whether in terms of pecuniary benefits or the full range of personal and nonmarket benefits. The point of that deconstruction is to undermine the role of preferences as a determinant of individual behavior and as a basis for the classical liberal order.

The attack on the use of preferences in legal and social theory has also been launched from another quarter. The claim now is that the theory of *individual* preferences does not take into account the difficulties of coordinating the preferences among separate individuals. In some cases, it is said that complex forms of individual psychology require us to think carefully about "preferences about preferences," or metapreferences. The clear implication of this expression is that a simple one-dimensional model of orderly preferences on ordinary goods or services understates the complexity of ordinary human experience. In other cases, the classical theory is attacked on the ground that it does not take into account conceptions of relative preferences for income and other goods—whereby it is said that individuals care less about their absolute levels of wealth, and more about where they stand relative to their fellows in some reference group. Both of these arguments in the end dissolve, I believe, into claims that the standard Prisoner's Dilemma (PD) game represents a challenge that voluntary markets cannot overcome. That basic point is true, for the control of PD games can often yield large social gains. But I also believe that both of these arguments fall short of their intended purpose of discrediting market institutions, insofar as they rely on forced and contrived versions of the PD game. Let us take up the two points in order.

Coordinated or "Meta" Preferences

In his essay "The Impossibility of a Paretian Liberal,"[1] Amartya Sen seeks to show by simple examples why it is impossible to reconcile a belief in the liberty of individual choice with the achievement of social efficiency, as measured by the familiar Paretian standard, which holds that state A of a (two-person) world is superior to state B when at least one prefers state A to state B, and the other is at least indifferent between them. Obviously, state A is Pareto superior if both individuals prefer state A to state B. For these purposes, at least, the fraction of the gain going to each is immaterial.

Sen's attack on the use of this standard revolves around the hypothetical question whether Prude or Lewd, or both, should read D. H. Lawrence's *Lady Chatterley's Lover*. In order for his example to work, each individual has preferences not only about his own well-being but that of the other, a so-called external preference. Prude's first choice is that neither read the book at all, but if push come to shove, he would rather read it himself than have it read by Lewd, who could easily be led astray by its content. His last choice is that both read it. Lewd's first choice is that both men read the book, but if push comes to shove, then Lewd would rather Prude read it in order to open his mind and soften his heart. But if Prude cannot read it, then he would choose to read it himself. His last choice is that neither read the book.

Given these preference orderings, it is evident that the two parties are at loggerheads over whether both or neither read the book. Lewd prefers the former, and Prude the latter. But they do have a limited area of agreement in that both men prefer that Prude not Lewd read the book if only one does. In this austere universe, however, Lewd reasons that he cannot compel Prude (as a free agent) to read the book, so Lewd has no reason not to read it himself. Prude realizes that he cannot stop Lewd (also a free agent) from reading this book, so he sees no point in reading it himself. The principle of liberty is thus said to lead to an outcome that neither prefers: Lewd, not Prude, reads the volume. Sen claims that his example exposes the weakness of the theory of revealed preferences, because neither party is able to realize his first choice when both parties wish to do so.[2] The ostensible difficulty with "revealed preferences" arises solely with the fact that each knows that, as a free man, he is forced to settle for his second best alternative. Sen claims to get a good deal of mileage from this example: "If someone takes the Pareto principle seriously, as economists seem to do, then he has to face problems of consistency in cherishing liberal values, even very mild ones."[3]

But why? The original example did not assume a libertarian universe, for neither of the participants is allowed to trade with the other.[4] Relax the prohibition and allow trade, and the paradox begins to unravel. Now the simplest deal is that Lewd proposes to Prude that Prude read the book and Lewd not. If these are the only choices on the table, then both sides should assent since each is better off than before. The conclusion that one draws from this is not the impossibility of being a Paretian liberal, but the *necessity* of being a Paretian liberal with an unwavering commitment to free trade.

Sen acknowledges the possibility that trade upsets his supposed imbalance, but then tries to shift ground by claiming that on matters of morality both sides will reject trade for moral reasons, making, as lawyers say, the subject matter of the deals *res extra commercium*. "[T]he Prude or the Lewd may refuse to enter such a trade despite utility gain, if he is libertarian enough to see no gain in the 'trade' (namely the 'deal' involving the Prude reading a book that he detests to prevent the Lewd reading it with pleasure)."[5] It is odd of course to call this position "libertarian," since the usual libertarian takes exactly the opposite position, namely, the offense that he takes at someone else's conduct offers no justification for prohibiting that conduct unless it involves the use of force and fraud against another.[6] That said, the complications come in the terms of the trade. If the only options on the table are those set out by Sen, then the deal should go through because both sides benefit from, as it were, this instance of barter. But once side payments are allowed, the outcome then becomes cloudier because now both Prude and Lewd could each bluff a bit in the hopes of getting the other to throw in a side payment to close the deal. Here is one instance in which the use of compensation slows up matters and makes the game more complex.[7]

The supposed moralisms in the case could, however, block the use of side payments just as they block the possibility of barter. For our purposes, however, we can put both cash and barter aside to consider a third possibility not open to the strict libertarian, but open to anyone like myself who thinks that the state may force (at least some) exchanges between private persons. Thus, if Lewd and Prude resent having to consent to a transaction that each regards as immoral, then the state can initiate the transaction by barring Lewd from reading the book and forcing Prude do so, knowing that the compensation needed to make each better off comes from the simultaneous exaction that it imposes on the other. The usual scope of forced exchanges does not extend to exercises of personal liberty, but are confined to the taking of private property when the holdout position of its owner (of land critical to the completion of highway) is largely impregnable. One of the reasons why forced exchanges are limited to property transactions is that no one quite believes that anyone really holds the peculiar preferences that animate Sen's example. But by stripping away all the empirical uncertainty and endowing his imaginary people with interactive preferences that guarantee dissatisfaction and preclude trade, Sen is setting up the ideal circumstance for a guarded extension of the eminent domain option. Of course, his hypothetical could be rejiggered to postulate that both sides loathe state intervention, but then what becomes the point of the case: Why should we demand that any legal theory provide for a Pareto improvement when the only two conceivable means to achieve it—voluntary and forced exchanges—are banned by the specifications of the initial example?

The issue can be put into somewhat better perspective if we strip the moralisms out of the case and assume that each party, when faced with an either/or choice picks his less favored choice because he recognizes that he cannot count on the cooperation of his opposite number. As Sen rightly recognizes, viewed in this light, the impossibility of finding the Paretian liberal provides us with nothing more than a PD game in which the dominant strategy of both parties is to defect from the cooperative solution. "It can be seen that in terms of the basic preference structure the Paretian Liberal paradox has the same ordering as the Prisoners' Dilemma."[8] And so it does. Without cooperation Lewd thinks that it is best for him to read the book, for he gains in that regard whether Prude chooses to read *Lady Chatterley's Lover* or not. Prude for his part decides not to read the book because nothing he can do will influence Lewd not to read it.

What is left, therefore, is a caricature of a strict libertarian system in which trade, here in the form of coordination, is prohibited. The impossibility of Sen's argument is tantamount to an assumption that the transaction costs are infinite, which by assumption *always* makes it impossible to achieve all the potential gains from trade. Calling this predicament an inability to handle metapreferences tells us nothing about the psychological attitude of individuals who are about to be faced with a PD game that both would like to avoid. No need to wallow in their complex preference structures; just work out some routine arrangement to avoid this destructive cycle.

The hard question for a legal system is what institutional arrangements will overcome the corrosive effects of a PD game. Sen does not offer any positive program of his own, but is content to show that the austere libertarian position is unable to cope with these examples. On this point he is surely correct. But Sen's lack of interest in looking at alternative institutional arrangements leads him to overlook the role of forced exchanges in overcoming PD games when appropriate. It is critical to identify the set of circumstances where such might be the case.

In the simplest scenario, the only individuals who care about the outcome of the game are the immediate players to it. With no spillovers, positive or negative, the maximization of the two-person game ensures maximization of the overall social gain as well. Perhaps this is the best way to understand the game between Prude and Lewd, but it is certainly a very odd way in which to understand most games with moralisms. If the Prudes are members of fundamentalist religions and the Lewds organize themselves into political movements, lots of people are likely to take more than a passing interest in the outcome of this particular struggle. The one thing that we can say with confidence is that no one will ever be able to oppose a sensible solution to any of these questions if trade on the one hand and forced exchanges on the other are both systematically ruled out of bounds.

It is, therefore, more fruitful to examine other PD games whose external effects are amenable to compensation, as is the case generally with most forms of economic regulation. Once these external effects are taken explicitly into account, then both their direction and magnitude matter. Thus, suppose that a group of firms recognize that unless they fix prices or divide territories among themselves, they will enter into a cycle of destructive rivalry as price gets driven down to the competitive level. Their losses surely count as an element of the social calculus, but so too do the interests of consumers who suffer losses, including those from forgone transactions, that exceed the gains derived by the members of the cartel. Here the Kaldor-Hicks test inspires us to make sure that the market players do *not* escape the PD game, given the beneficial social consequences that it generates on net. And the older common law rule that refused to enforce contracts in restraint of trade surely advanced that end.

The analysis must go further, however, under a Paretian standard that blocks any movement from one social state to the next if *any* individual (including a cartel member) in the second state is worse off than he was in the first. That Paretian deadlock exists in principle no matter what the size of the gains to the winners and the losses to the losers. But this requirement does not impose an insuperable obstacle to tackling this problem. The ideal social solution is *not* to break up the cartel by compensating

its members for the loss of their monopoly profits. That route only encourages the formation of other cartels in a general social free-for-all.[9]
Rather, the better approach recognizes that by reverting back to some
original position, we have a choice of either allowing or banning these
monopoly practices *before* any specific cartel is formed. Over all states of
the world, all individuals in this *ex ante* state are better off with the gains
of competition (when these can be feasibly obtained) than with the dislocations that monopoly induces. Across the board, any needed compensation thus comes in an in-kind form (without invoking the moralisms in
Sen's in-kind Paretian example), so long as a consistent policy is followed
from the outset. Contracts to cartelize are banned, and the PD game is
encouraged to run its course. The Rawlsian veil of ignorance tempers the
rigors of a libertarian world.

Generalizations, however, must be made only with caution, for some
PD games have destructive consequences across the board. The tragedy
of the commons arises from the excessive consumption of common pool
resources when each individual gains the full amount of what is taken
out but suffers only a fractional loss to the resources that remain in the
common pool.[10] All players would prefer a world in which they agreed to
limit their consumption, but so long as that result is unattainable, their
best strategy is to overconsume, which (as self-interested actors) they do.
It is Lewd and Prude all over again. For the players, this PD game has
exactly the same consequences as the failure to form or to enforce a marketing cartel. But unlike cartels, this PD game has only negative external
consequences, so state intervention to stop this destructive game in its
tracks should be welcomed. Compensation is awarded only if the restrictions imposed do not offer each claimant to the common pool resources
rights to extraction or use that equal or exceed the value of the naked
capture right that has been surrendered.[11]

In the usual situation, such as the extraction of the oil and gas, the
state can adopt a number of strategies, which are designed to reduce the
number of wells that operate within a given field. These desired social
arrangements create strong gains. The total costs of extraction are reduced by a limitation on the number of wells drilled; yet the amount
of oil and gas recoverable increases as the disturbance from the field is
also reduced. In the aggregate, we have more of a standard commodity
produced for a lower cost—a world in which subjective preferences for
unique goods plays no role at all. If each party is required to reduce its
activities by a proportionate amount, then every one is left better off, so
no one landowner need receive cash compensation from anyone else to

improve his position relative to the preregulatory baseline. But let the efficient output be achievable only if some persons are barred from drilling at all, then side payments from those who continue to drill can equalize the rate of return so that once again all parties are better off than they were in the preregulated state. Either way, state control of this PD game is capable of generating net positive consequences.

In practice, industry members treat these two bargaining situations as though they present the same problem: control of their own losses. They are largely indifferent to the question of whether the sign on the social externality is either positive or negative. Not surprisingly, therefore, the hard mixed case arises when the control of a natural resource problem in the field is extended politically to facilitate the creation of a cartel arrangement for marketing oil and gas collected from multiple sellers. Just that outcome is possible in the hurly-burly of partisan politics. In one famous example, the Texas Railway Commission undertook two tasks: the first was to control the level of drilling from Texas oil fields; the second was to set the prices for oil at the railhead. The former prevents the PD game with negative externalities; the latter prevents the PD game with positive externalities. The institutional arrangements have from time to time deliberately used the one to conceal the other.[12] The issues here are not new. In principle, they are identical to the ones that arose in chapter 5 in the discussion of unconstitutional conditions. It is permissible for the state to regulate highway use to maintain the roads and prevent accidents. It will not do for the state to use its power to cartelize the shipping industry.

It seems clear, then, that Sen's conclusion holds only insofar as he rejects the strong libertarian position that precludes all types of forced exchanges. But it hardly follows that once that position is rejected we must fall into the deadly embrace of a legal system that allows the unlimited use of political power to overcome PD games. Rather, exposing the weak underbelly of libertarian thought should push Sen to opt for state regulation and state condemnation to overcome this coordination problem so long as each party is left better off, by his subjective lights, than he was before. If the subject matter is the pollution of public waters, the maintenance of a uniform public appearance, or the organization of a sensible system of recordation, of course government action makes sense even though none of its targets have used force or fraud against another individual. At this point, Sen's examples show nothing about either the fallibility of individual preferences or the inability to organize social behavior. They only show the need for a legal system that provides for public goods, itself a point forcefully been made by Mancur Olson in his 1965 classic *The Logic of Collective Action*. The constrained choices left to the unreconstructed libertarian explains why I defend a system that allows the government to orchestrate forced exchanges for the overall benefit of the common good.

The operation of PD games is not restricted to natural resources, but also occurs in labor markets, where again the issue could be, following Sen, described as a matter of metapreferences. All workers would at the metalevel prefer to band together in dealing with management, but since they cannot satisfy this preference, they compete with each other until wages drop to the competitive level. Collective bargaining eliminates this PD game and allows workers to satisfy their higher order preferences—for example, the attainment of monopoly rents. Of course, there is little doubt that unionization can, at least under certain conditions, advance the welfare of (most of) its members. (The conclusion is uncertain because of the real conflicts of interest among union members—for example, old versus young—that are exacerbated by regulation.) But here again, the case for regulation is *not* established even by showing the improbable, namely, that *all* workers are better off under the arrangement. Consequences to third parties matter as well. Using collective bargaining to inject monopoly power into an otherwise competitive industry slights the interests of the firm, its shareholders, and its nonunion employees. It adds to the costs for its current and potential consumers. It increases, especially in service and transportation industries (where output cannot be stockpiled), the risks of disruption of markets. These massive disruptions to third parties are classic externalities that dwarf in size any wage gains to union workers, so that collective bargaining agreements (which are now protected under the National Labor Relations Act) should be greeted with the same hostility as cartel arrangements in product markets. The broader context makes the worker PD game welcome from a social point of view.

Expanding the PD Game: Enter Relative Preferences

Raising the Stakes

The PD game in and of itself is neither desirable nor dangerous. But in many contexts its negative consequences justify the use of forced exchanges that leave all parties (including nonplayers) better off than before. The question, then, is how widespread are the occasions in which destructive PD games arise? In my view, the major role of the doctrine lies in preserving natural resources located in the commons and in providing standard public goods, while hampering the organization of cartel and collective bargaining arrangements in various product and labor markets.

But other writers take a much more aggressive view of the dangers of these PD games in order to argue for a far broader role for state regulation of what, on more conventional views, count as competitive market behavior.

The writer who has pushed this line of argument the hardest is the economist Robert H. Frank, who finds a fatal PD game lurking in virtually every complex social setting.[13] In order to make his case, Frank seeks to explode the naïve view that individual preferences are set solely, or even largely, by reference to what individuals find, either more or less, in their own discrete basket of goods, services, and personal satisfactions. Rather, for him, the key determination is the *relative* size of the market basket of any individual relative to some *reference* group to whom the subject compares himself.[14] Stated in the simplest terms, the naïve "absolutist" view of individual preference formation holds that in comparing two different social states each person cares about only what he possesses but is indifferent to what is possessed by others. Frank puts the point in ways that distance himself from the economics profession: "But outside the world studied by economists, everyone knows that people are much more concerned about how the economic pie is distributed than about how large it actually is."[15]

Frank makes this point about common knowledge in two distinct contexts. In the narrower sense it is meant to show that economists do not understand the popular moral prohibition against theft when they treat it simply as a transfer of wealth from one party to the other—itself a wash—for which the real social losses come in the resource costs of either seeking to defend property from theft or to acquire it from another.[16] He is right that the moral intuition ignores the collateral issue of the costs of securing or resisting transfer. What is more difficult, however, is to imagine any case in which the institution of theft could thrive without those collateral costs. Over the broad run of cases it is impossible to envision a world of theft in which those expenditures do not take place. It follows, therefore, that in the theft case, a lack of concern about the size of the pie is perfectly consistent with the adaptation of legal rules that expand the size of that pie maximally. The moral intuition is a perfect proxy for the social loss calculation, so there is no survival pressure on individuals to distinguish between them. Quite the opposite, the categorical rule based on the simple observable is better able to ensure behavioral regularities and social sanctions than any appeal to collateral social consequences that invites empirical disputations about the underlying empirical assumptions of the model. We have but another instance of the persistent cleavage between the vocabularies of ordinary life and the more precise, but more remote, language of utilitarian theory.

The harder question has little or nothing to do with the allocative or distributional consequences of theft. Rather, it has to do with the sentiments about the trade-off between total output and distribution in settings where theft plays no part. In one situation the changes in position are brought about by voluntary trade, and in the second they are brought about by some state coercive action that cannot count as theft, precisely because both actors to the situation are left better off than before. In the initial situation, the usual common law rule holds that the terms of the bargain are for the parties to determine, so that the distribution of the joint surplus raises no social issues. As a social matter we accept all Pareto improvements, without inquiring into their relative proportions.

That position is of course qualified whenever one party enjoys a monopoly position; but rather than concentrating on that situation separately, it is convenient to consider it as part of the larger problem in which state power is used to effectuate the change in social position. Thus assume now that the wages of workers are determined in part by a collective bargaining agreement that by a *deus ex machina* allows us to place two new choices on the table. The first alternative allows the move from the initial position to a labor market in which A and B each enjoy 15 units of wealth. The second alternative involves a movement from that initial position to one in which A has 12 units and B has 18. In both cases, greater wealth implies greater individual utility for the party who enjoys it. The array thus looks as follows:

	Person A	Person B
Initial State	10	10
Alternative 1	15	15
Alternative 2	12	18

The question is how to rank these alternatives. The traditional view assumes that a move from the initial state to Alternative 1 should be regarded as an unambiguous improvement insofar as both parties are made better off in the same proportions. We have the best of both worlds relative to the initial state: an improvement in the absolute position of both parties without any alteration in their relative positions. But the next question is why do we prefer the 15/15 outcome to one that might have yielded 12/18, when the totals are the same in both cases. Why the persistent if inarticulate distributional preference for the even outcome over the disproportionate rates of return. The answer stems at least in part from its instrumental virtues. This world (especially in collective bargaining arrangements) has no *deus ex machina* to shift wealth and opportunities across individuals, so that the uneven outcome of the second alternative is regarded as a telltale sign that something was amiss in the politicized processes that worked the transformations in question. Unless some assumption of this sort is introduced, then we are faced with the anomaly that the 15/15 distribution from Alternative 1 will in fact be regarded as inferior to the 12/18 distribution of Alternative 2 if the initial distribution had been 8 units for A and 12 units for B, instead of 10 for each (12/18 is the proportionate increase from an 8/12 distribution). In a sense, therefore, 15/15 is both better and worse than 12/18. The puzzle resolves, however, only when our view of the process of transformation links final outcomes to the initial states. Yet if these instrumental concerns were banished, it is easy to see how someone could come to prefer the 15/15 division of the spoils no matter what the initial distribution. The diminishing marginal utility of wealth would treat the equalization of outcomes as the best of all Pareto improvements.

Thereafter, we come to a traditional quandary: whether one should move, if at all, from the initial state to Alternative 2 if Alternative 1 is blocked by technical reasons, that is, for reasons that preclude any appeal to political intrigue that underlie the initial presumption for equal improvements. On the conventional view, both parties prefer to change from the initial state to Alternative 2, because each is better off under that switch. But once *relative* preferences are introduced in the situation, the outcome becomes murky. The perceived differences in position create a perceived "positional externality,"[17] in all cases where "subjective well-being depends on relative wealth" compared to other persons. The point here is not that A is envious of B, although that might be the case. Nor does the argument necessitate that higher income leads to some improvement in relative status, or signals some kind of superior reputation, although these might be true as well. "People care about maintaining relative position not only because of envy, status-seeking, signaling, or reputational concerns; a particular important point is that the *frame of reference* for evaluating many goods and services is set socially rather than individually, and inevitably so."[18] The point is that it is a psychological truth of sorts that the simple knowledge that others have more makes what you have seem as though it were worth less, wholly apart from any instrumental reason, that is, any consequence that this difference might have in the way in which a person interacts with another. The one-bedroom apartment that seemed so spacious now feels cramped when everyone else lives in a three-bedroom ranch home. If, therefore, A finds the loss in relative position distasteful, then he concludes that the higher absolute endowments under Alternative 2 need not make any Pareto improvement over the initial state. B's new higher position is now the source of some palpable harm to A under this most elastic version of Mill's famous harm principle. The stakes, therefore, are very high. Affording a central place to relative preferences makes it difficult, if not impossible, to judge alternative social states by the standard Pareto or Kaldor-Hicks criterion, and it guts the Millian harm principle[19] by making it virtually impossible to identify a set of individual acts that do not result in harm to another. Nonetheless, this position and its implications should be rejected for a wide range of conceptual, empirical, and practical reasons.

Conceptual Difficulties

At the conceptual level, this broad definition of harm cannot be introduced solely to secure the equality of positions between persons. Once harm covers positional changes in one case, then it must do so in all. Thus, any systematic analysis requires asking whether B's welfare has increased some increment over 18 units, precisely because of the added satisfaction of seeing her material condition improve beyond that of A. Yet no one knows how these two magnitudes compare in seeking to evaluate the desirability of these relative states of affairs. But abstractly, it is very hard to imagine a world in which relative position, stripped of all extraneous elements of envy, status, signals, and reputation, matters deeply to the person who has less but is of no consequence to the person that has more. The relative loss experience by A must in part be offset by some parallel gain to B. Yet once that possibility is admitted, we have to revisit the modest earlier conclusion that Alternative 1 counts as a Pareto improvement over the Initial State. After all, either A or B, or indeed both, could think they *deserve* greater wealth than the other, and thus resent the even distribution of the gain. Likewise, many people may simply rejoice in the success of others, even if it increases gaps in relative wealth because they think that success in overcoming obstacles is a testament to the power of the human spirit. In a world in which subjective preferences are unconstrained, equality does not become a focal point to which all individuals converge.

Matters with relative preferences become only more mysterious when the attitudes of outsiders are introduced. When A and B advance in lockstep progression, that change could trigger (relative) losses in C and D, who are left behind. Or it could leave them sad because E and F have enjoyed larger gains. Indeed, every distribution of wealth and every change in distribution creates a situation in which someone has harmed someone else. Relative preferences create multiple reference points for comparison precisely because they are said to be unconnected to such important determinants of individual behavior as envy, status, and reputation. The question of *which* reference group counts, and to what extent, is not answered empirically by posing arbitrary groupings that are limited to a given firm, industry, or social or national grouping. This positional model preserves its consistency only if any change in wealth for X requires us to record, positive or negative, the corresponding change in utility for every other individual within the social system. The empirics behind the theory of relative preferences may show a (weak) tendency for some people to prefer lockstep progressions in, for example, wage levels. Yet even that is more closely related to implicit process concerns that are difficult to isolate in particular cases. But the evidence does not come close to establishing an iron law that relative wealth trumps absolute wealth, or even matters a great deal.

Implicit in the last argument is the view that relative preferences matter only when the differences between the two individuals are small, so that each party perceives itself as playing in the same "league" as the other.[20] The point here is that ordinary people do not know how to evaluate their own comparative position with that of John D. Rockefeller or Bill Gates, so they concentrate their concerns around individuals with whom they are in close contact. But this point is odd because it cuts against the usual rationale for either compulsory or voluntary redistribution: the declining marginal utility of wealth is such that the very rich will suffer small declines in utility relative to the large increase in utility gained by the far poorer recipients of the transfer. This instinct itself is subject to uncertainty, for it is never quite clear whether what matters to the social case of redistribution is the extreme want of the recipients or the relative difference in their status. Under the extreme want standard, the case for redistribution is strongest when the initial distribution is 1 versus 10—where 2 units are needed for survival, then it is for 10 versus 100, in which case the ratios are the same but both parties are above the survival line.

But either way, it seems clear that the focus should be placed on the large gaps found between unrelated individuals and not the small gaps found within, say, the ranks of clerical employees within the firm. In fact, people are concerned about these smaller differences in local environments, but not for reasons independent of status or envy. They treat them as markers of progress and cross-subsidies, which matter for very different, but quite ordinary, rational choice reasons.

Empirical Evidence

The restrictive definition of relative preferences makes it exceedingly difficult to find any empirical evidence that bears on the claim that relative preferences should be given great weight in formulating social policy. The traditional theories of individual self-interest work well enough to give some account of the proper social response to envy, status, signaling, and reputation, even if we suppress the idea of pure relative preferences altogether. Envy, generally speaking, is a destructive human emotion because it posits that one individual regards himself as better off precisely because other people have been made worse off. The point is distinguishable from relative preferences, for the envious person is quite happy to see a diminution in status or fortune of persons whose position is perceived as superior to their own. The social condemnation of envy lies in part from the fear that envious people will take steps to reduce the position of others even at some cost to their own tangible welfare. It is easy to see why social sanctions against envy can improve overall social position.

Similarly, status matters on any account of individual well-being. The person who enjoys high status receives preferential social treatment; he is ushered into restaurants, asked to preside over ceremonial events, offered attractive business deals, and introduced into elite social circles. These connections are of value in any society regardless of its overall wealth, and are a component (along with wealth) in virtually everyone's personal utility function. To understand what actions create and maintain personal status, and what actions undermine or destroy it, is something that everyone should care about. To the extent that differences in income or wealth are signs of social status, they matter because of the way in which they influence someone's life's projects. Signaling and reputation are part of the same package. Status is a social conception whose value is only realized through communication; reputation helps determine the number of individuals who are willing to deal with a given individual, and thus his chances of social success. People commonly invest time and money to build their reputations and to obtain high social status. The legal system works to protect these investments by allowing defamation suits against persons whose false statements reduce the reputation of the plaintiff, and thereby deter other individuals from dealing with him.

The inescapable relative nature of status leads Frank to treat it as a commodity that is distributed in a zero-sum game. On matters of status, there has to be a loser for each winner.[21] But this bleak Malthusian view badly misses the psychological dynamics within any social institution. To be sure, it may well be in some cases that a rise in status for one person is offset by a loss in status for another, but nothing says that the group has no incentive to minimize any social dislocations. One sensible response is for larger groups to organize themselves into subgroups that specialize in different areas, so that each person can think of himself as part of an in group that confers extensive social status on its members relative to an anonymous, if larger, whole. This task of internal division can take place through voluntary means. All members within the group (say a high school or college class) opt for those activities to which they attach the greatest value: theater, debate, sports, student government, and the like. The cohesion within the group allows them to enjoy high self-esteem against outsiders who are hardly troubled by the fact because their own internal scales attach greatest weight to the activities of the subgroups of which they are a part. Each group looks with puzzlement on the value scales of the others, and all profit in consequence. To be sure, this inward/outward strategy will not ease hard feelings in a close contest for group leader, but it does indicate that abundant possibilities remain for group activities to work like positive-sum games.

There are other ways in which groups can work to reduce the costs of status deprivation. It may well be that, by definition, all individuals cannot attain high levels of relative status in a firm or club. But it hardly follows that the self-esteem or self-respect connected with one's association with a firm or a voluntary organization is limited to some single, mystical dimension, let alone one perfectly correlated with income. The mélange of attitudes and tastes within a firm cannot be pressed into Frank's narrow mold. One secret of good management is that cooperative behavior can improve everyone's self-esteem, even if it can do nothing to eliminate hierarchies based on income. Simple gestures of respect to workers—hello, good morning, how are you?—go a long way to making people think that they are not invisible, that they matter in the day-to-day operation of the business. Keeping people informed about key decisions in the firm or group; asking for advice about specialized tasks; lending a helping hand when there is a problem at home; throwing holiday parties; giving special recognition to meritorious employees—these are all part of the picture in a well run firm. On Frank's parsimonious view of the world, all workplaces have to look equally bleak under the iron law of status.

But the differences in productivity and morale across workforces show that psychological compensation can come in multiple coins, and often determines the success of the venture as a whole.

In one sense, therefore, relative preferences have the same mysterious presence as the adaptive preferences discussed in chapter 6. They never appear in pure form in any important institutional setting. Unlike concern with monopolies and public goods, the first task is to isolate a pure case of relative preferences by stripping away the confounding elements. I have already indicated that it is impossible to consider status in isolation from mutual respect and esteem within a given firm. Equal complications arise when the principle of relative preferences is applied across firms or industry. Just ask the question of how the workers in one firm are likely to respond when they learn of large salary increases at a rival firm. One possibility is that they think that their own relative status is thereby diminished. But they make take the exact opposite position because this action contains information that may augur well for their own prospects: if wages move up for one, then others like him may find that their employers will follow suit. Far from a sense of relative deprivation, the uptick in fortune for members of close reference groups could be treated as a harbinger of good things to come. The pure reference group component of the analysis is overshadowed by the good (or bad) information that changes in wage or wealth levels carry to other individuals in the same firm or profession.

The upshot is that the strength of any relative preferences are attenuated when changes of wealth are embedded in some concrete social situation, as in practice they always are. It is this difficulty that makes it hard to interpret the kinds of sociological evidence that seeks to correlate happiness with wealth or status. There is no doubt that richer people within one country are happier than poorer individuals; and their high status only magnifies the social differences that are otherwise attributable to wealth.[22] It is, however, far more difficult to interpret findings that indicate that overall levels of happiness in society do not improve with increases in overall wealth. In general, people are asked this question in something of a void. Any answer they give does not draw on their experience and understanding about their business, their family, or their social interaction with friends. Here it would be hard to give an *absolute* answer to the question, even if one tried, because of the acontextual nature of the question. The obvious procedure is for everyone to assume that happiness within the overall population follows some kind of normal distribution in which most people are tolerably happy, so that any estimation of personal happiness is done off that implicit baseline. Under these circumstances, we should expect these answers to be highly invariant across cultures. But let the question be "Are you prepared to go back to the standard of living that your parents enjoyed a generation ago so long as others in your society were prepared to make the same move?" and comparisons over time become explicit, especially to anyone over the age of fifty. People may wish for the quiet life, but their are no signs that they will give up the advantages of modern medicine, entertainment, transportation, communication, nutrition, and so on. Rather, they will buy a country place, and remain in contact with their friends by email. It is far more plausible to assume that the words "quite happy" refer to rather different states of affairs in 2000 than in 1950. Perhaps there are people who would prefer to feed horses and carry out manure in the dead of winter as was done in 1900, but I suspect, survey or no survey, few people would opt to return to a time when the average standard of living was, at a guess, about one-sixth of what it is today. The argument here is not one against survey research. It is against that subclass of surveys used to measure happiness as an abstract state of mind.

Nor can defenders of relative preferences take any comfort in the experimental work that indicates, for example, that "proposers" who play the ultimatum game are willing to share their winnings with their "responders."[23] In the usual version of this game, the controller offers the proposer the option to divide a sum, say $100, between himself and the second player. That responder, in turn, has the right to reject any offer that is proposed. In principle, the proposer could claim $99 for himself, and, if the neoclassical model of absolute preferences holds, the second player will accept the offer because he is left $1 better off than if he rejected the offer himself. But typically the offers call for an even or close to even split of the wealth, which might indicate the importance of relative preferences. The right response here is not to reject that classical approach; it is to incorporate all the elements needed for sound choices. These experiments clearly involve an interaction between the two players, such that the acceptance of a paltry sum could easily be taken as a sign of a lack of self-respect or desperation for money. If so, then these experiments cannot rule out status, signaling, or reputational effects, and hence do not isolate the pure influence of relative position.

More important, the general movement toward more or less even division depends on the social setting in which the game is played. The initial ultimatum game made it appear that the $100 is a *windfall* to which *neither* party has any claim under a labor theory of value. The results appear to be sensitive to that initial condition. Thus, as studied by Binmore et al., the proposer typically becomes much more aggressive in his demands when instructed at the outset to maximize his gains from this transaction.[24] With someone looking over the shoulder, as it were, the second player is offered only minimal payment, so that self-interest appears to win out over altruism. The same reversion to standard assumptions of individual self-interest has also been observed by Hoffman and Spitzer when the initial proposer has to win some small game, in which case he typically captures a much larger fraction of the take.[25]

This second round of experimentation does not negate the possibility of some positional effect. But it reduces the explanatory power of these positional claims in real-world settings. Nor should that come as a surprise. The legal system generally has a difficult time setting up rules for "windfall" gains precisely because (as the name suggests) these are solely created by acts beyond the control of all parties. Thus, the rules for dealing with abandoned or lost property, with treasure troves and other finds, all have an inescapable arbitrary quality: do they go to the finder? to the owner of the site on which they were found? to the state?[26]

The reason for this massive uncertainty is that it is hard to see what useful incentives can be created one way or the other by fine-tuning the legal rules allocating windfalls when neither party has invested either labor or capital to acquire it. But the finder situation, which the typical ultimatum game mimics, is rare in the grand scheme of things. In virtually all negotiation cases, the gains from a joint venture have to be allocated among multiple participants, each of whom make substantial contributions in either labor or capital to the joint venture. In those cases, all parties will perceive themselves as "entitled" to make strong claims on the returns from the investment under the usual commonsense theories that condemn theft as a wrong in itself. The division of profit will clearly reflect the resources, the talents, the risk preferences, the monitoring skills, and the track record that each party brings to the table. The instructions offered by Binmore et al. and the simple game proposed by Hoffman and Spitzer reflect these realities even if they do not capture the full array of possibilities. But they do a better job than the uncontextualized ultimatum game played when only windfall profits are on the table.

Practical Applications

Employment. The tenuous hold that relative preferences have on basic behavior is revealed in the employment context, the very setting in which these preferences are thought to exhibit powerful effects. Take the simple case of the workers who bring different endowments to their jobs, for which they receive different wage levels. It would be an odd reading of the theory of relative preferences to assume that all workers would prefer to receive equal wages regardless of skill levels. The far more sensible reading is that workers like, *ceteris paribus,* to see equal wages for equal work because the *uniform* pay scale gives them some protection against favoritism of the boss. It would be a blatant overstatement to claim that all secretaries resent their bosses' higher pay. Yet it would be quite predictable for any individual secretary to experience strong resentment if she did all the work while her boss took all the credit. Yet to make the point in that fashion implies that we are no longer talking about pure positional externalities. Rather, it forces us to address the far more serious problem of preserving workplace *morale* when it is widely perceived that some privileged employees are free riding on the talents of others.

"Morale" at long last is a term that is starting to come into its own in general economic theory. (Economists and lawyers often take too long to discover that ordinary people actually know their own businesses, even if they cannot run anyone else's.) It plays, for example, a central place in Truman Bewley's detailed account of why employers do not cut wages during a recession.[27] As noted earlier, this term suggests that the perceptions of workers depend on their interactions with their coworkers, a sense that management takes their interests to heart, a feeling of being treated with dignity and respect, a sense of candor and open communication with the workforce, the ability to make sure that everyone is "on the same page" with respect to the purpose and mission of the job—in sum, all those things that Frank excluded in his one-dimensional definition of status. Making these things work is no easy matter, because in the true sense of the word, management is not economics. The marketplace, writ large, is more rational than the firm, and the firm is more rational than the individuals who compose it.

The theory of economics cannot demonstrate that all individuals are rational or always act "as if" they were. What it can say is that those people whose behavior is less rational stand a greater risk of falling by the wayside. What it can propose is that the creation of incentives increases the odds that individual gain will be aligned with social advantage. In the grand scheme of things, the overall system is likely to be nudged in the right direction. But economic incentives, like personal hints, are sometimes ignored in particular settings. In understanding firm management, it should be treated as a self-evident truth that workers bring all sorts of personal baggage to their job, of which some disembodied taste for relative preferences is at best a tiny sliver.

Good managers weed out and control these emotional and human forces so that the firm's operation can begin to approach (though it will never fully achieve) the ideal efficiency that firms constantly seek in a competitive environment. That work starts with responding to justified resentments that eat away at firm morale and individual self-respect. A good manager has to root out any imbalances between effort and reward; lazy bosses have to be instructed or replaced; diligent clerical and manual workers have to receive raises and promotions; all forms of pettiness, slights, rudeness, backbiting, and personal nastiness have to be curtailed in order to set the tone of the plant or office. These concrete passions and palpable irritations swamp any academic fascination with relative preferences.

In some cases, of course, the firm might wish to control some of these tensions between workers by keeping wages to a lockstep progression. That strategy *might* work in settings where both the training costs of workers and the variation in worker quality are low. But that strategy will surely fail when these conditions do not hold, because of the near certainty that rival firms will cream its undercompensated workers and leave the firm with the dregs of its initial distribution. The recalibration of wages with an eye to productivity (including good relations with others) induces superior workers to stay; the inferior workers are not likely to find better alternatives elsewhere, and if they do, then it is best for all concerned that they shift jobs.

Similar considerations apply in dealing with *layoffs* in times of economic stress. Here, the basic empirical truth is that wages remain sticky, that is, do not trend downward for current workers, and some workers are laid off.[28] This type of anomaly is difficult to explain by conventional economic theories that postulate a smooth downward trend in wages with few if any layoffs. But whatever the failings of the traditional account, relative preferences do not come close to filling the gap. At the very least, that theory would suggest that the employer would treat all workers the same, that is, adopt proportionate pay cuts or reduction in hours, which is exactly the opposite of what occurs when selective layoffs are the order of the day. The wage stickiness for the remaining workforce might be explained at least in part as the honoring of an "implicit contract" that employers would provide wage cushions during bleak times in exchange for workers' not pushing for outlandish raises during good times. The employer thus bears more of the residual risk in both good times and bad. Or, in the alternative, it is highly likely that firm morale has much to do with the situation. As Truman Bewley described his extensive interviews, he was told by employers that "cutting pay would have almost no impact on company employment, that hiring new workers at reduced pay would antagonize, that reducing the pay of existing employees was nearly unthinkable because of the impact on worker attitudes, and that the advantage of layoffs over pay reductions was that they 'get misery out the door.'"[29] To which he might have added that it is far harder to manage a workforce when everyone has idle time on their hands than when a smaller cohesive force is hard at work. But even here, there are many choices to be made about severance packages, about timing, about out-placement assistance, about the prospects of rehiring on the one hand and new recruitment on the other. The complexities abound at every corner, and clearly the soft stuff plays an enormous role in shaping these decisions. But each of these variations can be taken into account by recognizing the importance of nonwage terms and workplace interactions within the framework of a neoclassical theory. As with the experimental literature, these elements drown out any role for relative preferences.

Nonetheless, it is possible to construct models in which the relative preferences appear to dominate, and then to use these improbable constructions to draw just the wrong inference on the need for external regulation of the labor markets. Thus Frank and Sunstein, in addressing this problem, write:

> Assume that relative rather than absolute economic position is what most workers care about—that worker well-being would not be decreased by (say) a decrease in annual wages of $250, $500, or $1000, so long as all workers face the same annual decrease. In that event some nonwaivable terms, such as a right to job security, might be justified on the ground that the consequence of the new term is to decrease absolute income but to hold relative income constant, thus imposing little or no welfare loss on workers, while at the same time giving workers a substantial benefit, such as job security.[30]

The analysis is far-fetched at every turn. Start with the brute empirics. In this instance, we have little need to draw elaborate inferences from generalized surveys on happiness or experimental games. The powerful field evidence, *directly on point,* is wholly inconsistent with the proposition that relative preferences matter much, if at all, in real-world world settings. Frank and Sunstein cite Bewley for the generalized proposition that "[f]ew workers have a precise notion of market wages or wages that are fair in some absolute sense. Rather, they make comparisons with their own past pay and with the pay of co-workers."[31] But that passage referred solely to workers in the secondary sector, that is for "short-term positions" such as waiters and waitresses, clerks, taxi drivers, and the like.[32] Clearly, these individuals need to know about relative wages in order to determine whether they are getting paid the market rate for their endeavors. But even if they detect any wage differences, it does not necessarily follow that they will act on that information. The question of whether two workers are "alike" is not all that easy to answer in the abstract. It is, therefore, possible that the employer could explain the differences by pointing out some difference in skills or performance that might justify the difference. The norm that speaks of like pay for like work is in its application necessarily presumptive.

The social practices are quite different, however, for primary sector jobs where, as Bewley meticulously documents, employers vigorously resist a strategy of across-the-board pay cuts in favor of selective layoffs. The explanations offered are clear: "People can't explain a pay cut at home, whereas if they are laid off they can draw unemployment benefits and look for new work. A pay cut is like a criticism or an insult. A pay cut is so closely associated with self-worth that a cut is taken personally." The external reference groups do care about the decline in living standards, and they do attribute a "social meaning" to pay cuts that strikes to the core of their self-esteem. "A pay cut would be interpreted as a punishment, even if it were done across the board." "Morale suffers from a pay cut for psychic reasons. It says, 'I am doing badly,' even if everyone gets a pay cut."[33] The "even if" clause puts the kibosh on the theory of relative preferences. That conclusion is only strengthened when the same survey data suggests that at most 10 percent of firms dabbled with some pay cuts (not necessarily for all levels) even in hard times.[34] And the major layoffs—for example, Boeing and American Express—after the September 11, 2001, terrorist attacks show that the traditional preference for layoffs is alive and well in corporate America. Once the dust settles, moreover, we should expect to see a fall in overall wages. Many of the laid-off workers will only obtain new jobs at wages lower than those of their former positions; and the increased supply of labor should have ripple effects throughout the entire market. The overall wage pattern will tend to show a persistent slowing or downward trend, which is consistent with the discontinuous layoff decisions.

It is, however, important to keep Bewley's points in perspective. There is nothing about his argument that necessarily makes layoffs the dominant solution in all cases. Pay cuts are common on Wall Street, for example, where the basic compensation package often consists of a relatively low salary coupled with a substantial year-end bonus. In cyclical businesses, it is often highly inefficient to fire people in January only to have to hire them back in large numbers in June. Sharp cuts in bonuses, as happened on Wall Street in 2001, are the obvious way to divide risks between the firm and its employees. Clearly, similar strategies are followed implicitly for shoe salesmen who work on commission. But for our purposes, we need not give a precise account of which firms will choose what mix between layoffs and pay cuts—or for that matter, reassignments—in response to hard times. It is easy to imagine high levels of variation in practice across different industries and lower levels of variation within each industry. The key point is that the necessary variation in personnel practice across different market niches only shows how difficult it is to fashion any single rule that works for the full range of employment. There is no reason to believe that pay cuts instead of dismissals should be imposed—such is the force of the term "nonwaivable"—on industry groups. The unhappiness within any firm does not disappear because other firms are plunged into similar discord. What value are nonwaivable rights to job security in a firm that is driven into bankruptcy?

Nor should we expect matters to be otherwise from a theoretical point of view. Even in its own terms, the quoted passage offers no idea as to the wage interval over which relative preferences dominate absolute ones. Everyone rejects out of hand a wage cut to zero for all workers, even if it resulted in perfect parity. How then do we know that a wage decrement of $250 to $1,000 is a matter of (absolute) indifference? It is far more probable that utility functions are continuous so that any decline in wages carries with it some decline in utility, even if not at a one-for-one level. In principle, someone might be able to construct a complex utility function whereby the individual worker attaches X percent of his weight to his relative utility and $100 - X$ percent to his absolute wealth position, where X could shift with wage levels. But the ability to outline the shape of a mathematical map of an individual utility function does not tell us what values to attach to X for any given wage level, or why. Nor is there any reason to indulge in the additional complication when a simpler explanation for the relevance of wage comparisons—the concern with implicit cross-subsidies—is independently available. The additional complexity has little explanatory traction.

More generally, the entire scheme here presupposes that it is possible to get something for (nearly) nothing. But even if that form of economic alchemy were possible, the punch line is still missing. Let these odd assumptions about the role of relative preferences be true, and still no case for state regulation—nonwaivable terms—can be made out. Start with the relative preferences that are most visible: those within a firm. In one sense the Frank-Sunstein construction treats the workers as part of a giant PD game in which all workers individually cannot achieve the security that they collectively prefer. Were that the problem, however, then any employer has both the motive and the means to solve it. If relative preferences matter, then let the firm follow the same strategy that Frank and Sunstein urge upon the regulator. The *firm* lowers the wages across the board and then offers a security package that costs the firm less than the wages saved but is worth more to the workers than the wages forgone.

All this possible maneuvering rings a familiar chord because trade-offs between risk and wages are a staple of the neoclassical model even if we dispense with the idea of relative preferences. The ultimate question in both settings is whether the trade-offs make sense. Of course, the odds shift in favor of making this trade-off if it can be fueled by the "free" cash from painless wage reductions. Rational employers should leap at this chance, but in fact no employer bites. When push comes to shove, employers usually insist on the contract at will or some variation thereof (including one that tenders some measure of job security by allowing workers some multiple of weekly wages when dismissed from the job).[35] Even if the Frank-Sunstein position were right about relative preferences, they make no showing of how it *dominates* all the traditional problems of workplace management while a legal rule that guarantees some form of firm-wide job security remains. No one quite knows what the definition of good cause is, how the burdens of proof are to be assigned, what should be done with workers while their status is under investigation, or what measure of damages should be given in the event that a dismissal is treated as wrongful. No one knows how the rule should apply to reassignments or demotions. The administrative drag of this civil service regime can easily push marginal firms over the edge into a world where bankruptcy operates as dismissal for cause.

Nor would any firm have reason to relent in its attitude on learning that its rivals were uniformly subject to the same legal regime. Nothing is more common than the observation that rules that are neutral on their face can have powerful disparate impacts on the parties subject to its regulation. The burdens associated with complying with the for-cause rule differ vastly with the composition of the workforce. Firms with young workers with high turnover may be able to weather the storm. Firms with an older workforce may find the burden ruinous. Similarly, the for-cause rule could hurt those firms that are labor intensive relative to those that are capital intensive. Bankruptcy or lost profits, *pace* relative preferences, has at most a faint silver lining when others are brought to their knees by the same ill-advised rules: think only of the situation of the Enron employees whose pensions were wiped out. Nor do firms in regulated industries have an immutable preference for uniform treatment. I much prefer being slightly hobbled by a tax of 2 percent when my rival faces a 1 percent tax, if the alternative is a uniform 20 percent tax that drives us both out of business. To be sure, it is easier, judicially, to review and strike down taxes or regulations that are overtly discriminatory: there is ordinarily no reason that justifies even a small level of discrimination. But it hardly follows that petty discriminations are always more potent than draconian uniform rules. It is a hard question to decide whether courts or legislatures should incur the additional costs to ferret these out. But judicial passivity on this point does nothing to justify any misguided uniform rules.

Ironically, the for-cause rule often makes little sense even from the *employee's* side. The usual model of the PD game is that each person is in the identical position. After all, it is hard to imagine anyone who prefers a longer to a shorter prison sentence. But we cannot make any placid assumption that all workers within a firm attach equal weight to job security and wish for it to be extended to all. Many workers within a firm are rightly opposed to job security for *all* workers. The simple calculations are not those of two prisoners in separate cells. Workers differ in skills and temperament. It takes only *one* worker with a bad attitude to destroy morale within a workplace.

The able employee, therefore, reasons as follows. She has little reason to value any nonwaivable security for herself because she knows that strong work performance will minimize the risk of her wrongful dismissal. Her eyes are on promotion—which will be thwarted by any scheme of lockstep progression—or on exit to a better job, which strong performance facilitates. By the same token, she knows that the weaker worker has no hope of promotion and few, if any, viable exit options, and therefore will value job security more than she will. She will further reason that the employer's reduced ability to fire a troublemaker will reduce her enjoyment from the job, increase the likelihood that her own work will founder, and strain her relations with other coworkers as they all try to size up their options to cope with the fallout from the one bad apple protected by civil service laws.

Owing to the fundamentally different initial positions, therefore, there is no PD game here, much less any second-order preferences: the players do not find themselves similarly situated but incapable of realizing their common objective. Rather, profound conflicts of interest often divide employees, so that the employer provides an important service of keeping morale high in the workplace by disciplining weak workers. The boss who lacks the courage to fire a disgruntled or disruptive worker lets down the rest of his employees and will suffer from deserved loss of, respect, status, and influence. It is wholly romantic to assume that employee solidarity works in the interest of employees as a class.

In a sense, the situation is still worse than this. A preoccupation with positional externalities and relative preferences does nothing to spur production. At the same time, any firm has to worry about giving signals to workers about their long-term prospects, for which wage differentials are a powerful tool. Wages are but one part of the package. Firms must give workers offices, equipment, and perks. There is often real status in eating in the officer's dining room, traveling first class, or getting a company car or palm pilot—and real danger in using these tools in the wrong fashion. Any regulatory decision to standardize wages or to provide job security (however defined) weakens the use of wage and status changes as a signaling device. Accordingly, these perks and collateral terms take on greater significance now that other clear signals are dampered. Unfortunately, the necessary information about differentials in worker status and prospects will have to be communicated by less efficient signals than those available to the unregulated firm. The standard neoclassical model holds that the function of the firm is to internalize the externalities among workers. That is just another way of saying that PD games cannot arise within the firm so long as communication can take place through its hub. Nothing about relative preferences, or supposed worker indifference to proportionate wage cuts, makes the state a better candidate for discharging this job than the firm. The ostensible phenomenon of relative preferences does nothing to undermine the superiority of private ordering of the workplace.

Nonemployment Contexts. The same conclusion, moreover, applies to many other ingenious examples that Frank advances on the strength of this model. He sees, for example, a destructive PD game when individuals each strive to build ever-larger homes than before solely to get ahead of, or to keep up with, the Joneses. His view is that the additional expenditures count as social waste productive of no additional gains, with the clear implication that a stiff dose of progressive taxation is needed to curb these counterproductive displays of conspicuous consumption.[36] But Frank's result is sheer speculation at best. Does it really follow that people experience *no* (absolute) gain in utility when they move from a two-thousand- to a three-thousand-square-foot house? Ask the child who now gets her own room, or the dad who has a separate space for his workshop, or the mom with an airier kitchen or a larger garden, or the elderly parent who can now visit or move in. In these cases, it seems almost perverse to argue that relative preferences dominate the improvements in convenience and comfort that come with increased wealth or large size.

Nor is there any reason to assume that people build or buy homes with the arms-race mentality of topping their neighbor. Quite the opposite, the usual advice given, for example, to purchasers of new homes or condominiums is to avoid being the outlier by wealth or preferences in the subdivision or high-rise. It is not wise to be richer by far than other members of a subdivision, or to be the only couple with children in a development dominated by adults. The sensible course is to choose a neighborhood populated by other homes of like size and quality, which is of course the way in which new tract houses are generally organized. In part, it is easier to bond with other homeowners who share similar backgrounds. That commonality of interest further expresses itself in the interaction between the private goods of home owning and the public goods—police, schools, parks, streets, lighting—shared with one's neighbors. Generally speaking, the public goods that most individuals want are loosely correlated with their wealth: hence the homogeneity of the population along that dimension reduces the discord that this community—be it a local township or a gated community—finds in the selection of public goods. The model of relative preferences ignores this constraint that leads to a constructive convergence of preferences, not a destructive escalation of pointless consumption.

Finally, the model of relative preferences is wholly insensitive to all overarching issues of administration raised by any ambitious system of regulation. As a formal matter, Frank and Sunstein are correct to say that a PD game is a PD game whether we deal with pollution or relative preferences. "Analytically, positional externalities are no different from ordinary environmental pollutants."[37] Practically, however, it hardly follows that the case for regulation is of equal strength: so PD games look the part, while others (such as among workers in a firm) do not. And even when PD games do exist, it hardly follows that the law should take a uniform response to them. Much depends on the size of the social losses that follow from the failure in coordination and on the cost of remedying any perceived shortfall. Analytically the point can be made simply by looking at two PD games with the same structure but different values in the various cells.

	Game 1			Game 2	
	A	B		A	B
A	10, 10	2, 15	A	100, 100	20, 150
B	15, 2	5, 5	B	150, 20	50, 50

The structure of these two games is identical, where the stakes in the second game are just ten times larger across the board than they are in the first game. But it hardly follows that the case for regulation is the same in both. The net gains from regulation in Game 1 are limited to 10 units, 5 for each player. The net gains from regulation in the Game 2 are 100 units, 50 for each player. The clear implication is that if regulation costs 25 units in both systems, then it is a bad investment in the first game and a wise investment in the second game, for the prosaic reason that 10 < 25 < 100. The sober lesson that one learns is that sometimes, but not always, the cure is worse than the disease.

This question of magnitudes tells us a lot about the parallels between the two PD games with pollution and relative preferences. With ordinary nuisances we all understand the drill. These were regarded as torts between neighbors long before anyone thought of the dangers that particulate emissions had to ambient air quality. The ordinary private suit does not present a PD game given that it has only one polluter and one victim, and seeks only to shut down the latter. But with air pollution there is a well-nigh complete overlap between the (large) class of polluters and the (large) class of victims. One reason why it is feasible to regulate pollution is that all of us do not create it all the time. Rather, it comes from factories and automobiles and other defined sources and activities. There is not, however, apart from government, any individual or organization that can coordinate activities on the various spokes through a hub.

Once, therefore, it becomes clear that countless individuals bear only a tiny cost of the pollution they create, then it is easy to identify the PD game for which there is no private monitor: all persons are better off (that is, satisfy some higher-order preference, if you will) with some restraints on pollution in light of the health benefits they receive in exchange. Since the regulated quantity is relatively observable, regulation on environmental matters becomes easy to defend, at least in principle. But there is much slippage in implementation. In the ordinary traumatic injury, such as a blow to the skull, it is easy to isolate the single cause of the particular harm. Environmental changes are not amenable to such simple explanations. There is a raft of variables that can work to advance or retard such complex phenomena as global warming and destruction of coral reefs, so that it becomes incumbent to develop sound science to determine even the direction of simple variables: Do increases in carbon dioxide increase or reduce levels of global warming? Once this causal thicket has been navigated, then much attention must be devoted to sound system design, taking account, for example, of the interrelationships between command and control mechanisms, tradable permits, taxes, subsidies, and the like. Matters are not made any easier by virtue of the great temptation for regulators to serve some illicit distributional goal—such as protection of eastern producers of high-sulfur coal[38]—which could easily lead to the adoption of highly inefficient systems of regulation. But even with the pitfalls that always loom large, the huge potential social gains justify the overall venture.

Even here a note of caution is in order, for in many cases it is better to ignore pollution than to regulate it. Most notably that result holds when pollution arises from high-frequency, low-level invasions that are reciprocal in nature. In this context, the rule of live-and-let-live[39] weeds out from the system those low-level interferences (backyard conversation, play, and barbecues) that on balance do more *good than harm,* while focusing the attention of the law on those larger dislocations (soot from factories, massive discharges into streams and lakes) that count as harm in anyone's book.

Yet what about the relevant trade-offs in the world of relative preferences? In my opinion, all relative preferences should be uniformly handled by a live-and-let live rule: collectively, we ignore them. The very existence of these preferences is a hotly debated topic, on which the stronger evidence is decidedly against. The best that one can say is that, like quarks, they are not found in nature in unbound form; the worst that one can say is that they are like the ether of old, which means that they will never be found at all. Any analysis of their supposed harm rests on a selective suite of experiments and social surveys, subject to multiple interpretations. It is virtually impossible to find a pure positional externality in any social setting, given that wages, prices, and collateral terms all have functional purposes: there are ample reasons why people who are indifferent to relative preferences in the abstract deeply care about their wages and working conditions relative to their coworkers and neighbors. Any effort to regulate labor or other markets is likely to have all sorts of unintended and negative spillover effects on the morale of workers, the investment and hiring strategies of the firm, and the long-term operation of the market in general. Likewise, the extravagant fear that some misguided individuals will engage in conspicuous consumption of their wealth is likely to have strongly negative effects on the ability of individuals to create and amass wealth in the first place. We should not base public policy on a strong puritanical sense.

The strategies that work with pollution do not work here. These preferences are not observable: no one breathes them in. Any adverse consequences, if we can find them at all, are likely to be small and evenly distributed. Their content is likely to be far more heterogeneous than pollution, and thus much more amenable to regulation within the firm. The public costs of curbing them are likely to be large. With relative preferences, it is not possible to imitate a regulatory stance—"We shall tax you on the level of emissions from your plant; now you take the steps to minimize the level of production"—thereby imposing on the firm the job of deciding when the additional costs of prevention become higher than the fines that are imposed. Nor is it possible to create anything analogous to tradable pollution rights.

The common law has long taken a leaf from Roman law with its adoption of the famous category of *damnum absque injuria*—harm without legal injury. At one level this term looks like a paradox, but in reality it is the soul of good sense. Harms to competitors are real even if economists like to dismiss them from analysis with the epithet "pecuniary." That said, when these harms are taken into account for analytical purposes, they are nonetheless rightly ignored in practice for the long-term good they produce when the gains to the winners are taken into account.[40] In those cases we should not want to eliminate the losses in question, even if we could do so at zero cost, for to do so is to eliminate the greater gains. With relative preferences, the case is not so clear cut for it is at least possible to conceive of some infrequent states of affair in which it would be better to eliminate them if we could. But in this context the cure will prove worse than the disease. Any effort to regulate preference formation is likely to be counterproductive, so that we are all better off giving a massive legal pass to the relative disappointments suffered by others. The PD games that arise out of controlling natural resources, protecting the environment, developing network industries, and securing a competitive market structure offer enough challenges. The rest should be left on the cutting room floor.

8   Behavioral Anomalies

Many Forms of Irrational Behavior?

THE LAST OF THE MAJOR ASSAULTS on the classical liberal model concerns neither moral nor conceptual issues. Rather, the focus now shifts to more behavioral questions of whether the model of rational self-interest is able to explain the frequent anomalies that lead to biases in human behavior—biases that might provide the justification for further government regulation of economic and social activities. These biases go to the way in which people calculate probabilities or integrate their knowledge of specific cases with that of general rules. They involve criticism of the economic theory of sunk costs, whereby bygones are bygones, or of the asserted equivalence between the amount that some individual is prepared to pay to receive a good and the amount that he will demand to be paid in order to part with it.

In order to deal with these behavioral challenges, this chapter and the one that follows have three related missions. The first is to question the strength and pervasiveness of the full range of cognitive and psychological biases in ordinary human activities. On this point, I think that the biases are likely to exert their greatest power where they matter the least and recede in importance as the stakes become higher, the frequency of their occurrence increases, and the social context in which decisions are made become better defined. All these conditions are more likely to be satisfied in thick markets with professional traders. But when the stakes are high enough, individuals can make any needed adaptations even without a full awareness of their own conceptual deficits. The Eskimos who built igloos in a way that maximizes heat conservation did not have the foggiest notion of the general physical principles that validated their choices; nor could they apply those principles outside the areas of their own experience. In many real-world settings, high stakes lead to *specific* adaptive responses to these biases that largely neutralize their effect. No experimental work could duplicate either the level of repetition or the size of the stakes, both of which improve the odds that trial and error will overcome the weaknesses of rational or deliberative processes.

The second task is to ask how these behavioral anomalies, to the extent that they do survive, are consistent with an evolutionary view of human psychology, an enterprise that assumes that the forces of natural selection operate as much on the emotional and cognitive domains as they do on physical and chemical structures. Do these biases have some survival value, if not under current conditions, then at least on the primitive conditions under which much of human evolution took place? In general, there are reasons why psychological tendencies that seem maladaptive today worked better in more primitive human settings.

The third inquiry is whether proof of these cognitive biases or behavioral anomalies strengthens the case for government regulation. Even if we recognize, as in some cases we should, the existence of these psychological anomalies and biases, their presence does nothing to undermine the basic theory of private rights and limited government. Indeed, in most cases the explicit confrontation with these biases only *strengthens* the case for decentralized power as the preferred means to diffuse or neutralize their effects.

In order to show how this argument progresses, I group the various kinds of behavioral data into several classes. In this chapter, I undertake two inquiries: the first is to explore whether people fall prey to the fallacy of sunk costs. The second investigates the extent of the endowment effect's influence on human behavior in ways not anticipated by the traditional economic theory. Chapter 9 examines the full range of cognitive biases that shape the way individuals (and institutions) make decisions under conditions of uncertainty both in ordinary personal decisions and in financial markets.

Before delving into the particulars, it is useful to frame the basic problem of why and how rationality matters. In his book *Guns, Germs and Steel,* Jared Diamond turns to the opening passage in Leo Tolstoy's *Anna Karenina* to launch his trenchant discussion of the domestication of wild animals.[1] "Happy families are all alike; every unhappy family is unhappy in its own way." So, historically, it was with domestication of animals. Domestication can succeed only if everything clicks, but that fragile enterprise can fail in many distinct ways. Carnivores will eat you out of house and home; elephants take too long to reach maturity; cheetahs and vicunas will not breed in captivity; grizzly bears and zebras are too nasty and dangerous to tame; gazelles, when frightened, will bolt into concrete walls; male antelopes will not stay in herds during breeding season. Let an animal fall short in any single dimension and domestication fails, no matter how great its other virtues. Early on, sheep, goats, cows, pigs, and horses all made the cut, as did some more localized species such as camels, llamas, reindeer, donkeys, and water buffaloes. But no other species of large animals has been domesticated since around 2,500 B.C., and it seems that none ever will.

The domestication of animals offers an instructive parable for the behavior of self-interested human beings. There are many forms of irrational behavior, each distinctive in its own way. But there is only one way for people to engage in "rational behavior" as that term is understood in classical economic theory: they must hold and act on a consistent set of preferences. To achieve their ends, they must obey the dictates of "expected utility" theory.[2] They must form estimates of probabilities of uncertain events, attach payoffs to each of those outcomes, and choose the correct strategy. They must be relentless in their forward-looking perspective. For them, opportunity cost is all that matters; bygones are bygones, the fallacy of "sunk costs" never darkens their decisionmaking prowess.[3]

On the austere assumptions of this model, people must reach the one right answer to the calculations they perform.[4] Unhappily every other answer is wrong in its own unique way. But, in a concession to imperfections of human kind, it is not necessary for individuals to make these calculations in a conscious and explicit fashion. Milton Friedman and Leonard Savage argued in 1948 that individuals act "as if" they were aware of, and had mastered, the basic rules of probability,[5] just as they have mastered other facets of their life. This emendation saved (or at least strengthened) the theory of rational behavior and made it conform to common sense. Friedman and Savage spoke of the expert billiard player who can make all the caroms, with and without English, even though he cannot articulate the rules of Newtonian physics that dictate how billiard balls move. The same conclusion holds for the outfielder who takes off at the crack of the bat in total ignorance of the laws governing the flight of a batted ball.

In a strict probabilistic sense, deviations from optimal behavior should be expected, simply because there are many choices that offend the dictates of expected utility theory, while only one can conform to them. The truth of this observation, moreover, is *not* tied to the naïve assumption that individuals possess perfect information about the probabilities and payoffs of their choices. It is quite enough to require them to reach the best possible outcome with whatever imperfect information they possess, in light of their own subjective desires. It takes no deep knowledge of psychology to realize that no individual can perform calculations with the rapidity and accuracy of computers, so we are constantly required to economize on information by using rules of thumb, rough and ready proxies, or, somewhat more grandly, "heuristics."

"Bounded rationality," a theme developed by Herbert Simon,[6] presupposes only that people do the best they can with the limited cognitive facilities that they possess; it marks a sensible concession to the shortness of life. Far from undermining the theory of rational choice, it lends plausibility to it, for it makes eminently good sense for rational agents, knowing their limited capacities, to substitute rules of thumb for precise calculation. The businessman or planner who uses heuristics is no more irrational than the unskilled chess player who concentrates on the center of the board and the key squares under attack, thus ruling out most moves—sometimes, the best moves—from the look and feel of the board. A better player, with more ability to process information, will look further afield with better results, understanding the role of "quiet moves" to build a strong position. Even he must in the end make some intuitive assessment of this last position unless, of course, the outcome is certain to be a win or draw. The weaker player who imitates that strategy will simply make larger blunders.

This logic of successive approximation (which, as we have seen, has such importance in moral reasoning) is not limited to chess, but carries over to the ordinary experiences of everyday life, where it helps explain the behavioral adaptations of imperfect agents. Decisions do not take place in a vacuum; actors are typically not asked to figure out how to maximize the difference between total gains and total losses by pure intellectual reckoning. Rather, most decisions are made in a context where one incremental change (say in price) is likely to yield some incremental improvement (say in profit). So long as people have an accurate sense of direction, they can take a cautious but useful first step to readjust on the strength of new information. Even a move in the wrong direction is likely to exert quick feedback so as to allow the actor to reverse course, especially when the cost of error is more than linear.[7] When, therefore, the external environment is relatively stable, as it often is, these successive adjustments should lead individual actors closer to their perceived optimal strategy. People may never reach their target, but usually they will converge on it through trial and error. The only open question revolves around the rate of convergence from the initial position to the desired one.

Sometimes, however, the currents move so rapidly as to swamp those who navigate by trial and error. At this point, customary practices will tend to falter and different forms of adaptive responses will be invoked. Inexperienced actors will attempt to leave these treacherous waters, so that more experienced players can assume the critical risk-bearing and risk-managing roles. Few amateurs trade in derivatives or commodities any more than they go solo on rough water rafting expeditions. But many ordinary people purchase mutual funds or go on rafting trips led by others. In both cases, people purchase expertise to offset their own known limitations. To be sure, this solution is not foolproof: the agent may turn out to be faithless or incompetent. To minimize that risk, some resources must be spent in choosing agents and monitoring their behavior, which is one of the reasons why branding, through firms, is so important. So long as those costs are lower than the expected costs of acting individually, then these transactions should produce gains for both sides. The shuffling of roles operates as a sorting mechanism, where the principle of comparative advantage helps people overcome their known cognitive limitations, or indeed limitations from any other source, such as lack of experience or nerve. The theory of rational choice thus helps us understand the institutional structures chosen by individual agents to offset their own shortcomings.

The objections to rational choice theory, however, go beyond the obvious concern of limited computational powers and the adaptive responses they generate. Today, as for some considerable time, a large and distinguished academic industry has been devoted to exploring the ways in which individual behavior fails to conform to the optimistic assumptions of the rational choice model, even after the role of bounded rationality is acknowledged. In this view of the world, the decisions of individual actors do not, at least in any obvious fashion, conform to the usual postulates of standard economic theory. Rather, they deviate from the strict mandates of expected utility theory, and do so in predictable ways. It is for this reason that Richard Thaler has described this view of the world as "quasi-rational" economics.[8] In some instances, common heuristics may lead to outcomes that are not biased in one direction or another, as happens when individuals equally overrate, from the *ex ante* perspective, the possibility of remote contingencies in either direction, as happens under the standard model of prospect theory. Those unbiased errors could easily lead to mistaken behavioral choices, for example, by encouraging individuals to invest excessive sums in the prevention of worst-case scenarios. In some cases the biases are more severe: from the *ex ante* perspective people could adopt strategies that lead them to misestimate both the mean and variance of a distribution; from the *ex post* perspective, they could miscalculate the underlying distribution from which the observations had been drawn. The entire history of statistics shows the enormous difficulty in coming to grasp with what (in retrospect only) seems to be the simple and attractive properties of the normal distribution.[9] It is also well known that individuals often overrate the probability of remote events by ignoring underlying base rate information about the frequency of the phenomenon under investigation.[10] These heuristics and biases (which in many cases are linked together in spite of their internal differences) are not products of hatred or impatience, but rather stem from a naked cognitive inability to make or act on the appropriate expected utility calculations.

The topic of behavioral anomalies would be short indeed if the only point at stake were the use of instructional techniques in guiding the perplexed through the maze. To be forewarned is to be forearmed, even in this bias-plagued world. The punch line here is quite different: psychological observations of human behavior point to far more worrisome concerns than the use of rules of thumb to overcome information shortfalls. First, there is some real question about the coherence of ends to which rational choices are directed. I have already discussed some of these issues in connection with adaptive preferences, but the list of potential anomalies goes beyond the philosophical to include how individuals weigh and choose their desires.

In dealing with these ostensible deviations from the rational actor model, I think that it is important to distinguish between two different attitudes toward the issue. On the one hand, I think that it is critical to incorporate into our understanding of the rational actor those deviations that should be expected on the strength of the model of evolutionary psychology and development.[11] It was just this line of criticism that counts as the strongest part of Richard Posner's broadside against behavioral economics generally.[12] The model of individual self-interest may be a useful approximation in certain settings, such as those where individuals interact or transact with strangers, but it is a very poor descriptive model of human conduct generally. More specifically, only a slice of human experience is tied into voluntary exchanges with strangers in labor or product markets. Much of it has to do with familial organizations in which the level of biological interdependence accounts for a higher level of sharing and sacrifice. Precisely because these constraints were, and are, of such importance, we should expect them to influence any overall account of human behavior, conceived in both its individual and group senses.

The use of evolutionary theory also explains why we should expect to find some systematic differences between the observed patterns of human behavior and the dictates of any theory of individual rational self-interest. The natural conditions in which human reason and emotions were formed are a far cry from those that exist today. Life expectancy was short; danger was everywhere; every kilocalorie mattered; and sex roles were sharply divided. The need to estimate compound probabilities was slight, and that to calculate the expected value of securities nonexistent. In such circumstances, we should expect the emergence of those character traits tailored for short-term survival, such as the ability to distinguish friend from foe. Yet once the conditions of human life change by the introduction of property, writing, and technology, those initial traits may no longer be perfectly adapted to their new environment. The pace of change, especially in the last several thousand years, has been so rapid that it would be foolish to expect that strong evolutionary pressure has changed human temperament much from the hunter-gatherer days. The theory of evolution is not invoked to explain why behavior today must be rationale (even if it helps to explain why it is self-interested in the inclusive fitness sense). But it can give some genetic explanation as to what motivates individual behavior and why that behavior should deviate systematically from the dictates of rational choice theory. The exact role of these differences is, moreover, difficult to state in the abstract because of the uncertain weight of basic instincts on the one hand and conscious human adaptations and belief structures on the other. But whatever the precise balance, it seems naïve to urge that modern behaviors are slaves to, or emancipated from, these evolutionary behavior. Rather, we should expect evolutionary influence to be more pronounced in some areas and less in others. The trick is to figure out which areas and why.

This approach contrasts, I think, with that taken by much of behavioral economics that uses experimental evidence to suggest directionless, if persistent, deviations from the predictions of rational choice theory. In these cases, the behavioral anomalies are not tied to any alternative theory of human behavior, that is, to any conception that asks who (the person) or what (the gene) is seeking to maximize—for example, some measure of fitness. Rather, what develops is a loose assemblage of behaviors that are thought to be accounted for by experimental evidence, often conducted on college or graduate student subjects. One major purpose of this and the following chapter is to contrast these two approaches.

Some experimental evidence suggests, for example, that people consider sunk costs when making ordinary decisions, even though classical economic theory focuses exclusively on (forward-looking) opportunity costs.[13] Moreover, individual behavior may respond strongly to an "endowment effect," by which "the value of a good increases when it becomes part of a person's endowment," that is, when it becomes something that he owns rather than something that he wishes to acquire.[14] That bias, in turn, is said to follow from the "loss aversion" effect, whereby individuals seek to avoid uncertainty in the domain of gains (that is, in cases where they are given a choice between receiving a fixed sum and a chance of a somewhat larger sum) but prefer uncertainty in the domain of losses (so that they will take a higher uncertain loss over a smaller certain one).

In addition, individuals fall prey to errors that infect their capacity to use and interpret statistical data. There are biases about hindsight, about availability, about representativeness, about background conditions, about base rates, about sample size,[15] about conjunction,[16] and about overconfidence. In fact, we can find a bias fit for just about every occasion. In each case, the standard form of expected utility theory predicts that individuals should choose certain decisions, but much experimental data suggests that people are led astray in their sensible quest for rules of thumb to economize on high information costs. The central finding of the psychology of cognitive bias is that individuals resort to strategies that systematically violate the basic principles of rational behavior and the accepted rules of probability, and they do so even when the stakes are high and their motivations to succeed are unambiguous.[17]

The collection of this information has both its descriptive and normative implications. The former concerns its accuracy, and the latter its central implication for the roles of markets and government. Where individual behavior does not conform to the traditional economic model of expected utility theory, it becomes far more difficult to afford foundational status to autonomous individual choices under conditions of uncertainty. To what extent, therefore, should these foibles and frailties of the human mind lead us to reevaluate the attachment to classical liberal theory defended in chapter 2? Clearly, these cognitive issues should give us pause, for as human beings behave less efficiently, our social institutions become ever creakier. But the key question is not whether the classical approach yields the optimal outcome under all situations, but whether it works at least as well as any of the alternatives. Let us start with sunk costs and then turn to the endowment effect.

Sunk Costs

Irrelevant?

The standard economic models, as noted above, assume that individuals at each point in time seek to maximize their future economic gains. The necessary corollary is that they can distance themselves from their past mistakes and take into account only their future gains and losses, systematically ignoring their historical costs. The business that invests in heavy equipment that has no alternative use and no salvage value should continue to use that equipment so long as its future revenue will cover its variable costs. So if a firm invests fifty thousand dollars, it continues to deploy the asset in the firm even if it plummets 50 percent in value the next day. "There is no need to fret over spilt milk, burnt toast, or yesterday's business losses."[18] Regret and remorse should not influence human behavior.

Clearly, however, these emotions are too powerful and ubiquitous to be denied their role in human affairs, hence the empirical evidence that gives sunk costs a salience that general economic theory denies them. One well-known experiment observed the behavior of two groups of theater patrons, randomly divided into one group that received discounts on pre-paid season passes and a second that did not. Because the passes had already been paid for, both groups faced the same forward-looking costs for the attendance of the events, measured for example by time used to attend the show. Yet the experimental results showed that those individuals who received the discounts were less likely to attend the performances than those who had paid full price for their tickets.[19] The sunk costs (that is, the price already paid for the tickets) apparently influenced choices, contrary to the standard economic theory.

As with so many behavioral experiments, this question abstracts from many of the social problems that make sunk costs relevant. Thus it is notable that the situation does not present any problem of precommitment for any decisionmaking process that takes place over two periods. Nor does any decision to use or not use the tickets serve as a likely predictor of one's overall level of professional competence or personal character, given that the choice here is largely a *consumption* decision that hardly speaks volumes of future prospects. Indeed, the experiment depends on an artificial sorting of individuals into groups, which removes from them the responsibility for making the initial decision in the first place. They can therefore choose to use the tickets or skip the show without it being a reflection of their prior behavior.

At this point, the key psychological question is whether people will in general do better if they abandon small investments more readily than larger ones. The prompt response is that evaluation of investments should depend on their present value, not their historical cost, and the value in the case of the two theater tickets is the same regardless of cost. But it may well be that individuals who paid more for the ticket thought themselves more heavily invested in the situation, and thus were more likely to attend the performance in order to avoid the somewhat greater costs of psychological reexamination that would be prompted by skipping the event. After all, people who don't readily bail out of costly transactions will be more careful in selecting these ventures in the first place. They will also find it easier to secure trading partners (and mates) for whom their constant character signals a low probability of breach. It is not for nothing that marriage vows speak "for better or for worse."

Yet this last point is not conclusive, because the ability to sense rapid changes in the external environment and to respond accordingly before it is too late also has a powerful survival value. The conclusions that one reaches on this issue are clear on only one point: so long as past behavior helps evaluate and improve future conduct, sunk costs will never be regarded as irrelevant. But it is far harder to decide either the purposes or the ways they are taken into account. One doesn't need behavioral economics to be of two minds on the question.

Self-Knowledge

In light of this experiment, it might be wise to revisit the question of whether standard rational choice theory requires us to treat sunk costs as irrelevant wholly without regard to behavioral economics. Whatever the "need" on these occasions, nothing seems more self-evident than the proposition that people routinely kick themselves, literally and figuratively, for spilling milk, burning toast, and botching past business decisions. Yet at the same time, they also recognize that they cannot dwell on these mistakes forever, but must start over again and put these errors out of their mind if they are to make the best of their next opportunity. The entire task of psychological self-management is something of a balancing act: all individuals have to work hard to separate their future actions from these historical costs but are in the end reluctant to endorse or accept the complete separation. Why?

The first point in the reconstruction is to recognize the powerful difference between the position of the firm and that of the individual employee who decided to purchase the asset that suddenly lost value. For the firm, the choice of how to deploy the asset is indeed easy. A machine that cost fifty thousand dollars should not be junked because it is only worth twenty-five thousand any more than a bearer bond that cost fifty thousand dollars should be thrown away because its value has dropped by half. But even under neoclassical theory, employees should use the information about the outcome of the manager's decision to evaluate both its internal procedures and his position within the firm. Thus, suppose that the firm head had to choose between one of two project managers for promotion, the first of whom purchased equipment that lost half its value, and a second who had purchased equipment that doubled in value. The choice, presumptively, looks easy. At this point, the first project manager *should* fret about the outcome so long as he thinks his past performance offers some evidence of his ability to do this job or others like it.

It is, of course, a mistake to judge performance of one's self or others solely by *ex post* results in a single case, when the proper measure is the expected *ex ante* value of the full range of individual endeavors. But that response does not render information about past performance irrelevant, even if it sets up red flags about its use. It is important to know whether the decision was sound at inception, even if it turned out badly in hindsight. It is critical not to view a single decision in isolation but to evaluate the record as a whole. The firm that decrees that a single error can end a career will have miserable feedback and timid managers. It is the portfolio that counts.

Yet even with these sensible mediating devices, bad outcomes still count as negatives in the record no matter how the ultimate judgment is made. People, therefore, have reason to fret, and through fretting they have reasons to learn from their past mistakes in order to improve their future prospects. In the end, the concern with "sunk costs" is a misnomer, for what is at stake is future prospects, to which fretting is the right emotional response. Those who fret will improve or shift lines of work. Unhappiness from failure is a powerful internal stimulus for self-improvement; so too pleasure from success. Human motivation cannot be solely all carrots or all sticks, given the diminishing rate of effectiveness of each device taken in isolation. Both sets of emotions working together in moderate proportions will do better than either fretting or elation standing alone, which is why the process of evolution has moved us so sharply in this direction.

Precommitments

Thus far I have spoken about reasons for taking sunk costs into account in order to make better judgments as to future prospects. In other contexts of ordinary life, rational individuals should take sunk costs into account as an effective device of self-regulation. For these purposes, it is instructive to look at the process of grief and mourning for the death of a loved one. One possible view is to say that those who have died are gone, and their memories should be ignored in all future calculations. That sentiment is expressed in more muted tones by the proposition (to which all eventually accede) that one "just has to get on with life." But why not do this right away, since no future actions can bring the dead back to life?

In this instance, evolutionary psychology seems to offer a partial explanation of the continued survival value of grieving over losses—for example, the investment in a child—that are technically sunk. In order for human beings to survive as a species, parents must invest enormous resources in the rearing of their offspring to maturity. At a psychological level, both carrots and sticks are used to meet, as just noted, the diminishing marginal returns from using each alone. The tenth, or one hundredth, carrot will be less effective than the first psychological stick. The usual pressures of natural selection should incline individuals to feel both pleasure from the success of their offspring and pain from their failures. Roughly speaking, the pleasure and pain should cut deeper when attributable to the efforts of the parent, so both pride and guilt contribute to the propagation of the species. Yet these same responses should also be present, perhaps at less intense levels, even when the parent has not brought about the desired or feared result. Just knowing that good or bad things could happen to one's offspring could spur greater parental involvement with their lives.

These simple considerations help explain why ostensibly rational individuals do not obey the standard economic injunction to ignore sunk costs. The internal spur for taking risks for the survival of a young infant depends partly on how horrible its parents will feel afterward if that offspring is injured or killed. Yet that emotional mechanism will not kick in if parents *know* today that they as (hyper)rational beings will suffer no anguish should that adverse consequence occur tomorrow. It is the dread of future shock that drives much of current behavior. At a less dramatic level, the same dilemma arises with anticipated benefits. Parents will not work as hard for the success of their offspring if they know today that they will take no satisfaction from their offspring's future achievements. "Let bygones be bygones" is therefore a rational strategy for survival only if an actor has a single mission: to continue with his life once the good or bad outcome has manifested itself. But it is not a reliable maxim given the actor's need before that moment to take steps to avert bad outcomes and promote good ones.

At this point, the optimization problem in this *two*-period game involves the familiar trade-offs. To bind oneself to optimal behavior in the first period is to precommit to emotional paralysis in the event of an adverse outcome in the second period. To preserve optimal discretion in the second period undermines the ability to bind one's self in the initial period. That balance across periods cannot be obtained by any rational choice, for then the whole system would unravel. To avoid that difficulty, individuals are, as it were, programmed to split the difference. Reduce the regret in the second period until the increased flexibility of future action offsets the weakening of the bonds in the prior period. As this game goes on period after period, emotional precommitment becomes a necessary human strategy; accordingly, rational agents should not systematically ignore what are sometimes called "sunk costs." And they don't.

The basic position, then, is that the problems of information and self-bonding make it incorrect to assume that rational actors necessarily avoid sunk costs. Here, of course, one could quibble over the definition of "rational," positing that no rational person is prey to emotions in the first place. But the better sense of rational simply asks whether individuals devoid of emotional impulses will do better in this world than those who respond to emotional stimuli. On that proposition the work of Antonio Damasio shows that the evolutionary verdict is in the negative. Human beings with damage to the emotional centers of their brains are congenitally unable to make ordinary decisions no matter how frequently they process information.[20] Much of the work in behavioral economics is suspicious of the ostensible axiom that rational persons ignore sunk costs, but it takes its cue not from biological concerns, but from experimental ones.

Investments and Joint Ventures

Thus far this analysis of sunk costs has largely focused on personal and consumption choices. There is, however, good reason to think that sunk costs influence business decisions in certain investment contexts as well. Consider allocation of profits and losses in a joint venture situation. If the parties could have perfect knowledge of the payoff options for each participant in each revealed state of the world, there would be no second-stage negotiation over the division of gains or losses. That result requires the parties to be able to write a complete contingent state contract. While that exercise may be brought close to fruition in certain discrete transactions, for example, cash sales, it is hardly possible with these joint venture situations, where twists and turns are always the order the day, and some form of "relational" contract is need to resolve these differences. These contracts typically require a renegotiation of gains and losses at some subsequent stage when the outcomes of the earlier investments are revealed. In these settings, Lorne Carmichael and Bentley MacLeod,[21] have suggested that the parties may use sunk costs as a proxy to allocate the gains from the transaction, or, I would add, the losses from a transaction where the residual investments are still greater than zero.

This need for renegotiation is common knowledge in the venture capital business. The challenge is to devise a set of rules with two overlapping properties: first, the outcomes of the process must be regarded as fair by the participants, not in some abstract sense, but as consistent with their expectations of the deal going in. Fairness here is a proxy for confidence that makes people willing to commit to transactions in which renegotiation is an anticipated part of the process. It is also a precondition for avoiding litigation in the second stage of the deal. Second, the rules in question must be sufficient to limit the bargaining range so as to reduce the level of jockeying between the parties and speed up the renegotiation process. The one convenient focal point that satisfies both of these conditions calibrates (both for positive and negative sum projects) the returns to make them across the board *proportionate* to the total level of prior investment. Here, the system will only work to the extent that these investments—whether in cash, kind, or labor—are observable by the other parties. That looks like a plausible but not perfect assumption in joint venture cases where monitoring is built into the basic structure.

The ability of this proportionate standard to serve as a focal point for both gains and losses helps explain not only why it is the intuitive baseline in ordinary discourse but also why it has a key role to play in constitutional settings. The parties subject to regulation are regarded as compensated (with their fair share of surplus) when the gains are proportionate to their initial investment. More precisely, the proportionate impact test for regulation becomes a test for whether individuals have received compensation for losses sustained through government action,[22] and whether they have received their fair share of the surplus in positive-sum projects.[23] This rule is, for example, far superior to one that gives a fixed dollar rate of return to all participants, and thus skews the rate of return in favor of small investors. Yet by the same token, it does not eliminate all disputes that could arise in deciding the level of contribution made by each member of the group (labor is hard to value; money has a risk that could vary with time of contribution; and so on). But these embedded problems only point to the larger conclusion. Here, one does not need to move to behavioral economics to find a role for sunk costs. Once we leave the world of pure competitive regimes with full information, those costs play a role in preventing the dissipation of unappropriated rents in any renegotiation game.

The overall situation is frequently muddled, for it is possible to identify multiple reasons, some better than others, why individual actors will choose to ignore sunk costs. But the question still remains, does the introduction of this complexity alter the appropriate balance between the market and the state, and if so, in which direction? On this point, it seems clear that major firms can learn that they should not take into account historical costs in deciding to continue with projects that, in hindsight, they wish not to have begun in the first place. It takes only a few well-placed individuals to understand the economic reasons for disregarding sunk costs, and it takes only a little ingenuity to recognize that different considerations apply to the question of personnel management. Once the basic point is internalized in the firm, project managers will quickly adopt the correct protocols. The firm is thus more rational than the individual.

In principle, government agencies could reach the same conclusion, so at this point the question of *relative* advantage turns to the question of which type of organization can respond more readily to the dangers in question. That comparative advantage, moreover, seems far greater in those cases where ostensible sunk costs are used to evaluate internal procedures or personnel. A government civil service is not as likely to get the right balance on these issues as the firm because it works in a monopolistic environment without a clear profit function. Firms have stronger feedback on their mistakes, and workers are more likely to exercise their exit options if the business is poorly run. Once we understand that one purpose of the firm is to constrain the odd behavioral patterns of the individual, we are back to the familiar question: If irrational decisions hurt overall performance, who is likely to pick them up sooner? On this point, one is hard pressed to think of a form of government regulation that could outperform good management sense. The only practical implication of behavioral economics is to strengthen the case for private institutions.

Let me now develop one parallel. The uneasiness of behavioral economists regarding sunk costs is matched in large measure by their uneasiness with the assumption that individuals maximize their own self-interest, a proposition that appears to deny the presence of altruism in a world that sports not only great cruelty but also magnificent generosity.[24] These two concerns are different: one goes to the question of whether the welfare of others falls into anyone's utility function; the other question (concerning sunk costs) asks how people should act to maximize whatever goal (individual or group) that they wish to advance. I have just addressed the matter of sunk costs,[25] so I now ask whether we can explain any deviations from the economic principle of self-interested behavior. Recall that biological self-interest is not individualistic, but turns on *inclusive* fitness, whereby each person takes into account the welfare of their familial connections weighted by their genetic distance. Precisely because genes are selfish, individuals are not. Caring for others is a built-in part of the human condition. That said, the imperfect nature of evolution requires a balance between two types of error: excessive benevolence and excessive egotism. An agent that acts in a benevolent fashion toward strangers (that is, persons with no common genes) may reduce its own inclusive fitness by expending resources on others that could be used to advance its own genetic complement. The agent that fails to show adequate concern for the fate of its offspring runs, however, a reciprocal risk, that of failing to protect and promote their interests, which are critical to genetic success.

Which error is likely to prove more costly? This issue is too important for choices to be attributable to some mistake as to the genetic relatedness of the parties being helped. In some species the level of kin recognition is quite high (as when elephant seals all give birth on the same beach), and in other cases, such as human beings, there are easy ways to track offspring at birth in relatively isolated circumstances. It seems better, therefore, to postulate that all organisms work with reliable information. In this environment, the better guess is that neglecting one's own will prove more costly than any occasional burst of misplaced generosity. Extending care to distantly related or unrelated individuals consumes some resources. But it also offers an opportunity to learn the altruistic behaviors that can be subsequently used in family situations, and it may well lead to forms of reciprocity by other individuals who think they are likely to benefit a second time by doing a good deed of their own. The level of care that one observes in these more distant situations is likely to be far lower than that devoted to one's own kin. But the ability to cut down on external commitments increases one's confidence in the judgment that casting the net too wide has fewer risks than casting it too narrowly. Stated otherwise, in marginal cases the cost of benign neglect could easily exceed that of misplaced generosity. If this is the case, then we can postulate some evolutionary pressures that lead us away from the Hobbesian model of relentless self-interest and toward the Humean model of individual self-interest tempered by "confin'd generosity," which is the philosophical forebear of the empirical claims for limited individual self-interest.

This biological account of the overall practice is not meant to favor either behavioral or traditional economics. Rather, its aspirations are more modest. It is easy to postulate some individual welfare function to which the general expected utility theory can be applied. But it is crucial not to choose oversimplified models solely to make the mathematics tractable. Nor should these models be chosen simply to advance the agenda of one economic point of view; they should rest on plausible assumptions from outside the field. Within economics, self-interest is a working assumption; within evolutionary biology, it is an outgrowth of the theory of natural selection. Evolutionary biology will not explain every manifestation of generosity or selfishness, but it does help explain why some deviations from the individual model of rational choice are more descriptively accurate than others.

Endowment Effect

Setting the Stakes

The issues regarding sunk costs carry over, as we might expect, to the closely related problem of the endowment effect. The endowment effect, it will be recalled, asserts that individuals will attach higher values to those items that they own relative to those that they do not. Stated in other terms, the endowment effect postulates a systematic gap between the willingness to pay (WTP) and the willingness to accept (WTA),[26] or as it is sometimes called, the "bid/asked differential." No matter what the terminology, the former of these two quantities represents the amount that individuals are willing to pay to acquire something they do not possess. The latter represents the amount of money that they must receive to part voluntarily with something that they do possess. The naïve assumption of many neoclassical writers has been that the two figures will generally converge so that the differences between them can safely be ignored in dealing with public policy analysis.[27] Once that is done then the usual prescriptions of the Coase theorem will apply, and we can be confident that voluntary exchanges will direct the resource to its highest value use no matter what its initial allocation.[28]

One object of a system of free exchange is to move resources to higher valued uses. Unfortunately, that task is compromised if the value of the good depends on who owns it, for then the social program now appears circular. Under the traditional analysis, if some good is valued more by A than by B, then A will keep it if he already owns it; but if he does not, then he will buy it from B for a price that leaves both parties better off. Thus, if A values the good at $100 and B values it at $80; A will buy it from B if she has it, and keep it if he already possesses it. If the values are reversed, B will buy it from A if he has it, and keep it if she possesses it. So long as transaction costs are zero, ultimate location of the good depends on who can make the best use of it, not on who initially owns it.

These optimistic Coasean outcomes may be confounded, however, if ownership of a good counts, for some reason, as a constituent element of its own value. Suppose we can say that if A already has the good then he will value it at $100, while B, who does not possess it, will value it at $80. A will keep possession even if transaction costs are zero. But now suppose that B has possession of the good. Now the endowment effect makes a reverse valuation plausible, so that A will value the good (simply because he does not own it) at $80, while B values it at $100. This time, no trade will take place. Any cleavage between WTP and WTA implies that the initial assignment of the good, however obtained, may well determine its ultimate allocation even when transaction costs are zero.

In one sense, that result seems to be perfectly benign, for even if we recognize the endowment effect, it hardly leads to inefficient allocations, given the subjective nature of human preferences. Rather, it only reduces the number of occasions in which voluntary transactions are needed to correct some initial error in the assignment of resources. The difficulties become more serious, however, when the initial resource ownership is un-determined. One intuitively sensible way to allocate such resources is by way of auction.[29] In principle, however, the endowment effect could lead to odd inversions that subsequent market transactions could not correct. Suppose A would value a good at $100 if he already possessed it, and at $80 if he did not. Yet B would value it at $120 if she already pos-sessed it, but $70 if she did not. If both parties have sufficient funds to bid for the item, A will win the auction, for $80 is greater than $70. Yet if B had won the auction, once in possession she would attach a greater value to the good, since $120 is greater than $100. It follows, therefore, that the auction will not necessarily lead to the optimal resource alloca-tion. The same result obtains for a different reason if B lacks sufficient wealth to bid for an item that she would choose not to sell if she already possessed it.

The first question about this model is whether one can imagine a set of empirical circumstances that render it plausible. One possibility appeals to the idea of a wealth effect. Let two identical people start with the same wealth, after which one gets some particular item. At this point his greater wealth reduces his relative preference for dollars so that he will hold out for the higher price. But the explanation has little persuasive force because the observed cases of the endowment effect occur even in experiments that involve small increments to wealth. At this point the mystery only deepens, for the inversion outlined in the previous example works only if A and B have no knowledge of their WTAs when they bid for the goods. If that assumption does not hold, then B's higher WTA should lead her to raise her WTP to a sum just below that amount, at which point there is a puzzle to explain why there is any endowment effect at all.[30] The empirical question, then, is whether B's surge in WTA on acquisition comes without any forewarning. As with so much of behavioral economics, a good deal of ingenuity is expended to *identify* an effect, let alone ascertain its magnitude. It is conceivable that sometimes people will have no real sense of their attachment to particular goods until they obtain possession of them. That response is common for couples with newborn children (not, of course, acquired by auction) who, even when forewarned, typically underestimate the enormous wrench that childbirth has on their psyches. But why believe that all changes in endowments generate that jolt? Any WTA/WTP differential rarely matters for goods consumed in the ordinary course of one's life. Clumsy private resales are rarities next to organized merchant sales. In ordinary markets, the phenomenon is most likely to arise, if at all, with costly consumer durables such as artwork or furniture. In any *particular* case, an endowment effect may take hold. But when experienced time after time, the lesson learned should kick to impel people to raise their bids. How many surprises does it take until people adapt? As with adaptive preferences, there is some good reason to doubt the role of this phenomenon in a wide range of ordinary transactions.

For the moment, however, let us assume that the endowment effect operates in the way that is described. Even so, we should be wary about drawing institutional implications from theoretical considerations. The numbers set out in the above example with A and B were necessarily hypothetical, and we have no empirical way to verify them short of survey evidence that itself presents genuine difficulties in collection and interpretation. It should, moreover, give us pause before asserting that one individual will consistently have a substantially greater spread between his WTA and WTP than another. The more plausible working assumption is that the ratio will be roughly fixed in any population: where the WTP is greater for A than for B, the odds are pretty good that A's WTA will be greater than B's as well. If so, then the bid prices offer reasonably good proxies for the asking prices, so the naïve auction usually should lead to mostly efficient outcomes, punctuated by some mistakes.

Why worry? Auctions are likely to be mildly inefficient even when WTA is identical to WTP. Thus, suppose that bids in a standard auction rise in $100 increments. A has bid $1,000 for the item, which B values at $1,050. A will win the auction even though B attaches the higher value to the good; and the outcome would have been different if B had made the $1,000 bid, which A would not raise. Yet no one thinks that this imperfection should force art houses to abandon auctions. Sotheby's might want to switch to smaller intervals when the bidding tapers off, but Christy's may fear smaller intervals will prolong auctions in ways that reduce customer interest in the overall list. So each house is left to chart its own course, just as individual bidders plot their own strategies. (If the misallocation is pronounced, then it just might be corrected by a private sale from A to B.)

Similar imperfections can be found in competitive markets, as when foodstuffs are sold for fixed prices in the supermarket. Sometime quantities run out under a first-come, first-served regime. The last lucky customer may have a lower consumer surplus than the first customer to leave empty-handed. Some small inefficiency results. No side transaction is likely to fill that gap. But if markets survive these reversals, then they can survive the endowment effect as well. Institutionally, it is one thing to identify a weakness *in principle* and another thing to devise a method to correct that weakness *in fact*. Certainly, one could not run an auction by asking individuals to state truthfully their WTA, even assuming they could know it, for a good that they had not yet acquired. What would prevent systematic overstatement of one's WTA? Nor is there any other reliable political fix to this revelation problem. The existence of the endowment effect may add yet another complication to auctions and other markets, but it hardly suggests, let alone compels, the adoption of some alternative mechanism.

In Market Transactions

Thus far I have offered reasons to be skeptical about the long-term role that the endowment effect has in ordinary markets for goods and services. It is now useful to examine the empirical evidence, largely from experimental studies, for the effect's existence and significance. The best known experiment involves a comparison of behavior in the use of tokens and mugs.[31] In the first half of the experiment the subjects were each given different individual prices at which identical tokens could be redeemed by the experimenter. They were then allowed to trade these tokens among themselves for cash. The transaction costs were essentially zero (negative, if the game resulted in consumption), and the markets cleared in accordance with the dictates of neoclassical theory. A would pay B $1.00 for a token that he, A, could redeem for $1.25. C would sell to D for $1.00 a token that she, C, could redeem for only $0.75. All tokens gravitated to the hands of those individuals with the higher bidding prices, as the economic theory predicted.

That outcome was *not* replicated, however, when a similar experiment with tradable (Cornell) school mugs, which again could be redeemed at different prices. Trades still occurred but at a lower frequency than before, for some individuals exhibited strong attachments to the mugs they initially received. (Apparently, prior experience had not prepared the students for these experiments.) A large spread developed, as the WTA often exceeded the WTP by a factor of two: that as, experimental subjects demanded twice as much money to part with their mug as they were prepared to pay to acquire the identical mug from someone else. For want of any alternative explanation, this differential result is arguably attributable to the endowment effect, which asserts itself before the subjects had any reason to develop any subjective attachment to a mug that was designated theirs, not through individual effort, but through random assignment.

The same phenomenon has been observed in other contexts. In one study, jury instructions for personal injury actions were framed in two different ways.[32] The first set of instructions asked the jury to decide how much money it would take to secure the *ex ante* consent of an individual for the injuries inflicted on him. That "selling price" approach asked the jury, in effect, to calculate the WTA. The alternative instructions stressed the amount of money that was necessary after the fact to make the victims whole. This "make whole" test was designed to elicit the WTP, the amount that the injured party would pay to be indifferent between the loss of his health and having his injuries undone, assuming that this could have been done instantaneously in the first place. Both these measures run into certain real puzzles in any case of death or personal injury.[33] A person who dies has no use for the money that he might receive apart from a bequest motive of uncertain strength. A person with serious injuries could have few medical expenses, but no opportunity to use wealth for ordinary consumption activities. It would be odd for one therefore to think of selling one's body for a high purchase price when that sale would necessarily compromise the ability to enjoy the wealth received in exchange. It is perhaps for that reason that courts have always been leery of adopting a formula that uses *either* the WTA *or* WTP measures for damages,[34] preferring instead an artificial index of damages that sums up (with appropriate fudge factors) lost earnings, medical expenses, and pain and suffering to arrive at a damage award.

Any asserted correspondence between WTA and the "selling price" approach (and between WTP and the "make whole" approach) also does not quite capture the situation, for in the first case, the jury is instructed to give independent weight to the autonomy value that each person has in choosing his or her own fate. The second set of instructions implicitly valued that right of self-control at zero. But, even with these caveats, experimentally the two sets of instructions evoked different jury responses too powerful to ignore. The "make whole" approach produced a (logarithmic) mean of $151,448 and a median of $290,000, while the "selling price" approach yielded a (logarithmic) mean of $331,042 and a median of $527,000.[35]

A similar pattern has been observed in experimental work directed to environmental issues. One instructive study by Boyce and others[36] of Norfolk Island pines—a small house tree that could be easily moved—showed that under a variety of conditions it took more money to get an individual to part with a tree than to acquire it. Boyce and her colleagues examined WTP and WTA under two different scenarios. In the first, the experimental subject either acquired (WTP) or surrendered (WTA) the tree in question, knowing that the tree would be kept alive in either case. In these two "no-kill" settings, the experimental subject who owned the tree demanded a mean price of $8.00 to give it up. Yet he would only pay $4.81 to purchase the same tree so long as he thought it would not be killed by its present owner. But once the destruction of the tree was built into the experiment, so that the subject thought that the failure to transact would result in the death of the tree, *both* figures got higher: $18.43 for the WTA and $7.81 for the WTP. The endowment effect may explain the differentials in each experiment, while the independent concern with nature explains the higher figures for both WTA and WTP in the "killing" scenario.

The immediate follow-on questions are these: Can these results be replicated? Can these results be generalized? There are doubts on both points. On the first score, Shogren and his colleagues ran a careful experiment that substituted Iowa State mugs for Cornell mugs over ten trials and found an initial disparity in which WTA exceeded WTP, only for the gap to close (and slightly reverse) by the end of the run.[37] The bidding systems involved were slightly different from those employed in the Cornell experiment in that they used a Vickrey second-price sealed bid auction, which is designed to elicit the reservation price that the bidder (or the minimum price for the owner) has for the goods. The great advantage of this system is that it forces all bidders to think about the relationship between WTP and WTA in ways that are likely to make the two numbers converge.[38]

Shogren and coworkers presented further evidence to argue that the endowment effect is much more likely to persist when ordinary individuals are asked to deal with "commodities" that are not easily tradable in ordinary markets. They thus found a far greater WTA/WTP disparity when the "good" to be bought or sold was a sharp reduction in the level of health hazard (for example, bacterial infection from roughly one part in 100 million to one part in 125,000) from the sale of ordinary household goods. Their hypothesis is that so long as one good is cheaply substitutable for another, then WTA/WTP differentials are likely to become insignificant, but they will remain robust (and highly variable) in other setting with nonmarket goods. Market actors normally try to cover this risk by offering a warranty of fitness, either express or implied,[39] for food that is either sold in containers or served in restaurants, so as to reduce the burden on consumers to estimate the probability of contamination in the first place.[40] Shogren's approach also helps explain something about the persistence of the WTA/WTP differential in the Boyce example, where once again the protection of trees against destruction is not a standard tradable market commodity. It also helps again to explain the results with jury instructions as well, when the role of individuals is to evaluate behavior, but not participate in ordinary markets.

There is yet another set of reasons why we should systematically expect the endowment effect to be weaker in market settings than even the Shogren experiments suggest. Even in the mug experiments, no effort is made to mimic the behaviors found in ordinary market transactions. The subjects are just asked whether they wish to buy and sell, wholly without regard to any purpose. Not surprisingly, therefore, it is virtually impossible to identify any business, commercial, or consumer dispute in which either side has appealed to the endowment effect in order to bolster its own position.

For good reason. Take the simple case of a dealership in automobiles or even artwork. It would be odd to think that the endowment effect inhibited their sales efforts. The entire purpose of both businesses business is to first acquire and then to sell inventory. Each day that an automobile, say, remains on the showroom floor it depreciates. Carrying costs mount while payroll has to be met and rent paid. It is hard to conceive how any dealer could stay in business if he developed an instantaneous attachment to a car that cost him $15,000, such that his WTA leaped to $20,000 so that he could not accept the offer from a customer whose WTP was $18,000. The whole mission is to buy cheap and to sell dear, so that a dealer would fire any sales representative who fell under the spell of the endowment effect. Art dealers labor under the same imperatives, notwithstanding their strong personal identification with the artists whose work they sell. No turnover, no survival.

These imperatives seem to apply to every supermarket and financial institution, and are quickly communicated from owners to employees. As such, they point broadly to two effects that the earlier experiments do not try to capture. The first is that business imperatives create strong *incentives* to reduce the effect of any possible endowment effect. Second, the endowment effect, like any other, is not uniformly distributed in nature. Therefore, a *selection* effect will also tend to weed out of these various selling positions any endowment-sensitive individuals who might exhibit strong retentive attachments to the goods and services that they are supposed to sell. In these markets, on common experience we should reject the view that the WTA is consistently higher than the WTP on a priori grounds.

Some recent experimental research tends to confirm this point of view. One study by John List involved two types of sports memorabilia that had roughly equal market value.[41] In the first run, these memorabilia were distributed randomly among individuals with little or no trading experience. It turned out that the parties were reluctant to trade the goods that they received, which could be attributed either to an endowment effect or simply to a reluctance to exchange for fear of being duped in a market in which they had little experience. The attractive bid from a buyer could represent either his own unique use for the good in question, at which point the well-advised seller should leap forward, or it could represent better knowledge of the overall market situation, at which point the inexperienced seller should hold back. The seller who does not know which scenario (or which scenario in what proportion) holds will be rightly cautious, especially if he knows that the potential buyers are aware of his inexperience.

In light of these general observations, it should come as no surprise that the reluctance to trade (whether or not attributable to an endowment effect) disappeared when the goods were given to dealers in these memorabilia. Collectors with extensive trading experience exhibited behaviors closer to that of dealers than to that of collectors with little experience. If the endowment effect explains the initial reluctance to trade, it is driven out by experience. One possible explanation of the effect (if it exists) is as an instinctive device that protects uninformed traders from being duped. But no matter what its function, the implications of this last experiment seem clear for overall industry behavior. Markets are dominated by dealers and experienced traders. Inexperienced individuals know that they work at a disadvantage and often seek guidance from people who are more experienced. The selection effect thus drives out the novices who do not learn. In equilibrium, some new people are always entering and leaving a market that is dominated by survivors whose behavior conforms to the postulates of rational choice theory.

The same basic result has been confirmed in another setting. Arlen, Spitzer, and Talley[42] sought to determine the extent to which corporate agents would exhibit an endowment effect while conducting business for the firm. They found that control subjects (who did not act for another) exhibited an endowment effect similar to that found in the prior literature, but experimental subjects who were instructed to act as agents did not. The endowment effect likewise did not appear to influence their behavior in negotiating compensation for positions that they might take within the firm. Here again, the market setting tends to drive out the endowment effect.

As Arlen and her colleagues recognize, their findings undercut yet another attack against the contract at will in employment. Here, the basic suggestion is that under a sound default rule worker job attachments count as elements of the initial endowment that may merit protection against arbitrary employer dismissal.[43] Thus, suppose that a worker attached $1,000 to security if it were included in a default rule, but only $300 if it were not. Conversely, the employer might attach a value of $750 to the at-will rule if it were part of the default regime, but only $200 if it were not. In this case, the choice of the initial default rule would determine the ultimate allocation for the same reasons outlined above.[44] No employer would pay $1,000 to acquire what he values at $200; no worker would pay $750 to acquire what he values at $300. But it looks as though these differentials do not survive in market settings for labor, so that the supposed stickiness of the default rule disappears.

Nor should we expect otherwise, for the existence of any endowment effect seems far weaker with a default rule than a property right. A default rule does not allocate rights; nor does it even set the baseline for contractual negotiations. It is only a gap filler when negotiations are silent. Suppose one switched (mistakenly in my view) to a for-cause default rule. Let the employer post a sign in the hall outside the hiring room that says all contracts shall only be at will, and that state-created default term is history before a single prospective worker walks through the door. What worker endowment effect could possibly survive that posting? Should one make this posting illegal because of the elements of value that it destroys, at which point the default rule verges on one of positive law? Of course, no employer is entitled to have his way simply by posting his hiring conditions. And so too the employee. Neither side can claim an endowment effect during the course of negotiations.

Acquisition and Taking of Private Property

The question then arises as to whether we can identify any contexts in which endowment effects do matter. Here, I think that it is possible to find two areas in which they may count, neither of which involves ordinary forms of market transaction. These involve (1) the rules of the initial acquisition of property rights under a rule of capture and (2) the rules that govern the awards of just compensation for the taking and/or regulation of property. These cases present special difficulties precisely because market systems cannot organize the rules that govern the emergence of private property or those that structure their involuntary conversion or limitation by government coercion. In both these cases, moreover, the arguments from behavioral economics, to the extent that they have any traction at all, tend to *strengthen* the case for a regime with strong property rights and limited government power that is already defensible on other grounds. Let us consider the points in order.

First Possession. Thus far I have cautioned against appealing to the endowment effect to undermine classic allocation devices such as the auction. The effect also leads to a useful reexamination of the case for some of the critical common law rules. The standard principle of first possession has long been attacked as an arbitrary system of allocation that confers an enormous advantage on those individuals lucky enough to "grab" property for themselves.[45] As noted earlier, it is mistaken under standard economic theory to attack the rule for its supposed unbridled individualism, for that transition rule supplies an easy means for taking resources out of the state of nature and reducing them to private ownership, which in turn facilitates their orderly consumption, use, or disposition.

Ironically, the endowment effect only undergirds the common law rule by offering an additional explanation as to why the initial possessor attaches a greater value to a resource than any subsequent party. The experiment with the mugs suggests that the element of desert is not strictly necessary for developing an attachment, insofar as people are willing to attach higher values to goods even if they have done nothing to earn them. But there could easily be a useful survival feature in this outcome, for it helps explain why the new owner is instantly prepared to defend his claim against the entire world, and may have done so with some success even before the advent of public institutions to secure property rights.

More specifically, it is possible to postulate a strong evolutionary advantage to the first possession rule, and through it of any endowment effect. As ever, all psychological mechanisms are subject to two kinds of error. Here, the attachment to an object already possessed could develop either too early or too late. The former vice might well lead an organism to expend excessive resources to defend things of little value, but places at risk the early investment in things that an organism wishes to keep for its own. In nature we would not expect to see too many weird wind-fall situations, so the dangers of premature attachments are accordingly reduced. So long as the selection of things taken into possession is not random, and depends on some informed estimation of the value of the thing acquired, the former error looks on balance to be less costly than the latter. Better to develop a few unexplained attachments in odd social settings than to undercut those attachments that really matter. A strong first possession rule, therefore, becomes justified not because of the "labor" added to the thing acquired, but because of the additional value (that is, the endowment) that it preserves when things are separated from the commons.

The rule gains in its salience, moreover, when placed in a larger social perspective. In ordinary lawsuits it is too easy to presume that the only competition that counts takes place between the two parties who litigate, typically the first possessor and a rival who had previously commenced hot pursuit. I shall return to the importance of that situation, but for the moment the first possession rule is best understood as setting up a focal point in an otherwise disorderly state of nature, not only with humans but with any conspecifics, that is, with any species of its own kind. Any competition over food, prey, or territory is probably not confined to two parties, but likely extends in varying degrees to all members of the group. A practice that assigns rights of priority based on a direct comparison of individual characteristics thus runs into difficulty when multiple contenders lay claim to a single good. How does one determine which of ten animals dominates on any given occasion, especially when they are about the same size?

The rule of first possession goes a long way to obviate that impasse among approximate equals. By allowing the first possessor to control a resource, a cheap signaling rule works to solve an important coordination problem in the context of repeat play. The signal becomes credible because, *ceteris paribus,* possession confers some advantage to the possessor in any random confrontation that might otherwise arise; he knows the territory or has the prey in his grasp. In any specific interaction, therefore, the odds are tilted toward the first possessor. Over many iterations of the game, avoiding risky or lethal confrontations early on allows both loser and winner to compete successfully in later rounds.

It is, of course, possible to imagine individual organisms evolving strategies that deviate from this implicit first possession norm.[46] In the most simplified form, assume that one group of players adopts an aggressive strategy to an unclaimed resource while a second group follows a timid one. The result is a two-by-two matrix with the following payoffs. A conflict between aggressive versus timid will yield a clear outcome whereby the aggressor wins. But the outcome of a confrontation of aggressive versus aggressive is likely to prove harmful to both contestants, leaving each vulnerable in subsequent encounters, even against otherwise timid players. Timid versus timid avoids that risk, but that outcome is not ideal either, because in some cases both parties will leave some valuable resource unclaimed.

A uniform rule of conflict resolution collapses the matrix into a single box with positive payoffs for one player and no negative payoffs for the other. When embodied in the first possession rule, it goes a long way toward eliminating any practical difference between the two types of players, and thus helps reduce the potential losses from confrontation and underutilization. The first possession rule may not gain universal adherence, but its centralizing tendency remains strong. The costs of aggressive confrontations are likely to be very high, so this strategy will prove dangerous to any one player so long as a small fraction of the population adopts it. Once fewer players adopt that more cooperative strategy, then there is less reason for anyone else to remain timid, inducing convergence on a single behavioral standard from individuals who start out as either timid or aggressive.

All independent decisions carry with them substantial risks that no system of evolution can overcome. In this case, the major problem could arise when *each* player, for whatever reason, thinks that it is the first possessor. In these cases where the property rights are unclear, each will take the aggressive strategy, leading to conflict. In 1978, John Maynard Smith reported on an earlier experiment by N. G. Davies about the speckled wood butterfly who gained energy from evanescent cones of light formed among the branches of the forest—one butterfly to each cone.[47] The number of possible confrontations was likely to be high, but the number of available cones was large and their durability was short, so that no single loss was necessarily ruinous. In that environment, the first possession rule offers an effective way to resolve multilateral conflicts. The experimenters duly reported that once occupation had been established, other butterflies tended to stay away. If they challenged, there was a brief ritual in which both butterflies spiraled to the top of the cone, and then the challenger flew away. Thereafter, it was discovered that the contests became somewhat more intense when the scarcity of the sunspots increased. One possibility was that the behavior in question only reflected the prior dominance of the first possessor: that is, that the first to occupy was in some sense fitter prior to the occupation. But when the roles between them were reversed, even in very short intervals, the new possessor prevailed after going through the same ritual. Nor could that result be explained by some advantage that was acquired by virtue of the occupation itself, for the rule held even when butterflies had just acquired, or lost, their spaces. Fierce conflicts arose, however, when each thought that it was the first possessor: mistake thus induced the aggressor versus aggressor scenario in a limited number of cases. In these circumstances, both butterflies adopted the hawk strategy because each thought it had pride of place. The most sensible explanation, therefore, is that the taking position works to provide a general *signal* respected by others to avoid what would otherwise be ruinous confrontations.

Natural experiments help explain the importance of the first possession rule as a conflict resolution device in human societies. Its importance looms especially large in primitive societies where state power is weak and self-help a daily necessity. In this specific context, the endowment effect is not just an odd behavior posited by psychologists. It may also supply a working solution to potentially deadly conflicts. To wait until some attachment to a resource forms after possession gives an uncertain signal to those who follow as to the strength of one's attachment to things within his possession. That uncertainty opens the door to conflict when two parties come to the same land or animal in rapid succession. It is also no small wonder that the most difficult cases in the law are precisely those where the claims to possession are conflicted, as when the initial pursuer loses out to the crafty interloper: the imprinting of oneself on external objects could take place before actual occupation is attained, so that the rule that ignores hot pursuit (and the customary practice that sustains it) could prove to be inferior to one that takes refuge in the greater certainty afforded by first possession.[48]

An endowment effect helps explain not only the importance of possession as a means of acquisition, but also supplies an additional reason to recognize continued ownership of discrete things. On this score, the legal rules uniformly allow an owner to retain possession without repeating the affirmative actions that led to its acquisition. It is, therefore, no accident that David Hume, in his account of private property, identified the stability of possession as a major pillar of a strong legal system,[49] as a complement to the basic rule of occupancy for the acquisition of property.[50] It dovetails well with the ordinary sentiments of mankind, whose biological origins are only reinforced by a dominant social convention that has proved more tenacious than the intellectual affection for it.

Takings and Habitat Regulation. These first possession cases also suggest how the endowment effect might influence modern conflicts over environmental protection. The common law rules on this subject are clear. The habitat was part of the land, and no individual owned the wild animals that depended on it for survival. Thus, the owner could eliminate the habitat, and any individual could capture or kill the wildlife. It is no surprise that in modern times both parts of this synthesis have been attacked. State protection of wild animals from death or capture is justified by the mismatched incentives when a single hunter captures all the gains but bears only a fraction of the social loss, a standard common pool situation well accounted for without any reference to behavioral economics. Excessive capture inexorably leads to extinction, which is in no one's interest, and only a firm system of social control can prevent this problem. In this world, the WTA/WTP differential only reinforces the basic argument. The individual actors have not gained possession of the natural resource, so preventing them from acquiring it only implicates WTP values (or, more accurately, willingness to capture values), which are more easily compensated than WTA values for animals already reduced to possession. So the only change in the basic argument for public intervention is that the level of compensation owed individual actors for the loss of their right to capture is lower than might otherwise be supposed, and thus more easily satisfied by allowing them limited rights of capture in a more stable stock.[51]

The next question is how the proper treatment of habitat preservation is influenced by the WTA/WTP differential. Wholly apart from any endowment effect, it is always difficult to offer valuations for environmental resources in which the ownership rights are not clearly defined. One common strategy is to resort to contingent valuation whereby social surveys help determine how much a representative portion of the population values a certain environmental good or service for which, typically, there is no ready market equivalent.[52] Ordinary market choices require people to actually forgo one thing in order to acquire another. But with survey research what is received is clearly in view while nothing visible is surrendered. The temptation to overvalue the known good is strong when the question posed gives individuals systematically better knowledge of what they are to receive than what they may be asked to surrender. It may, ironically, suffer from the availability heuristic.[53] It is, therefore, hardly surprising, but somewhat unnerving, that individual estimated values on various natural resources vary with the exact phrasing of the question on the order of 300 to 2,000 percent, depending on the exact form of the problem.[54] Piled onto the implicit difficulties of survey research, the size of these evaluations may well depend on whether respondents are asked to give their (higher) WTAs or their (lower) WTPs, when the context leaves it unclear whether the public owns or only aspires to own the resource in question. Whatever cognitive biases infect market transactions are magnified within survey studies.

Choosing between WTA and WTP is treacherous business if the question at hand is the protection of the ozone layer or the preservation of the scenic beauty of the Grand Canyon. But less global valuation disputes also arise in the administration of many more focused environmental programs, such as the Endangered Species Act,[55] in which habitat preservation plays an essential role. The basic statutory prohibition makes it an offense for any person to "take" members of endangered species.[56] "Take" is defined in the Act to cover all direct attacks on animals—"to harass, harm, pursue, hunt, shoot, wound, kill, trap, capture, or collect, or to attempt to engage in any such conduct."[57] Thus far, the logic of the Endangered Species Act tracks the standard common pool problem in perilous circumstances where any diminution of the stock increases the risk of the total destruction of the species. But, by administrative regulation, upheld by the Supreme Court in *Babbitt v. Sweet Home Chapters of Oregon,*[58] the Secretary of the Interior extended the definition of "harm" to "include any significant habitat modification or degradation where it actually kills or injures wildlife by significantly impairing essential behavioral patterns, including breeding, feeding or sheltering."[59]

For these purposes, we can safely assume that habitat on private land is essential for preserving endangered species. But should that habitat be taken, as it were, by regulation, or should the state buy the relevant habitat or compensate an individual landowner for his property losses? Traditional economic analysis exposes a powerful asymmetry between species and habitat destruction. The former must be prevented by the use of force, for any decision to compensate individuals for not killing species will bring forth legions of potential killers demanding compensation. For just this reason, compensation is not paid to people who refrain from stealing, killing, and raping. But this threat of follow-on violations does *not* exist for habitat preservation, because the only parties who can tender habitat to the state are those who already possess that limited resource, and inducing more of that behavior does not retard but advances the social interest. The indirect social benefits from species preservation—the knowledge that the species will survive for future human enjoyment, for example—are widely distributed. Why then use regulation to concentrate the burdens of that system on a few isolated individuals? Committed private parties can always purchase habitat for preservation purposes, and, if they choose, can lease limited use rights to raise the capital for further acquisition of sensitive lands. The government can, by appropriate deliberative processes, chime in with additional purchases of its own in the voluntary market, or forced purchases through its eminent domain power.

Unfortunately, the alternative system of regulation may well induce private individuals to quietly destroy private habitat to avoid the onerous restrictions that come with its ownership—a result that benefits neither private owners nor the public at large. These incentives seem powerful in theory, and one careful empirical study of these private preemptive strikes showed that their effects should not be ignored. The red-cockaded woodpecker (RCW) lives in old growth southern pine throughout the southeast.[60] The passage of the Endangered Species Act induced the harvesting of trees at a younger age—a reduction of nine years from a forty-eight-year mean.[61] It also induced a more rapid destruction of stands of trees near RCW colonies, increasing that rate from 40 percent to 53 percent (a 62 percent increase).[62] Why should one be surprised when the two hundred acres of habitat for a single colony of RCWs holds timber worth nearly $200,000?

Under any economic analysis, offering compensation turns habitat from a private liability into a private asset. Properly calibrated, it should undo the landowner's incentive for a preemptive strike. The point is, moreover, important even in the traditional framework, for there are many cases, the endowment effect aside, in which the value in use to the present owner exceeds the value in exchange, which is why all property is not perpetually for sale. The gap between WTA and WTP modifies the analysis in three ways. First, in cases of voluntary acquisition, the reservation price of the owner is likely to be somewhat higher than conventional economic analysis predicts. Second, in those cases in which compensation is granted, the appropriate level should be ratcheted up to reflect this additional component of private value. And third, the social costs of denying compensation altogether are greater because of the increased private losses that are not taken into account in this imperfect social calculus.

Taken together, these arguments about the WTA/WTP differential reflect a decided preference for the vested rights, which in this case include the ordinary rights of husbandry associated with private land. Unlike the biosphere, there are no hidden conflicts as to which person assumes what role. As such, the owner is not a purchaser, for whom the WTP becomes the operative number, but the owner, for whom the higher WTA controls. Denying compensation results in WTA losses for the owner that would still not be redressed under the ordinary fair market value test, which ignores, of course, any increment of the owner's subjective value. Matters are made only more difficult if environmentalists think that habitats located on private lands are somehow to be regarded as public resources, for then each side sees victory by the other as dispossession of its protected ownership interest. It would be the case of the battling butterflies transferred to the human context. But it is hard to see why this complication alters the basic logic on compensation. The environmentalists who claim that their position implicates WTA should be able to raise funds that compensate landowners for their own WTA valuations: after all, the higher values they attach to the habitat should raise their willingness to pay.

More generally, the WTA/WTP spread is relevant when evaluating any restrictions on proposed land use. Suppose the question is whether a landowner is denied the right to develop land that he possesses. As with habitat preservation, we can no longer draw the sharp dichotomy between owner and buyer that is found throughout the experimental literature; the lines are blurred. Do we treat the landowner as though he always owned the rights to develop the land, so that their value to him is the WTA? Or do we regard the landowner as not yet having reduced these potential development rights to possession so that they are rightly valued at some lower WTP figure? To the owner, the former figure looks appropriate precisely because one central purpose of property is to create stable expectations for its future use, as Bentham argued.[63] That result seems especially plausible where an owner delayed development in early years in explicit reliance on the legal rule that preserved the development option for future years, which is one of the key advantages of the indefinite time horizon of the fee simple ownership. If so, then the modern land use case law that postpones the time of "vesting" (after which land development rights can be no longer denied) to the moment that land is actually used clearly conflicts with the experimental literature.[64] The rights are vested upon occupation and should presumably be valued under a WTA rule. The WTA/WTP split in this context calls, as several writers have already noted, for boosting the level of compensation in takings cases to reflect the WTA.[65] In sum, postulating an endowment effect seems most plausible at both ends of the property continuum. It lends additional support to first possession rules in the acquisition of property and points to higher levels of compensation when private property is taken for public use.

9 Cognitive Biases

The Cognitive Biases of Everyday Life

How Pervasive?

THE PROBLEMS WITH SUNK COSTS and the endowment effect, examined at length in chapter 8, raise only a small sample of the deviations between the presumptions of rational choice theory and the actual behavior of ordinary individuals. Also important are the cognitive errors that arise when intelligent but naïve subjects draw inferences about decisions made under conditions of uncertainty. The important issues, however, do not relate to how these biases manifest themselves, but rather to how both the legal system and the actors within it should respond to these cognitive challenges. How difficult is it to root out these errors and to correct them? What are the incentives for so doing? And what is the likelihood that the corrective response will emerge under different sorts of institutional arrangements? Since these biases are cognitive only, by definition they do not provoke emotional or motivational resistance to the adoption of corrective rules (unless of course they interact with other biases). The only issue is whether they are so ingrained that it becomes difficult, if not impossible, to develop personal or institutional strategies to counter them. The challenge to rational decisionmaking is once again all pervasive. In this chapter, I first examine how these issues play out in personal interactions and then discuss the questions as they relate, in connection with the efficient market hypothesis (EMH), to the operation of financial markets.

One Failed Experiment

Most of the major work in the identification of cognitive biases comes from the use of survey devices or tests that ask people to make simple, but tricky, estimations of probabilities on matters of great importance to them. For the most part, the individuals in question are drawn from the ranks of undergraduates or graduate students in economics and law (which itself raises a real question of the selection bias), who are asked to work out the solutions to some well-recognized problems. In these unstructured environments, it is easy to fall into traps. My introduction to the field occurred when I cheerfully fell victim to a hypothetical posed nearly twenty-five years ago by Daniel Kahneman and Amos Tversky at a workshop at the National Bureau of Economics in late 1977 or early 1978. Their example ran as follows:

> You are a fighter pilot who runs a risk of being killed by enemy fire. You can be killed in one of two ways: either by flak or by burns. You may also wear a jacket that will protect you entirely against one hazard, but is useless against the other, that is, you may wear a flak jacket or a burn jacket, but not both. Two-thirds of casualties result from flak; one-third from burns. You can wear either jacket all or part of the time. Which jacket do you choose to wear and why?

As a member of the audience (who had taken, but obviously not mastered, graduate courses in probability theory and statistics), I leaped to the challenge, responding (over)confidently: "Use the flak jacket two-thirds of the time and the burn jacket one-third of the time." The intuition behind my answer was that you proportion your behavior to the relative frequency of the risks.

Nice try, old chap, but quite wrong. The bias to which I, and others, succumbed was in assuming that uncertain risks require mixed responses. The correct answer to this stripped-down hypothetical is to *always* wear the flak jacket. If you wear that jacket all the time, you will survive two-thirds of the time, dying only from the burns. But if you split your jackets, you will be saved only two-thirds of the time you are wearing the flak jacket, or four-ninths of the time overall. Similarly, you will be saved for only a third of the time that you wear the burn jacket (that is, a third of one-third of the time overall), or one-ninth of the time. Four-ninths plus one-ninth total five-ninths, which is less than the two-thirds (six-ninths) survival rate if you only wear the flak jacket. Quite simply, each and every time you should adopt the dominant strategy, as a mixed response gives up something and gets nothing for it in return. That answer could be modified in a more complex world where your choice of protective jacket influences the enemy's choice of ammunition, at which point all bets are off. But for our purposes, these cognitive biases highlight the risk that some hasty pilots, left to their own devices, will make some fatal mistakes if allowed to do so.

What implications should be drawn from this example? At one level it confirms what statisticians have always known. All students do not ace (or even pass) statistics examinations even after they have been tutored in the subject. Ask a group of naïve subjects whether there is a greater probability of (1) the second to last letter in any given word being an "n" or (2) a word ending in "ing," and some will instinctively answer the latter because it is easy to identify "ing" words. But a moment's reflection shows that words ending in "ing" are a proper subset of words whose second to last letter (as in the word "second") is "n," so that the conclusion is sadly in error. No one should make this mistake, at least a second time.

That said, wrong answers and some incorrect decisions will necessarily be part of any behavioral landscape, and it is fruitless to argue that social institutions can be designed as though these mistakes never existed. But these individual tales of woe also contain a powerful institutional moral similar to that derived from our discussion of the endowment effect (whose empirical foundation is far weaker). The key question concerns the determinants of the rate of correction, which we should expect to be rapid. There are strong incentives to learn from mistakes, and powerful selection effects are likely to finish off those who do not heed the warning signals. To see how it works, we should assume that at least one person can figure the correct answer. Let us assume further that the outcome matters, as in the choice between flak and burn jackets, and turns on more than the relative frequency of "ns" and "ings." Once the error is exposed, it can be shown to be just that—an error. The military person, whether pilot or underling, who detects the error has no reason to keep his findings secret from his copilots, nor to resist changing his own behavior. Any Air Force officer in charge of the overall situation can respond by ordering the change if the risks are uniform across all cases, or by informing the pilots of the proper risk calculation so that they can make a responsible choice if it is not. Armed with the background information individual pilots decide whether and when the two-thirds/one-third ratio applies to their circumstances. Thus, once any *single* person figures out what the error is, then, by a reverse Gresham's law, the good information drives out the bad, precisely because there is no emotional resistance to overcoming cognitive biases. The more widespread the information about these biases, the more rapid the institutional response. The extensive attention this body of work has received becomes the best antidote for the dangers posed for the unwashed and unenlightened.

The key question is how the choice of institutional structure affects the dissemination of accurate information. For example, suppose that the Air Force adopted a strict hierarchical principle that assigned to one person complete command and control over all decisions. Pilots just took orders and flew, without any feedback mechanisms. In such situations, cognitive bias is a much more deadly enemy. If the leader does not detect the error, he will not correct it, and no one else can fill the void. The advantage of a military organization that tolerates debate and promotes feedback is evident. The point gives, as it were, a good functional explanation why deliberation is not only a democratic virtue but also an instrumental one, which explains why it is a feature of private governance structures, both profit and nonprofit. Discussion increases the odds of error correction and the rate of dissemination of the corrected information.

Yet the Air Force is still prey to one weakness. It is a government monopolist, so that correction must come, if at all, from within the institution. A competitive industry, however, is more likely to give rise to people who detect and correct these cognitive biases. To be sure, industry firms could organize along democratic or hierarchical lines, but the high variation in competitive markets makes it likely that at least one firm will develop open internal lines of communications, even in the unlikely assumption of practical or legal barriers to the sharing of information. Once the cognitive error is detected and corrected, the firm will then be in a superior position relative to its uninformed rivals. If the undetected bias led a firm to underestimate certain kinds of risks, it can now invest greater resources to correct the error or to price it into its goods or services. These higher prices will immunize it from the greater risk of bankruptcy faced by other firms. With time, only those firms that understand the nature of the risk will survive; other firms that do not correct for the risk will be forced from the market. Alternatively, if some bias leads an errant firm to overprice its goods and services, it will also lose market share by not matching the lower prices offered by its better informed competitors. No matter what the direction of the error, better information will spread through the market with great rapidity. Competition, therefore, offers two mechanisms to control cognitive bias by promoting the dissemination of information within the firm and competition across firms. Working together, these market forces should do a better job in countering risk than any government commands.

The point here does not apply only to this particular cognitive bias, but to any similar error, regardless of its nature or origin. Indeed, so long as firms know that some kinds of error can creep into their calculations, they can afford to adopt compensating mechanisms to guard against such error, even if they are uncertain about its precise mode of operation.[1] Engineers and architects can make their precise calculations and then build in the extra margin of error, not only solely as a response to cognitive biases, but also as a safeguard to defects in materials and workmanship that cannot be detected by ordinary inspection methods. The smaller the needed extra margin of error in the system, the more efficient its overall operations. Any precaution taken to prevent the obvious error will do double duty by preventing other kinds of errors, including those attributable to cognitive biases.

The ability to guard against cognitive bias, therefore, does not presuppose any precise knowledge of the source of these errors. Indeed, it is instructive to note that Herbert Spencer spent much time addressing the biases that he thought infected the overall social system, speaking at length about the various objective and subjective difficulties in the social sciences, with explicit reference to biases in, or from, education, patriotism, class, politics, and theology.[2] Viewed within their larger institutional framework, cognitive biases offer but another illustration of the basic Hayekian insight regarding the importance of decentralization in social affairs: the partitioning of responsibility (analogous in its own way to separation of powers with checks and balances in both public and private organizations) again functions as an error-correction mechanism. A decentralized system may not respond as quickly as a centralized command and control system when things are going well. But it will respond better, as a brake against mistake, when things are going badly. The theory of cognitive bias shows that bad decisions can arise in institutional environments where they are least expected. If so, then decentralized market forces will respond better than monolithic governments. In an odd sense, the concern with cognitive bias helps explain the need for certain forms of institutional protection to guard against unknown forms of error.

Hindsight and Tort

The above argument deals with cognitive biases in their most general form. It is, however, helpful to see how this argument plays out in connection with the specific biases that have been identified in the literature. Start, for example, with the hindsight bias.[3] The literature on this point confirms the same systematic result, which in my view (in contrast to the endowment effect) resonates with ordinary experience. Individuals tend to exaggerate their predictive powers and thus treat what happened as though it had to happen. Ordinary people tend to assign higher probabilities to the events that did happen after the fact than a neutral observer would assign to those events if forced to estimate the odds before the fact. The original experimental example of this bias postulated a group of individuals who were told (in the early 1970s) of Nixon's trips to Moscow and Peking, and then given different accounts as to the outcome of the meetings. No matter what the particular outcome in question, the subjects tended to assign higher probabilities to the outcome that they were told had happened than to others that might have. In effect, it was easier to invent explanations for why what happened had to be the case than to invent explanations for why what did not happen might have been the case.

The institutional lesson from this and similar examples of the hindsight bias relates to the choice of legal rules for making different kinds of decisions. To see why, substitute for diplomatic trips to Russia or China the rules used to determine liability for ordinary accidents in a wide range of settings. In the simplest cases, where one party damages the person or property of a stranger, the usual question is whether liability for accidental harms is strict, so that the defendant is judged by the outcome of his action, wholly without regard to his antecedent negligence, or whether the plaintiff has to prove the defendant's negligence that led up to the injury.[4] In principle, the two systems will tend to converge when measured by their incentive effects, for either way the rational defendant will tend to take precautions only against those accidents where these efforts are cost effective. Otherwise (at least if his own safety is not in issue) it will be cheaper to pay for the liability after the fact than it would be to incur the precautions before it.

Nonetheless, these two rules do have very different properties in light of the potential risk of the hindsight bias. The strict liability rule only asks whether it is possible to link up the defendant's action to the plaintiff's harm, so that questions about the influence of precautions on *ex ante* probabilities are no part of the jury's task. But the negligence form of liability, either explicitly or implicitly, requires that some judgment be made of the reasonableness of defendant's conduct from an *ex ante* perspective. In cases of harm to strangers, the customary care afforded by defendants in like situations will not generate a reliable rule of thumb as to the efficient solution because it will tend to undervalue the losses to other individuals.[5] The open-ended cost-benefit analysis eliminates that error, but only at the cost of asking jurors to reconstruct the probability of an accident after the fact, where the hindsight bias (such as it is) only compounds all the other difficulties in assessing the probabilities and severity of some hypothetical accident and the costs of precaution needed to curtail it. Some estimate of probabilities is, of course, invariably necessary when the issue on the table is that of injunctive relief, which is generally confined to cases of imminent peril. But in the domain of completed harms, the strict liability rule offers a mechanism to evaluate defendant's conduct, which operates better than any rules that might be devised to limit expert testimony or to instruct the jury. A quick look at the litigation on expert evidence shows that the resolution of the issue of admissibility is always fraught with difficulty.[6] At present, the 2000 revision of the Federal Rules of Evidence allows for the admission of evidence "if (1) the testimony is based upon sufficient facts or data, (2) the testimony is the product of reliable principles and methods, and (3) the witness has applied the principles and methods reliably to the facts of the case."[7] It is no slight to the drafters of these provisions to say that they contain loose margins: words like "sufficient" and "reliable" always raise issues of degree. Alternative tests may move the margins one way or the other, but never eliminate the basic confusion. Clearly, a legal rule that makes certain questions of fact irrelevant helps to reduce jury discretion (and indeed judicial discretion) in ways that are fully welcome for many reasons, of which containing the hindsight bias is only one.

In most stranger cases, the scope of the choice between these two rules is sharply limited because of the requirement that a plaintiff establish both that the defendant caused the harm *and* could have taken steps to have avoided it.[8] Thus, a typical case involves a showing that the defendant ran down the plaintiff (the element of physical causation), which he could have avoided had he traveled at a lower speed (the element of avoidance). The great expansion of tort liability, however, has occurred precisely in those cases in which the defendant is placed under a duty to take reasonable care to prevent harms that have been caused physically by others. A humdrum automobile accident takes on a different hue when the driver of the car sues the manufacturer for supplying an "uncrashworthy" vehicle, that is, one that failed to provide him with sufficient protection against such external harms as being hit by a drunk driver or even driving the car into a telephone pole. Now, physical causation no longer resides in the defendant but in the plaintiff or some third party. The earlier common law cases adopted a general "no-duty" rule and held that the driver assumed, as against the manufacturer, the risk of these collisions: those who wanted more protection could drive a bigger car.[9] Even with the expansive attitude toward tort liability in the late 1960s, a precipitous move from no liability to strict liability appealed to no one, for no one "expects" any automobile to withstand the dangers of hurtling off a mountain road at a hundred miles per hour. At common law, therefore, the operative standard in the new crashworthiness cases was the ordinary negligence standard previously applied in some stranger cases: under the circumstances, did the defendant take reasonable care to prevent harm?[10]

Once again, the economic interpretation of reasonableness is whether the costs of prevention are justified in terms of the savings from accident prevention, measured by the reduction in accident levels multiplied by the anticipated severity of the accidents averted.

Probability determinations permeate these lawsuits. Thus, one question might be whether a gas tank, to protect against a side collision, should be located in the center rear of the vehicle or located on one side or another. That choice depends on the probability of rupture and explosion as a function of the location choice, multiplied by the severity of the accident for each location.[11] It is easy to imagine situations where the greater risk comes from the tank located in the center rear of the car rather than on the rear right, where the expected dangers, given the impact, are lower. (Or for these purposes the actual facts could be reversed.)

It is possible to lodge many objections against the use of jury trials to decide design defect cases. Juries do not have the technical expertise, for example, to pass on all the design choices that go into making a complex product. It is possible, therefore, to take exception to the common law crashworthiness doctrine without making any appeal to the hindsight bias. But that bias surely increases the risk of jury error in deciding which of the available design alternatives should have been adopted by the defendant. Again, note the importance of institutional setting. The finders of fact in the first instance are ordinary juries. In contrast to regulatory bodies, juries are not continuous bodies called on to assess large numbers of similar cases from which they could start to form reasonably sensible estimations of the relevant probabilities of alternative accidents. Instead, each case has its own panel, its members separately chosen by lawyers who are not interested in some dispassionate search for the truth. It was to restrain erratic jury behavior that Holmes defended the practice of having judges take cases from juries when confident in their own assessment of the applicable community norms.[12] Nor do juries benefit from any strong feedback mechanism. They make their decisions and go home. Unlike potential drivers, they do not have to live with the consequences of choosing an inferior design over a superior one. Therefore, what incentives do they have to overcome any bias, hindsight or otherwise, under which they might labor? Smart lawyers for defendants in such a case always take the position that the jury must consider more than the pecuniary cost of taking the proposed precaution. Using money in this context, particularly for precautions that are cheap when viewed individually but costly when taken in combination, only exposes the large manufacturer to the determined harassment of the populist plaintiff lawyer who knows how to intone: "Send corporate America a message," or "Don't let big automakers get away with murder on the highway," and the like.

Given these institutional realities, defendants are usually well advised to present evidence that, from the *ex ante* perspective, the plaintiff's proposed design exposes the driver and passenger of the automobile to greater alternative risks from different sorts of accident. That course of action is all the more imperative when a standard cost-benefit analysis, even correctly conducted, will often expose the defendant to the risk of punitive damages on the ground that only the callous or malignant are prepared to trade off dollars for lives.[13] The appropriate defense strategy is that the trade-off is not dollars versus lives (which leaves a defendant naked before a jury) but lives versus lives, where the rap on the plaintiff is that his proposed alternative design will cause more deaths and injuries than it prevents.

That argument raises its fair share of factual disputes in individual cases. But no matter how those doubts are resolved, the defendant operates under the genuine disadvantage of having to downplay the *ex ante* risk of the harm that did occur while stressing the magnitude and severity of hypothetical harms that may well have been avoided in some unrelated case. Let jurors suffer from a bias that overweighs the case presented to them, and it is clear that the law is structured in a way that once again increases the probability of an erroneous outcome.

One possible justification for tolerating this bias is to counterbalance the risk that a defendant will take insufficient precautions because of (over)confidence in its ability to evade the sanctions.[14] That concern might apply to individual automobile drivers who may escape detection or have few assets to satisfy tort claims. But it hardly rings true for wealthy and immobile institutional defendants who can be reliably identified from the wreckage. Even if that risk did occur, it need not be of the same order of magnitude as the hindsight bias; and it could well aggravate some other bias within the judicial setting.

Nor is it clear that hindsight bias is eliminated with bench trials, for individual judges also lack the necessary incentives and feedback mechanisms to make the proper adjustments. In sum, we cannot identify any reliable procedural antidote to this particular bias; and we cannot control the risk that different juries will, responding to different accidents, impose inconsistent design requirements, all of which could not be satisfied when the car was made. The negligence standard itself necessarily immerses the jury in a swamp of probabilistic calculations that oozes hindsight bias. No manipulation of the rules of admissibility, burdens of proof, expert qualifications, and jury instructions makes much of a dent in the process. Given their institutional isolation, jurors are not able to make reliable risk-utility trade-offs from the necessary *ex ante* perspective.

In contrast to these half measures, alternative institutional arrangements should be able to counter both the jury's lack of technical expertise and its hindsight bias. One approach would return to a regime of voluntary contracts whereby the buyer of an automobile, for example, takes the risk of all accidents for any vehicle that conforms to its own design specifications. Under this regime, the buyer and the seller escape the hindsight bias by making decisions at the point of purchase before the type of accident is revealed. But this method will not work for passenger injuries. A more general alternative holds that all vehicle occupants take the risk of accidents that are either obvious or commonly known, returning to the earlier common law rule. This position, to my mind, makes a good deal of sense because the key variable in accidents involve the weight of the automobile, which is easily observable. What is striking about most individual design defect cases is that the obvious factor is always put aside and much more attention is paid to the details of a door assembly, or the placement of a steering column, which are by no stretch of the imagination the primary determinants of safety.

The efforts to counter this initiative rely either on private contract or on the proposition that an open and obvious condition cannot be regarded as a product defect.[15] Under current law, the contractual alternative is blocked, and the open and obvious defense enjoys but limited acceptance.[16] Whatever their merits, any reliance on private contract or obvious dangers may be attacked in principle on the ground that buyers and passengers lack the knowledge to make informed judgments at the time of purchase or entering a vehicle for the first time. But even if these objections carry the day, the National Highway and Traffic Safety Commission could set comprehensive standards that all automobiles must satisfy before sale, after which compliance with the initial standard confers an *absolute* immunity against a crashworthiness suit based on the soundness of the design. (Ordinary suits for construction defects in individual cases would of course remain.) Such public regulation is not costless. Not only does it require the extensive administrative approach that is already in place, but it could also easily require safety precautions more extensive than those desired by informed consumer demand. Regulatory zeal (born perhaps of some other bias) could thus impose an implicit tax on the purchase of newer automobiles equal to the difference between the cost of the mandated benefit less its value to the particular consumer. By retarding sale of new vehicles, the regulation prolongs the use of older and more dangerous vehicles already in service, with the consequent increase in accident levels. But at least that regulatory process escapes the hindsight bias, for administrators must act before any harm occurs, and thus have no incentive to overweigh one set of future harms while unduly slighting another. Nor can an agency soft-pedal the risk of inconsistent standards, for, unlike freewheeling juries, it knows that all its standards must be simultaneously satisfied before sale is allowed.

Note the conservative doctrinal implications. The current judicial approach treats administrative regulations as "minimum standards" subject to political bias. It thus allows plaintiffs a second bite at the apple through individual tort actions that rely on a general risk-utility analysis.[17] Given the hindsight bias, it is more likely that biased juries will undercut the plausible *ex ante* judgments of professional agencies, and more money will be spent to get less reliable decisions. The proper rule, therefore, is one that affords defendants a complete defense if their products comply with statutory standards, unless (as occasionally happens) clear evidence shows that the defendants used fraudulent means to secure the adoption of a favorable administrative determination.

Parallel arguments apply to duty-to-warn cases, where again the dominant position today rejects the position that statutory warnings should be regarded as sufficient to insulate a firm from claims it breached its duty to warn. The current situation invites error by asking juries with wide discretion to evaluate in hindsight the true level of the risk *ex ante*. The decision that represents perhaps the high point in this trend is *MacDonald v. Ortho Pharmaceutical Co.*[18] The defendant sold an oral contraceptive (Ortho-Novum) that was obtainable only by women who first obtained a prescription from a gynecologist. The pills were sold with detailed warnings preapproved by the FDA that spoke to the risk of death or serious injury, including those from blood clots that "may threaten life if the clots break loose and then lodge in the lung, or if they form in other vital organs, such as the brain." The warning did not use the word "stroke" which, after the fact, the plaintiff claimed would have, if included, deterred her from the use of the pill in question. The court held that this warning lacuna created a triable question of fact on the adequacy of the warnings.

As in design defect cases, the key function of any warning is not to generate liability *ex post* but to give plaintiff an accurate assessment of the relative risks *ex ante*. It is, therefore, surely proper to provide warnings about the potential downside of medical treatment to counter individual overoptimism (yet another bias). The behavioral economics literature, however, offers no reason to believe that this is the *sole* bias that operates in any individual case. The vividness of the warnings could easily lead some individuals to so overstate the level of the risk that it becomes necessary to decide how to deal with two biases with uncertain magnitudes and opposite signs. The risk of people not taking medicines with expected positive effects is every bit as important.

The consequences are far from ideal. The stern rules on warnings, which offer a detailed enumeration of the adverse effects of given treatment, are likely to lead individuals (especially those who are both anxious and ill) to the wrong conclusion by leading them to overrate the downside of treatment. Thus, the simple statement that a drug user has a 1 percent chance of death or serious injury from a given product is probably *more* instructive from the bottom line point of view than a detailed catalogue of all the unrelated causes that sum to that final tally. The cumulative weight of the negatives could easily deter even optimistic folks from taking treatment. But after the fact, the weak system of jury controls allows individual plaintiffs to reach a jury by arguing, against the odds, that the addition of one word (stroke) would have led them to abandon treatment or switch therapies when the parade of horribles admittedly presented to them had no influence on the choice of conduct.

Some cases have noted the danger in question and have concluded, rightly in my view, that simpler warnings are more effective. Thus, in *Cotton v. Buckeye Gas Products* (a case involving flammable gas containers),[19] Judge Steven Williams noted that these "failure-to-warn cases have the curious property that, when the episode is examined in hindsight, it appears as though addition of warnings keyed to a particular accident would be virtually cost free." But this innocuous policy could be ruinous if implemented from the *ex ante* perspective when the blanket warning must separately identify each adverse contingency in order to provide legal protection. As with design changes, the cumulative impact of too many warnings could leave people uncertain as to which peril matters the most, and, in cases where user precautions do matter, as in dealing with dangerous equipment, to misdirect their efforts from major to minor perils.

In order to deal with these issues sensibly, it is necessary to be able to inform users and consumers of two sorts of risks, one that is intrinsic to the product sold, and the other that is unique to its particular user. In the case of prescription pills, a drug insert could handle the question of generic risk, while a consultation with a physician could take into account the particular health profile of the patient that considers, for example, the use of alternative contraceptive devices. With industrial equipment, the manufacturer's warning could focus on the inherent risks of the product, and the employer's instruction could focus on the special risks of using the product in a particular environment, addressing such matters as the clothing to be worn, the ventilation to be used, the places to avoid, the on-site personnel to consult, and the like. One way to reach that result with prescription drugs is to have a system that contains warnings to both patients and physicians, and then relies on physicians as "learned intermediates" to supply the information unique to the condition of the individual plaintiff. The regime in question, therefore, couples preset warnings on original distribution with unique warnings at the patient level. On balance, it does a better job in communicating information than the alternative regime that seeks to rely on the remote supplier to provide full information to all customers. The administrative transfer of information is not flawless, and warnings may well have to be updated to take into account new information that reflects a perceived increase or reduction of risk. But the current system of *ex post* judgments on the adequacy of warning will, in general, lead firms to overwarn against risks in the first place by giving full rein to any hindsight bias.

Availability

This analysis of the hindsight bias carries over to another important cognitive bias, the so-called availability heuristic. As stated by Kahneman and Tversky, "people assess the frequency of a class or the probability of an event by the ease with which instances or occurrences can be brought to mind."[20] As the authors go on to explain, particular occurrences of a given event that an observer sees tend to be those that are most easily recalled. From that, people mistakenly draw the further inference that these familiar events are also the most common. Yet all too often vivid but infrequent events receive great coverage. Are people more likely to die from shark attacks or falling airplane parts? Although deaths from shark attacks receive greater coverage, those from falling airplane parts are more frequent by a factor of 30.[21] Similarly, contrary to the relatively scarce media coverage they receive, diabetes and stomach cancer kill nearly *twice* as many Americans annually as homicide or car accidents, and lightning strikes claim more lives than tornadoes do.[22]

What relevance does this bias have to the sound operation of ordinary markets? One possibility is that mistakes of this sort contaminate consumer decisions. The potential Volvo purchaser might shy away because a close friend was killed when his Volvo collided with a large truck. By rating that information more highly than the car's overall safety record, he will be led to buy a less-safe model—a market failure based on imperfect information. But, ironically, this argument falls prey to the common mistake of assuming that single causes have only single effects. A more likely scenario is that our hypothetical consumer will be spurred to look more closely at auto safety in general. If so, his search may confirm the safety of Volvos and thus lead him to return to his initial choice. But even if he does not, he is less likely to shift from a Volvo to a Volkswagen, and more likely to buy a Saab. If so, then his error (if error there be) is likely to be relatively small. It will be smaller still if the potential buyer seeks out information about other accidents, which may prompt a greater concern about safety, and perhaps some systematic examination of the topic, leading to a more informed choice, especially if his original preference for a Volvo was for some reason unfounded. And if similar biases affect most buyers, it could just be that random accidents shift a few drivers from Volvos to Saabs, or from Saabs to Volvos. The overall market shares of the two vehicles are unlikely to shift very much.

The availability heuristic, however, could have much more powerful effects in litigation when it operates in tandem with the hindsight bias. Juries told of a single fiery accident could easily assume that the car in question has a higher rate of accidents than any of its rival brands. This is precisely what happened in the famous trials over the Ford Pinto, whose safety record was average for its class.[23] The litigation over the Bjork-Shiley heart valve also revealed this risk.[24] Occasionally, some models of the valve would rupture inside the user, leading to death in over half the ensuing episodes. But the overall rate of valve failure was in fact lower than many other models that failed in less conspicuous ways—such as deprivation of oxygen from inefficient transfer, clotting of blood, and the like. Here again the vividness of the breakage led to lawsuits not only when the valve failed, but also in suits for emotional distress where it had yet to malfunction.[25] Yet the greater compensating benefits of this valve did little to alter the trajectory of the overall litigation.

The same distortions also arise within the legislative process. Jolls, Sunstein, and Thaler offer an account of the passage of Superfund that centers on the public hubbub over Love Canal, which placed the solid waste problem in high relief.[26] In their view, the availability heuristic played a key role in securing the passage of the Act, which in many ways has proved a colossal blunder. Their account prompts two responses. First, if true, it shows that the availability heuristic is likely to do more damage in legislative than market processes. Second, the availability heuristic must share center stage with a healthy dose of old-style interestgroup politics.[27] Much of the publicity that surrounded the Love Canal story, later discredited,[28] was orchestrated by the Environmental Protection Agency (EPA), which sought to expand its influence by redoing its image from a "bugs and bunnies" operation into an agency dedicated to the preservation of public health.[29] The EPA lobbied Congress every step of the way, and Superfund was enacted into law by a lame-duck Congress that President Jimmy Carter called into session after Ronald Reagan had won the 1980 presidential election.[30]

What makes matters worse is that in all the search for the right political answer, the drafters of the Superfund never asked the right question about the key remedial element of the statute: its preference for cleanup over more modest sanctions such as fines for trivial risks. The right question to ask is whether we should spend public funds to clean up these risks if we knew that they derived from purely natural origins. Normally that would not be done when the costs are high and the benefits small, as it is with the constant level of background toxins that are part of the natural environment. That judgment should only be strengthened when it becomes more costly to obtain a cleanup owing to the need to institute litigation to establish the culpability of the defendant, or more commonly, the group of defendants who were responsible for the discharges. Unfortunately, the current law is so far off course that defendants are ordered to clean up harmful substances from all sources, even when their own discharges are "orders of magnitude below ambient or naturally occurring background levels."[31] But it makes no sense. If the public at large endures these natural harms, then the appropriate remedy against small private polluters should be damages tied to the incremental losses from the defendant's discharge—not the total losses in question.

It is difficult to attribute so large a miscalculation to any cognitive bias when the interest group politics are so rife. But it is useful to note that one way in which to address this problem is to integrate the relationships between public and private law on the granting of injunctions. In the normal case, any individual landowner would have to show imminent peril in order to stop a harm that had not yet occurred and could under no circumstances compel the cleanup demanded under the Superfund with its treatment of remote risks. The shift from individual to collective action is fully justified when large numbers of individuals cannot coordinate their efforts to block some particular action that could be enjoined by any single individual who bears the brunt of all the anticipated harm. But it is critical to ensure that the shift in forum does not result in a shift in substantive standards. Yet all too often the move from the judicial to the political arena results in taking both steps instead of concentrating on the coordination problem alone.

The hard question is what countermeasures, if any, should be taken against the biases of the political process. Today it is futile to raise constitutional objections against these misguided schemes given the massive judicial deference to legislative action in environmental matters. But, in principle at least, the same tools used to judge government action in other areas that affect private rights should be available here as well. The first (large) step is to note that all forms of regulation and liability are takings that under our constitutional system of government must be justified or compensated.[32] In this context, compensation (either cash or in-kind) is never offered, so the case turns on public justifications for the use of the police power. Here, the government end—the prevention of nuisance— is beyond challenge. But if the analysis above is correct, then the means chosen are woefully inadequate for the task at hand precisely because of the government's refusal to attach equal weight to losses of natural origin. Without that commitment, there is no fit between the means chosen and the ends served. The clear import of this test is to introduce a system of honest valuation into the measurement of environmental risk. Means/ends tests are routinely applied on substantive matters relating to speech, to equal protection claims, and to issues surrounding the allocation of power between federal and state governments under our constitutional system. They could surely be applied with moderation here to root out these excesses. So here is another useful role for behavioral economics: to dramatize the defects in political behavior that led to the passage of Superfund. The upshot is more diligent supervision of the legislative process in the environmental arena.

Most mainline constitutional scholars will dismiss this proposed constitutional foray as both misguided and futile. But the intellectual lesson should not be forgotten even as the constitutional claim lies in ruins. So long as we can uncover defects in legislative behavior, we should strive to correct them. In this context, that points strongly to a return to the common law rules that require the actual or threatened causation of substantial harm before any cleanup remedy is ordered. At this point, we are more likely to take into account the background probabilities of injury that are too easily overlooked when the marching orders that regulators receive ask them to make a worst-case analysis of the situation in question.

Overoptimism

Yet another common bias is that people are overoptimistic about their chances of success in any venture they choose to undertake. It is commonplace to note that 50 percent of every entering class says that they will finish in the top 10 percent, or that all the graduates of a program expect to get teaching jobs after graduation. Their implicit frame of reference leads them to overstate the gains of their ventures, and hence their prior willingness to enter into them. The strength of this bias is surely open to question in light of the heavy subsidies that most colleges and universities routinely offer students to attend their institutions. But subsidies or no, it is doubtful the extent to which the publication of the "true" background probability for the group will dissuade individuals of their preferred position. There is little uncertainty, moreover, that a bias of this sort, especially if widespread, could lead to the following wedge: the actual expected value of the venture is less than its costs, but the perceived expected value of the enterprise is greater than its costs. Errors in judgment, therefore, lead to errors in conduct, which in turn have negative effects of resource allocation.

Once again, it is hard to know what to make of this proposition, even if it is true. It is very difficult to obtain field estimations of the magnitude of the error or, in some cases, of its expected cost. Thus, suppose that students overstate their anticipated class rank but would still have enrolled in school if they feared that they would finish near the bottom of their class. The rude awakening may well be the source of psychological discomfort, but it will not lead to *ex post* regret. Stated otherwise, the individual who thought that his expected surplus from a venture was 10 over his next best choice would not have changed his decision once it is revealed to him that the net gain was only 5. And the dangers here may well be further reduced if the same person had overstated the potential gains from his next best alternative. So long as the two move in rough lockstep proportion, the *relative* errors will tend to cancel out, although no one can say with confidence what the net error is likely to be. Nor in some cases would a person want a brutal assessment of the situation going in, especially if a dose of overconfidence *improved* his performance relative to what it would have been if he had known just how heavily the odds were stacked against him.

There are, moreover, steps that individuals can take, tailored to their own circumstances to deal with these risks. It is one thing to get information from a prospective employer or graduate program about its prospects. It is another to ask independent third parties for their assessment of the overall risk, or to find reliable information about job placement or promotion for graduates of different programs. Here, furthermore, the cognitive biases are to some extent offset by the natural suspicion that everyone has about the "puffery" that is present in self-promotion, for which a bit of caution offers far better remedy than the legal system could provide by regulation.

So what then should be the response of the legal system if the intrinsic bias, such as it is, is not fully overcome by awareness of the basic situation? In most cases it is hard to think of a form of intervention that, net of cost, is worthwhile. It seems clear at present that the current legal position does not require individuals to correct the cognitive errors that others have made. Owing to the potential pervasiveness of the problem, it would create a wholesale onslaught in which just about everyone could sue just about everyone else. Even in more specific contexts, it would be generally unwise to toughen the law that relates, for example, to nondisclosure or concealment, for one could never be quite sure whether the more extensive amount of information will further dull the cognitive capacity.

Financial Markets

The Efficient Market Hypothesis

The role of cognitive basis, and the field of behavioral economics more generally, are not limited to the decisions of businesses or everyday life. One obvious testing ground for the strength of cognitive biases are financial markets. In one sense, these ought to be where rational choice models work to their greatest power. The instruments that are traded—stocks, bonds, options of all kinds and description—are designed in such a fashion to make them fungible one to another. The creation of corporate shares and debt instruments, for example, allows for the rapid exchange and accurate valuation of the underlying assets over which they provide a fractional claim. Unlike many forms of personal property (for example, homes, books, memorabilia) few, if any, market participants find any subjective value in holding one numbered share of General Motors stock relative to another; indeed few individuals care about the company whose stock they hold, independent of its prospects for its capacity for future gains realizable by dividends, liquidation, or sale. The large number of market participants and the huge array of instruments available seem to create the ideal conditions for competitive markets and, in turn, for a set of efficient outcomes under the most rigorous definition of Pareto optimality.

In line with this general approach to competitive markets, the efficient (capital) market hypothesis (EMH) was posited as the dominant economic paradigm.[33] In its strongest version, EMH assumes that all market participants are rational actors who are capable of assimilating and acting on all relevant information that affect stock values. When this exercise is complete all individuals arrive at the same valuation of these stocks, so that, with *homogeneous* expectations, demand for them is perfectly elastic in that no (rational) investor would pay a penny more for the stock than its risk-adjusted value required, and none would accept a penny less for the stock they held.[34] Ceaseless movements in prices come solely from the revelation of new information that is quickly incorporated into the stock price. Individual variations on matters of valuation have no place; nor, a fortiori, is there any room for mistakes in the valuations made.

One key question is how much systemwide rationality is needed to make the EMH model work. Clearly the assumption that all players in all markets are wholly rational is as much a stretch in financial markets as it is in the market for clothing or vacations. Some slippage is surely a part of the overall picture. To deal with this point, much of the financial literature follows the sensible path often taken in evaluating regular markets. Markets will do well in organizing the delivery of goods and services because the system has a collective rationality greater than the rationality of its individual members. Generally, more rational players will tend to outperform less rational players and will set the prices at which other individuals will trade. Thus, one variation on EMH postulates that its optimistic conclusions survive insofar as imperfectly rational actors—so-called noise traders—entertain beliefs that vary randomly from the ideal, so that their market decisions cancel each other out, allowing prices to be determined by the rational players who grasp the basics of the situation. In a still weaker form of EMH, originally attributable to Milton Friedman and developed by Eugene Fama, these nonrational players often had strong biases that pulled in one direction or another, but arbitrageurs—individuals who buy and sell the same or similar securities in different markets at mutually favorable prices—enter the market to take advantage of their unhappy errors.[35] In the end, the market is brought back to equilibrium so that each asset is priced uniquely, and the key variable (under the capital asset pricing model, or CAPM) is the risk premium demanded in order to offset the undiversifiable variation in risk level—its beta—associated with the stock.[36]

The Behavioral Critique

The empirical evidence on this topic is vast, and not easy to summarize in a short compass, but the bottom line appears to be that large chunks of market behavior do not correspond with the predictions of any version of EMH. Much evidence suggests that the volatility of stock prices is far greater than would be expected if markets were able to incorporate new knowledge at a rapid rate.[37] Further evidence suggests that several years of large run-ups and large declines are followed by periods of correction.[38] The easy explanation is that investors get over- or underoptimistic before the painful truth sets in (if indeed it ever does). Still further evidence suggests that the rates of return on stocks located in the largest decile in the New York Stock Exchange between 1926 and 1996 equal 9.84 percent, while that for the smallest decile was 13.83 percent. Under the theory of efficient markets, their rates of return should converge over time. In addition, much evidence has accumulated that companies that have high market-to-book-value ratios (which are thus considered "growth stocks") in general have lower rates of return than stocks with a low market-to-book value (which are thus considered to be "value stocks").[39] Finally, some evidence suggests stock prices react to what some have called "non-information," so that the simple decision to include a stock in the S&P 500 (when, for example, a current firm in the index is acquired by merger) raises its value in both the short and long run on the order of 3 percent.[40]

The ragged nature of these asset returns and their inclusion of variables that do not fit snugly into the capital asset pricing model have led for the search for other explanations for investor behavior, including approaches that rest on behavioral economics. Thus, one point of departure starts with the observation that the common errors in computing probabilities that operate in other contexts carry over to financial markets. Individuals do not know how to calculate complex probabilities that depend on Bayes's formula; they fall prey to the dangers of representativeness; they have inconsistent attitudes toward risk that lead them to depart from the principles of expected utility; they suffer from a variety of "framing problems," such that they do not give identical valuations to the same issue of probability when stated in a somewhat different fashion; and they suffer from risk aversion and myopia that induce them to hold on to losing stocks too long even after they have lost value, and in some instances to avoid the stock market altogether, even though it yields in the long run far higher premiums than the bond markets.[41]

The Critique Critiqued

The question now arises as to how to evaluate these claims. The first and simplest point of the evaluation is to examine any *non*behavioral objections that could be raised to the optimistic conclusions to the EMH, which might account for some of the observed results. In order to frame the discussion, it is useful to recall two alternative accounts of the virtues of competitive markets generally. The common textbook version of these markets has a wonderland quality that assumes that transaction costs are close to zero and that all parties have perfect information about the goods and services that are subject to exchange. Starting with those optimistic assumptions, it is hard to resist the view that voluntary markets clear and generate desirable social outcomes that cannot be trumped by following any other course.

If we really believed these assumptions about the capacity of ordinary individuals to gain information, then we would be hard pressed to explain why (benevolent) government officials could not use their perfect information to organize the knowledge in society. It was just this simple point that led Hayek to insist that the superiority of markets lay in their ability to harness through the price system the bits and pieces of information held, apparently haphazardly, by each individual actor. The clear implication is that markets do not fare well under any criterion of ideal perfection, but deserve support only under the view that they offer a better shot at overcoming, on a transaction-by-transaction, industry-by-industry basis, the social problem of dispersed and incomplete knowledge.

In this view, the diagram of perfect competition represents an ideal to which ordinary markets strive, but never reach: equilibrium represents determined efforts that never quite hit a moving target. The empirical inquiry concerns the *relative* efficiency of particular markets in chasing that ideal position. On this point Hayek's basic view was that customary markets involving only traders who specialize in given products or services were most likely to evolve a set of customs, norms, and specific contractual provisions that allowed them to transact relatively reliably and at low cost. This position helps explain the common law deference to industry custom for internal industry trade disputes. More critically, however, it does *not* treat these informal norms and customs as the ultimate authority in any contractual dispute. Rather, any such custom has to give way to any clear expression of intent in any written contract. In dealing with these provisions in commercial and financial contexts, courts understand that to trifle with the provision of standard form contracts is to risk throwing financial markets into disarray. However leery contract theorists are of standard form contracts in other contexts, that attitude mercifully disappears in financial markets where huge numbers of fungible instruments are issued and traded. As Ralph Winter writes: "[B]oilerplate provisions are thus not the consequence of the relationship of particular borrowers and lenders and do not depend upon particularized intentions of the parties to an indenture. . . . [U]niformity in interpretation is important to the efficiency of capital markets."[42] Hence, the usual desire to individuate specific financial instruments through private negotiations and parol evidence cannot survive when these are rapidly traded. Likewise no *class* of bonds or debentures can be given rights over future transactions (for example, redemptions) unless they are subject to a uniform interpretation.[43] This tough-minded attitude works best in closed markets with experienced repeat players; larger and unspecialized markets perform less well than these well-defined trade groups. To be sure, they contained a larger number of individuals and thus took on the appearance of thick markets, but they worked less well because the persons who participated in these markets were ordinary consumers—noise traders, as it were— and not sophisticated traders. Accordingly, they could be counted on to be less confident and more hesitant in the execution of trades.

That same approach should be carried over with profit in order to understand the pitfalls of financial markets. Thus, one oddity about EMH is that it becomes difficult to explain why individuals engage in any kind of market research at all. The preferred strategy should be to adopt passive investment strategies, which save on transaction costs, by investing in index funds.[44] But it takes little wisdom to show that, however good this strategy may be for some, it cannot work for all. Information is a costly good, and someone has to collect and sort the information if markets are to budge in response to changes in prices.[45] At this point, the only real battle is just how many people are going to spend how much money to ferret out investment opportunities. The more the passivity by some, the greater the opportunity for gains by others.

At this point, it becomes necessary to ask just how large a deviation is needed to keep markets efficient. Once again, ordinary product markets provide some indication. Individuals who search for a new car or a new home often spend a good deal of time deciding what they want and what purchase will satisfy those desires. Investors may not have to worry about the consumption decisions for their stock purchases, but they do have to worry about the way in which their investment portfolio ties in with their earned income in a world in which loans (to equalize income across periods) are expensive to calculate and make. And, by the way, investors are also concerned with whether or not they will make money.

The difficulties grow quickly deeper once financial decisions are seen as efforts to improve one's position in a world of imperfect information. More concretely, the first of EMH's assumptions to go overboard has to be the idea that any person (let alone all people), even if they expend their own effort, can incorporate *all* the latest information about any firm into *uniform* expectations of its future course. In this context, the difficulty does not lie with the plausible distinction between the use of public and insider information about the firm: even if all information were publicly disclosed, why expect all potential investors to *interpret* it in the same fashion? Markets are like a giant game of Texas Hold'em, where the common table cards (which are treated as part of every player's hand) have value only in relation to the cards that each player has in his own hand. A nine and three on the table may be worthless to some players, but for the player with two nines and one three in his hand they effect a full house, while the fellow with three aces gains nothing at all. Suppose that a company makes widgets, which are complements to gidgets but substitutes for didgets. The person who understands the gidget market would have one take on changes in the price or composition of widgets. The person who understands didgets might well have a quite different take. The person who is engaged in the secret development of ridgets could see the ramifications of these changes in a different light from all others. Two traders can acquire *inconsistent* information from different sources within the same firm. It is the difference in opinions that make a horse race, and a stock market. Or to switch analogies yet again, intelligence in markets is no different from intelligence in espionage. The information that is acquired only makes sense in light of the information that is already known.

Once new information is evaluated in light of what is already established, it becomes hard to distinguish, as EMH seems to require, between "stale" and "fresh" information, much less to posit that stale information, however defined, has no place in the calculation of share values. Information does not necessarily depreciate with time: some old discarded bit of information may provide the needed clue to evaluate some new project or development. Unless one wants to assume that all individuals have the same static, outside information base, then it is impossible to assume, even approximately, that all individuals react to the identical body of public information in exactly the same way. Sophisticated people are certain to form "heterogeneous expectations" about the prospects of a given firm even if they apply the same techniques for valuation to the same public data. These differences become only more pronounced when it is recalled that complex firms undertake literally hundreds of projects that intersect in odd ways with multiple ventures both under the firm umbrella and beyond it.

These observations make it far more problematic to write as though the world divides itself dichotomously into rational traders and noise traders, or that the law could devise any rule that *ex ante* decides which traders fall into which camp. Not only are their many gradations in the skill of various traders, but it is equally plausible to assume that different rational traders will have different takes on the prospects of the same firm (just as skilled scouts differ on major league prospects), so that it is no longer a simple matter to determine which traders are gumming up the operation of the markets and which express the difference in opinion that makes for an honest horse race. I am aware of no important social phenomenon in which there is not some variation within a population under study. The entire theory of natural (and artificial) selection depends on the ability of nature (or society) to throw up populations that differ from each other along some critical dimension, and then explore the implications as they compete for scarce resources. Finance markets are subject to the same dynamic.

Once these heterogeneous expectations are introduced into the model, then we must ratchet down our expectations of how efficiently an efficient market will behave. More concretely, as Lynn Stout has so forcibly argued,[46] it is no longer proper to assume with EMH that the demand for stocks is ever perfectly elastic, or even nearly so. Shares are fractional claims on the assets held within the firm; any difference in the estimation of the value of the underlying assets should lead to differences in the evaluation of the shares, so that the demand curves for stock will look like those for all kinds of other goods. They will be negatively sloped, such that some individuals will find that a stock is "cheap" at the market price, while others will think that it is too "pricey." Both investors could be willing to bid up the price of the stock until their risk-adjusted rate of return meets the dictates of the CAPM model. But so long as they have different estimations of the earnings per share over future periods, then they should have different valuations of the same security even if they demand (for the sake of argument) the same risk-adjusted rate of return from their investments. That difference of opinion will lead some investors to sell the stock (if its price minus the transaction cost of selling is greater than their subjective evaluation) while others continue to bid the price upward, even if no new information changes the equilibrium price. The market price of stock thus becomes the *minimum* valuation of people who continue to hold the stock with a full range of alternatives. At this point it becomes almost idle to speak of a convergence of expectations. What we have is a system that induces individuals to invest in finding out information to guide their investments, and to do so in ways that work toward the production and supply of goods and services that satisfy consumer demand. The world was neither tidy nor linear before the advent of securities markets. It did not become so with their arrival. EMH sets itself up for a fall by claiming a set of strong results that no human institution could achieve, in securities markets or anywhere else.

The parallels between financial markets and ordinary markets for goods and services can be strengthened. Recall the Hayekian position that specialized markets often function more efficiently than generalized markets, even though they are more concentrated. The same conclusion seems to hold to financial markets as well. One of the criticisms of EMH is that it cannot make good on its claim that arbitrageurs are able to overcome nonrandom pressures that are generated by so-called noise traders. As Shleifer develops the argument, arbitrageurs work best (as does everyone else) when close substitutes are available for any particular stock or commodity. He writes: "[T]he central argument of behavioral finance states that, in contrast to efficient markets theory, real-world arbitrage is risky and therefore limited."[47]

We are now left to wonder about the definition of behavioral finance (as a subset of behavioral economics). Shleifer's argument looks correct on its face, but it has no specialized behavioral overtones about it, unless we assume that behavioral finance covers any and all evidence that undermines EMH. But clearly what is intended is not a substantive outcome, but a methodological approach, and Shleifer's point about the inability to arbitrage the market sounds like orthodox finance theory. Thus, it seems clear that close substitutes may be available in connection with particular stocks, where it is possible to hedge positions with options, derivatives, and (more dubiously) stock of other firms in the same industry.

At this juncture, it becomes important to distinguish between a "lock" where a person buys in one market and sells in another and thus is guaranteed (probability one) a profit no matter which way the market moves, and a "correlation" where the arbitrageur counts on a continuation of historical trends showing, say, a close relationship between German water bonds and the Italian lira. It is one sign of the (relative) efficiency of capital markets that locks are very hard to find these days. Any evident disparities that run across markets in identical securities (and their derivatives) are quickly observed and eliminated just as EMH would hold. At this point, the arbitrageur has to enter the difficult and more risky game of correlations, which led to the demise of Long-Term Capital Markets, when certain historical patterns disappeared and left its leveraged hulk in ashes.[48]

The difficulties with arbitrage, moreover, become most apparent with efforts to evaluate the market as a whole. Quite simply, there is no hedge for the entire market itself. "An arbitrageur who thinks that stocks as a whole are overpriced cannot sell short stocks and buy a substitute portfolio, since such does not exist."[49] Riskless strategies that might work for an individual stock do not work for the market as a whole. At this point, the arbitrageur can no longer count on acting like the prudent bookie who has balanced his bets and wins no matter what the outcome of the event. So long as there is any nonrandom pressure on the market, then he has to take the risk that the market will run against him. This observation, to repeat, is not behavioral economics; it is simple economics. All that is needed for the problem to arise is a strong division of opinion on the future of the world, even among sophisticated traders, on the question, for example, of whether future attacks, such as that on the World Trade Center, will lead to a worldwide economic recession. The matter is not made any easier if inexperienced noise traders take (what in hindsight appears to be) the "wrong" view of matters.

The problem that the arbitrageur faces is quite simply this: once we know that behavior in the short term can, for whatever reason, deviate from the rational solution, then there is no reason to think that such deviations will not happen in the long run as well. The simplest explanation is that the individuals who continue to hold the wrong views in period one will (call it the persistence bias) hold them in period two. At this time, they may be joined by other individuals who share, for good reasons or bad, the same set of expectations so that the prices continue to hover above their "fundamental" levels. At this point, it is no longer clear what strategy the fully rational player should adopt to maximize his returns. One clear possibility is to switch sides in the short term, participate in the market rise, and then sell out at just the right time before the new consensus somehow (note the deliberate vagueness of the term) forms that will bring stock prices back to their rational and proper level. But at each instance in time, who decides just how long this bubble will last? The mere fact that some skilled traders will adopt this short-term strategy will first induce more of those nameless noisy traders to enter into the market, which in turn makes it all the harder for arbitrageurs to hold on in the long run, and all the wiser for them to switch sides in the short term.

In this environment, it remains an open question as to when the return to fundamentals will reemerge. In some cases it could happen when some traumatic public event forces its attention on all traders, regardless of skill level or orientation, to take notice. At this point, the correction could well be dramatic and abrupt, as the information is too clear to support the differential expectations that pervaded the market only moments before. But even in a placid external environment, the bubble could burst when a small number of key traders decide that now is the time to pull out, and in so doing lead others to make a reevaluation of their positions. Those quiet events are never tracked in event studies, but they might explain why bubbles burst in financial markets, so long as we relax the assumptions that arbitrageurs can costlessly hedge the market no matter what others think or do. Shleifer's observation on inefficient hedging does not require that one become a behavioral economist. It only requires one to assume the same heterogeneity in expectations and strategies that define every other market.

The point can be pressed by looking at the efficiency of more limited markets. As noted above, my prediction is that these submarkets, with fewer but more experienced players, could easily outperform larger markets. One piece of evidence in that direction involves the patterns observed in risk arbitrage situations that emerge in pending takeover situations, where the acquiring corporation commonly has to pay a healthy premium in order to succeed with its tender offer. The well-known study of Keown and Pinkerton notes that cumulative abnormal returns for takeover candidates hover around zero until news starts to leak out about the pending bid, such that these tend to rise, ever more rapidly from 0 to 12 percent in the two weeks or so before the announcement rate, after which they shoot up to around 28 percent and level off for the next thirty days.[50] These findings seem to be consistent with anyone's definition of efficient markets, which is as it should be. The takeover offer is such a powerful piece of information that it sweeps aside all subtle differences that might otherwise exist, given that it is relatively easy to give a respectable estimate of the final offer price. In addition, the takeover will or will not take place within a short finite period so that arbitrageurs do not have to worry about weathering the storm before the equilibrium is reached.

Legal Reforms

The question then arises of what, if any, legal intervention should be taken on the strength of these various observations. One great compliment for Shleifer's dispassionate treatment of the subject is that he proposes *no* major reforms that might alter the operation of these financial markets. The nature of the pressures that influence these long-term decisions is not well understood by anyone: there are too many possible candidates for behavioral anomalies to know which ones matter and which do not. We also know that legal reforms in general are costly and any legislative reforms could well magnify these biases instead of eliminating them, assuming that we could find statutory language that targets them at all. Thus it seems almost pointless to adopt some general legal requirement that excludes noise traders from markets, because that would require us to identify them before, not after, the fact. Nor could we hold back the tides by requiring all traders to take a course in Bayesian analysis before allowing them to trade securities. We could encourage individuals to invest in mutual funds and similar vehicles, at least on the assumption that these managers could read or study with Shleifer and Thaler (both of whom run investment funds) and avoid their mistakes.

It does not follow, however, that all possibilities for reform are misguided. One key element, of use in limited contexts, is the control that exchanges place on the trading behavior of their members. Exchange rules do not simply allow any persons to trade at will. At the minimum, there are rules that govern when trading may be stopped on the floor in order to prevent cascades from developing. In addition, the exchanges could designate certain market makers, or insist that traders be certified as to levels of experience or net worth. These, and other expedients, might help create the needed pool of experienced traders that will resemble Hayek's highly textured customary markets. Individual brokerage firms could establish rules indicating the kinds of positions they are willing to take for certain classes of clients. Naïve individuals could be kept away from derivatives and steered into mutual funds. Here again, the benefits of decentralization and experimentation seem larger than those of direct regulation, a familiar theme that needs no elaboration.

The insights gleaned from rejection of EMH might also help in dealing with certain level reforms in corporate law. Lynn Stout, for example, has argued, persuasively in my view, that it would be inappropriate for the law to take the position that target management has to remain passive in the face of an outstanding takeover offer, as urged by Easterbrook and Fischel.[51] I think that on balance this position of mandated passivity is wrong for three reasons that relate to the discussion here. First, it implicitly assumes that any price over the prebid market price counts as a premium. That result is true only if one rejects the possibility of heterogeneous expectations; once those are recognized then the ostensible premium is necessary to compensate individuals for the (higher) value that they attach to the stock. Indeed, it is hard to explain why anyone would ever choose to offer a premium at all if demand for shares were perfectly elastic. The one possible explanation is that the required public announcements under the securities law would prompt ordinary holders of shares to revalue their stock. But that explanation does not explain why these premiums seem to occur in a wide range of regulatory setting. If all estimations of value converged, then any small bump-up should clear the market when there is no independent news to justify the increase in prices.

Second, this passive-only position also assumes that in any complex negotiation the first and best offers are synonymous. Yet ordinary individuals who bargain over the sale of unique assets choose from a wide range of strategies; they certainly do not accept the first offer as a matter of course. To be sure, a passive response increases the probability of getting offers, just as it lowers the prices that will be received for any offer that is made. That approach looks desirable when (as is surely sometimes the case) target management is inept and needs to be kept in line. But the same restrictions on target management could be devastating if the takeover is of a successful business run by top-flight people. The precise trade-off between success and premium is hard to measure, and need not cut the same way in all cases.

That last observation leads to the third point. The selection of the "proper" rule for target management should not be a matter of positive law at all. At most, the law sets (without fear of tumbling over an endowment effect) a default provision, which could be varied by corporate charter. In the easy case, the matter will be resolved on formation of the corporation so that all will know the rules under which the game will be played. In other contexts, the policy should be chosen by the directors, subject in general to a shareholder vote to guard against the dangers of an entrenched directorate. As is so often the case, the nature of the firm, the distribution of shares, and the attitudes of top management could easily lead to differences in rules across corporations.

A similar analysis applies to going-private transactions in which the insiders acquire some shares voluntarily and then complete the takeover by exercising what amounts to a private right of condemnation at the prebid share price, again championed by Easterbrook and Fischel.[52] They note rightly that the easier route to takeover allows the minority shareholders to buy in at a lower price, albeit at the cost of lower buyout. But there is no a priori reason to prefer one combination over the other. That said, the basic caveat about the use of the eminent domain power applies: don't give all the advantages to the party that invokes the state use of force. That warning is especially timely when the prebid share price could be below the price that dissident shareholders attach to their holdings. The practice should be allowed to go forward if authorized in the original charter or in any amendment thereto that enjoyed broad support across all shareholder groups. But in the event of charter silence on this issue, I think it is a mistake to assume that the prebid market price leaves the dissident shareholders no worse off than they were at the outset of the transaction.

Finally, there is some question of what is the proper response to insiders who trade on the strength of information they have acquired through their work with the corporation. In principle, there seems little that behavioral finance offers by way of instruction. These are not markets where any cognitive bias is likely to survive. As with takeover bids, the critical question should be that posed by the conventional analysis: whether the initial charter, or some charter amendment with shareholder approval, authorizes or prohibits the use of inside information. The matter should not be a matter of positive law, as is currently the case, but of private contract.[53] How any corporation should answer this question is, however, far from clear, for it is no easy matter to explain why all, or some, insider trading should be prohibited in the first place.[54] It is not clear who is harmed by insider trading when all are aware that it can take place. Nor is it axiomatic that all investors should have equal access to information if they were prepared to waive any such claim on the formation of the corporation. In addition, trades by insiders might have some positive advantage in moving a market closer to its equilibrium price without having to disclose information (for example, potential acquisitions of assets) that would lose value if made public knowledge. It may well be the case that shareholders will be more concerned about insiders who dump stock on the receipt of bad news than they are with their acquiring additional shares on the receipt of good news. If so, a charter provision could prohibit sales of shares, or require notice that insiders are selling (or buying) without requiring them to disclose the reasons for their actions.

Ironically, it is far easier to see why law firms and other businesses that assist corporations agree not to trade on the strength of the information they receive about the shares of *other* corporations. Here, the fear is that the insiders will bid up the price in competition with the firm's own tender offer.[55] But in these cases, it is hard to see any danger to the market at all, for these trades raise no complications when done with the approval of the employer, who is in a position to impose sanctions (fines, dismissal, disgorging of gains) as part of the employment contract. These sanctions seem, moreover, sufficient in and of themselves, so that with all forms of trading on insider information, caution seems to be the order of the day. It is hard to demonstrate any systematic benefits to the current prohibitions on trading that justify the heavy costs of administration.

A Summing Up

This last discussion frames the central theme of these last two chapters. One critical issue with behavioral economics is a matter of perspective and proportion. The current fascination with behavioral insights has powerful things to say about the glitches in personal behavior, conduct that is hard to regulate in any case. But it has far less to say about the sensible regulation of public markets. On these matters, the importing of behavioral insights is often risky business because of the inordinate energy that has to be spent just to establish that certain effects (for example, the endowment effect) exist. But even when biases do operate, they do not in my view do much to undermine the classical liberal synthesis that I have defended in this book. The endowment effect, for example, can easily be understood as furnishing an additional reason to protect private property from confiscation, and to supply generous compensation when it is taken for public use. But lest we be blinded by the novelty of these arguments, it is always wise to remember that the traditional concerns that led to the need for the creation of the state do not disappear. The control of force and fraud are still the first order of business of any society that values ordered liberty. Nothing from behavioral studies alters that view or the mix of sanctions, public and private, that should be directed against such asocial behavior.

The second great problem of the social order is that of monopoly power, either public or private, and the difficulty of adopting some sensible social response to that issue. Yet nothing in behavioral economics undermines (or much informs) the classical liberal synthesis. Behavioral theories do not offer any explanation as to why monopolies outperform competition, or why state actors outperform private ones. Nothing in behavioral economics requires us to jettison the strong results of traditional economic theory. No behavioral phenomenon justifies rent controls, price controls, or wage controls. None should cause us to ignore the destruction of common pool resources, to cast a kind eye toward monopoly behavior, to overlook the temptations of faction and self-interest in public life. On the issues that really matter, the traditional accounts of human behavior deserve our continued allegiance.

Staying the Course

IN THIS BOOK I HAVE SOUGHT TO MAKE OUT a modern case for a return to the system of classical liberalism, resting as it does on the twin pillars of strong property rights and limited government, and organized in ways to protect and support the property rights so created. In order to develop that system, it is necessary to begin, as the classical writers began, with a somber and detached assessment of the psychological strengths and weaknesses of human beings, one that neither romanticizes nor demonizes their capabilities. The basic lesson one learns from this inquiry is that some form of limited self-interest (which includes the interest of family and loved ones) is the best guide to human behavior. But that guide is uncertain, for variations in individual character and temperament guarantee that self-interest will manifest itself differently in different people. Commonsense observation tells us that variation in individual self-interest is what we should come to expect. Some people will find it part of their human nature to help other individuals in need, just as some take perverse glee in the misfortunes of others.

Yet knowledge of these variations in human temperament provides us with a sensible agenda for developing those social institutions that will suppress the worst and bring out the best of what counts, when all is said and done, as the human condition. According to that agenda, it is necessary to control violence and production and exchange. The first portion of this exercise is easier to state. The individuals who lust for power constitute a small minority of any population; yet they must be treated firmly in order to create the necessary space that enables other individuals to develop their faculties and talents to their fullest. Ninety-nine percent compliance with a social norm against the use of force will not cut it if the remaining 1 percent of the population can prey at will on the rest of the population. The bottom portion of the distribution must never be allowed to dictate the behavior of everyone else.

How then to respond? The applicable social imperative requires all individuals to refrain from the private use of force as a means to achieve their private ends. It recognizes that fraud and deceit are often used in two ways. First, in their additive capacity they make the use of force more effective. Feint before you punch; lead your opponent into traps. Second, in some cases they work as a close substitute for force. Why bother to take the risk of a strong-arm robbery if you can sweet-talk your victim out of something of value?

No system of uncoordinated individual responses can deal with the menace of aggression. It requires some coordinated effort—a monopoly of force by well-socialized individuals to prevent the aggressive few from calling the shots for us all. The entire structure of constitutional government must respond to the danger of internal unrest and external aggression. Yet it must do so in a way that prevents the concentration of state powers to work for the advantage of the aggressive few. We need therefore to set power against power, so that no small group of individuals can ever gain complete control of the instruments of government. The separation of powers and the principles of checks and balances are born of these concerns. The sad truth is that even the limited government called for by laissez-faire is a large and complex undertaking that is not made any easier in light of the all-pressing need to combat both the threat and the use of force. That task takes imagination, dedication, perseverance, resources, and self-discipline. My great fear is that as we divert public resources into state enterprises of doubtful merit, we weaken the ability of government to deal with the obvious perils that are its first obligation to counteract. Strong government within a limited compass should be our watchword. The twin tasks of maintaining social order and providing, when needed, social infrastructure is big business even for the minimal state.

The need for the state to constrain internal unrest and protect against external aggression is only half the story. It is also necessary to ensure that government is confined to the tasks it can do well. The many tasks that the state cannot do well include everything from writing novels to building machine tools. Public force may be necessary to quell the darkest impulses of some human beings. But no system of government control will ever be able to unleash or spur the creative or entrepreneurial elements of the human spirit. It is therefore incumbent that any government should seek to facilitate but not direct these efforts. The best and the brightest will be able to succeed only if they receive breathing room for their own activities. They can receive that space only if our collective power and intelligence support and nourish systems of private property, on which the advancement of public welfare so heavily depends. In creating these institutions, we must stress the strong distinction between markets and mercantilism. The strong rights of property allow individuals to keep exclusive control only of their own assets, both physical and intellectual. Property rights do not allow them to bar others from acting as their direct competitors.

The question then arises as to how it is possible to preserve a set of institutions that uses its power solely for the limited ends for which they are called into being. Constitutions can certainly help to improve the odds that various societies will be able to strike the correct balance between collective control and individual choice. But our world is littered with constitutional failures, which are, alas, all too easy to explain. No set of man-made institutions can achieve the right balance between social control and individual choice on its own. Constitutions do not appear out of thin air. They are part of a complex web of political and social institutions that define what is best and worst about any set of political institutions. James Madison wrote in Federalist No. 10 that we cannot design our institutions on the assumption that enlightened statesmen will always be at the helm. His basic insight was that political institutions need to be designed more with an eye to weathering rough seas than to sliding majestically through smooth waters. It is, if anything, more important to structure political institutions to obstruct the ambitions of the unfit than to unleash the capabilities of wise and true leaders.

Yet what Madison left unspoken in that brief passage is more troublesome by far. Limited governments of perfect design will surely fail if enlightened statesmen are *never* at the helm. And they won't make it to the top without the assistance of an informed public led by an informed and deep set of business, political, and intellectual elites. A succession of bad or mediocre leaders—no need to think of Adolf Hitler when Juan Perón will suffice—will, with time, surely undermine the political and social institutions on which both human liberty and human security depend. Bad leaders will treat the principles of limited government as weak presumptions that can be discarded for weak or foolish reasons. Horrible leaders will in turn treat public office as a private hunting preserve instead of a public trust in which they have to test their every actions against an unflinching standard of public welfare. High-sounding rhetoric when paired with venial and corrupt actions can quickly sap the vitality of public institutions and breed a popular cynicism regarding the capacity of political leaders to govern. Government could become a parade of bread and circuses where short-term appeals to one faction or another become the order of the day. Regulation and taxation can then snuff out the creative impulses in arts and businesses even in a country that pays lip service to freedom of speech.

What, then, is the antidote to the all-too-familiar story of great expectations followed by ready decline? Legal and political institutions can take us only so far. Sadly, the numerous political failures around the world should warn us that there is no automatic safeguard against the scourges of Nazism, fascism, communism, and fundamentalism. All that we can hope to do is to improve the odds, and toward that end the most powerful bulwark is a determined citizenry that internalizes the basic lessons of human history. That understanding makes it necessary to educate anew each generation to understand the uses and limits of government. Alas, the outcome is very much in doubt in light of the strong obstacles that lie in the path of market liberalization. One sure sign is the rise of special pleading for concentrated interest groups. It is an ominous sign for the United States to see how *both* political parties in America can disregard the case for open markets, most recently by levying high tariffs on steel imports, by doling out large subsidies for farmers, and by concocting new entitlement programs for jobs and medical benefits.

What is so difficult to fathom is how political knowledge ebbs and flows while scientific and technical knowledge is able to grow and progress in continuous, if not wholly orderly, fashion. We are confident that the best and the brightest physicists and biologists in one generation *know* more about their work than their predecessors. It is not that today's scholars and scientists are smarter or more creative than their predecessors. If anything, our huge knowledge base, peopled by so many learned experts, leads to genuine expertise in peptides and base metals. It is highly unlikely that any single scientist or researcher will ever again have the impact of an Archimedes, Newton, or Einstein. But rigorous application of the scientific method allows them to combine theory and evidence in ways that advance the cause of human knowledge.

Notwithstanding their formidable intellectual requirements, science and technology have jobs easier than those of law and political theory. Science can prosper so long as its technical standards are transmitted to the practitioners of each particular discipline. Politics, including the political institutions that support basic scientific research, cannot succeed by taking over some small community. Unless some commitment to fundamental principles is widely shared throughout society, political institutions remain always in danger. Education cannot be confined only to the best and the brightest, but must be extended to everyone who has a stake in the future of society—which is to say, to everyone. That educational mission will fail if it loses sight of the fundamental principles of sound government, which leads us back to the familiar themes of private property and limited government.

In writing this book, I have not sought to answer the fundamental question of how to *implement* these principles, for I am at a loss to answer whether legislators, administrators, or judges are most likely to lead us astray. My own preference is to divide power among the various branches in order to achieve two objectives. The first is to reduce the concentration of power, and the second is to slow down the pace by which law has been made. But this book is concerned with the climate of intellectual opinion that leads to the erosion of the beliefs necessary to support the creation and preservation of free institutions. In order to counteract that trend, it is necessary to set out for our generation the modern case to support a series of classical institutions. That is why it is so important to describe the functional justifications for traditional institutions and understanding, which are too often and too casually attacked as unformed relics of the past. For that reason I have sought to lay out a set of principles that responds to the dangers of negative externalities and holdouts that bedevil any modern state. I have then pursued the critics of these principles in order to show that the use of modern economic and legal theory does not require us to back down on any of the three pillars for a coherent and just society: we should never think that our intuitions are so unsatisfactory that we drown in a sea of moral relativism; we should never be so cavalier about the use and coherence of language that we think it an impossible feat to articulate, in clear and unambiguous ways, the rules that define a sound legal system or the agreements and practices that it should undergird; and we should not think that people are so unformed in their preferences that they cannot, on average, be counted on to make decisions that advance their own interests when given the power and right to do so.

Any sound legal order has its moral, conceptual, and psychological underpinnings. All these have been attacked in recent years, often in search of an expanded role for state power. Yet we are rightly cautious about making any new concession to government power that rests on the claim that governments are better able to make choices for individuals than they are able to make for themselves. In the endless challenge to preserve both liberty and social order, moral, conceptual, and behavioral clarity will in the long run outperform any form of moral, conceptual, or behavioral skepticism. Wrongly understood, skepticism undermines freedom. Rightly understood, skepticism and freedom form an indissoluble pair.

◼ NOTES

Introduction

1. See David D. Friedman, *The Machinery of Freedom: Guide to a Radical Capitalism* (2d ed. 1989); David D. Friedman, *Hidden Order: The Economics of Everyday Life* (1996).

2. Hernando de Soto, *The Mystery of Capital: Why Capitalism Triumphs in the West and Fails Everywhere Else* (2000).

3. 1 William Blackstone, *Commentaries on the Laws of England* *39–*40.

4. Louis Kaplow & Steven Shavell, *Fairness versus Welfare* (2002).

5. Gaius, *Institutes*, bk. 1, 1 (Francis de ZuLueta ed., 1946). The analogous passage of Justinian is in *Institutes*, bk. 1, 1.2.

6. Gaius, *Institutes*, bk. 1, 1.

7. Justinian, *Institutes*, bk. 1, 3.2.

8. Richard A. Epstein, *Takings: Private Power and the Power of Eminent Domain* (1985); Richard A. Epstein, *Bargaining with the State* (1993).

9. For the dogmatic assertion that it does, see *The Selective Service Cases*, 245 U.S. 366 (1918).

10. David Hume, *A Treatise of Human Nature* 495 (L. A. Selby-Bigge ed., 1888).

Chapter One

1. See Cass R. Sunstein, *One Case at a Time* (1999).

2. Immanuel Kant, *Ground for the Metaphysics of Morals* 46 (1993).

3. Oliver Wendell Holmes Jr., *The Common Law* 1 (1881).

4. See, e.g., G. E. Moore, *Principia Ethica* 116–26 (1903). For discussion, see W. D. Ross, *The Right and the Good* 93–100 (1930).

5. See David Hume, *A Treatise of Human Nature* 469–70 (L. A. Selby-Bigge ed., 1888).

6. See, e.g., Aristotle, *Politics* 1256b40–1258b8, in *The Basic Works of Aristotle* (Benjamin Jowett trans., R. McKeon ed., 1941).

7. Justinian, *Institutes*, bk. 1, tit. 2 (J. B. Moyle trans., 5th ed. 1913).

8. See, e.g., Gaius, *Institutes*, bk. 2, 66.

9. *Digest*, 9.2.4.pr. (My translations are all taken from F. H. Lawson, *Negligence in Civil Law* [1950].)

10. For my more extensive elaboration of this theme, see Richard A. Epstein, *Principles for a Free Society: Reconciling Individual Liberty with the Common Good* (1998).

11. See, e.g., John Locke, *The Second Treatise of Civil Government*, ch. 3, "Of the State of War," ch. 5, "Of Property," and ch. 6, "Of Parental Rights" (1689).

12. H. L. A. Hart, *The Concept of Law* 193 (1961).

13. For a powerful account of how socialization within families is a precondition for "homo economicus," see Jennifer Roback Morse, *Love & Economics* (2001). The point was not lost on Locke whose chapter on Paternal Power began with the assertion that these obligations bound father and mother alike, without distinction. Locke, *Treatise*, ch. 6, ¶ 52.

14. See Mancur Olson, *The Logic of Collective Action* 2 (1965) (emphasis in original). Much of his book is then devoted to explaining how various groups that operate at the substate level overcome the tendency to free ride.

15. Id. at 13.

16. See, e.g., Norman Frohlich & Joe A. Oppenheimer, "Experiencing Impartiality to Invoke Fairness in N-PD: Some Experimental Results," 86 *Public Choice* 117 (1996). During the initial period, however, the use of external sanctions reduced short-term levels of defection. Clearly, every society must choose the optimum mix of the two types of sanctions, taking into account the "crowding out" effect that external sanctions have on internally developed rules. See Bruno S. Frey, "How Intrinsic Motivation Is Crowded Out and In," 6 *Rationality and Society* 334 (1994).

17. On the intuitive capacity to generate language and grammar, see Steven Pinker, *The Language Instinct* (1994).

18. See 1 F. A. Hayek, *Law, Legislation and Liberty* (1973), where the first chapter is entitled "Reason and Evolution."

19. Elinor Ostrom, "Collective Action and the Evolution of Social Norms," 14 *J. Econ. Persp.* 137, 143 (2000).

20. For a more elaborate discussion, see Epstein, *Principles for a Free Society*, ch. 9.

21. Duncan Kennedy, "Form and Substance in Private Law Adjudication," 89 *Harv. L. Rev.* 1685 (1976).

22. Mark Kelman, *A Guide to Critical Legal Studies* 3 (1987).

23. For discussion, see Louis Kaplow, "Rules versus Standards: An Economic Analysis," 42 *Duke L. J.* 557 (1992).

24. See, e.g., Duncan Kennedy's treatment of precontractual duties, "Form and Substance," 89 *Harv. L. Rev.* at 1694–1701, or Kelman's demonstration of Richard Posner's exaggerated claims of the efficiency of the ostensible common law rule of negligence. Kelman, *Guide to Critical Legal Studies*, at 115–18.

25. For discussion, see Clayton P. Gillette, "Commercial Relationships and the Selection of Default Rules for Remote Risks," 19 *J. Legal Stud.* 535 (1990).

Chapter Two

1. Jacob Viner, "An Intellectual History of Laissez-Faire," 3 *J. Law & Econ.* 45, 45 (1960).

2. Charles Murray, *What It Means to Be a Libertarian: A Personal Interpretation* 36–41 (1996).

3. See, e.g., Grant Gilmore, *The Death of Contract* 103 (1974).

4. Stephen Holmes & Cass R. Sunstein, *The Cost of Rights: Why Liberty Depends on Taxes* (1999).

5. David D. Friedman, "Private Creation and Enforcement of Law—A Historical Case," 8 *J. Legal Stud.* 399 (1979).

6. *McCulloch v. Maryland,* 17 U.S. 316, 431 (1819).

7. Liam Murphy & Thomas Nagel, *The Myth of Ownership: Taxes and Justice* (2002).

8. Id. at 32.

9. I develop these arguments at greater length in Richard A. Epstein, *Bargaining with the State* 28–32 (1993).

10. See Harold Demsetz, "Why Regulate Utilities?" 11 *J. Law & Econ.* 55 (1968).

11. Justinian's *Institutes,* bk. 1, ch. 2, 2.

12. John Locke, *Of Civil Government (Second Treatise),* ch. 2 (1689).

13. See, for the importance of communication in the articulation of property rules generally, Henry E. Smith, *The Language of Property* (2001) (unpublished manuscript).

14. John Rawls, *A Theory of Justice* (1971).

15. See David Hume, *A Treatise on Human Nature* 502 (L. A. Selby-Bigge ed., 1888).

16. The key American case on the right to conquest is *Johnson v. M'Intosh,* 21 U.S. 543 (1823), which has generated an enormous discussion on the status of rights of indigenous people everywhere in the world. For a discussion on the relationships between the United States and the Indian tribes, see Terry L. Anderson & Fred S. McChesney, "Raid or Trade? An Economic Model of Indian-White Relations," 37 *J. L. Econ.* 39 (1994).

17. For a fuller discussion of these points, see Richard A. Epstein, *Principles for a Free Society: Reconciling Individual Liberty with the Common Good,* ch. 9 (1998).

18. For a discussion, see *Keys v. Romley,* 412 P.2d 529 (Cal. 1966).

19. For a discussion, see *Robinson v. Ariyoshi,* 753 F.2d 1468 (9th Cir. 1985).

20. See J. Mark Ramseyer, "Water Law in Imperial Japan: Public Goods, Private Claims and Legal Convergence," 18 *J. Legal Stud.* 51 (1989).

21. See Gaius, *Institutes,* bk. 3, 97–98.

22. For a related discussion on coercion, see pages 110–14.

23. Immanuel Kant, *Ground for the Metaphysics of Morals* 37 (1993).

24. On their use, see John O. McGinnis & Michael Rappaport, "Still a Solution: In Further Support of Spending Supermajority Rules," 40 *William and Mary L. Rev.* 527 (1997).

25. For a discussion, see Frank H. Easterbrook & Daniel R. Fischel, *The Structure of Corporate Law* 126–53 (1991); Robert C. Clark, *Corporate Law* 141–57 (1986). Note that the list of topics that address this issue is long: it includes at the very least self-dealing, executive compensation, corporate opportunities, insider trading, freezeouts, and buyouts.

26. Isaiah Berlin, *Four Essays on Liberty* (1969); for a sympathetic explication, see

John Gray, *Isaiah Berlin* (1996), noting Berlin's skepticism about the dangers of forming any comprehensive system, id. at 7–9, a warning that I have obviously not heeded.

27. See pages 94–95.

28. For a parallel development that covers these four rules, but refuses to go much beyond them, see Randy Barnett, *The Structure of Liberty* (1998), criticized in Richard A. Epstein, "The Libertarian Quartet," *Reason,* January 1999, at 61.

29. Murray, *What It Means to Be a Libertarian,* at 20.

30. See *Vincent v. Lake Erie Transp. Co.,* 124 N.W. 221 (Minn. 1910), discussed in greater detail in chapter 4.

31. For a fuller treatment of the subject, see Richard A. Epstein, *Principles for a Free Society: Reconciling Individual Liberty and the Common Good,* ch. 10 (1998).

32. See, for judicial recognition of the point, *Duquesne Light Co. v. Barasch,* 488 U.S. 299 (1989).

33. On which see *AT&T v. Iowa Utilities Bd.,* 525 U.S. 366 (1999).

34. For its most powerful recent expression, see the Telecommunications Act of 1996 § 254, which expands the obligation beyond its earlier contours. For a discussion of the difficulties, see Eli Noam, "Will Universal Service and Common Carriage Survive the Telecommunications Act of 1996?" 97 *Colum. L. Rev.* 995 (1997).

35. See "Taking Flight," *Economist,* Feb. 22, 1997, at 73; Wendy Zellner, "Can American or Its Pilots Afford This Game of Chicken?" *Business Week,* Feb. 17, 1997, at 38; Michael Arndt, "The Industry Will Pay for United's Deal with Pilots," id., Sept. 18, 2000, at 52.

36. See Linda Babcock, Xianghong Wang & George Loewenstein, "Choosing the Wrong Pond: Social Comparisons in Negotiations That Reflect a Self-Serving Bias," 111 *Q.J. Econ.* 1 (1996).

37. Garry Wills, *A Necessary Evil* 16 (1999).

38. Id. at 297 (emphasis in original).

39. See Frank Easterbrook & Daniel Fischel, *The Economic Structure of Corporate Law* 1–7 (1991), treating the corporation as a network of (relational) contracts among shareholders and other principal players. For example, a stock dividend to some shareholders but not others functions as an implicit transfer between the two groups of shareholders.

40. Adam Smith, *The Wealth of Nations,* bk. 5, ch. 2, pt. 2 (Modern Library ed., 1937).

41. Aristotle, *Nicomachean Ethics,* bk. 5, ch. 3, 1131a, 30.

42. John Locke, "Of Civil Government" in *First Treatise of Government* ¶ 140 (1689).

43. Friedrich A. Hayek, *A Constitution of Liberty* 314 (1960).

44. Richard A. Epstein, "Taxation in a Lockean World," 4 *Social Philo. & Pol.* 49 (1986); Richard A. Epstein, "Can Anyone Beat the Flat Tax," 19:1 *Social Philo. & Pol.* 140 (2002).

45. For a partial endorsement of this position, see *Lucas v. South Carolina Coastal Comm'n,* 505 U.S. 1003, 1022–32 (1992).

46. For a comprehensive argument to this effect, see John Lott Jr., *More Guns, Less Crime* (1998).

47. My thanks to David Friedman for pressing this point, as he has so many others.

48. For one such account, see Joseph Story, "Natural Law," an unsigned article in *Encyclopedia Americana* (1836).

49. For a discussion, see Martin Olasky, *The Tragedy of American Compassion*, ch. 1 (1992).

50. *Clark v. Community for Creative Non-Violence*, 468 U.S. 288 (1984). As ever the problem of administration of public spaces is always far more difficult than first appears. Campgrounds clearly allow for overnight use, but setting (below market) charges for their use often makes their allocation inefficient.

51. 291 U.S. 502 (1934).

52. Thomas DeLeire, "The Unintended Consequences of the Americans with Disabilities Act," 23:1 *Regulation* 21 (2000).

53. Murray, *What It Means to Be a Libertarian*, at 47–54. For his earlier critique of that system, see Charles Murray, *Losing Ground: American Social Policy 1950–1980* (1984), which provides a more exhaustive account.

54. For more recent evaluations, see, e.g., Yong Back Choi, "Misunderstanding Distribution," 19:1 *Social Philo. & Pol.* 110 (2002).

Chapter Three

1. F. A. Hayek, *The Constitution of Liberty* (1960).

2. Each volume bears its own title. Volume 1, published in 1973, is titled *Rules and Order;* volume 2, published in 1976, is *The Mirage of Social Justice;* volume 3, published in 1979, is *The Political Order of a Free People.*

3. F. A. Hayek, *The Fatal Conceit: The Errors of Socialism* (1988).

4. 2 *Law, Legislation and Liberty*, at 8. "The expression 'the Great Society,' which we shall frequently use in the same sense in which we shall use Sir Karl Popper's term 'the Open Society,' was, of course, already familiar in the eighteenth century" (1 ibid., at 148 n. 11).

5. F. A. Hayek, "The Use of Knowledge in Society," 35 *Am. Econ. Rev.* 520 (1945).

6. The phrase comes from one of Holmes's great decisions that denied the possibility that federal courts could pluck out some principles of common law to apply to ordinary private law disputes usually governed by state law. See Holmes's dissent in *Southern Pac. Co. v. Jensen*, 244 U.S. 205, 222 (1917). His views eventually prevailed, so that today, roughly speaking, the federal courts in diversity cases normally apply the applicable state common law, and not some version of federal common law. See *Erie R.R. v. Tompkins*, 304 U.S. 64 (1938).

7. For a recent, and relentless, dissection of Holmes's skepticism, see Albert W. Alschuler, *Law without Values: The Life, Work, and Legacy of Justice Holmes* (2000).

8. See, e.g., Oliver Wendell Holmes, "Ideals and Doubts," 10 *Ill. L. Rev.* 1, 2 (1915).

For exhaustive and very different accounts of Holmes, see Richard A. Posner, *The Essential Holmes* (1992).

9. 250 U.S. 616, 624 (1919) (Holmes, J., dissenting). For an exhaustive account of the historical setting, see Richard Polenberg, *Fighting Faiths: The* Abrams *Case, the Supreme Court, and Free Speech* (1987).

10. John Henry Wigmore, "Abrams v. United States: Freedom of Speech and Freedom of Thuggery in War-Time and Peace-Time," 14 *Ill. L. Rev.* 539 (1920).

11. *Abrams,* 250 U.S. at 630.

12. For the manifold interpretations that this passage allows, see Alschuler, *Law without Values,* at 69–81. See also David Luban, "The First Amendment in Its Forgotten Years," 90 *Yale L. J.* 514 (1981), for an account of the early history of the First Amendment. For a close examination of the indictment in *Abrams* from the point of view of the criminal lawyer, see James Boyd White, "Legal Knowledge," 115 *Harv. L. Rev.* 1396, 1411 (2002).

13. 249 U.S. 47, 52 (1919).

14. *Abrams,* 250 U.S. at 630. There is no question that Holmes's statement of the principle in *Abrams* was more restrictive of government practice than his earlier remark in *Schenck:* "The question in every case is whether the words used are used in such circumstances and are of such a nature as to create a clear and present danger that they will bring about the substantive evils that Congress has a right to prevent" (249 U.S. at 52).

15. Note that inducement of breach of contract is not just some newly concocted tort to attack political speech. Its origins go back to *Lumley v. Gye,* 2 El. & Bl. 216, 118 Eng. Rep. 749 (Q.B. 1853); for a general account of the issue, see Richard A. Epstein, *Torts* § 21.2–21.5 (1999).

16. *Brandenburg v. Ohio,* 395 U.S. 444 (1969), handed down just in time to prevent criminal prosecution of protestors of the Vietnam War.

17. 198 U.S. 45 (1905).

18. Id. at 75.

19. Id. at 76.

20. It was made by Justice Pitney in *Coppage v. Kansas,* 236 U.S. 1, 17 (1915): "[T]he contract is made to the very end that each may gain something that he needs or desires more urgently than that which he proposes to give in exchange."

21. See, for a discussion, Richard A. Epstein, "The Mistakes of 1937," 11 *George Mason L. Rev.* 5 (1988).

22. See *Addyston Pipe & Steel Co. v. United States,* 175 U.S. 211, 228–29 (1899), allowing the application of the Sherman Antitrust Act to territorial divisions among producers.

23. Jacob Viner, "An Intellectual History of Laissez-Faire," 3 *J. L. & Econ.* 45, 45 (1960).

24. *Caldor v. Bull,* 3 U.S. 386, 388 (1798) (per Chase, J.).

25. For some of the early criticism, see, e.g., Roscoe Pound, "Liberty of Contract," 18 *Yale L. J.* 454 (1909).

26. For a popular account, see Philip K. Howard, *The Death of Common Sense* (1994); for a more technical account of the differential interest group pressures on OSHA, see, e.g., Ann P. Bartels, "Direct and Indirect Effects of Regulation: A New Look at OSHA's Impact," 28 *J. L. & Econ.* 1 (1985).

27. See Alschuler, *Law without Values*, at 151–54 for a discussion of the debate, which began with Holmes's famous essay "The Path of the Law," whose stated intention was to "dispel a confusion between morality and law." Oliver Wendell Holmes, "The Path of the Law," 10 *Harv. L. Rev.* 457, 459 (1897).

28. H. L. A. Hart, "Positivism and the Separation of Law and Morals," 71 *Harv. L. Rev.* 593 (1957) (for the strict separation); Lon Fuller, "Positivism and Fidelity to Law," 71 *Harv. L. Rev.* 630 (1957) (insisting on the minimum requirements for natural law).

29. F. A. Hayek, *The Road to Serfdom* 4 (1944). "It is necessary now to state the unpalatable truth that it is Germany whose fate we are in some danger of repeating." Hayek also announced that "he has become increasingly convinced that at least some of the forces which have destroyed freedom in Germany are also at work here and that the character and the source of the danger are, if possible, even less understood that they were in Germany" (id. at 5).

30. See Richard A. Posner, "The Problematics of Moral and Legal Theory," 111 *Harv. L. Rev.* 1637 (1998), expanded into book form under the same title, Richard A. Posner, *The Problematics of Moral and Legal Theory* (1999). For his evident adulation of Holmes, see also *The Essential Holmes* (Richard A. Posner ed., 1992).

31. See generally, Ronald Dworkin, *Law's Empire* (1986).

32. Richard A. Posner, *The Problems of Jurisprudence* 28 (1990).

33. Id. at 26 n. 40.

34. See Richard A. Posner, *Economic Analysis of Law* (1st ed. 1973).

35. Id. at 341–47. He cites Richard A. Epstein, "The Utilitarian Foundations of Natural Law," 12 *Harv. J. L. & Pub. Pol'y* 713 (1989).

36. Posner, *Economic Analysis of Law*, at 346–47.

37. See James W. Ely Jr., *The Chief Justiceship of Melville W. Fuller, 1888–1910* (1995).

38. James W. Ely Jr., "The Oxymoron Reconsidered: Myth and Reality in the Origins of Substantive Due Process," 16 *Constitutional Commentary* 315, 320–22 (1999) (relying on Edward Coke's readings).

39. Howard Gillman, *The Constitution Besieged: The Rise and Demise of* Lochner *Era Police Powers Jurisprudence* (1993).

40. Id., carefully rehearsing the arguments in *Lochner*, at 126–31. See, e.g., *Adair v. United States*, 208 U.S. 1 (1908) (striking down a collective bargaining statute for federal railroad workers as outside the scope of the police power).

41. H. L. A. Hart, "The Nightmare and the Noble Dream," 11 *Ga. L. Rev.* 969 (1977).

42. See Richard A. Epstein, *Simple Rules for a Complex World* (1995).

43. Id.

44. Posner, *Problems of Jurisprudence,* at 236.

45. Posner, "Problematics of Moral and Legal Theory," 111 *Harv. L. Rev.* at 1644–45 (emphasis added).

46. The literature on the Nuremberg trials is voluminous. For Posner's own (pragmatic) views on Nuremberg, see Richard A. Posner, *Law and Legal Theory in the UK and USA* 4–6 (1996). For some recent exhaustive accounts, see Matthew Lippman, "Crimes against Humanity," 17 *B.C. Third World L. J.* 171, 177–233 (1997); "Essays on the Laws of War and War Crimes Tribunals in Honor of Telford Taylor," 37 *Colum. J. Transnat'l L.* 693–937 (1999). For a prosecutor's perspective, see Bernard D. Meltzer, " 'War Crimes': The Nuremberg Trial and the Tribunal for the Former Yugoslavia," 30 *Val. U. L. Rev.* 695 (1996).

47. Posner, "Problematics of Moral and Legal Theory," 111 *Harv. L. Rev.* at 1644.

48. For a condemnation of suicide, see, e.g., John Locke, *Second Treatise of Government,* ch. 2, § 5: "though man in that state have an uncontroulable liberty to dispose of his person or possession, yet he has not the liberty to destroy himself;" chiefly for theocratic reasons that human life is a gift of God. Usually suicide is taken as a sign of mental instability, but that need not be the case with assisted suicide for terminally ill patients. See, for the rejection of the constitutional right of assisted suicide, *Washington v. Glucksberg,* 521 U.S. 702 (1997), and *Vacco v. Quill,* 521 U.S. 793 (1997); for my views (against the constitutionalization of assisted suicide), see Richard A. Epstein, *Mortal Peril: Our Inalienable Right to Health Care?* 329–43 (1997).

49. See, e.g., Adam Smith, *The Theory of Moral Sentiments,* pt. 3, ch. 4 (1759), a book that appears to have made a well-deserved comeback in recent years. See also John Rawls, *A Theory of Justice* (1971), for his take on the veil of ignorance question.

50. Discussed recently in Peter Gay, "Inside the Third Reich," *New York Times Book Review* (review of Victor Klemperer, *I Will Bear Witness: A Diary of the Nazi Years 1933–1941*), Nov. 22, 1998, at 15, 16.

51. Posner, "Problematics of Moral and Legal Theory," 111 *Harv. L. Rev.* at 1643.

52. See Posner, *Problematics of Moral and Legal Theory,* at 6.

53. Posner, "Problematics of Moral and Legal Theory," 111 *Harv. L. Rev.* at 1640.

54. See Alschuler, *Law without Values,* at 1, quoting Holmes to Lady Pollock, Sept. 6, 1902, in 1 *Holmes-Pollock Letters* 105 (Mark DeWolfe Howe ed., 2d ed. 1961).

55. H. L. A. Hart, *The Concept of Law* (1961). This account is hardly original with Hart. As he notes, "This empirical version of natural law is based on Hobbes, *Leviathan,* chs. 14 and 15, and Hume, *Treatise of Human Nature,* Book III, part 2; esp. ss. 2 and 4–7." He hardly could have picked better jumping off points.

Chapter Four

1. See J. L. Austin, *Sense and Sensibilia* (1962), an obvious take-off on the great concern of the time with sense data, as opposed to things, as the ultimate constituents of the percep-

tual universe. See, e.g., A. J. Ayer, *The Foundations of Empirical Knowledge* (1940); C. I. Lewis, *An Analysis of Knowledge and Valuation* (1946). See also J. L. Austin, *Philosophical Papers* (J. O. Urmson & G. J. Warnock ed., 1970), containing such masterpieces as "A Plea for Excuses," at 123, and "Ifs and Cans," at 153.

2. See H. L. A. Hart & A. N. Honoré, *Causation in the Law* (1st ed. 1959); this approach had extensive influence on my own earlier work. See Richard A. Epstein, "A Theory of Strict Liability," 2 *J. Legal Stud.* 151 (1973).

3. See, e.g., Bruce A. Ackerman, *Private Property and the Constitution* (1977).

4. W. D. Ross, *The Right and the Good* (1930).

5. The trade-offs involved in this communication game have recently received much more attention. See, e.g., Henry E. Smith, *The Language of Property* (2001) (unpublished manuscript), noting that property rules binding the world have to have simple dimensions, while contract relationships, with designated persons, can assume more complexity because they reach a narrower audience. See also the discussion of rules versus standards in chapter 1.

6. Richard Courant & Harold Robbins, *What Is Mathematics? An Elementary Approach to Ideas and Methods* 298 (1941).

7. C. S. Lewis, *The Case for Christianity* 3 (1943). My thanks to Albert Alschuler for pointing out these passages.

8. Id. at 3.

9. For a discussion see Richard A. Epstein, "Pleadings and Presumptions," 40 *U. Chi. L. Rev.* 556 (1973). For its early invocation in the Roman law, see Gaius, *Institutes,* bk. 4, pt. 1, §§ 115–29 (Francis de ZuLueta ed., 1946) (noting the use of the replication as a way to admit new matter that overcomes what would otherwise be a valid exception to the prima case). The replication made its way into English law as well. See Ralph Sutton, *Personal Actions at Common Law* 78, 190, 198 (1929).

10. See, e.g., Ross, *The Right and the Good.*

11. Id. at 21.

12. Id. at 18.

13. Id. at 19.

14. Id. at 22.

15. For a more detailed discussion, see Richard A. Epstein, "The Static Conception of the Common Law," 9 *J. Legal Stud.* 253 (1980).

16. "Law, in its most general and comprehensive sense, signifies a rule of action; and is applied indiscriminately to all kinds of action, whether animate, or inanimate, rational or irrational" (1 William Blackstone, *Commentaries on the Laws of England* *39–*40).

17. Élie Halévy, *The Growth of Philosophic Radicalism* 6 (Mary Morris trans., 1928). "In this moral Newtonianism the principle of the association of ideas and the principle of utility take the place of the principle of universal attraction."

18. See Justinian, *Digest,* 9.2.51, the *Lex Aquilia* with the reference, *si culpa quis*

occiderit—"if only kills negligently (*culpa*)," as translated in F. H. Lawson, *Negligence in the Civil Law* 83 (1950). Lawson's title shows his clear preference for the negligence system, and his own translation leaves *culpa* sounding clearer in English than it does in Latin, as Lawson acknowledges. Id. at 36–43.

19. Richard A. Epstein, *Simple Rules for a Complex World* 92–97 (1995).

20. See Restatement (Second) of Torts § 431, comment a, noting that the law does not use the term "causation" "in the so-called 'philosophic sense,' which includes every one of the great number of events without which any happening would not have occurred."

21. *Fletcher v. Rylands*, L. R. 1 Ex. 265 (1866), *aff'd sub nom. Rylands v. Fletcher*, L. R. 3 H.L. 330 (H.L.E. 1868).

22. For one notable attempt at their resolution see, e.g., H. L. A. Hart & Tony Honoré, *Causation in the Law* (2d ed. 1985); for my view, see Richard A. Epstein, *Torts*, ch. 10 (1999).

23. For the Roman illustration, see Justinian's *Digest*, 9.2.9.4: "But if persons are throwing javelins by way of sport and a slave is killed, the Aquilian action lies; but if when others are throwing javelins in a field, a slave crosses it, the Aquilian action fails, because he ought not to have made his way at an inopportune time across the field used for javelin-throwing. However, anyone who deliberately aims at him is, of course, liable to the Aquilian action." For the parallel English principle, see *Robert Addie & Sons (Collieries) v. Dumbreck*, [1929] A.C. 358. For a fuller exposition, see Epstein, *Torts* § 12.3.

24. *Digest* 9.2.4–9.2.5; for the common law rules, see Restatement (Second) of Torts §§ 63–73. Section 71 deals with excessive force. Other sections cover defense of others (§§ 74–76) and defense of property (§§ 77–87).

25. See Milsom, *The Historical Foundations of the Common Law* (2d ed. 1981).

26. Saul Levmore, "Variety and Uniformity in the Treatment of the Good-Faith Purchaser," 16 *J. Legal Stud.* 43 (1987).

27. For the modern statement of the rule, see U.C.C. 3–104, Negotiable Instruments.

28. For the modern statement of the rule, see U.C.C. 2–403, Goods.

29. See *Ploof v. Putnam*, 71 A. 188 (Vt. 1908).

30. Similar questions arise under the law of general average contribution used to allocate losses between ship and cargo owners when partial salvage has been made. Here, again, the principles of necessity help explain the cases. For discussion, see Richard A. Epstein, *Principles for a Free Society: Reconciling Individual Liberty with the Common Good* 122–23. For earlier treatments, see Grant Gilmore & Charles Black, *The Law of Admiralty* §§ 5.1–5.2 (1975); William M. Landes & Richard A. Posner, "Salvors, Finders, Good Samaritans, and Other Rescuers," 7 *J. Legal Stud.* 83, 106–8 (1978).

31. See, e.g., *Post v. Jones*, 60 U.S. 150 (1856).

32. Id. at 159.

33. Id. at 160.

34. Id.

35. For a general discussion, see Epstein *Torts* § 11.3.

36. See *Buch v. Armory Mfg Co.*, 44 A. 809 (N.H. 1897).

37. James Barr Ames, "Law and Morals," 22 *Harv. L. Rev.* 97, 110–13 (1908); Earnest Weinrib, "The Case for a Duty to Rescue," 90 *Yale L. J.* 247 (1985).

38. For a version of this argument, see Leslie Bender, "A Lawyer's Primer of Feminist Theory and Tort," 38 *J. Legal Educ.* 34–35 (1988).

39. See, e.g., *Eckert v. Long Island R.R.*, 43 N.Y. 502 (1871). Suppose the victim on the tracks has a 100 percent chance of being killed without the rescue, but that the rescuer has a 40 percent chance of saving the victim and a 40 percent chance of coming out alive. Presumptively at least the rescue does not meet the standards of rationality because it results in an expected increase in the number of deaths from 1 to 1.2. The legal system does not adopt the strict quantitative approach, but allows the rescuer to recover unless his conduct was "rash."

40. See A. M. Rosenthal, *Thirty-Eight Witnesses* (1964), for the hair-raising account.

41. See Judith Jarvis Thomson, "The Trolley Problem," 94 *Yale L. J.* 1395 (1985).

42. In defense of this proposition, see, e.g., Richard A. Epstein, *Mortal Peril: Our Inalienable Right to Health Care?* 249–82 (1997), advocating a market for organs for live donors. For more limited proposals, see Lloyd R. Cohen, "Increasing the Supply of Transplant Organs: The Virtues of a Future Market," 58 *Geo. Wash. L. Rev.* 1 (1989), updated and reissued as *Increasing the Supply of Transplant Organs: The Virtues of an Option Market* (1995); Henry Hansmann, "The Economics and Ethics of Markets for Human Organs," in James F. Blumstein & Frank A Sloan, eds., *Organ Transplantation Policy, Issues and Prospects* (1989).

43. For an early statement of this position, see Richard A. Epstein, "Substantive Due Process by Any Other Name: The Abortion Cases," 1973 *Sup. Ct. Rev.* 159, using the naïve version of the Millian harm principle to attack the idea that abortion rights are simply an exercise of the mother's autonomy.

44. Judith Jarvis Thomson, "A Defense of Abortion," 1 *Phil. & Pub. Affairs* 47 (1971), written before *Roe v. Wade*, 410 U.S. 113 (1973).

Chapter Five

1. For a discussion, see A. W. B. Simpson, "The Analysis of Legal Concepts," 80 *Law Q. Rev.* 535 (1964).

2. For some sampling of the confusion and difficulty, see Barry Nicholas, *An Introduction to Roman Law* (1962); Frederick Pollock & Robert S. Wright, *Possession in the Common Law* (1888): Carol M. Rose, "Possession as the Origin of Property," 52 *U. Chi. L. Rev.* 73 (1985). For my views, see Richard A. Epstein, "Possession," *The New Palgrave Dictionary of Economics and the Law* 62 (1998). For its consequences for behavioral economics, see chapter 8, pages 219–23.

3. Ray Andrews Brown, *The Law of Personal Property* 19–22 (W. Raushenbush ed., 3d ed. 1975).

4. See, e.g., Oskar Lange & Fred M. Taylor, *On the Economic Theory of Socialism* (1938), for some extent of the confidence of these economic claims. The editor of the above-mentioned volume wrote: "By a mathematical demonstration using simultaneous equations, Barone, following suggestions of Pareto, was the first to demonstrate that it was possible for a socialist economy to make a rational allocation of resources." Benjamin E. Lippincott, intro. at 12. Dream on. For the decisive refutation, see F. A. Hayek, "The Use of Knowledge in Society," 35 *Am. Econ. Rev.* 519 (1945).

5. Barbara H. Fried, *The Progressive Assault on Laissez Faire: Robert Hale and the First Law and Economics Movement* (1998).

6. See, e.g., Robert L. Hale, "Bargaining, Duress, and Economic Liberty," 43 *Colum. L. Rev.* 603 (1943).

7. Alan Wertheimer, *Coercion* 6–7 (1989).

8. Robert L. Hale, "Coercion and Distribution in a Supposedly Non-Coercive State," *Pol. Sci. Q.* 470, 472–73 (1923).

9. Id. at 474.

10. Fried, *Progressive Assault,* at 214. She is not alone in that praise. See also Mark Kelman, *A Guide to Critical Legal Studies* 103–4 (1987).

11. Fried, *Progressive Assault,* at 211–12.

12. See, e.g., *Tarleton v. McGawley,* 170 Eng. Rep. 153 (K.B. 1793).

13. For a more systematic account of the tort, see Richard A. Epstein, *Torts,* ch. 18 (1999).

14. See *The Mogul Steamship Co. v. McGregor, Gow & Co.,* 23 Q.B.D. 598 (1889), aff'd, [1892] A.C. 25. For further discussion, see Richard A. Epstein, *Principles for a Free Society: Reconciling Individual Liberty with the Common Good,* ch. 3 (1998).

15. Thomas Hobbes, *Leviathan* 103 (M. Oakeshott ed., 1962 [1651]).

16. 1 William Blackstone, *Commentaries on the Law of England* *125.

17. Id. at *130. Note again the appeal to "natural right" just when the going gets rough.

18. Franklin D. Roosevelt, *Nothing to Fear* 387 (1946).

19. Id. at 389.

20. Id. at 396.

21. F. A. Hayek, *The Road to Serfdom* 132–33 (1944).

22. Id. at 133.

23. Id. at 134.

24. A couple of examples. Article 6 of the ICESCR provides the following:

> 1. The States Parties to the present Covenant recognize the right to work, which includes the right of everyone to gain his living which he freely chooses or accepts, and will take appropriate steps to safeguard that right.
> 2. The steps to be taken by a State Party to the present Covenant to achieve the full realization of this right shall include all technical and vocational guidance and training

programmes, policies and techniques to achieve steady economic, social and cultural development and full and productive employment under conditions safeguarding fundamental political and economic freedoms to the individual.

ARTICLE 11(1) provides as follows:

The States Parties to the present Covenant recognize the right of everyone to an adequate standard of living for himself and his family, including adequate food, clothing and housing, and to the continuous improvement of living conditions. The States Parties will take appropriate steps to ensure the realization of this right, recognizing the essential importance of international co-operation based on free consent.

25. See, e.g., Cass R. Sunstein, *After the Rights Revolution: Reconceiving the Regulatory State* 21–22 (1990).

26. Hayek, *The Road to Serfdom*, at 141. For a similar recognition of the risks of political guarantees, see David Schmidtz, "Guarantees," 14 *Soc. Phil. & Pol.* 1 (1997).

27. For a discussion, see "Special Issue: The Stanford University Conference on Social Treatment of Catastrophic Risk," 12 *J. Risk & Uncertainty* 99 (1996).

28. Hayek, *The Road to Serfdom*, at 134.

29. Florida's law featured two central provisions. Emergency Rule No. 4-ER93–18 and Chapter 93–401 of the Laws of Florida called for mandatory renewal of insurance policies. Section 215.555 called for mandatory participation in the Hurricane Catastrophe Fund.

30. See John B. Shoven, "Social Security Reform: Two Tiers Are Better Than One," in Henry J. Aaron & John B. Shoven, *Should the United States Privatize Social Security?* 23–24 (Benjamin M. Friedman ed., 1999).

31. For a detailed discussion, see Richard A. Epstein, *Mortal Peril: Our Inalienable Right to Health Care?* 185–215 (1997); for a far more sympathetic account, see Theda Skocpol, *Boomerang: Clinton's Health Security Effort and the Turn against Government in U.S. Politics* (1996).

32. See chapter 1, pages 29–30.

33. 12 East 525, 104 Eng. Rep. 206 (K.B. 1810). For a discussion, see Epstein, *Principles for a Free Society*, at ch. 10. The common law concerns with monopoly most obviously extended to cases of state-created monopolies. But it also carried over to the less frequent cases of natural monopolies that were stable, not because they were propped up by state power, but because they were the initial entrant in a field that was characterized by uniform declining marginal costs of production over the relevant range of output. That low marginal cost of production would block the second entrant unless he could capture all the market.

34. Robert L. Hale, "Unconstitutional Conditions and Constitutional Rights," 35 *Colum. L. Rev.* 321 (1935).

35. For the assertion of state power, see *Buck v. Kuykendall*, 267 U.S. 307, 314 (1925).

36. See, e.g., *Hess v. Pawloski*, 274 U.S. 352 (1927) (allowing state to demand that foreign drivers assent to local jurisdiction over highway accidents); Opinion of the Justices, 251 Mass. 569, 147 N.E. 681 (1925) (allowing mandatory insurance for use of highways).

37. For my more detailed analysis of the issues discussed in the rest of this section, see Richard A. Epstein, *Bargaining with the State* (1993).

38. See the discussion in chapter 3, pages 69–73.

39. See *Frost & Frost Trucking v. Railroad Comm'n of California,* 271 U.S. 583, 591 (1926). That decision was gutted six years later in *Stephenson v. Binford,* 287 U.S. 251 (1932), when similar regulation was allowed on the ground that the Texas statute explicitly authorized the regulation of private carriers.

40. See, e.g., *Western Union Tel. Co. v. Kansas,* 216 U.S. 1 (1910), striking down a discriminatory tax on Western Union's local business within the state.

41. The key decision was *NLRB v. Jones & Laughlin Steel Co.,* 201 U.S. 1 (1937). For my criticism, see Richard A. Epstein, "The Proper Scope of the Commerce Power," 73 *Va. L. Rev.* 1387 (1987).

42. See *Hammer v. Dagenhart,* 247 U.S. 251 (1918). The issue here is not whether the market or the government controls the use of child labor (however important that question might be), but whether states or the federal government are given that authority to regulate. To the extent that ordinary manufacturing enterprises were involved, that task fell upon the states. The implicit conflict in the *Hammer* decision was whether competitive federalism exercised a proper limitation on state power. As one might expect, the state limitations on child labor were less stringent than those contemplated under the federal act. *United States v. Darby,* 312 U.S. 100 (1941).

43. For the genesis, see *Griswold v. Connecticut,* 381 U.S. 479 (1965) (preventing state from blocking sale of contraceptives to married couples). For a defense of this capacious definition of liberty, see Charles Black, "The Unfinished Business of the Warren Court," 46 *Wash. L. Rev.* 3, 32 (1970), fearing that without *Griswold* "[v]irtually all the intimacies, privacies and autonomies of life would be regulable by the legislature." Note that the defenders of freedom of contract could easily defend the outcome in *Griswold*. Under the traditional accounts of the police power, state regulation should be upheld only if it bears a direct and tangible relation to safety and health, which in this case it clearly does not.

44. Adam Mossoff, "Rethinking the Development of Patents: An Intellectual History, 1550–1800," 52 *Hastings L. J.* 1255, 1294–1302 (2001), describing the Lockean and natural law influences on the development of patent law.

45. See, e.g., Liam Murphy & Thomas Nagel, *The Myth of Ownership: Taxes and Justice* (2002), discussed in chapter 2, pages 33–34.

46. See, for this view, Joseph L. Sax, "Takings and the Police Power," 74 *Yale L. J.* 36 (1964); Joseph L. Sax, "Takings, Private Property and Public Rights," 81 *Yale L. J.* 149 (1971) (with a more expansive view of public rights than his earlier article).

47. G. A. Cohen, *Self-Ownership, Freedom and Equality* (1994).

48. Robert Nozick, *Anarchy, State, and Utopia* (1974).

49. *Coppage v. Kansas,* 236 U.S. 1, 30–31 (1915), which struck down labor legislation that undid the common law right of an employer from insisting that its workers agreed not to become members of a union so long as they worked for their employer.

50. Nozick, *Anarchy, State, and Utopia,* at 160–64.

51. The "ultimately" is inserted to allow for the possibility that differential status (elderly widow against commercial sophisticate) will be important in deciding in fact whether fraud or undue influence might exist.

52. Nozick, *Anarchy, State, and Utopia,* at 177–78.

53. For the historical origins, see William Letwin, "The English Common Law Concerning Monopolies," 21 *U. Chi. L. Rev.* 355 (1954).

54. See, e.g., Lord Coke: "[A] mans trade is accounted his life, because it maintaineth his life; and therefore the monopolist that taketh away a mans trade, taketh away his life, and therefore is so much more the odious." 3 Edward Coke, *Institutes of the Laws of England* 181 (1797 [1644]). Similar views were expressed by Samuel Pufendorf, *De Jure Naturae et Gentium (Of the Law of Nature and Nations)* 27 (Basil Kenner trans., 1703 [1672]). Note that the explanation offered does not distinguish between the trader who loses out to a monopolist from the one who loses out in open competition. The point here is that the private loss to the rival is not the ultimate measure of the claim: it is the social loss of the practice.

55. See, e.g., *United States v. United States Gypsum Co.,* 438 U.S. 422 (1978) (noting the presumptive adverse effects of secret communications between sellers in the same market).

56. *United States v. Citizens and S. Nat'l Bank,* 422 U.S. 86 (1975) (recognizing a limited exception with communications among correspondent banks); *Cement Mfrs. Protective Ass'n v. United States,* 268 U.S. 588 (1925) (sharing of price information to prevent fraud in certain limited cases).

57. See chapter 1. For one estimation, see Michael Trebilcock, *The Common Law Restraint of Trade: A Legal and Economic Analysis* (1986); for my views, see Epstein, *Principles for a Free Society,* at 87–90.

58. Nozick, *Anarchy, State, and Utopia,* at ix.

59. Cohen, *Self-Ownership, Freedom and Equality,* at 38.

60. "And therefore, as long as this natural right of every man to every thing endureth, there can be no security to any man, how strong or wise soever he be, of living out the time, which nature ordinarily alloweth men to live." Hobbes, *Leviathan,* at 103.

61. Cohen, *Self-Ownership, Freedom and Equality,* at 55–56.

62. Id. at 55.

63. Richard Pipes, *Property and Freedom: The Story of How through the Centuries Private Ownership Has Promoted Liberty and the Rule of Law* (1999); Bernard H. Siegan, *Property and Freedom: The Constitution, the Courts, and Land-Use Regulation* (1997).

64. Cohen, *Self-Ownership, Freedom and Equality,* at 94–95.

65. For an early, unselfcritical expression of the rule, see Gaius, *Institutes,* bk. 2, 66: "But it is not only those things that become ours by delivery that we acquire under natural law, but also those that we acquire by occupation (by being the first takers), because they were previously no one's property, for example everything captured on land, in the sea or in the air."

66. John Locke, *The Second Treatise of Civil Government*, ch. 5, ¶ 28: "And will any one say he had no right to those acorns or apples he thus appropriated, because he had not the consent of all mankind to make them his? Was it a robbery thus to assume to himself what belonged to all in common? If such a consent as that was necessary, men had starved, notwithstanding the plenty God had given him." Note that Locke gives comfort to collectivist impulses by treating each acorn as being owned in common, in opposition to the Roman and common law rule that treated it as a *res nullius,* and not a *res commune.*

67. For a discussion of the relevant rules, see Richard A. Epstein, *Simple Rules for a Complex World* 67–70 (1995).

68. Cohen, *Self-Ownership, Freedom and Equality,* at 43.

69. For discussion, see Epstein, *Simple Rules for a Complex World,* at 116–18 (1995); for the recent attempt of the American Law Institute to restate the law of Restitution, see ALI, Restatement (Third) of Restitution, Preliminary Draft (2000).

Chapter Six

1. John Locke, *An Essay Concerning Human Understanding,* bk. 2, ch. 27, § 10 ("consciousness makes personal identity").

2. Id. at § 18 ("objects of reward and punishment").

3. See chapter 1, page 18.

4. Gary S. Becker, *The Economic Approach to Human Behavior* 14 (1976).

5. Id. at 5.

6. See Joseph LeDoux, *The Emotional Brain* (1996). For a discussion of the implication of this division of responsibility in the separate spheres of the brain, see H. Lorn Carmichael & W. Bentley MacLeod, *Fair Territory: Bargaining, Property Rights, and Framing Effects* (unpublished manuscript).

7. Used to great dramatic effect in the movie *The Culpepper Cattle Company* (1972).

8. See, for discussion, Andy Clark & Annette Karmiloff-Sith, "The Cognizer's Innards: A Psychological and Philosophical Perspective on the Development of Thought," 8 *Mind and Language* 487 (1991).

9. Jon Elster, *Sour Grapes: Studies in the Subversion of Rationality* 25 (1983).

10. Jon Elster, "Sour Grapes—Utilitarianism and the Genesis of Want," in Amartya Sen & Bernard Williams, eds., *Utilitarianism and Beyond* 219 (1982), which tracks the argument in his book. Elster, *Sour Grapes,* at 109.

11. Elster, *Sour Grapes,* at 220.

12. "The Fox and the Grapes," in *Aesop's Fables* 118 (Lewis Rhead trans., 1927).

13. Isaiah Berlin, *Four Essays on Liberty* xxxvii–xl (1969).

14. Elster, *Sour Grapes,* at 229.

15. Id. at 133–40.

16. 347 U.S. 483 (1954).

17. Cass R. Sunstein, *After the Rights Revolution: Reconceiving the Regulatory State* 38–42 (1990).

18. Suzanne Daley, "New Rights for Dutch Prostitutes, but No Gain," *New York Times,* Aug. 12, 2001, at § 1, p. 1.

19. Restatement (Second) of Contracts § 2 (1978) (emphasis added). This section follows the definitional provision: "§ 1. Contract Defined. A contract is a promise or a set of promises for the breach of which the law gives a remedy, or the performance of which the law in some way recognizes as a duty."

20. Restatement (Second) of Contracts § 151 (1978). The rule was otherwise in the First Restatement. See Restatement of Contracts § 71, illus. 2 (1932). If A uses the word "horse" when he means cow, and B knows of that mistake, nonetheless no contract is made.

21. Cass R. Sunstein, "Social Norms and Social Roles," 96 *Colum. L. Rev.* 903, 913 (1996) (emphasis added).

22. Id. at 905, 948. Sunstein celebrates the lower level of smoking among white teenagers in 1993. But since that time, the number has soared. A theory of social norms that explains the decline has to be robust enough to explain the increase.

23. See Deborah Solomon, "Jackson Pollock Finally Goes Postal," *New Yorker,* Jan. 11, 1999, at 24.

24. *West Virginia State Bd. of Educ. v. Barnette,* 319 U.S. 624 (1943) (no compulsory flag salute); *Abood v. Detroit Bd. of Educ.,* 431 U.S. 209 (1977) (compulsory dues may be used to support union's collective bargaining activities, consistent with the First Amendment); *Lehnert v. Ferris Faculty Ass'n,* 500 U.S. 507 (1991) (dues may not be used to support political positions unrelated to contract issues).

25. For the classical discussion, see R. Duncan Luce & Howard Raiffa, *Games and Decisions: Introduction and Critical Survey* 12–38 (1957). "Often when one is made aware of intransitivities of this kind [in preference orderings] he is willing to admit inconsistency and to realign his responses to yield a transitive ordering" (id. at 25).

26. See Amartya K. Sen, "Behaviour and the Concept of Preference," in *Choice, Welfare, and Measurement* 54, 55 (Kelvin J. Lancaster ed., 1982).

27. For the original demonstration here, see Kenneth J. Arrow, "Rational Choice Functions and Orderings," 26 *Economica* 121, 123 (1959).

28. See Elster, *Sour Grapes,* at 27, who credits the point to Howard Raiffa, *Decision Analysis* 78 (1968).

29. The example comes from Paul Anad, "The Philosophy of Intransitive Preferences," 103 *Econ. J.* 337, 344 (1993), discussed in Bruce Chapman, "Law, Incommensurability, and Conceptually Sequenced Argument," 146 *U. Pa. L. Rev.* 1487, 1498–1507 (1998).

30. "Context-Dependence in Legal Decision Making," 25 *J. Legal Stud.* 287 (1996), reprinted in *Behavioral Law & Economics* 61 (Cass R. Sunstein ed., 2000).

31. Joseph Raz, *The Morality of Freedom* 322 (1986).

32. Elizabeth Anderson, *Value in Ethics and Economics* 8–9 (1992).

33. See Raz, *The Morality of Freedom*, at 345–53; Margaret Radin, "Compensation and Commensurability," 43 *Duke L. J.* 56, 65–66 (1993). It was Radin who added in the dollar figure, which gives the example much of its bite.

34. George Loewenstein, Ted O'Donoghue & Matthew Rabin, "Projection Bias in Predicting Future Utility," in *Conference on Behavioral Economics, Organizations and Law* (USC Center in Law, Economics and Organization, Caltech Division of Humanities and Social Sciences 2001).

35. Duly noted in Richard A. Posner, *Aging and Old Age* 264 (1995).

Chapter Seven

1. Amartya Sen, "The Impossibility of a Paretian Liberal," in *Choice, Welfare, and Measurement* (Kelvin J. Lancaster ed., 1982), at 285, originally published in 78 *J. Pol. Econ.* 152 (1970).

2. See Amartya Sen, "Behaviour and the Concept of Preference," in *Choice, Welfare, and Measurement*, at 54, originally published in 40 *Economica* 241 (1973).

3. Sen, "Paretian Liberal," at 290.

4. For one account of the point, see James S. Coleman, *Foundations of Social Thought* 335–41 (1990). As Coleman notes, the odd point about this paradox lies in its implicit assumption about human preferences insofar as it assumes that each person cares more about the welfare of someone else than of himself. Id. at 337. Cases like that are not likely to come up in nature.

5. Amartya Sen, "Personal Utilities and Public Judgments," in *Choice, Welfare, and Measurement*, at 343–44, originally published in 89 *Econ. J.* 537 (1979).

6. See, e.g., H. L. A. Hart, *Law, Liberty and Morality* 42–47 (1963). In speaking of the broad definition of harm, Hart writes, correctly in my view: "The fundamental objection surely is that a right to be protected from the distress which is inseparable from the bare knowledge that others are acting in ways you think wrong, cannot be acknowledged by anyone who recognises individual liberty as a value" (id. at 46).

7. For an early recognition of the possible complexities introduced by side payments, see R. Duncan Luce & Howard Raiffa, *Games and Decisions: Introduction and Critical Survey* 110–11 (1957).

8. Amartya Sen, "Choice, Orderings and Morality," in *Choice, Welfare, and Measurement*, at 82.

9. For the same position with regard to government contracts, see Daniel Fischel & Alan Sykes, First Issue, 1 *Am. L. & Econ. J.* 1 (1999), who argue that protection under the Contracts Clause will lead self-interested actors to expend resources to acquire socially wasteful contracts in the first instance. The correct response, in my view, is not to deny enforcement of state contracts, but to allow third parties to attack within a short period of time after bidding the contracts on the ground that they represent a sweetheart deal in

which state assets have been given away without receipt of a fair *quid pro quo*. See generally Richard A. Epstein, "The Public Trust Doctrine," 7 *Cato J.* 411 (1987).

10. H. Scott Gordon, "The Economic Theory of a Common Property Resource: The Fishery," 62 *J. Pol. Econ.* 124 (1954).

11. For discussion, see Richard A. Epstein, *Takings: Private Property and the Power of Eminent Domain* 216–28 (1985).

12. For a clear sense of the difference, see *C. C. Julian Oil & Royalties Co. v. Capshaw*, 292 P. 841, 847 (1930). "In my judgment the Legislature is empowered with the right to pass laws having for their object the conservation of the natural resources of this state. . . . Conservation statutes [however] must not become the vehicle of monopoly of supply or of prices." For a collection of materials on the regulation of extraction and price of oil and gas interests, see Charles Donahue Jr., Thomas E. Kauper & Peter W. Martin, *Property: An Introduction to the Concept and the Institution* 352–59 (1974). The same view of extraction is found in *Frost & Frost Trucking v. Railroad Comm'n of California*, 271 U.S. 583, 591 (1926), which prohibited regulation designed to control competitive conditions, but allowed it for the preservation and conservation of the highways. Note that with the greater the level of judicial deference, the greater the likelihood that the two will be confused. See also chapter 5.

13. See, e.g., Robert H. Frank, "The Frame of Reference as a Public Good," 107 *Econ. J.* 1832 (1997); Robert H. Frank, "The Demand for Unobservable and Other Nonpositional Goods," 75 *Am. Econ. Rev.* 101 (1985).

14. See, e.g., Richard H. McAdams, "Relative Preferences," 102 *Yale L. J.* 1 (1992).

15. Robert H. Frank, *Choosing the Right Pond: Human Behavior and the Quest for Status* vi (1985).

16. See Gordon Tullock, "The Welfare Costs of Tariffs, Monopolies, and Theft," 5 *W. Econ. J.* 224 (1967).

17. See Robert H. Frank & Cass R. Sunstein, "Cost-Benefit Analysis and Relative Position," 68 *U. Chi. L. Rev.* 323, 364 (2001).

18. Id. at 327. See also id. at 367.

19. "The principle is, that the sole end for which mankind are warranted, individually or collectively, in interfering with the liberty of action of any of their number, is self-protection. That the only purpose for which power can be rightfully exercised over any member of a civilised community, against his will, is to prevent harm to others." John Stuart Mill, *On Liberty, in Utilitarianism, Liberty and Representative Government* 72–73 (Ernest Rhys ed., 1929 [1910]).

20. Frank, *Choosing the Right Pond*, at 8–9.

21. Id. at 4, 42.

22. For one early account, see Richard A. Easterlin, "Does Economic Growth Improve the Human Lot? Some Empirical Evidence," in Paul A. David & Melvin W. Reder, eds.,

Nations and Households in Economic Growth: Essays in Honor of Moses Abramovitz 89 (1974).

23. See generally Werner Guth, Rolf Schmittberger & Brend Schwarze, "An Experimental Analysis of Ultimatum Bargaining," 3 *J. Econ. Beh. & Or.* 367 (1982).

24. Ken Binmore et al., "Testing Noncooperative Bargaining Theory: A Preliminary Study," 75 *Am. Econ. Rev.* 1178 (1985).

25. See Elizabeth Hoffman & Matthew Spitzer, "Entitlements, Rights and Fairness: An Experimental Examination of Subjects' Concepts of Distributive Justice," 14 *J. Legal Stud.* 259 (1985).

26. For the general rules, see Ray A. Brown, *The Law of Personal Property* (Walter B. Raushenbush ed., 3d ed. 1975); for additional references, see Jesse Dukeminier & James Krier, *Property* 99–116 (4th ed. 1998). For some of the complications with finders, and the contest between the owner of the place and the casual finder, see *Hannah v. Peel*, [1945] K.B. 509, awarding a brooch to the lance corporal who found it while in military service and not to the owner of the house, who had not taken possession of it before it was requisitioned from the Crown.

27. See Truman F. Bewley, *Why Wages Don't Fall during a Recession* (1999). One concrete implication of this theory is that corporate mergers often flounder because of the difficulties in realigning the culture of the two different organizations. See, e.g., Roberto A. Weber & Colin Camerer, "Cultural Conflict and Merger Failure: An Experimental Approach," in *Conference on Behavioral Economics, Organizations and Law* (USC Center in Law, Economics and Organization, Caltech Division of Humanities and Social Sciences 2001). The difficulties are no doubt increased because the choice of cultures within different firms also exerts a selection effect in that different types of individuals will gravitate toward different firms in response to cultural signals. It is, therefore, not just a question of getting people to follow one common set of rules. Getting two different types of people, each preferring different regimes, to conform to a single set of norms means that *neither* side is likely to prefer the postmerger to the separate premerger norms.

28. Bewley, *Why Wages Don't Fall during a Recession*, at 41–56.

29. Id. at 16.

30. See Frank & Sunstein, "Cost-Benefit Analysis," at 373.

31. Id. at 342, quoting Bewley at 310.

32. Bewley, *Why Wages Don't Fall during a Recession*, at 18.

33. Id. at 173.

34. Id.

35. For a discussion of these alternatives, see Richard A. Epstein, "In Defense of the Contract at Will," 51 *U. Chi. L. Rev.* 947, 962–77 (1984).

36. See Robert H. Frank, *Luxury Fever* 211–26 (1999).

37. Frank & Sunstein, "Cost-Benefit Analysis," at 364.

38. On which the standard account continues to be Bruce A. Ackerman & W. T. Hassler,

Clean Coal/Dirty Air, or How the Clean-Air Act Became a Multibillion-Dollar Bailout for High Sulfur Coal Producers and What Should Be Done about It (1981)—but wasn't.

39. For discussion, see *Bamford v. Turnley*, 122 Eng. Rep. 27 (Ex. 1863), which I have long regarded as one of the most sophisticated common law analyses of a tough legal problem. See Richard A. Epstein, *Principles for a Free Society: Reconciling Individual Liberty and the Common Good* 191–96 (1998); Richard A. Epstein, "For a Bramwell Revival," 38 *Am. J. Legal Hist.* 246, 269–83; Richard A. Epstein, "Nuisance Law: Corrective Justice and Its Utilitarian Constraints," 8 *J. Legal Stud.* 49, 72–77 (1979).

40. For a longer discussion of this point, see Epstein, *Principles for a Free Society*, ch. 3.

Chapter Eight

1. Jared Diamond, *Guns, Germs and Steel: The Fates of Human Societies* 157 (1997). The title of the chapter is "Zebras, Unhappy Marriages and the Anna Karenina Principle." He leaves dogs and cats out of his analysis, even though they are both domesticated and useful.

2. John von Neumann & Oskar Morgenstern, *Theory of Games and Economic Behavior* (1944).

3. For one exposition, see Richard A. Posner, *Economic Analysis of Law* 6–7 (5th ed. 1998). For a critique, see Christine Jolls, Cass R. Sunstein & Richard Thaler, "A Behavioral Approach to Law and Economics," 50 *Stan. L. Rev.* 1471, 1482–83 (1998).

4. I put aside here the complications for those games in which the equilibrium condition calls for some mixed strategy, which are found, for example, in the chicken game, when both players should ideally play hawk and dove strategies 50 percent of the time. The point here is that this mixed strategy follows from the rational choice analysis.

5. Milton Friedman & Leonard J. Savage, "The Utility Analysis of Choices Involving Risks," 56 *J. Pol. Econ.* 279, 298 (1948).

6. Herbert A. Simon, "A Behavioral Model of Rational Choice," 69 *Q. J. Econ.* 99 (1955).

7. To illustrate: suppose that we had a simple function in which the payoff equals 100 $- x^2$, where x is the distance from the ideal solution, which is the zero point. The player who moves from 4 to 5 sees his utility drop 9 units from 84 $(100 - 4^2)$ to 75 $(100 - 5^2)$. The player who moves one unit closer increases only by 7 from 84 to 91 $(100 - 3^2)$. My own weak empirical sense is that most error functions behave in this fashion, so that most people first recognize that something has gone astray and then test the waters to see which direction to move. If they are far afield, they will receive strong feedback from the initial adjustment as to which way they should go.

8. Richard A. Thaler, *Quasi Rational Economics* (1991).

9. See, e.g., Stephen Stigler, *The History of Statistics*, ch. 2 (1986).

10. For some notable landmarks, see Amos Tversky & Daniel Kahneman, "Judgment under Uncertainty: Heuristics and Biases," 185 *Science* 1124 (1974); Daniel Kahneman &

Amos Tversky, "Prospect Theory: An Analysis of Decision under Risk," 47 *Econometrica* 263 (1979); Richard Thaler, "Toward a Positive Theory of Consumer Choice," 1 *J. Econ. Behav. & Org.* 39 (1980). For more general accounts, see Robin M. Hogarth, *Judgment and Choice: The Psychology of Decision* (1980); Scott Plous, *The Psychology of Judgment and Decision Making* (1993). The field also has its detractors. See, e.g., Gerd Gigerenzer, "How to Make Cognitive Illusions Disappear: Beyond 'Heuristics and Biases,' " 2 *European Rev. Soc. Psychol.* 83 (1991).

11. For my earlier defense of this view, see Richard A. Epstein, *Principles for a Free Society: Reconciling Individual Liberty and the Common Good*, ch. 2 (1998).

12. Richard A. Posner, "Rational Choice, Behavioral Economics and the Law," 50 *Stan. L. Rev.* 1551, 1561 (1998), appealing explicitly to the idea of inclusive fitness. But there are specific points of disagreement. I do not think that "our instincts are easily fooled" into loving adopted children, in what must be a much more complex set of conscious decisions made for multiple explicit reasons. But even if I do not follow Posner on his views of what an evolutionary theory entails, I have long agreed with the basic position that rational economic theory must take into account these basic evolutionary pressures.

13. Daniel Kahneman, Jack L. Knetsch & Richard H. Thaler, "Experimental Tests of the Endowment Effect and the Coase Theorem," 98 *J. Pol. Econ.* 1325 (1990); Hal R. Arkes & Catherine Blumer, "The Psychology of Sunk Cost," 35 *Org. Behav. & Hum. Decision Processes* 124 (1985).

14. See Plous, "Psychology of Judgment," at 96.

15. Daniel Kahneman & Amos Tversky, "On the Psychology of Prediction," 80 *Psychol. Rev.* 237 (1973).

16. Amos Tversky & Daniel Kahneman, "Extensional versus Intuitive Reasoning: The Conjunction Fallacy in Probability Judgment," 90 *Psychol. Rev.* 293 (1983).

17. Hillel J. Einhorn & Robin M. Hogarth, "Behavioral Decision Theory: Processes of Judgment and Choice," 32 *Ann. Rev. Psychol.* 53, 57–58 (1981).

18. James D. Gwartney & Richard L. Stroup, *Economics: Private and Public Choice* 418 (4th ed. 1987).

19. Arkes & Blumer, "The Psychology of Sunk Cost," at 127–28, discussed in Jolls, Sunstein & Thaler, "Behavioral Approach to Law and Economics," at 1482–83.

20. Antonio R. Damasio, *Descartes' Error: Emotion, Reason, and the Human Brain* (1994).

21. Lorne Carmichael & W. Bentley MacLeod, "Caring about Sunk Costs: A Behavioral Solution to Hold-up Problems with Small Stakes." Olin Working Paper No. 99–19, available at http://papers.ssrn.com/paper.taf?abstract_id=200776.

22. See *Armstrong v. United States,* 364 U.S. 40, 49 (1960).

23. See Richard A. Epstein, *Bargaining with the State* 91–103 (1993).

24. See Jolls, Sunstein & Thaler, "Behavioral Approach to Law and Economics," at 1479.

25. See pages 202–6.

26. For summaries of the literature, see Elizabeth Hoffman & Matthew L. Spitzer, "The Divergence between Willingness-to-Pay and Willingness-to-Accept Measures of Value," 71 *Wash. U. L.Q.* 39 (1993).

27. The usual citation here is Robert D. Willig, "Consumer Surplus without Apology," 66 *Am. Econ. Rev.* 589 (1976).

28. For discussion, see, e.g., Kahneman, Knetsch & Thaler, "Experimental Tests of the Endowment Effect"; Herbert Hovenkamp, "Legal Policy and the Endowment Effect," 20 *J. Legal Stud.* 225 (1991).

29. The position has much appeal in the philosophical literature as a device for avoiding the arbitrariness of the first possession rule. See Ronald Dworkin, *Sovereign Equality* 65–73 (2000).

30. My thanks to Gary Becker for pressing the point.

31. Kahneman, Knetsch & Thaler, "Experimental Tests of the Endowment Effect."

32. Edward J. McCaffery, Daniel J. Kahneman & Matthew L. Spitzer, "Framing the Jury: Cognitive Perspectives on Pain and Suffering Awards," 81 *Va. L. Rev.* 1341 (1995).

33. David D. Friedman, "What Is 'Fair Compensation' for Death or Injury?" 2 *Int'l Rev. L. & Econ.* 81 (1982).

34. See, e.g., *Zibbell v. Southern Pac. Co.*, 116 P. 513, 520 (Cal. 1911). "No rational being would change places with the injured man for an amount of gold that would fill the room of the court, yet no lawyer would contend that such is the legal measure of damages."

35. McCaffery, Kahneman & Spitzer, "Framing the Jury," at 1359.

36. Rebecca R. Boyce, Thomas C. Brown, Gary H. McClelland, George L. Peterson & William D. Schulze, "An Experimental Examination of Intrinsic Values as a Source of the WTA-WTP Disparity," 82 *Am. Econ. Rev.* 1366 (1992).

37. Jason F. Shogren, Seung Y. Shin, Dermot J. Hayes & James B. Kliebenstein, "Resolving Differences in Willingness to Pay and Willingness to Accept," 84 *Am. Econ. Rev.* 255, 265 (1994).

38. See William Vickrey, "Counterspeculation, Auctions, and Competitive Sealed Tenders," 16 *J. Finance* 8 (1961). Under this form of auction, each bidder (in a WTP context) is told that the highest bidder of the good is entitled to purchase the good at the price that is bid by the *second* highest bidder. The purpose of the system is to elicit the maximum bid from each bidder. Its logic runs as follows. The bidder who bids below that maximum price runs the risk of losing a profitable opportunity if any person enters a bid above his stated bid but below his reservation price. The bidder, therefore, has an incentive to raise his bid to his effective maximum to avert that potential loss. He loses nothing by following this strategy because he will still pay less if the second bid comes in lower than the reservation price, no matter how high it is. By the same token, if he bids above his reservation price, then he runs the risk of losing if the second highest bidder also comes in over his reservation price. Each bidder has the incentive to bid his highest price in order to maximize his expected surplus.

39. See, e.g., U.C.C. §2–314 (warranty of merchantability, such that goods "are fit for the ordinary purposes for which such goods are used").

40. Do not underestimate the difficulties of winning such lawsuits. Food poisoning can result from anything that has been ingested in the last twenty-four to forty-eight hours, including milk or ice cream that is left off ice by the consumer. Most institutional defendants will resist these claims unless there is a mass outbreak that is attributable only to their own product or services. But real difficulties can arise when a caterer, for example, supplies food to a host who also serves some of her own chicken (with mayonnaise) salad. If all the guests eat from both sources, determining causation is a genuine nightmare. Note that state regulation cannot easily reach the preservation of foodstuffs once they are in consumer hands.

41. John List, *The Effect of Market Experience on the WTA/WTP Disparity: Evidence from a Field Experiment with Sports Memorabilia* (April 2000) (unpublished manuscript), available at http://enviro.colorado.edu/class/4309/jlistwtawtpdec10—doc.pdf.

42. Jennifer Arlen, Matthew Spitzer & Eric Talley, "Endowment Effects within Corporate Agency Relationships," 31 *J. Legal Stud.* 1 (2002).

43. See Cass R. Sunstein, "Human Behavior and the Law of Work," 87 *Va. L. Rev.* 205, 220–24 (2001). Note that in his discussion of relative preferences with Frank, Sunstein argued that a plausible case could be made out for treating for-cause provisions as a nonwaivable term. See id. at 236–43.

44. See pages 210–11.

45. C. B. Macpherson, *The Political Theory of Possessive Individualism* (1962). For more moderate criticism, see Lawrence C. Becker, *Property Rights—Philosophic Foundations* 25–31 (1977).

46. H. Lorne Carmichael & W. Bentley MacLeod, *Fair Territory: Bargaining, Property Rights, and Framing Effects* (1997) (unpublished manuscript).

47. John Maynard Smith, "The Evolution of Behavior," 239 *Sci. Am.* 3, 176, 191–92 (Sept. 1978). The Davies experiment is written up in N. B. Davies, "Game Theory and Territorial Behavior in Speckled Wood Butterflies," 27 *Animal Behav.* 961–62 (1979).

48. For discussion, see Richard A. Epstein, "Possession as the Root of Title," 44 *Ga. L. Rev.* 1221 (1979). Note there are other reasons for preferring the hot pursuit rule, not the least of which is that it tends to reduce jostling as the two (or more) riders converge on a moving target.

49. David Hume, *A Treatise of Human Nature,* bk. 3, §§ 1, 2 (L. A. Selby-Bigge ed., 1888 [1740]). "Tis evident, therefore, that men wou'd easily acquiesce in this expedient, *that every one continue to enjoy what he is at present possess'd of*" (id. at 503–4, at 503 relying on "natural expedient" and "custom" that extend the rules in this fashion).

50. "Men are unwilling to leave property in suspense, even for the shortest time, or open the least door to violence and disorder. To which we may add, that the first possession always engages the attention most; and did we neglect it, there wou'd be no colour of reason

for assigning property to any succeeding possession" (id. at 505). This account offers no reason why certain resources, e.g., water, are left in the commons.

51. For a discussion of the doctrine of implicit-in-kind compensation as applied to a takings analysis of the common pool issue, see Richard A. Epstein, *Takings: Private Property and the Power of Eminent Domain* 216–28 (1985).

52. For a thorough review of the subject, see Daniel S. Levy & David Friedman, "The Revenge of the Redwoods? Reconsidering Property Rights and the Economic Allocation of Natural Resources," 61 *U. Chi. L. Rev.* 493, 494 (1994).

53. See pages 240–43.

54. Levy & Friedman, "Revenge of the Redwoods?" at 495. For a detailed examination of these variations, see Edward J. Yang et al., eds., *The Use of Economic Analysis in Valuing Natural Resource Damages* 30–32 (1984). The issue arises in connection with valuations needed under the Clean Water Act, the Clean Air Act, and CERCLA, or Superfund.

55. The Endangered Species Act of 1973, 81 Stat. 884, 16 U.S.C. § 1531 (1995).

56. § 1538(a)(1)(B).

57. § 1532(19).

58. 515 U.S. 687, 115 S. Ct. 2407 (1995). For my critique of the statute, see Richard A. Epstein, "Babbitt v. Sweet Home Chapters of Oregon: The Law and Economics of Habitat Preservation," 5 *Sup. Ct. Econ. Rev.* 1 (1997).

59. 50 C.F.R. § 17.3.

60. Dean Leuck & Jeffrey Michael, *Preemptive Habitat Destruction under the Endangered Species Act* (2000) (manuscript on file with author), available at http://www2. montana.edu/lueck/JLEpaper.pdf. For a similar study on the golden-cheeked warbler in Texas, see Charles C. Mann & Mark L. Plummer, *Noah's Choice: The Future of Endangered Species* 190–210 (1995), noting the fierce political struggles that resulted from proposals to designate large sections of several Texas counties as protected habitat. The Noah Principle refers to the proposition that all living species should be cherished solely "because they exist and have existed for a long time." See David W. Ehrenfield, "The Conservation of Non-Resources," 64 *Am. Sci.* 648, 654–55 (1976).

61. Leuck & Michael, *Preemptive Habitat Destruction,* at 18.

62. Id. at 20–21.

63. "Property is nothing but a basis of expectation; the expectation of deriving certain advantages from a thing which we are said to possess, in consequence of the relation in which we stand towards it." Jeremy Bentham, *Theory of Legislation* 111 (4th ed. 1882).

64. See, e.g., *Avco Community Developers, Inc. v. South Coast Regional Comm'n,* 553 P.2d 546 (Cal. 1976), which held that a developer's right to continue with a project in the face of new regulation did not vest merely because he obtained the necessary building permits and had made substantial subdivision improvements. For a complete account of the adverse consequences of land use restrictions on the California residential real estate market, see William Fischel, *Regulatory Takings: Law, Economics, Politics* 218–52 (1995).

65. Jack L. Knetsch & Thomas E. Borcherding, "Expropriation of Private Property and the Basis for Compensation," 29 *U. Toronto L. J.* 237 (1979); Robert C. Ellickson, "Bringing Culture and Human Frailty to Rational Actors: A Critique of Classical Law-and-Economics," 65 *Chi.-Kent L. Rev.* 23 (1989); William A. Fischel, "The Offer/Ask Disparity and Just Compensation for Takings: A Constitutional Choice Perspective," 15 *Int'l Rev. L. Econ.* 187, 192 (1995).

Chapter Nine

1. Chip Heath, Richard P. Larrick & Joshua Klayman, "Cognitive Repairs: How Organizational Practices Can Compensate for Individual Shortcomings," in 20 *Res. Organizational Behav.* 1 (Barry M. Staw & L. L. Cummings eds., 1998).

2. Herbert Spencer, *The Study of Sociology* (University of Michigan Press, 1961 [1871]). Spencer was, moreover, evidently influenced by Darwinian thought. See the introduction by Talcott Parsons in id. at vi–viii.

3. Baruch Fischoff, "Hindsight/Foresight: The Effect of Outcome Knowledge on Judgment under Uncertainty," 1 *J. Experimental Psychol.: Hum. Perception & Performance* 288 (1975). For its systematic application to law, see Jeffrey J. Rachlinski, "A Positive Psychological Theory of Judging in Hindsight," 65 *U. Chi. L. Rev.* 571 (1998).

4. For a more detailed comparison of the two systems, see Richard A. Epstein, *Torts,* ch. 4 (1999).

5. For a discussion, see Richard A. Epstein, "The Path to the *T. J. Hooper:* Of Custom and Due Care," 21 *J. Legal Stud.* 1 (1992).

6. Anyone eager to trace out the current confusion need only read *Daubert v. Merrell Dow Pharmaceuticals, Inc.,* 509 U.S. 579 (1993), outlining the tests for deciding when expert witnesses could introduce scientific evidence in a trial. At the time, the case (involving the dangers of Benedictin in early pregnancy) was remanded, and no one could decide who had won. On remand, the victory in that case went decisively to the defendants. See *Daubert v. Merrell Dow Pharmaceuticals, Inc.,* 43 F.3d 1311 (9th Cir. 1995), in a powerful opinion by Kozinski, J. *Daubert* was extended to all forms of expert evidence in *Kumho Tire Co. v. Carmichael,* 526 U.S. 137 (1999).

7. Fed. R. Evid. 702 (as amended eff. Dec. 1, 2000).

8. See the discussion on pages 94–95.

9. See, e.g., *Evans v. General Motors,* 359 F.2d 822 (7th Cir. 1966).

10. For the first of the cases, see *Larsen v. General Motors,* 391 F.2d 495 (8th Cir. 1968), now followed everywhere.

11. See *Carroll Towing Co. v. United States,* 159 F.2d 169 (2d Cir. 1947). The leading defense of the economic interpretation of this formula is Richard A. Posner, "A Theory of Negligence," 1 *J. Legal Stud.* 29 (1972).

12. Oliver Wendell Holmes Jr., *The Common Law* 120–24 (1881).

13. See W. Kip Viscusi, "Corporate Risk Analysis: A Reckless Act?" 52 *Stan. L. Rev.* 547 (2000).

14. See Christine Jolls, Cass R. Sunstein & Richard Thaler, "A Behavioral Approach to Law and Economics," 50 *Stan. L. Rev.* 1471, 1524 (1998).

15. Restatement (Third) of Torts: Products Liability § 18 (1998): "Disclaimers and limitations of remedies by product sellers or other distributors, waivers by product purchasers, and other similar contractual exculpations, oral or written, do not bar or reduce otherwise products liability claims against sellers or other distributors of new products for harm to persons."

16. Contrast *Micallif v. Miehle Co.*, 348 N.E.2d 571 (1976) (disallowing categorical defense against worker who injured his hand while "chasing a hickie"—i.e., trying to remove a blemish—without shutting down a high-speed printing press); *Linegar v. Armour of Am.*, 909 F.2d 1150 (8th Cir. 1990) (allowing defense to seller of a bullet-proof vest known not to cover his entire trunk). The Restatement (Third) of Torts: Products Liability enigmatically approved of both decisions. See § 2, comment d, illus. 3 (*Micallif*) and illus. 10 (*Linegar*).

17. *Stevens v. Park, Davis & Co.*, 507 P.2d 653 (Cal. 1973).

18. 475 N.E.2d 65 (Mass. 1985).

19. 840 F.2d 935, 937–38 (D.C. Cir. 1988).

20. Amos Tversky & Daniel Kahneman, "Judgment under Uncertainty: Heuristics and Biases," 185 *Science* 1124, 1127 (1974).

21. See Scott Plous, *The Psychology of Judgment and Decision Making* 121 (1993). Note in this case at least one could quibble with the question, for the estimate of the frequency could well be higher if the event in question were described as "deaths to persons on ground from airplane crashes," which has more vividness of its own. The phrase "falling airplane parts" suggests a wheel that falls off a plane. It does not suggest a plane that shatters into a million pieces on impact. For a more general attack on the cognitive bias theory from just this point of view, see Gerd Gigerenzer, "On Narrow Norms and Vague Heuristics: A Reply to Kahneman and Tversky," 103 *Psychol. Rev.* 592 (1996), noting similar linguistic objections to other asserted biases.

22. Plous, *Psychology of Judgment*, at 122.

23. See Gary Schwartz, "The Myth of the Ford Pinto Case," 43 *Rutgers L. Rev.* 885 (1991).

24. See, e.g., *Khan v. Shiley Inc.*, 217 Cal. App. 3d 848, 266 Cal. Rptr. 106 (Cal. App. 1990).

25. Id.

26. See Jolls, Sunstein & Thaler, "Behavioral Approach to Law and Economics," at 1520–21. For an earlier version of the same general point, see Roger G. Noll & James E. Krier, "Some Implications of Cognitive Psychology for Risk Regulation," 19 *J. Legal Stud.* 747 (1990).

27. Marc K. Landy, Marc J. Roberts & Stephen R. Thomas, "Passing Superfund," in

Marc K. Landy, Marc J. Roberts & Stephen R. Thomas, *The Environmental Protection Agency: Asking the Wrong Questions* (1990).

28. See "False Alarms Caused by Botched Study," 212 *Science* 1404–7 (June 19, 1981).

29. For an account, see Marc K. Landy & Mary Hague, "The Coalition for Waste: Private Interests and Superfund," in Michael S. Greve & Fred L. Smith, eds., *Environmental Politics: Public Costs, Private Rewards* 71 (1992).

30. See Comprehensive Environmental Response Compensation and Liability Act of 1980, 42 U.S.C. §§ 9601 et seq. For a brief history of CERCLA's hasty enactment, see Robert V. Percival, Alan S. Miller, Christopher H. Schroeder & James P. Leape, *Environmental Regulation: Law, Science and Policy* 279–82 (2d ed. 1996).

31. See *United States v. Alcan Aluminum Corp.*, 964 F.2d 252, 256 (3d Cir. 1992).

32. For the longer version of the story, see Richard A. Epstein, *Takings: Private Property and the Power of Eminent Domain* (1985).

33. For a highly lucid account of the basic evolution, see Andrei Shleifer, *Inefficient Markets: An Introduction to Behavioral Finance* (2000), on which I have relied for much of the empirical information summarized in this section.

34. For a collection of references, see Lynn A. Stout, "Are Takeover Premiums Really Premiums? Market Price, Fair Value, and Corporate Law," 99 *Yale L. J.* 1235, 1236, 1240 (1990).

35. Milton Friedman, "The Case for Flexible Exchange Rates," in *Essays in Positive Economics* (1953); Eugene Fama, "The Behavior of Stock Market Prices," 38 *J. Bus.* 34 (1965); Eugene Fama, "Efficient Capital Markets: II," 46 *J. Fin.* 1575 (1991).

36. See, for a discussion, Richard A. Brealey & Stewart C. Myers, *Principles of Corporate Finance* 195–203 (6th ed. 2000). The basic formula reads as follows:

$$r = r_f + \beta(r_m - r_f),$$

where r_f is the riskless rate of return, β is the level of riskiness relative to the market as a whole, and $r_m - r_f$ is the risk premium for holding assets that have uncertain rates of return.

37. Shleifer, *Inefficient Markets*, at 16–17.

38. Werner F. M. DeBondt & Richard H. Thaler, "Does the Stock Market Overreact?" 40 *J. Fin.* 793 (1985).

39. Werner F. M. DeBondt & Richard H. Thaler, "Further Evidence on Investor Overreaction and Stock Market Seasonality," 42 *J. Fin.* 557 (1987).

40. Shleifer, *Inefficient Markets*, at 21–22.

41. Shlomo Benartzi & Richard Thaler, "Myopic Loss Aversion and the Equity Premium Puzzle," 110 *Q. J. Econ.* 73 (1995).

42. *Sharon Steel Corp. v. Chase Manhattan Bank, N.A.*, 691 F.2d 1039, 1048 (2d Cir. 1982).

43. See, e.g., the long-term debt securities in *Katz v. Oak Indus., Inc.*, 508 A.2d 873 (Del. Ch. 1986) (85 percent of company's debt securities had to accept exchange offer for stock).

44. See, e.g., John H. Langbein & Richard A. Posner, "Market Funds and Trust-Investment Law, part I & II," 1976 *Am. B. Found. Res. J.* (1977).

45. See Sanford Grossman & Joseph Stigletz, "On the Impossibility of Informationally Efficient Markets," 70 *Am. Econ. Rev.* 393 (1980).

46. See Stout, "Are Takeover Premiums Really Premiums?" 99 *Yale L. J.* 1235.

47. Shleifer, *Inefficient Markets*, at 13.

48. See, on the infamous bankruptcy of the hedge-fund Long Term Capital Markets, Daniel R. Fischel & Randal C. Picker, "A Firm That Failed Well," *Wall Street J.*, Oct. 12, 1998, at A18. For a critical assessment of the performance of the fund, see Andrew Marshall, "They Seemed Like Masters of the Universe, the Gods of Investment Banking," *The Independent*, Oct. 15, 1998.

49. Shleifer, *Inefficient Markets*, at 13–14.

50. See Arthur Keown & John Pinkerton, "Merger Announcements and Insider Trading Activity," 36 *J. Fin.* 855 (1981), cited in Brealey & Meyers, *Principles of Corporate Finance*, at 360; Shleifer, *Inefficient Markets*, at 8.

51. For the defense of the position, see Frank H. Easterbrook & Daniel R. Fischel, "The Proper Role of Target Management in Responding to a Takeover Offer," 94 *Harv. L. Rev.* 1161 (1981); see also Frank H. Easterbrook & Daniel R. Fischel, *The Economic Structure of Corporate Law*, ch. 7 (1991).

52. See Easterbrook & Fischel, *The Economic Structure of Corporate Law*, at ch. 6. They take the position that demand curves are indeed close to horizontal, thus bolstering the case for awarding only the prebid price to dissidents. Id. at 153 n. 10.

53. See Dennis W. Carlton & Daniel R. Fischel, "The Regulation of Insider Trading," 35 *Stan. L. Rev.* 857 (1983); for an opposite view, see Ronald Gilson & Reinier Kraakman, "The Mechanisms of Market Efficiency," 70 *Va. L. Rev.* 549 (1984).

54. For a lucid summary, see Robert C. Clark, *Corporate Law* 266–80 (1986).

55. See *United States v. O'Hagen*, 521 U.S. 642 (1997).

TABLE OF CASES

INDEX

Aaron, Henry J., 277n. 30
Able and Infirm, parable of, 134–35
abortion, 103–7
Ackerman, Bruce A., 273n. 3, 284n. 38
age discrimination laws, 61, 121
agricultural subsidies, 29, 61, 119, 262
Alschuler, Albert W., 269n. 7, 270n. 12,
    271n. 27, 272n. 54, 272n. 7
altruism, 83, 208–9
Ames, James Barr, 275n. 37
Anad, Paul, 281n. 29
Anarchy, State, and Utopia (Nozick), 129
Anderson, Elizabeth, 281n. 32
Anderson, Terry L., 267n. 16
animals: becoming property, 2, 38;
    domestication of, 195–96; Endangered
    Species Act, 224–25; state protection of
    wild, 223
antidiscrimination laws, 35, 105
antismoking campaigns, 147, 151–52
antitrust law, 34, 131, 132
arbitrage, 246, 252–53
Aristotle, 20–21, 54
Arkes, Hal R., 286nn. 13, 19
Arlen, Jennifer, 218
Arndt, Michael, 268n. 35
Arrow, Kenneth J., 281n. 27
art dealers, 216
assumption of risk, 96
at-will rule, 218
auctions, 211, 212–13, 215, 287n. 38
Austin, J. L., 84, 272n. 1
Australian aborigines, 39
automobiles: design defect cases, 234–38;
    endowment effect and dealers in, 216;
    Ford Pinto, 241
autonomy of the individual: in better
    forms of consequentialism, 77; as

building block of private law, 35–38;
    in classical liberalism, 2; state power
    for protecting, 46; as universalizable,
    36–37. *See also* individual liberty
availability heuristic, 240–43
Ayer, A. J., 273n. 1

Babcock, Linda, 268n. 36
bankruptcy, 35
Barnett, Randy, 268n. 28
Bartels, Ann P., 271n. 26
battered wives, 82
Bayes's formula, 247, 255
Becker, Gary, 141, 287n. 30
Becker, Lawrence C., 288n. 45
behavioral economics: in critiques of
    neoclassical economics, 11, 200, 258;
    Posner on, 199; on sunk costs, 206. *See
    also* cognitive bias
behavioral finance, 252, 257
Benartzi, Shlomo, 292n. 41
Bender, Leslie, 275n. 38
beneficence, duty of, 59, 89, 90
Bentham, Jeremy, 226, 289n. 63
Berlin, Isaiah, 46, 145, 267n. 26
Bewley, Truman, 182, 183–85
bias, cognitive. *See* cognitive bias
bid/asked differential, 210
bin Laden, Osama, 93
Binmore, Ken, 181
birth defects, abortion in cases of, 104–5
Bjork-Shiley heart valve, 241
Black, Charles, 274n. 30, 278n. 43
Blackstone, William, 3, 94, 114, 118, 119,
    273n. 16
Blumer, Catherine, 286nn. 13, 19
Blumstein, James F., 275n. 42
body, control over our own, 127, 133

Made in the USA
Middletown, DE
09 January 2020